Ambrose Bierce
and the Period of
Honorable Strife

Ambrose Bierce
and the *Period of* *Honorable* Strife

The Civil War and
the Emergence of
an American Writer

Christopher Kiernan Coleman

Knoxville /
The University of Tennessee Press

Copyright © 2016 by The University of Tennessee Press / Knoxville.
All Rights Reserved. Manufactured in the United States of America.
First Edition.

The paper in this book meets the requirements of American National Standards Institute / National Information Standards Organization specification Z39.48–1992 (Permanence of Paper). It contains 30 percent post-consumer waste and is certified by the Forest Stewardship Council.

Library of Congress Cataloging-in-Publication Data

Names: Coleman, Christopher Kiernan, 1949-
Title: Ambrose Bierce and the period of honorable strife : the Civil War and the emergence of an American writer / Christopher Kiernan Coleman.
Description: First edition. | Knoxville : The University of Tennessee Press, 2016. | Includes bibliographical references and index.
Identifiers: LCCN 2015039994 | ISBN 9781621901792 (hardcover : alkaline paper)
Subjects: LCSH: Bierce, Ambrose, 1842-1914? | Bierce, Ambrose, 1842-1914?—Criticism and interpretation. | Authors, American—19th century—Biography. | Soldiers—Indiana—Biography. | United States—History—Civil War, 1861-1865—Influence. | United States—History—Civil War, 1861-1865—Literature and the war. | United States. Army. Indiana Infantry Regiment, 9th (1861-1865) | Indiana—History—Civil War, 1861-1865—Regimental histories. | United States—History—Civil War, 1861-1865—Regimental histories. | Mississippi River Valley—History—Civil War, 1861-1865. | BISAC: BIOGRAPHY & AUTOBIOGRAPHY / Editors, Journalists, Publishers. | HISTORY / United States / Civil War Period (1850-1877). Classification: LCC PS1097.Z5 C65 2016 | DDC 813/.4—dc23
LC record available at http://lccn.loc.gov/2015039994

*To my beloved wife Veronica
and to my devoted children,
for all their help and support.*

"They were honest and courageous foemen, having little in common with the political madmen who persuaded them to their doom and the literary bearers of false witness in the aftertime. They did not live through the period of honorable strife into the period of vilification—did not pass from the iron age to the brazen—from the era of the sword to that of the tongue and pen. Among them is no member of the Southern Historical Society. Their valor was not the fury of the non-combatant; they have no voice in the thunder of the civilians and the shouting. Not by them are impaired the dignity and infinite pathos of the Lost Cause. Give them, these blameless gentlemen, their rightful part in all the pomp that fills the circuit of the summer hills."

—Ambrose Bierce, *A Bivouac of the Dead* (1903)

Contents

Preface XIII
Acknowledgments XV
Introduction 1
 1. Green and Salad Days 11
 2. Bad Boys Make Good Soldiers 25
 3. On a Mountain 39
 4. Unfamiliar Landscapes 51
 5. What He Saw of Shiloh 63
 6. Excursions and Alarums: Corinth, Owl Creek, and Perryville 79
 7. Stones River 95
 8. Sitzkrieg to Blitzkrieg 109
 9. Chickamauga 121
 10. Besieged 139
 11. Lieb und Krieg 159
 12. Crimes and Misdemeanors: The Atlanta Campaign 165
 13. Casualties of War 177
 14. What Happens: The Road to Franklin 187
 15. A Son of the Gods: The Battle of Nashville and After 199
 16. In High Cotton: Carpetbaggers, Confederates, and Corruption 211
 17. Phantoms and Presentiments 219
Epilogue: The Difficulty of Crossing a Battlefield 227
Appendix I. What Albert Bierce Saw: A Little Bit More of Chickamauga 231
Appendix II. Major Bierce's Critique of Confederate Strategy 235
Appendix III. Ambrose Bierce's Journal of the Carolinas Campaign 241
Notes 249
Selected Bibliography 279
Index 289

Illustrations

Figures

Lucius Varus Bierce   18
Kentucky Military Institute   20
Colonel Robert H. Milroy   29
General Benjamin F. Kelley   33
The Battle of Philippi   35
The Battle of Laurel Hill   38
General William B. Hazen   54
General Ulysses S. Grant   57
The Army of the Ohio Crossing the Duck River   59
Defeat and Retreat   67
Pittsburg Landing   69
A Fight for the Cannon at Shiloh   71
The Gallant Charge of the Nineteenth Brigade   75
The Advance on Corinth   80
The Occupation of Corinth   81
Union Train Destroyed by Guerillas   86
Confederate Raiders Attacking Union Supply Wagons   88
The Ninth Indiana in Danville, Kentucky   91
General William S. Rosecrans   96
Palmer's Division, Battle of Stone's River   101
Burial of Colonel Garesche   103
Searching for Wounded by Torchlight   104
The Hazen Monument   105
Bound and Gagged   114
General Steedman at Snodgrass Hill   130
Thomas's Command Defends Snodgrass Hill   136
Union Encampments, Chattanooga   140
Chattanooga during the Siege   141
Amphibious Assault on Brown's Landing   145
The Capture of Orchard Knob   151
Grant and Officers on Orchard Knob   153

Colonel Foy   155
Attack on Mission Ridge   156
Capture of Rebel Guns on Missionary Ridge   157
The Battle of Resaca   168
Captain John Eastman   179
Officer's Hospital in Nashville   182
Casualty of War   183
Rebel "Guerilla/Deserter"   190
Officers Observing the Battle of Nashville   202
"Hurry Up and Wait," the Battle of Nashville   203
The Battle of Nashville   204
Company A, 9th Indiana   233

Maps

Brown's Ferry   142
Battle of Resaca   167
Battle of Pickett's Mill   172

Preface

This is a book about a man, a regiment, an army, and a war. The man was Ambrose Gwinnett Bierce; the regiment, his regiment—the Ninth Indiana Volunteer Infantry; the army in which it served, the Army of the Cumberland; and the war in which he and they fought, our American Civil War.

Encompassed within four years of mass bloodletting were clashes great and small on a scale hitherto unimagined. The Army of the Cumberland was neither the most illustrious nor the most chronicled of that conflict; but surely it was one of the hardest fighting and battle tested. In that army, the "Bloody Ninth" amply earned its epithet in action many times over. Of that illustrious band of brothers, one soldier went on to fame in civilian life as a chronicler of the human condition and of the frequent inhumanity that it entailed: Ambrose Bierce.

In those four short years an idealistic youth was transformed in the forge of war; annealed by deprivation, death, and suffering; and emerged as the man we are familiar with from his literary fluorescence. But as modern as his prose may seem to us, he was still very much a man of his times.

During this, the sesquicentennial of the Civil War, we take the opportunity to reflect on that war, its meaning, its consequences, and the manifold ways in which it is still with us today. It was the watershed event in our entire existence as a nation, and the long shadows it has cast can still be seen and felt. In a sense, the war did not really end in the 1860s; rather it endured into the twentieth century, when the promises of the Thirteenth, Fourteenth, and Fifteenth Amendments were finally fulfilled—and are today again under siege.

Ambrose Bierce, his life, and his works are in many ways a window into this era, just as they are a window into the human soul. By looking at the man and this crucial era of his life and the life of the nation, we hope not only to understand him better, but perhaps ourselves as well.

Acknowledgments

I would like to thank the following institutions and organizations for their resources and help with my research regarding Ambrose Bierce's Civil War odyssey: the Elkhart County Historical Museum, Bristol, IN; the Jasper County (IN) Public Library; the Kentucky Military Institute Alumni Associations; the Kosciusko Jail Museum (Kosciusko County Historical Society), Warsaw, IN; the Library of Congress, in particular their Digital Collections & Services division and its prints and photographs section; The Nashville Room and the Nashville Public Library Interlibrary Loan program; the National Archives and Records Administration; Tennessee State Library and Archives; Stanford University Libraries, Dept. of Special Collections, Ambrose Bierc Papers; UCLA Young Library, Dept. of Special Collections, Carey McWilliams Collection; and particularly the University of Virginia, Alderman Memorial Library, Ambrose Bierce Papers, Charlottesville, VA. I would like to thank S. T. Joshi for reviewing my manuscript and his suggestions, although he is not responsible for any possible errors written herein. I should acknowledge too that Stephen Hood's new research on his forebear led me to correct some errors in the text and temper my views on the Gallant Hood and his role in the Autumn Campaign. I also wish to acknowledge the help of the online resources of Don Swaim's Ambrose Bierce website, the Ambrose Bierce Project, the Internet Archive, and Son of the South websites. Last, but not least, I also wish to acknowledge all the staff of the University of Tennessee Press for their help and support in bringing this project to fruition.

Introduction

A century ago, Ambrose Gwinnett Bierce rode into Mexico, rode out of history, and entered the realm of legend. His mysterious disappearance has kept generations of his fellow journalists speculating, first as to his whereabouts, then later about his ultimate fate. However, unless like the unfortunate Mr. Williamson of Selma, Alabama, Bierce was sucked into a void in the "luminiferous ether," it may be assumed that the famous author is by now most certainly deceased. His legacy lives on, however.

Ambrose Gwinnett Bierce is widely regarded as one of the leading lights of American literature. One hundred years after his quixotic exit, Bierce remains one of the most highly regarded American authors. Generations of readers have appreciated his acid wit, his stark realism, and his mastery of the macabre. In his day, Author Bierce was called many things—iconoclast, cynic, misanthrope, devil, and even "Almighty God" (a play on his initials A. G.). Yet few who applied these varied labels ever included among them the epithet "war hero." To this day, most who read his works know him best as "Bitter Bierce."[1] In his youth, however, Ambrose Bierce was a young man of exceptional courage and bravery, someone who would instinctively risk his life to save others and who was cited for his outstanding service on several occasions. Moreover, there is substantial evidence that as a young man Bierce was also an unmitigated idealist who went to war for altruistic reasons. If we wish to understand the brilliant writer to whom those later labels were applied, we must first seek to understand this other Ambrose Bierce, the idealist and fearless warrior.

Some of A. G.'s previous biographers have understood the importance of the Civil War's influence on him, even if they generally glossed over it. Cary McWilliams, one of his earliest and best chroniclers, remarked that "only a few of the more important influences of the war on Bierce's character can be traced. It would be impossible to catalogue the ramifications of this experience. One cannot overestimate the importance of those years of soldiering; they must be kept constantly in mind."[2] Another early researcher, Napier Wilt, did delve into Bierce's military career, although his intent in so doing was primarily literary.[3] Over the years since these early biographers, academics have occasionally weighed in on Ambrose Bierce's military career, but almost all these specialized studies have viewed his wartime experiences

Introduction

from a literary perspective, not a historical one, which has resulted in erroneous conclusions.

Who was this young lion that marched off to war in 1861? What did he experience during the Civil War and how did those experiences affect him? What chain of circumstances might lead an idealistic youth to transform into a mature cynic? From his youth, when the clouds of war were still looming, through the early days of the war, to the full horror of the "blood-stained period" and finally into the scoundrel time of Reconstruction, this book will attempt to chronicle Bierce's war experiences and illumine how they influenced his transition from youth to manhood and indelibly colored his literature.

Ambrose Bierce's short stories are notable for their dearth of sentimentality, tales whose tone was notably out of character with the maudlin romanticism of his era. Bierce reveled in dark tales with a grim sardonic twist, intended to upset his contemporary reader's smug Victorian assumptions. Bierce was also renowned as a muckraking journalist, an acerbic humorist, a poet, and a keen observer of the passing scene. He excelled above all else as a writer in his realistic portrayal of war—not the vainglorious accounts so typical of his era, but in brutal, horrific and often bizarre portrayals of combat, where sentiments of romance and chivalry seemed absurd and futile. H. L. Mencken wrote that Ambrose Bierce was "the first writer of fiction ever to treat war realistically." His war stories possess a surprisingly modern tone. Ironically, however, at least one of his contemporary reviewers criticized him for his "unrealistic" accounts of war, a criticism he bristled at.[4]

Incongruously, alongside Bierce's gritty realism is an affinity for the bizarre, the uncanny and the irrational—traits seemingly at odds with this realism. Perhaps we should view this too as an outgrowth of his war experiences: an officer is court-martialed for obeying orders; a comrade murders his best friend out of affection for him; a son kills his father out of duty; a man previously executed for striking an officer answers an early morning roll-call; the ghost of a cavalryman warns his comrades of an enemy ambush; a man loses his life saving the man who seduced his wife; a corpse catches a chill on the battlefield. In Bierce, the real and the surreal often march together in an uncomfortable alliance with one another, as do life and death.

Admittedly, there were a select few other authors of the era, such as Stephen Crane, who also wrote realistically about war. Unlike the Major, however, they never experienced war firsthand. In the parlance of the time, in 1861 Ambrose Gwinnett Bierce went "looking for the elephant." He found it in spades. Bierce was embroiled in many of the bitterest and most bloody battles of the Civil War, witnessing at close quarters the horrors he so graphically described in later life. Furthermore, he was seriously wounded in combat, an event that likely had a profound and lasting effect on him. Despite being at the forefront of action throughout most of the war, however, Bierce eschewed the "how I won the war" genre of memoir, or for that matter, any book-length account of his experiences. His nonfiction and fictional war stories shun all hint of vainglory, exuding a notable cynicism regarding the entire enterprise of soldiering. In fact, Bierce's war stories frequently display a finely honed sense of the absurd more at home in late twentieth century fiction than late nineteenth. Although referred to as "Almighty" and similar inflated epithets by his acolytes, his autobiographical writings of war experiences more typically reflect a tone of humility with a hefty leavening of self-deprecating humor. When discussing the war, A. G. commonly expressed respect and reverence for the fallen—a sentiment he frequently extended to his former foes. Arrogance and humility, idealism and cynicism, venom and magnanimity: such contradictions in Bierce's character are but a few of the still-lingering mysteries about his personality.

Although most biographers acknowledge that Bierce's wartime experiences profoundly influenced his life and later literary career, historically they have glossed over that formative period of his life, concentrating more on the postwar era—the time of his literary flowering. In recent years, however, scholars have tried to rectify this oversight and have paid renewed attention to Bierce's war writings. The most recent general biography of Bierce, Roy Morris's *Ambrose Bierce: Alone in Bad Company,* does indeed devote several chapters to Bierce's wartime activities, though these chapters are largely based on Bierce's own episodic memoirs. Other scholars have taken up the banner as well, closely studying Bierce's war prose and analyzing it from the perspective of literary criticism. In the 1980s Cathy N. Davidson edited *Critical Essays on Ambrose Bierce,* which included several essays looking closely at Bierce's war literature and which remains a seminal collection. More recently, David Owens focused his doctoral thesis and subsequent book on Bierce's war literature, emphasizing in particular how Bierce's activities as a topographical engineer (mapmaker) during the war greatly influenced his writing.[5] It would also be remiss not to mention the *Ambrose Bierce Project Journal,* an estimable online academic e-zine which is of great value and well worthy of broader popular and financial support, and which, while mainly literary in focus, has nonetheless also published several articles that delve into aspects of Bierce's war career. Nevertheless, up until this present work there has been no in-depth exploration of Bierce's activities in the Civil War from a historical point of view, bringing to bear the documentary record as it regards Lt. Ambrose Bierce and placing his wartime activities within the broader context of the Civil War in the west.

To a certain extent, this oversight is due to Ambrose Bierce himself. Unlike many other Civil War veterans, Bierce consciously avoided writing

Introduction

a full-length memoir of his war service. His antipathy toward the bragging, self-serving distortions of many military memoirs of the era may have had much to do with this, though he likely had other motives as well. Indeed, despite writing extensively on the Civil War, when it came to his own participation Bierce could be circumspect. Even when he did pen essays about his personal experiences, he tried to avoid giving the impression of any great knowledge of events or that his own efforts were of any import: "What I Saw," "What Happens along a Road," "A Little of" and similarly circumscribed phrases pepper his autobiographical works. His style of writing, while vividly painting for the reader the physical and psychological experience of war, tells us less about his own experiences than we would want. Moreover, regarding many other aspects of his personal life, both in his youth and in later years, he kept his secrets well.

It is unfortunate that Bierce did not write a fuller account of his wartime service, for his eloquence and acute powers of observation make him an invaluable eyewitness to some of the most important events of the war. He is also a valuable primary source for the war's more pedestrian aspects, those "in small things forgotten," which are nonetheless quite insightful about life in America and in the South during and immediately after the conflict. While this text is meant to offer a documentary account of Ambrose Bierce's war service, it also seeks to verify his war writings as primary sources for historians to utilize. Previous writers have accused Bierce of fabrication in his nonfiction memoirs, and while literary license is certainly allowable in fiction, it would also be good to know just how much fact is behind his realistic war fiction.

In constructing a coherent narrative of Ambrose Gwinnett Bierce's wartime career, I have tried to make full use of what he himself had to say about the war and his participation in it. In so doing I utilize both his nonfiction and his fiction pieces as primary sources. At the same time, I also rely on available documentary sources that bear on his war service, both to verify and amplify his words. There is, of course, an inherent contradiction in this approach, in that I am both using the historical record to make sense of Bierce's writings and using Bierce's writings to make sense of the historical record. The situation is somewhat akin to the situation when, during the First World War, Lord Kitchener inspected the British Army in Egypt's defenses guarding the Suez Canal and somewhat derisively inquired whether the British army was guarding the canal or the canal was guarding the British army. In fact, both were true. So this is, admittedly, something of a balancing act. I will leave it to the reader to judge whether I have juggled both successfully.

Ideally, the chapters of this book should speak for themselves. Like Bierce, I aspire to achieve the virtue of brevity in prose; nevertheless, a brief word about the words that follow is in order, partly to illumine where this work order differs from predecessors in interpretation, but also to highlight controversies touched on in the narrative and to underscore some difficulties regarding Bierce's own writings on the subject. When I began this undertaking, I had only intended to chronicle Bierce's actual war years; what came before and after I felt had already been investigated and sometimes well-recorded by his other biographers. However, as I delved deeper into Bierce's early years, it became apparent that additional chapters were needed to properly explore both the period before and after his actual term of service in the war.

One thing was immediately apparent: if I were to assert that the Civil War was a transformative event for Bierce, I should include at least a brief description of who Ambrose Gwinnett Bierce was before he went "looking for the elephant" in April 1861. In his 1951 biography, *The Devil's Lexicographer,* Paul Fatout covered the Bierce family history quite thoroughly, tracing their genealogy back to their arrival on the Mayflower (at least his mother's Sherwood line) and emphasizing the poverty and peculiarity of his family upbringing, which Bierce rebelled against. While I acknowledge my debt to Fatout's research into Bierce's prewar years, in Chapter 1, my own interpretation of those same sources and of other primary sources relating to this period of Bierce's life differs significantly from that of Fatout and other biographers. While "Bitter Bierce" sometimes decried his early upbringing in his postwar writings, portraying it in negative terms, we should take that portrayal with a grain of salt. Marcus Bierce was a man of his time in many respects; moreover, contrary to received opinion, Marcus was neither poor nor peculiar. Marcus Bierce's love of literature and erudition may have been exceptional, but he was well-regarded in his community and far from indigent. Furthermore, the fact that Marcus and his wife had a large family was not in any way unusual in the early part of the nineteenth century; nor was their strict religiosity.

It is my thesis that, while young Ambrose may well have resented his parents' strict discipline, their reproofs to him may have at times been well earned. The mature Bierce's memories of his youth may have been colored and distorted. Moreover, circumstantial evidence points to Ambrose having inherited much of his father and uncle's moralism, at least in its political aspects. Bierce came from a family of staunch Abolitionists; his first employment was with a newspaper that was tied to a Republican Party political organ and I believe that, far from being an aimless youth seeking direction in 1861, Bierce joined the army out of ideological commitment.

All this being said, significant gaps remain in this phase of Bierce's life for which few sources are available. His sojourn at Kentucky Military Institute, in particular, is still a mystery. Besides basic military discipline and drill, how

Introduction

much military instruction did young Bierce receive? In a school that advertised its emphasis in engineering, did Topographical Engineer Bierce actually receive instruction on the subject during his time there? Did Ambrose Bierce, a fiery young Abolitionist, come into conflict with the Southern cadets there, some of whom held equally strong Secessionist sentiments? Alas, time and the postwar fires that plagued the Kentucky campus of KMI have rendered these and other questions problematical, if not unanswerable.

It is worth noting that many of the most significant events of the war in the Western Theater do not warrant any great attention from A. G. in his war writings, yet many lesser ones do. For example, in Chapters 2 and 3, I cover Bierce's participation in the campaign in western Virginia, which at best was a "sideshow" early in the war and which does not loom large among chroniclers of the Civil War. Yet this period of his service seems to garner disproportionate attention from Bierce in both his nonfiction memoirs and his short stories. To be sure, Private Bierce and his comrades first saw active service in this campaign and were exposed to danger and death in West Virginia (not then a state); but compared to the period of bloodletting that followed, this campaign made them seem more like like boys playing at war than men in combat. It was, perhaps, the scenic beauty of the region rather than Bierce's actual military service that affected him most. He poetically describes the mountainous terrain in his memoirs, and his writing about the region is at times wistful. One cannot help speculating whether this youthful sojourn in Appalachia did not influence Bierce's well-known affection for the mountainous scenery of northern California.

The Battle of Shiloh certainly looms large in he history of the war and in Bierce's war writings. Notably, "What I Saw of Shiloh" ranks not only as a classic of war literature but also as an important historical document. In Chapters 4 and 5, I attempt to amplify Bierce's own writings with the abundant sources available about his unit and the campaign in general. Shiloh remains a highly problematical battle for historians, and much of what Bierce alludes to, however briefly, has an important bearing on this ongoing debate. This phase of his military service warrants both his and our attention to it.

While historians of the Western Theater ignore the post-Corinth period, Bierce did not overlook it. Consequently in Chapter 6, I go into some detail about the period. Bierce's "An Occurrence at Owl Creek Bridge" is justly regarded as a classic of American literature, and while I leave it to literary scholars to interpret and analyze it as art, I attempt to provide some context behind it. By contrast, the ensuing Kentucky Campaign, which was both strenuous and bloody, and in which Bierce took an active part, was thoroughly ignored by him. I try to remedy that gap here, although it would have been better had I been able to do so in Bierce's own words.

Introduction

Similarly, in Chapter 7, I chronicle Bierce's considerable efforts relating to the Battle of Stones River. While he did write about the battle and its aftermath, here again, as to his own participation he is reticent. His short story, "A Resumed Identity," seemingly references the battle, yet closer analysis indicates that the story is a composite of different aspects of Bierce's wartime service and, obliquely, of his postwar pilgrimage there. The six months following Stones River was a seemingly dormant phase for the Army of the Cumberland and thereby for Bierce's unit; therefore, historians largely ignore it. This period figures in several of Bierce's short pieces, and during this time he was promoted to First Lieutenant and then appointed to General Hazen's staff as Topographical Engineer, both significant events. In Chapter 8, I illuminate this long period.

Of course, the Chickamauga Campaign and subsequent siege of Chattanooga looms large, both with historians and with Bierce. In Chapters 9 and 10, therefore, I thoroughly discuss both this period and the controversies surrounding it and Bierce. After this manuscript was completed, several new historical works that look at this campaign have been published, and while they don't affect our investigation of Bierce's experiences significantly, they do promise to stir further debate regarding some of the leading personalities of the campaigns. Whether these revisions to our understanding of this period will stand is a moot issue for now and will probably remain under debate by historians for some time. As a result, Bierce's own insights in this regard gain more importance.

In Chapters 11 and 13 I discuss aspects of Bierce's personal life during the war. For a man who never shied from expressing his opinions about women and marriage, the silence regarding his own personal life is deafening. His relationship with his first love, Fatima (also called Bernice) Wright is particularly obscure. While Bierce biographer Carey McWilliams did interview Fatima Wright late in life, unfortunately she had already burned Bierce's love letters some time before; moreover, it is clear from comparing McWilliams's article to what little documentary evidence is available that several aspects of his and other accepted accounts of their relationship is inaccurate and in need of correction. That Bierce's near-fatal wounding may have adversely impacted this relationship seems to me a likely thesis, and so does the possibility that it may have permanently affected his personality. Further enlightenment regarding the exact nature of Lieutenant Bierce's relationship with Fatima and its termination is greatly needed. While I believe I have elucidated some aspects of this relationship, what I have uncovered also raises more questions than it answers.

Chapters 14 and 15 cover Bierce's return to service after sick leave and his participation in the Autumn Campaign of 1864. Ambrose Bierce fortunately

7

Introduction

had much to say about this period in the postwar era. Here again, many aspects of this campaign were controversial even in the late nineteenth century. More recently, aspects of the campaign have undergone major reconsideration, especially regarding the generalship of Confederate Commander John Bell Hood. While none of this directly affects what we know of Lieutenant Bierce's participation in this campaign, it did cause me to seriously reconsider t many of the assumptions held by historians regarding General Hood and his leadership in this campaign, especially the controversies over his alleged use of alcohol and drugs and over the "Springhill Affair." Bierce was always magnanimous to his former enemies and so the bitter postwar recriminations regarding "the Gallant Hood" are entirely absent from his writings, although Bierce was certainly aware of the controversy. If John Bell Hood is not entirely blameless for the failure of this last and perhaps "most decisive" offensive campaign of the Confederacy, it becomes clear from both Bierce and from historian Stephen Hood's recent works that the Confederate commander was undeserving of much of the harsh criticism previously heaped upon him by historians. I also discuss, although admittedly without resolution, the conundrum of Bierce's official discharge from service. Officially his discharge occurred in late January 1865 in northern Alabama; yet from Bierce's own hand we know that he remained in active service, in some capacity, in Georgia and in the Carolinas until nearly April of that year. While I put forth theories to explain this enigma, conclusive proof is still wanting.

As previously mentioned, the last two chapters of this book were not part of the original schema. However, it became clear that aspects of Bierce's postwar life were as much a part of the story of his wartime experiences and also required some consideration. In particular, the almost picaresque period of his work as "agency aide" to his old war comrade Special Treasury Agent Eaton, rounding up contraband cotton, may have contributed to Bierce's notorious postwar cynicism as much as any single incident during the war. Moreover, this early phase of postwar Reconstruction is widely regarded by historians as, in effect, the terminal phase of the Confederacy in the Deep South.

After his work in Alabama, Bierce shook the dust of the South (and the Midwest) from his sandals and headed west trying to start life anew; as the years passed, however, the war exercised a strong hold over him. It is clear that in both his waking thoughts and in his dreams, the war haunted him and greatly influenced his literary output. I believe that the "period of honorable strife" (as he termed it once), may well have had a strong influence on Bierce's decision to undertake his final quixotic journey to Mexico.

Though Ambrose Bierce was reticent about his own achievements in his postwar writings, it does not imply that he did not hold strong opinions about the war and its conduct or that he was afraid to express those opinions. Throughout his postwar literary career, when it came to incompetent generals or those who made inflated claims of heroism—"the literary bearers of false witness"—Bierce unleashed the full venom of his considerable talents for invective and scorn. He was similarly critical of those who tried to romanticize war or portray it as a noble and chivalrous affair. In response to the hypocrisy, the lies, and the phony sentiment, Bierce strove to express the truth about the war as he saw it. I assert that what may seem to be purely literary text today, when refracted through the lens of history, can sometimes also be appreciated as factual accounts only thinly disguised as fiction. In other cases, Bierce borrowed incidents and anecdotes from different campaigns to cobble together a single story that was authentic in spirit but not in literal fact. I will try to elucidate those cases as well, lest the unwary fall prey to unwarranted assumptions regarding the good lieutenant's veracity. In several cases, Bierce changed names or details, either to protect the guilty, or to avoid libel suits, but his contemporary audience, especially his fellow veterans, would have been well aware of the context behind many of these stories. They would have easily understood the oblique references and pseudonyms in his stories; however, for modern readers these real subjects remain hidden behind his fictive veil. This present study restores some of that lost context as well.

Rising through the ranks from raw recruit to staff officer with the Army of the Cumberland, Ambrose Bierce was an active participant in nearly every major campaign of the Western Theater. In presenting more fully the background behind Bierce's war writings, I hope that the value of Bierce's literature as a historical source on the War will become more apparent. If indeed he is an honest chronicler of "the period of honorable strife" Bierce's writings—even his fiction—may prove to be an underappreciated primary source on aspects of the war often glossed over by other veterans more concerned with their reputations than with truth.

While not considered a "Southern writer," Ambrose Bierce nonetheless wrote extensively about the South of the 1860s—not just about the battles, but about the war's impact on civilians. Bierce's writings reflect a pivotal point both in his life and in the history of the South. He not only crisscrossed the South throughout the war; he was also eyewitness to the early chaotic phase of Reconstruction—that tragic terminal aspect of the war. The Civil War became the defining experience of Bierce's life, profoundly influencing all that came after it. In chronicling Ambrose Bierce's sojourn from youth to manhood, this book seeks to gain a greater appreciation of Ambrose Bierce, not only as the man who grew to become one of the most influential authors of American letters, but also as a man who was an observant and eloquent eyewitness to a pivotal period in American history. In the end this book hopes to help readers attain a deeper insight into the man whose postwar persona so often seemed at odds with the ideals of that young man who marched off to war in 1861.

1

Green and Salad Days

YOUTH, *n.* The Period of Possibility, when Archimedes finds a fulcrum, Cassandra has a following and seven cities compete for the honor of endowing a living Homer.

ZEAL, *n.* A certain nervous disorder afflicting the young and inexperienced. A passion that goeth before a sprawl.

Early on April 19, 1861, a toe-headed, blue-eyed youth lined up outside Theodore Mann's law offices in Elkhart, Indiana. Mann had just announced that he was opening enrollment for a volunteer company of infantry in response to Lincoln's call for volunteers. Eager Ambrose Bierce—called 'Brose or Brady by those who knew him—was second in line as the young men of the town flocked to Mann's offices to sign up. He was one among many young men to join, but time would prove him unique in many ways. What sort of person was this Brady Bierce who so hastily sought to join the looming conflict?

We know many things about Ambrose Gwinnett Bierce's postwar life, times, and work. Of his earlier years and careers, however, we possess far less information. In particular, regarding his formative years before the war, there exists a dearth of contemporary sources. There are, to be sure, sparse comments made by the adult Bierce about his youth, penned in the era when he received the epithet "Bitter Bierce." Further, much has been divined from his fictional works, which may be autobiographical—or not. But actual documentation dating to the prewar period is very sparse. Of course, this lack of fact has never gotten in the way of his chroniclers' speculations; to fill the gap about his early days, biographers have inferred—or assumed—much.

Of Ambrose Bierce's family history and ancestral background—which mattered little to the adult Bierce—we do have ample information, largely thanks to Paul Fatout, whose genealogical research uncovered much about 'Brose's lineage but less about the man himself. The Bierces and the Sherwoods (his mother's family) were venerable New England families, a long line of industrious Yankees whom on Bierce's maternal side could trace their forebears all the way back to the Mayflower. Descending from a long line of staunch Puritans, both of Bierce's parents were God-fearing—and apparently humorless—Congregationalists.[1] What the adult Bierce thought of his Puritan ancestry may safely be inferred from a bit of doggerel he penned in response to the rampant jingoism of the Gilded Age:

> Land where my fathers fried
> Young witches and applied
> Whips to the Quaker's hide
> And made him spring.[2]

Bearing the imperious name of Marcus Aurelius, Bierce's father was, by most biographers' accounts, a penurious and peculiar failure whose sole achievement was siring thirteen children. However, we should note that the mature Ambrose Bierce was hardly a model of filial piety; moreover, many of his later statements may have been uttered more to shock his late Victorian audience out of their smug complacency rather than to inform them of personal history. His spare comments about his family could easily imply that his father Marcus was a peculiar ne'er-do-well; that both he and his wife, Laura Sherwood Bierce, were cold, cruel, and uncaring parents; and that Ambrose grew up in abject poverty.

Marcus Bierce may have been eccentric, but in many respects he was also very much a man of his time. Like thousands of Americans in the early 1800s, Marcus packed up his family and headed west to seek a better life. Material life on the frontier could at times be quite spartan: the days were long, the work was hard, and there was no guarantee of success. Nonetheless, many men like Marcus in the early nineteenth century followed the paths westward, both north and south of the Ohio River. There is no doubt that Marcus Aurelius Bierce was deeply imbued with the Puritan ethic: work, constant prayer, accepting loss and suffering as God's will, and a parental philosophy of spare the rod and spoil the child. These and similar values were the moral tools that helped early Americans bring civilization to the wilderness. If Yankee pioneers like the Congregationalist Marcus were strict in their religious observances north of the Ohio River, south of the Ohio the hard shell Baptists were stricter still—and the dour Scots-Irish Presbyterians of the Southern Frontier even more so.

Following the lead of the irreligious and blasphemous adult Ambrose Bierce, twentieth-century biographers of A. G. have generally condemned his family's Puritanism. But the stereotype of the Puritans as irredeemably humorless or sexually repressed folk is largely a false one, foisted on the public by modern social activists, not historians. In regards to Brady Bierce's father, we may note that he was named after a pagan Roman emperor who penned a book of philosophy—this in an era when men were commonly given Old Testament first names. Outwardly, Marcus Bierce may have seemed but a humble dirt farmer, but in many respects such appearances were deceiving. In particular, Marcus's love of literature extended far beyond the confines of the Old Testament poetry of the King James Bible. Whether his religious scruples prevented him from attending the theater—had such a thing even existed on the early Midwestern frontier—is not certain, but it surely did not prevent him from reading secular plays and naming his son after a character in one.

It is almost certain that Ambrose was named after the leading character of a curious little contemporary play entitled *Ambrose Gwinnett: or a Sea-side Story*. Written by the British playwright Douglas Jerrold, this text in turn was based on an earlier story by the Irish dramatist Isaac Bickerstaffe. The play's plot involves a man who is hanged but somehow survives—a plot twist eerily similar to Ambrose's macabre Civil War masterpiece, "An Occurrence at Owl Creek Bridge."[3] We know that Marcus Bierce was quite fond of secular poetry, especially poems of that scandalous libertine poet Lord Byron, going so far as to name another son "Addison Byron."[4] We also know that Marcus devoured assorted secular novels, essays, and popular magazines that did not fit well with his "austere Puritan" stereotype. Even Ambrose admitted at one point that his father was "a man of considerable scholarship" who possessed the largest private collection of books in the county.[5] Marcus's love of literature was at least one trait that his son inherited; in later life "Bitter" Bierce, in a moment of candor, confessed that "to his books I owe all that I have."[6]

Whatever Marcus Bierce's personal failings may have been, hypocrisy was certainly not among them. Moreover, the Bierce clan's intense sense of morality extended into the political realm. Both Marcus and his more politically prominent younger brother, Lucius Verus Bierce, were staunch opponents of slavery. As the issue of slavery and its expansion into the western territories became an increasingly acrimonious political dispute, the Bierces' attitude opposing it become more militant.

The fact that Marcus Aurelius fathered thirteen children has often been cited as an indication of his peculiarity, as well as the cause of his family's alleged poverty. While we can assume that Marcus was uxorious—either that or he took the Old Testament injunction to "be fruitful and multiply" literally—it would be wrong to assume anything particularly unusual about the Bierces having a large brood. Large families were, in fact, the norm in America throughout the nineteenth century. Most Americans lived on farms up until the early twentieth century, and in a rural environment children were an asset, not a liability: more children meant more laborers to work the fields or help with household chores. Moreover, child mortality was often quite high in the early nineteenth century. That Marcus and his wife lost only three of their thirteen children marks them as more fortunate than many frontier families of the time.

Ambrose portrayed his childhood as one filled with poverty and hardship: "In the wilds of the far West we had to grub out a very difficult living."[7] This and similar remarks by Bierce have been accepted at face value by generations of biographers, who in turn assumed Ambrose's father was poor in addition to being a cruel ne'er-do-well. However Walter Neale, Bierce's publisher, biographer, and occasional drinking buddy, expressed a certain amount of skepticism about the accounts of early youth that Bierce related directly to him.[8] There is also documentary evidence that Bierce's later characterization of his early years is different from the facts—perhaps substantially so. In researching facts about Ambrose Bierce's birthplace, one diligent Ohio genealogist uncovered some interesting background information regarding the wealth and status of Ambrose's father For example, between 1818 and 1838 in Portage County, Ohio, the "destitute" Marcus bought and sold land no less than twenty-three times—often in tracts of one hundred acres each—and the tax records from that same county show that he paid substantial taxes on land, cattle, and horses.[9]

In the era before the Civil War, speculation in land was the main way that people grew their wealth. It was common practice on the frontier to buy land cheaply, develop it, sell it for a profit, and then move on and begin again. So in addition to working the land daily, Marcus Bierce was also something of a real estate entrepreneur. Many land speculators lost their fortunes during this era, but Marcus was not one of them. He may not have become immensely wealthy, but he was also not at the bottom of the socioeconomic ladder, as Ambrose's later recollections have led many to believe.[10]

Confirming Marcus Bierce's respected status in frontier Indiana society, evidence shows that he was inducted into the Masons in 1850, that he held positions of public trust such as property assessor and overseer of the poor for Wayne Township, and that he was elected vice president of the Kosciusko County Agricultural Society. A ne'er-do-well who is regarded as "peculiar" or abnormal by his neighbors is not admitted to an elite fraternal society or appointed and elected to positions of trust. Nor, in an era when few men possessed any more printed matter than a family bible, does Marcus's acquisition of a large private collection of books sound like the behavior of someone who continually had "to grub out a very difficult living."

Even more opaque than Bierce's early family life is the question of his early love life. Early biographers tell us that Brady was smitten with a charming girl named Bernice Wright, who, we are told, Bierce nicknamed "Fatima." It is said that he met her while attending high school in Warsaw and that he had a crush on her well before the war. In addition, his publisher, Walter Neale, also intimated in his "tell all" biography that the teenage Bierce had a sexual affair in Warsaw with an elderly female resident of the town—although most of Bierce's more reliable chroniclers doubt this last tale.[11] As with other aspects of his life before the army, details of Bierce's early love life in Warsaw remain vague and largely unverified.

Although Bierce's recollections of his youth do not quite square with the material facts, we may still grant that he chafed at his parents' strict discipline and religiosity as a boy. Tellingly, in one of his famous "definitions" Bierce observed that *disobedience* was the "silver lining to the cloud of servitude." That Brady may have occasionally deserved the corporal corrections he regularly received at his father's hand we learn from his older brother Albert, the only one of his twelve siblings with whom he was close. Albert Bierce (known affectionately to Ambrose as "Grizzly" or "Old Sloots") once confessed that he and his brother "did not make life as pleasant" for their mother "as we might have."[12] In fact, one gets the distinct impression that Grizzly played Huck Finn to Brady's Tom Sawyer in those days. In one instance, the two youthful mischief-makers disrupted an outdoor tent revival by draping a bundle of straw atop an old nag, setting the straw alight, and then whipping the horse into the tent. Instead of the usual fire and brimstone sermon common to such events, the boys delivered the fire without the brimstone to a highly agitated congregation. Needless to say, their parents were not amused.[13] In another instance, Brady sarcastically referred to one itinerant backwoods preacher sacrilegiously as "Saul of Cattarrhsus."[14] He also regularly skipped Sunday church services to be outdoors and commune with nature, which certainly did not endear him to the more staid members of the family. So when the hell-raising Ambrose expressed a desire to leave home and become a "printer's devil" with a newspaper, it is likely that his parents did not seriously object to his departure; they may well have breathed a quiet sigh of relief.

In later life Bierce recounted that he ran away from home to become a newspaperman in Chicago.[15] The story did have a grain of truth to it; shortly before the war, Bierce did indeed work at a newspaper—though it was in Warsaw, Indiana, not in Chicago. Indeed, *The Northern Indianian* was located only three miles from the old family homestead, which meant that Brady's leaving to work in Warsaw could hardly be described as "running away." *The Northern Indianian* came into being because the Republican Party, born in 1854, needed a newspaper to serve as its political mouthpiece within Indiana. Founded in 1856, *The Northern Indianian* has been described as an abolitionist newspaper by some Bierce biographers. Strictly speaking this isn't quite true; the paper was created explicitly as a propaganda organ for the Indiana Republican Party, and as such it shared the Republican Party's opposition to slavery as a key editorial platform. Unlike other crusading anti-slavery papers such as William Lloyd Garrison's *The Liberator*, however, *The Northern Indianian* did not solely seek to promote the abolition of slavery.[16]

The Bierce men had originally been Jacksonian Democrats—one of Marcus's older sons was even named after the famous Democratic president—and they presumably shared Old Hickory's staunch nationalism and his assertion of Federal authority over the doctrine of individual state sovereignty, or "Nullification." After the Jacksonian era, however, as the Democratic Party increasingly fell under the thrall of the Southern slave owners and their apologists, the Bierces, like many Free Soil Democrats, became disenchanted with their party over its pandering to the pro-slavery faction.

When the Republican Party came into being in the early 1850s, it not only attracted former Whigs such as Abraham Lincoln but also drew to its standard many other disenchanted factions in the nation: Free Soil Democrats, Socialists, militant Abolitionists, and other like-minded reform groups were drawn to its banner. By the mid 1850s, among the Abolitionist faction of the Republican Party in Indiana and Ohio could be counted both Marcus and his younger brother Lucius Verus Bierce. Ambrose was largely silent about what his political beliefs were at this time, but he was surely exposed to an earful of political talk at home from his both his father and from the influential Uncle Lucius when he visited.[17]

Young Brady's stint as a "printer's devil" at *The Northern Indianian* is generally placed around 1857–1858 by most of his chroniclers, beginning when he turned fifteen. However, Reuben Williams, who continued in the newspaper business well into the 1900s, dates Bierce's work at the paper to "the autumn of 1860" and puts his age at "about sixteen."[18] Reuben was writing in 1874, much closer to the time than his son's later secondhand recollection of Bierce's stint with the paper. Regardless of the exact chronology, Reuben remembered Bierce and his brief apprenticeship quite well. Reuben was already friends with Ambrose's father, who was "well known to nearly everybody in the county," so that when Bierce applied "for a situation to learn the printing business," he was readily accepted. During this brief period, Brady lived with the Williams family in Warsaw and was apparently an apt apprentice. Reuben Williams recalls that Bierce was educated "far in advance of other boys of his age" and that he learned the newspaper trade rapidly.

Bierce told an early biographer and friend that during his work at the paper he gradually worked his way up to the status of local reporter and contributor. His Boswell, the biographer in question, relates that Bierce's "overcritical and fierce expressions of the budding censor of public morals and political degeneracy" led the editor to frequently blue-pencil Bierce's articles. One of Bierce's biographers also claims that Bierce was unhappy with this editorial meddling and that this was the reason he abruptly quit the newspaper.[19] In any case, Reuben Williams gives us a very different version of Brady's departure from *The Northern Indianian*, relating that while young Bierce was industrious, "he was likewise pretty full of mischief." Bierce became entangled in a "scrape" with two or three other boys, and while Reuben does not specify the nature of the altercation, he does say that after investigating it he found Bierce to be "entirely innocent." Nonetheless, he advised Brady to leave town for a few days until things quieted down. Bierce never returned to the newspaper.[20]

Whether it was before or after his brief apprenticeship in journalism, Brady seems to have taken refuge with his Uncle Lucius for a time. Whatever abolitionist leanings Bierce may have absorbed from his father or from working at the Republican newspaper, he most certainly could not have avoided the politics of the anti-slavery movement while residing in the household of his activist uncle. Lucius Verus Bierce was more than a year younger than his brother Marcus, but in terms of public prominence and esteem, Lucius was by far the more advanced of the two. When he was only sixteen, Lucius decided to obtain a college education and for five years worked his way through Ohio University. Not long after graduating, he set out on foot for the South, where he studied law—and, apparently, slavery.

Although he obtained a license to practice law in Alabama, Lucius returned north. In 1824 he was admitted to the bar in Ohio and the next year was appointed District Attorney, serving in that capacity for eleven years. In addition to dabbling in politics and war, Lucius also had literary aspirations. He wrote a memoir entitled *Travels in the Southland,* which detailed his sojourn south of the Mason-Dixon Line, and he also penned other shorter pieces and gave numerous speeches.23 Like elder brother Marcus, Lucius was an avid reader and book lover; his personal library later became the basis for the University of Akron's first book collection. The university's Bierce Library is named in honor of him. Like his brother Marcus, Lucius joined the Free Masons; but Lucius was not content to simply socialize and network with fellow Masons like his elder brother had. As with all other aspects of his life, Lucius excelled, becoming Grand Master of the Grand Lodge of Ohio.[21] In the late 1830s, the restless Lucius led an abortive invasion of Canada in a quixotic attempt to make common cause with a local insurgency across the border. This filibuster expedition came to naught, but it did earn Lucius the self-anointed honorific of "General." His only other legacy from this Canadian misadventure was a stockpile of leftover swords and assorted arms.

Green and Salad Days

Lucius Varus Bierce. Abolitionist, adventurer, author, politician and self-appointed "general." Ambrose looked up to his flamboyant uncle and used him as his role model. Courtesy City of Akron.

Back home in Akron, Ohio, Lucius was elected mayor four times before the war—an indication of the way he was highly regarded by his fellow citizens.[22]

Lucius Bierce's anti-slavery beliefs took root when he witnessed firsthand how the institution was practiced in the Deep South. By the 1850s, General Bierce had become a militant abolitionist—as evidenced by his relationship with the notorious abolitionist John Brown. Although historians frequently refer to John Brown as "John Brown of Kansas," he was in fact for a time a neighbor of Lucius Bierce's in Ohio. Like fellow New Englander Bierce, Brown was a devout Congregationalist—and by all accounts a pacifist at first. However, when the murderous pro-slavery "Border Ruffians" threatened the lives of his children who had settled in the Kansas Territory, Brown had a crisis of faith.

Like any devout Congregationalist, John Brown turned to his King James Bible for answers. However, reading the New Testament, with its "turn the other cheek" philosophy, gave Brown no solace. Finally he turned to the Old Testament, where he found what he was looking for: "And the Lord said unto Saul, Go out and slay the Philistines." According to a contemporary witness who heard it directly from Brown himself, at that very moment John Brown saw a ray of light and then knelt with his wife in prayer. He heard the voice of the Lord in the upper part of the room saying, "John Brown, go to Kansas and slay the Border Ruffians!" Stopping in Akron on his way west to help his family, Brown solicited his like-minded friends—Lucius Bierce among them—for succor. About two dozen citizens of Akron donated money, equipment, and munitions. In addition to a shipment of new government-issue Sharps rifles and a twelve-pound cannon "lying about loose" that were diverted for the cause, General Bierce also donated two boxes of cavalry swords and pistols left over from his ill-fated Canadian invasion. These were the very same sabers that John Brown and his followers would later use against a number of pro-slavery "Philistines" during the notorious Pottawatomie Massacre.[24]

On December 2, 1859, John Brown was executed in Virginia for his famous (or infamous, depending on the point of view) attempt to start a slave revolt at Harper's Ferry. If any were in doubt about where the Bierces stood on this issue, Uncle Lucius clarified in a long public speech that very same day: "Call it fanaticism, folly, madness, wickedness, but until virtue becomes fanaticism, divine wisdom folly, obedience to God madness, and piety wickedness, John Brown, inspired by these high and holy teachings, will rise up before the world with his calm, marble features, most terrible in death and defeat, than in life and victory. It is one of those acts of madness which history cherished and poetry loves forever to adorn with her choicest wreaths of laurel."[25]

As with much else relating to his life prior to the war, Ambrose Bierce remained quiet as a sphinx regarding details of his relationship with his Uncle Lucius. However, as a longtime associate and biographer states, "There is no question but that Bierce fashioned his own life after his hero-relative."[26] That his flamboyant uncle was all that his father was not was obvious; Lucius's well-appointed library was an added bonus to the bookish adolescent Bierce. How much of his uncle's activism young Bierce absorbed can only be guessed at; likely it was considerable. At any rate, Uncle Lucius took his rebellious nephew under his wing. In addition to giving him shelter, he also volunteered to fund his further education.

The school chosen for young Bierce was the Kentucky Military Institute, or KMI.[27] KMI was founded in 1845 and was officially chartered by the state of Kentucky, the commandant of the military school technically being a Colonel in the state militia. The first such Kentucky Colonel of KMI was Robert D. P. Allen, West Point graduate and veteran of the Seminole Wars. Under his tutelage the institute quickly gained a reputation for its excellent instructors, strict discipline and demanding academic courses. The institute recruited all over the country, in particular from the Ohio Valley and the South. It was a full four-year college, but state militia officers could take a one-year course of instruction—already being officers, they just needed to learn how to become gentlemen.[28]

At the time that young Bierce attended, the institute was located on the old Farmdale Plantation in Franklin County, Kentucky, close to the state capitol of Frankfort. A mineral spring lay on the property, and before KMI was opened, the estate had housed a health spa where people came to be cured

Green and Salad Days

Kentucky Military Institute, prior to the Civil War. Although Bierce only attended for a year, he was thoroughly drilled in military discipline and may have received some instruction in engineering as well. His reasons for leaving remain cloudy, but may have been related to his and his family's abolitionist views. Library of Congress.

of their ailments by partaking of the waters. Farmdale proved less than successful as a health spa, but it did turn out to be an ideal locale for a military school. Young Brady certainly was not the first—or the last—"bad boy" to be sent to military school to be cured of rebelliousness.

Hard facts about Bierce's sojourn at military school are scant. Before relocating from Kentucky to Florida, the Kentucky Military Institute suffered several fires at Farmdale in the late nineteenth century. The fires destroyed most of KMI's early records; an elderly alumnus' testimony and a lone library card are the only hard evidence of Brady's presence there. But it seems certain that 'Brose did indeed attend. Scholars believe that he entered the institute in September 1859 and left in June 1860, never advancing beyond freshman level. The curriculum at KMI, one advertisement boasted, "is that taught in the best Colleges, with the addition of more extended courses in Mathematics, Mechanics, Practical Engineering and Mining Geology."[29] The school advertised its emphasis on an education in "engineering," but it is not certain how much such instruction Brady would have actually received during the first year. Among a collection of Bierce artifacts preserved in the county museum in Elkhart, Indiana is an edition of *Gillespie's Land Surveying*. Published in 1855, the book has the ex libris "AG Bierce" written on the inside. It is likely that Bierce acquired the surveying book during his time at KMI.[30]

We do know while that while at military school Brady would have had least one hour per day of parade ground drill and occasional instruction in military marksmanship. However, it is unlikely that Cadet Bierce would have been taught anything more advanced in the military arts than close order drill and similar basic martial instructions during his stay at KMI. The course "Duties of a Non-Commissioned Officer" was not taught until third year, and "Duties of a Commissioned Officer" was reserved for fourth year cadets. Likewise, "Military Engineering and Field Fortifications" was only offered in the second semester of senior year.[31]

Why Brady Bierce's military school education was cut short after only one year remains a mystery. It was not for lack of money for tuition, because Uncle Lucius was a successful lawyer and politician and could easily foot the bill. Homesickness is even less likely as a cause, given what we know of Bierce's home life. Moreover, Bierce's bookish nature and his natural aptitude for learning preclude poor academic performance as a reason. It is conceivable that one year of strict military discipline was about all that Bierce could stomach, though only a short time later he easily adapted to the strictures of military life as a member of the Ninth Indiana. During the war, Bierce demonstrated a positive preference for spit-and-polish discipline while serving under Brigadier William Hazen.

During this era, KMI's school seal shows two well-dressed young gentlemen shaking hands surrounded by the motto, "United we stand, divided we fall." Clearly, the school's original seal indicated the importance of leveling sectional differences between North and South. Kentucky, although a slave state, was very much a commonwealth of divided loyalties. While there was widespread Unionist sentiment in Kentucky, a very vocal Secessionist element also existed. Despite the institute's initially conciliatory motto, sectionalism and the debate over secession inevitably affected the student body. Attending school on the eve of the Civil War, Cadet Bierce may well have run afoul of the increasingly acrimonious dispute over slavery and secession among his classmates.

Exactly when Bierce's last day at KMI was is not known, but he was certainly present for the commencement exercise in mid-June, 1860. A contemporary newspaper report informs us that the entire student body attended. The ceremonies featured a "review, inspection, and drill of infantry, the latter eliciting the admiration of all the spectators." Upwards of one thousand persons, "a considerable portion of whom were ladies," attended the ceremonies. Numerous speeches were given to the graduating class and student body as part of commencement. The titles of some of these "orations" are suggestive: "Heroism Possible to All," "Ruin of Empires," "Virginia," "Anglo-Saxon Love of Land, Liberty and Law," "Self Government," and ""Kentucky's Illustrious Dead."[32]

Less than five months later, close on the heels of Lincoln's election as President and even as South Carolina prepared to secede, a brief notice was published that left no doubt as to where the majority of the faculty and student body of KMI stood regarding Lincoln's election and their reaction to it:

> Kentucky Military Institute,
> November 17, 1860.
>
> To His Excellency Governor Gist:
> The Cadets of the Kentucky Military Institute have this day, with unanimous consent, tendered their services to the citizens of South Carolina, and hold themselves in readiness for any emergency. Should our services be needed, we do hope that you will not fail to let us know immediately, for we are anxious to render the gallant State of South Carolina our services. As we are sons of the noble South, we are anxious to come and help defend our Southern rights. We do not wish to flatter ourselves, but still do we contend that, after being under strict military discipline for four years, we understand how to handle the musket.
>
> C. J. Ward, Adjutant[33]

Their neighbors in Warsaw regarded the Bierce family—father and sons—as being "strong-headed" men who "did not back down for anything."[34] Brady's outspoken nature and his family's steadfast abolitionism were well known. At Kentucky Military Institute Brady likely encountered more than one fellow cadet with an equally strong opinion regarding the virtues of slavery and Secessionism. Given the temper of the times—and Bierce's own temper—it is likely that their political discussions became heated; they may well have turned physical. While hard evidence is wanting, it is not an unreasonable inference based on the circumstances.

What is certain is that less than a year after Bierce left KMI, his fellow classmates did indeed express their political beliefs in violent terms. Most of the cadets joined the Confederate side, but a minority remained loyal to the Union cause. The Kentucky Military Institute would contribute several generals to both sides in the Civil War, and sixty-four alumni would die in the conflict.[35]

As the election of 1860 loomed, it did not take a prophet to see that the long-threatened sectional conflict was imminent. After leaving KMI and departing Reuben Williams's employ, Brady Bierce took up residence in Elkhart, Indiana. According to contemporary witnesses, his parents had already relocated there from their farm near Warsaw a few years before the war, and Ambrose was residing with them when Fort Sumter was fired on.[36] This move probably would have taken place sometime after the census-taker came through Kosciusko County since he listed them as still residing there in the 1860 census.[37] In any case, Bierce spent the ensuing months at Elkhart occupying himself with various odd jobs. Some biographers have interpreted those months as a period of Bierce's aimlessness, but it is more likely that his brief interlude in Elkhart was simply a way of marking time until the march of events caught up with his own militant sensibilities.[38] At any rate, Ambrose Gwinnett Bierce did not have a long time to wait.

2

Bad Boys Make Good Soldiers

> **RECRUIT**, *n*. A person distinguishable from a civilian by his uniform and from a soldier by his gait.

Coming as he did from a strict fundamentalist background, there is little doubt that Brady was regarded as the black sheep of the family. Young Bierce was indeed full of mischief growing up and apparently had a knack for getting into scrapes even after he left home and lived on his own. How "bad"[1] Bierce actually was, however, may have been more a matter of perception than reality. Nonetheless, in the spring of 1861, the Union Army cared little for the moral character of its recruits or whether the boys who were volunteering were good or "bad"—so long as they could carry a gun. Lincoln had summoned 75,000 men to suppress the rebellion and gave each loyal state a quota of troops to be met.

Since Lincoln's election in November, unrest had been unfolding with ever-increasing rapidity. Although the Buchanan administration still occupied the White House, slave states began seceding from the Union one after another. Long before Lincoln was inaugurated, Secessionists, with or without state approval, were seizing arsenals, forts, and other Federal property throughout the South. Even prior to this, however, militant "fire-breathing" Secessionists had already taken it upon themselves to organize in anticipation of enforcing their will at gunpoint should the 1860 election go against them.[2] The seceding states formed their own rebellious coalition and, harkening back to the early days of the Republic, to the feeble Confederation government of the 1780s, dubbed it the Confederate States of America. All this was done before Lincoln had so much as raised a finger against the South. The majority of Southerners before Sumter may have hoped for a peaceful resolution of their differences, but the Secessionists—even more than the Abolitionists—were not only a vocal minority; they were well organized and included in their number many men of power, wealth, and influence.

Lincoln's Inaugural Address on March 4, 1861 had been as conciliatory a speech as one could wish, given the circumstances. But even so, Secessionists would have none of it. Every conciliatory gesture was taken as a sign of weakness and every assertion of Federal authority was interpreted as a provocation. Finally, South Carolina's increasingly militant attitude against the small Federal garrison already occupying Fort Sumter erupted into open hostilities, and on April 12, 1861, armed Secessionist forces in Charleston began bombarding Fort Sumter. The War of the Rebellion had officially begun. Yet it was only when the fort fell two days later that Lincoln was finally moved to act, calling upon the states for volunteers on April 15 to suppress the rebellion.

Abolitionists such as the Bierces had long wished to take arms against slavery and the slave-owner oligarchy. Most of the country, however, held out hope for some sort of reconciliation long after such hope had proved vain. In 1861, few in the North would have gone to war simply over the issue of slavery. However, the Secessionists, in ignoring the results of a free and fair election, flaunting their defiance of the Constitution, and bombarding Fort Sumter, persuaded most of the Free States that it was necessary to suppress the rebellion by force.

Back home in Indiana, Lincoln's call for troops to defend the flag was readily answered in every town and village by patriotic Hoosiers. Among the throng who flocked to the flag, however, there were a few whose motives for enlisting went beyond simply preserving the Union. They, like the Bierces, had broader motives than patriotism. For example, Brady's former boss, Reuben Williams, decided that the sword was mightier than the pen after all and resigned as editor of *The Northern Indianian*. "The tocsin of war" reached Warsaw, Indiana at eleven o'clock on April 15, and by noon Williams was at the top of the list of volunteers for a company to represent Kosciusko County. Soon incorporated into the Twelfth Indiana Volunteer Infantry Regiment as Company E, the Kosciusko Guards more than proved their worth. Williams, beginning as a Second Lieutenant, rose to become Colonel of the regiment and led them through some of the bloodiest battles of the war.[3]

Meanwhile, Uncle Lucius Bierce, although too old for front-line military service, proved quite active in furthering the war effort for the Union. The old "general" outfitted and raised two companies of marines at his own expense and then personally delivered them to Washington, and he also raised a company of infantry for the Union army. He continued to occupy various important political and administrative offices, and Lincoln eventually appointed him Assistant Adjutant General of Volunteers, with the official rank of major. In this post he strove mightily to bring order out of chaos in organizing the vast manpower of the Republic.

As for young Brady, he was no less eager to serve—out of much the same motivation as his former boss and his uncle. Although the mature postwar Bierce was quite circumspect regarding his youthful ideals, at one point he did confess, "In my green and salad days I was sufficiently zealous for universal and unqualified Freedom to engage in a four years' battle for its promotion."[4] Elsewhere, Bierce also describes his military service as "soldiering for Freedom"[5]—not, one may note, as preserving the Union. Such adult comments reflect, albeit dimly, the attitudes of his youth—the young man nicknamed 'Brose—not "Bitter Bierce." While one would prefer more ample testimony from Bierce, it seems clear that at this point in his life Bierce was an idealist—perhaps even an ideologue—imbued with the same values that his father, his uncle, and his first employer shared, a zeal which included not only devotion to the Republican cause but, by 1861, an ardent opposition to slavery.

In Elkhart, where Bierce had been whiling away the months as the nation drifted toward war, Lincoln's call for volunteers did not go unheeded. On April 19, 1861, Theodore F. Mann, a prominent local lawyer in Elkhart, announced that he was organizing a company of volunteers to defend the Union. As soon as Brady heard the news, he rushed to Mann's to enlist. Bierce was only the second recruit to enroll in Mann's company; citizen Bierce was now Private Bierce, Indiana Volunteer Infantry. Of this newly formed band of volunteers, some were young men at loose ends and eager for change. Others had careers and were married with families to support. A few were older, but had heard the clarion call as clearly as the brash younger men. There were farm boys and townsmen, blacksmiths and laborers—there was even a man who had been a scout out west with Kit Carson.

Their motives for joining were varied: a few, like Bierce, were committed to freeing the slaves and saw the war as a means to that end. Many—perhaps most—were motivated by simple patriotism, responding to the call to defend the flag. Some joined to impress some comely young female they had been courting and believed that a few months of military service and a handsome new uniform would win her heart and hand. A few enlisted simply for adventure or to see someplace other than Elkhart, while others joined just for the sheer hell of it.[6] All had one thing in common though: none—officers and men alike—truly knew what was in store for them.

In addition to his devotion to abolition, however, Bierce may also have been motivated by other emotions, namely his desire to impress a certain young lady. Before he marched off to war, Bierce is believed to have sent her an anonymous love poem, expressing his affection for her. Since he addressed the poem to "Fatima"—a private pet name only he allegedly called her—Bierce assumed she knew who it came from. Walter Neale, Bierce's publisher, says Bierce told him that his first relationship with the opposite sex antedated his infatuation with young Fatima. He claims that Bierce confessed to a sexual liaison in Warsaw with a lady seventy years of age.[7] While most biographers have discounted Neale's piece of gossip, some suggest that Bierce may actually have told him this, though in the same way he told that he "ran away to Chicago" as a youth to work on a newspaper. Ambrose Bierce is known to have resided in England for a time during his postwar years; one can only speculate whether he also paid a visit to Ireland and kissed the Blarney Stone—or, more likely, some good Irish Whiskey—at least insofar as some of the things he regaled Walter Neale with are concerned.

It did not take long for the Elkhart volunteer company to reach full enrollment, at which point they headed for Indianapolis to be officially mustered in. The "Record of Events"—the regimental diary—indicates the company "marched" the 210 miles to Indianapolis to be mustered in. However, most of the personal accounts by veterans indicate that the various companies arrived by train rather than on foot. In any case, Brady and his newfound band of brothers arrived in Indianapolis on April 22, joining similar volunteer groups rapidly arriving to form one of six new ninety-day regiments that Governor Oliver P. Morton had promised President Lincoln.

Over the next few days, other companies appeared from outlying towns and cities: Captain Hannum's company from Delphi; Captain Blake's boys from Michigan City; Captain Dunn's unit from Logansport; Captain Segur's detachment from Fort Wayne; Captain Woodward's from LaPorte; Milroy and Moody's men from Rennsselaer; Captain Cameron and his group from Valparaiso; Andrew Andeman and his bunch from South Bend, and the Logansport Company under Captain Chase. All arrived in the city between April 22 and April 24 and were quickly banded together to form the Ninth Indiana Regiment of Foot Volunteers (Ninety Day), with the Elkhart Company being designated Company C.

At the head of the regiment was Colonel Robert Houston Milroy. Initially he had been the commander of the volunteers from Rensselaer, but his previous military experience and high social standing made him the natural choice for regimental commander. He had graduated from Captain Partridge's Military Academy in Norwich, Vermont in 1843 with a Bachelor of Arts and a Master's in Military Science, as well as a degree in Civil Engineering. In 1845, he went to Texas and volunteered for service with the Republic of Texas, but apparently had a change of heart and returned home to Indiana to study law. The outbreak of the Mexican War saw Milroy once more attracted to the Profession of Mars, and he led a company of Indiana volunteers with the First Indiana Regiment in that war. When his term of service expired in that outfit, Milroy volunteered to organize a company of mounted infantry, but he could get neither General Zachary Taylor nor the Governor of Texas interested in his offer. He therefore returned to Indiana to finish his law degree and in the intervening years not only built up a suc-

Colonel (later General) Robert H. Milroy was Bierce's first regimental commander. Called the "Grey Eagle," he was much admired by the men of the Ninth Indiana, although when it came to drill and discipline he was less strict than later commanders. Library of Congress.

cessful law practice but also became a person of some political prominence in Indiana.

As early as February 1861, Judge Milroy had sought to organize a volunteer company, but at first recruitment went slowly. With the fall of Fort Sumter, however, attitudes in Rensselaer changed dramatically. On the morning after the announcement of Sumter's surrender, while still dark, Milroy rang the Court-House bell and then, with a fifer and a drummer, roused the town and led them like the pied piper to his home where he completed registration of the Rensselaer volunteer company before breakfast. That same day Milroy reported to Governor Morton in Indianapolis. With his aquiline nose, his piercing dark eyes and a flowing mane of silver hair, Colonel Robert Milroy was popularly known as "the Grey Eagle." Although his later career as a general officer was somewhat checkered, he was a popular commander with the Ninth and his leadership of those ninety-day "wonders" proved spotless.[8]

Bad Boys Make Good Soldiers

While Governor Morton responded rapidly to Lincoln's call for troops, nothing could disguise the fact that Indiana was totally unprepared for mobilization. Only four volunteer militia companies existed throughout the whole state at the outbreak of war, and the captain of one of those companies joined the Confederate army. Not only did the state lack arms, munitions, and uniforms, but all the other impedimenta of war needed to equip a modern army were also wanting—even a place to assemble and train all the volunteers.

On April 17, the State Fairgrounds near Indianapolis were hastily commandeered and put into service as mustering ground and training camp for the new state units. Designated Camp Morton in honor of the governor, it consisted of thirty-six acres just north of the city, today bounded by Talbot Avenue on the west, Central Avenue on the east, Twenty-Second Street to the north and Nineteenth Street to the south. In 1861, the former fairgrounds—at one time known as "Otis' Grove" or "Henderson's Grove"—consisted mostly of open ground, with a scattering of oak and walnut trees and at least four freshwater springs. A creek also flowed through the grounds; originally called Fall Creek, it was simply the "State Ditch" by '62. Later in the war, it came to be called "the Potomac" by Rebel prisoners held at Camp Morton.

When Bierce and his Elkhart comrades arrived at Camp Morton on April 22, the camp was woefully lacking in the simplest amenities. There were a few buildings on the grounds left over from its use as fairgrounds, but little else. On the north side lay long, open-ended sheds that had been used to stable horses, while on the west end of the grounds were stalls for 250 cattle, some sheds to house sheep and hogs, and an exhibition hall. There was also a dining hall on the east end, while in the center stood a two-story office building. When Bierce and his comrades marched into camp, they were somewhat surprised to find their new barracks had lately housed livestock. Their billets were still redolent with the aroma of its former occupants.

Very quickly the stalls and sheds of the fairgrounds proved insufficient to house all the arriving troops. In short order, new barracks built out of green lumber were erected. These new buildings featured four tiers of bunks lining both sides of the long, shed-like building and extending seven feet into the middle of the room. Between these rows of bunks stretched long tables that served as a mess area where the troops could eat. Each barrack could house 320 men. As more men arrived at Camp Morton and supplies started to flow in, tents were pitched to house the growing mob. Whether the Ninth moved up to the newer barracks is not known; regardless, Bierce and his comrades had to deal with very cramped quarters during their stay at Camp Morton.[9]

If the living conditions were poor, the food was even worse. There was some talk at first that Rebel sympathizers had poisoned the food, so bad was their fare. As it turned out, the problem was more attributable to poor organization on the part of the Commissary General. The State Commissary initially had no money to work with and no official guidelines to adhere to in dealing with contractors. Incompetence on the part of the civilian staff also played a role. Eventually the adulterated coffee and short rations were remedied, and the recruits at Camp Morton began to fare better in terms of victuals.[10]

The Ninth Indiana was the first of the six regiments mustered into service by Governor Morton to deal with the secession crisis. Indiana's quota of troops had been set at 10,000 men, but in their enthusiasm to avenge Sumter and the flag, over 12,000 Hoosiers volunteered, showing up at Camp Morton within the span of two weeks—some without orders. In the end, realizing the Republic would need the surplus manpower and then some, Governor Morton did his best to retain as many of the excess volunteers as his military department could accommodate. Morton's prescience that the rebellion would last far longer than ninety days and need far more than the minimum quota would soon prove correct.

In the meantime, Private Bierce and the other newly minted soldiers of the Ninth attempted to learn the basics of soldiering within the crowded confines of Camp Morton—no easy task. The camp was overflowing with recruits and the buildings, and trees and tents that dotted the grounds made drill by large bodies of men difficult. In addition, local citizens started coming out from the city, finding the camp "a center of attraction." Likely there was a substantial portion of young females in the crowd—a further distraction for the young warriors.

Given the growing throng inside the camp, additional acreage was needed. Soon more territory was annexed nearby where Company C and the other units were able to carry out their parade-ground drills. For Private Bierce this all would have been familiar routine since he had already participated in about nine months' worth of daily drill. For Bierce's messmates, however, things as simple as attention, present arms, or marching in step would have been a foreign experience. The mysteries of close-order drill were beyond their civilian ken in even the simplest things: "It was said the technical terms 'right or left' were entirely above their comprehension, and it was necessary to substitute 'gee and haw.'"[11]

The Ninth's newly minted officers were likewise largely innocent of military discipline, tactics, and training. They scrambled to find copies of *Hardee's Infantry Tactics* in order to hastily learn how to turn a marching column into a line of battle and other simple maneuvers. With the exception of a few men such as Colonel Milroy, the Ninth Indiana—officers and men—were little more than an untutored mob of civilians in uniform—and initially not even that. In fact, Colonel Milroy and his officers had to take out personal loans in order to purchase uniforms and equip the regiment.[12] As the weeks passed at Camp Morton, the food improved, the variegate civilian costumes were replaced by military garb. The Ninth Indiana was not initially clothed in Union blue, however; Milroy purchased grey uniforms with black epaulettes, collars and cuffs.[13] Grey uniforms were common among Northern militia and volunteer units in the early days of the war, but it was a practice that led to a great deal of confusion in combat. The companies and regiments gradually learned to march in step, snap to attention, and otherwise present the illusion of trained soldiers. Finally, by May 29, the Ninth's time for graduation—if one could call it that—had come. Private Bierce, Company C and the other bands of brothers now collectively known as the Ninth Indiana marched to the railroad depot and entrained for points east.

It is a modern misconception that all folk north of the Mason-Dixon Line were opposed to slavery while all those south of it unquestionably supported the "peculiar institution" and Secession. In fact, all along the northern banks of the Ohio River there existed broad swaths of territory filled with those sympathetic to the Confederacy. Conversely, throughout the South and especially along the southern shores of the Ohio, there were substantial regions whose population had little affection for slavery and even less sympathy for Secession. One such region was western Virginia, inhabited by stubborn mountaineers whose livelihood was not dependent on slavery and who populated the thirty-five counties of northwestern Virginia. Traditionally, they had been slighted by the wealthy slave-owning oligarchy that firmly controlled the reins of state government. Fully a quarter of the white population of Virginia resided in this region and when the flames of disunion spread throughout the South, they were particularly vocal in their opposition to it.

The official tallies declared that Virginia voters were in favor of secession. But accusations flew that ballot boxes disappeared on the way to Richmond or else were stuffed with ballots different from the ones they originally contained; in any case, voters from the western Virginia counties rejected secession by a margin of three to one. Despite fervent pleas from western Virginians, the Lincoln administration was at first powerless to help. By April 1861, Washington, D.C., was virtually cut off from the rest of the loyal states as Secessionists sabotaged transportation and communications into and out of the capitol. Fortunately, Governors Morton of Indiana and Dennison of Ohio had an abundance of troops. When "Secesh" saboteurs cut the B&O Railroad's bridges, thereby cutting off Washington's last lifeline to the outside world, these Mid-Western governors and their military advisors resolved to act. So it was that Bierce and the Ninth were rushed east to the succor of the loyal Virginians.

By May 31, the Ninth Indiana arrived at Benwood, on the banks of the Ohio. That evening they crossed over into Virginia. Entering the town of Grafton right behind an Ohio regiment, the Ninth's arrival had more the air of a triumphal procession than that of a military occupation. The attitude of these Virginians was anything but rebellious: "Imagine a man reprieved under the gallows and restored in one stroke to an honorable position in society," wrote one breathless correspondent, "and you may conceive the feelings of the people of Grafton at their deliverance."[14] Drumming and fifing, cheering and singing greeted the young men of the Ninth. To show their appreciation at being liberated from the Secesh occupiers, the young women of the town donned "unique and appropriate costume," consisting of aprons made from the national flag. The blue field of stars was draped over their proud bosoms, while the red and white stripes hung vertically across their skirts. According to a correspondent embedded with the troops, the effect was "beautiful and striking"—no doubt many boys in blue felt proud at such a patriotic sight.

Even before the celebration had subsided, Colonel Benjamin F. Kelley, in command of the First Virginia Volunteers (Union), and General Thomas Morris, the overall Federal commander, had conferred over their force's next move. They knew that the Secessionist troops had withdrawn to the city of Philippi and believed that the Rebels were gathered there in strength. Colonel Kelley wanted to march immediately on Philippi, but General Morris urged caution and had his subordinate wait one day until additional

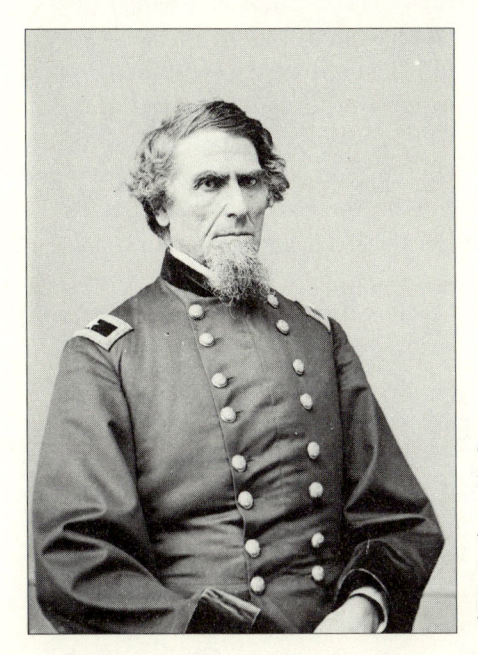

General Benjamin F. Kelley. Kelley initially commanded the First Virginia (US) Volunteer Infantry regiment but was soon put in command of the force that included Bierce's regiment during its initial stay in western Virginia (later West Virginia). Library of Congress.

troops could come up. On the evening of June 2, therefore, the Federals advanced on the town of Philippi in two separate columns with plans to encircle the enemy. One of the columns, under Colonel Dumont of the Seventh Indiana, was to advance on the town from the west, while Colonel Kelley's column, which included Bierce's regiment, would descend on the town with the main force from the opposite side; the whole expedition numbered about 1,600 men total—although Confederate reports later placed the total much higher.[15]

Night marches are not easy, even for veteran troops. At this stage of the war, no one on either side had had much experience with war—nor, it seems, with decent maps. By dark of night, the Ninth Indiana and the others advanced along winding country roads sticky with mud and across creeks swollen by heavy rain. Between the foul weather, the darkness, and a badly befuddled guide, Colonel Kelley's column lost its way and by four in the morning it was closing in on Philippi from virtually the same direction as Colonel Dumont's force. Fortunately, the Rebel garrison in the town of Philippi was as green as the Federals—and even more poorly equipped. At four A.M., when the Yankees descended on the town, there were no pickets guarding the approaches to town from any direction. The Secesh commander had indeed posted pickets at outposts the night before, but the same bad weather that had hindered the Union advance also persuaded the Rebel pickets to come into town and find comfortable lodging for the night. Unfortunately, no one bothered to inform the slumbering Rebel commander, Colonel George Porterfield, that his position was now undefended.

The Union plan was that, once all his troops were in position, Colonel Kelley would fire off a round from his revolver to signal the start of the attack. However, as one detachment of Federals approached the town, the irate mother of one of the young men in the Secessionist garrison took a pot-shot at the approaching Yankees, setting off the assault prematurely. In the shadowy darkness, the Federal infantry charged headlong into town even as an eager battery of Union artillery opened up on a nearby hill. Thus from the "high hill" the First Ohio Light Artillery fired merrily away at anything that moved in the shadowy valley below. In a short story partly based on this incident, Bierce suggests that in the dimness the Buckeye's shells fell indiscriminately among friend as well as foe. Fortunately, unlike the murderous Federal battery he chronicles in his story "One Kind of Officer," the Union artillerist's barrage did little damage to combatants on either side. It did, however, add greatly to the confusion in the enemy camp.[16]

The sole casualty from the Yankee cannon fire was one unfortunate Rebel—Private James Hanger—who had his leg taken off by a round. Bierce later made Hanger's acquaintance in 1903, when he visited his old battlefields. Hanger survived his injury and turned misfortune into fortune by inventing the artificial limb. An engineering student before the war, after his injury the young invalid set to work on providing an alternative to hobbling about on a peg-leg for the rest of his life. After months of solitude, he emerged from his room with the world's first artificial leg and set about manufacturing them. As the war progressed, tens of thousands of survivors of the internecine strife found themselves in a similar situation as Hanger, who enjoyed a booming business selling artificial limbs. The company he founded is still the world's largest purveyor of prosthetic limbs.[17]

The Ninth swept into town along with the other Federals, taking the Rebels by surprise and throwing them into a panic. The confused and outnumbered 800-odd Confederates hightailed it out of town any which way they could. Within half an hour of the beginning of the assault, the Rebels were in full retreat; so total and rapid was their rout out of town that the skirmish at Philippi was popularly referred to as the "Philippi Races." After the debacle at Philippi, the Rebels fled to Laurel Hill (or Laurel Hills) near the town of Belington, "in trying, Heaven knows why," Bierce recounts, "to get way from us."[18] Although the Secesh were in disarray, the Federals made little effort to follow up their triumph. Instead, they hunkered down around the town of Philippi as both sides took time to consolidate their positions and bring up reinforcements.

During the lull in action, there were occasional patrols and scouting forays. One member of the Ninth, Sergeant Dunham, was reputed to be "the

The Battle of Philippi—sometimes referred to as "The Philippi Races"—was more a comedy of errors that a real battle. Milroy's force got lost in the dark and then, when attacking the town, Bierce and his comrades had to dodge their own artillery shells as well as enemy bullets, an incident which Bierce later enshrined in a short story. *Leslie's Illustrated Weekly*, based on field sketch by Henry Lovie.

best scout in the service" and a former associate of the legendary Kit Carson. Toward the middle of the month he spent three days behind enemy lines, allegedly penetrating into their camp and returning with reports of enemy strength and dispositions.[19] Mostly, however, Bierce and his comrades simply whiled away the days entranced by this strange new land they found themselves in. To Bierce and his comrades, western Virginia was "a kind of dreamland." Even in later years, the hardened cynic inside Bierce evaporated whenever harkening back to these halcyon early days of the war: "In power of emotions nothing, I think, is comparable to a first sight of mountains. To a member of a plains-tribe, born and reared on the flats of Ohio and Indiana, a mountain region was a perpetual miracle. Space seemed to take on a new dimension; areas to have not only length and breadth, but thickness."[20] He continues, "Nine in ten of us had never seen a mountain, nor a hill as high as a church spire, until we had crossed the Ohio River."[21]

Having given their foes adequate time to rest and regroup, by the beginning of July the Federals were ready to advance once more. A force under Colonel Kelly—lately brevetted to Brigadier—marched toward Belington at the foot of Laurel Hills, where the Confederate forces had entrenched themselves. At two a.m. on Sunday morning, July 9, Milroy's column began to advance with the Ninth Indiana in the van. The road out of Philippi wound through sinuous valleys and ascended steep slopes that skirted the upper part of the Tygart's River Valley. Initially, the march was a pleasant one: "There came to us on the moist morning air the fragrance of the laurel and the azalea, and as our horses occasionally broke gaily into a trot . . . one might have had difficulty in imaging it aught else than a pleasant morning ride that had brought us on a road thus early."[22]

By about half past seven, the Ninth reached the outskirts of Belington, which Bierce describes as "little but a blacksmith's shop at a cross-roads." The two companies of skirmishers at the head of the Federal column soon ran into enemy pickets, which set off a running fight, the advance guard rushing the Rebels, who ran away "like quarter nags." As the other troops spread out on the flanks, the Ninth hurried to the base of the hill that overlooked the town. In the process, the Ninth suffered their first combat fatality of the war, William T. Girard. Girard was with the skirmish line chasing the Rebels into a nearby wood when an enemy bullet to his forehead put an abrupt halt to his morning exercise.

Within half and hour, the Ninth and the other units had deployed into a broad defensive line. Most of the first day was spent securing their line and making it ready to receive any assault from the Rebels ensconced beyond the town. Throughout the day, both sides kept up a "straggling fire." During the night, the Secesh troops even made a few attempts to rush the outlying pickets—to little effects.

On the morning of the tenth, the two sides kept up their random potshots at each other, and as the day wore on it gradually grew to "a regular bush fire." As the sun grew high in the sky, a substantial Rebel force occupied the woods opposite the Federals, making things hot for the "Swamp Devils"—as the Ninth was now known. When a Rebel sharpshooter dented a Union artillery officer's saber, the irritated subaltern quickly sighted his artillery piece and began lobbing shells in the sharpshooter's direction. About fifteen skirmishers from the Ninth—and perhaps a few more from the Ohio regiment—"grew tired of the resultless quarrel" between the two foes. Impulsively they ran across the road and into the woods to the foot of an acclivity, thick with laurel, that was known to the Yankees as Girard Hill. However, this reckless band of Swamp Devils—Private Bierce among them—soon discovered that Girard Hill was held by a full regiment of Georgia infantry, backed by some Southern cavalry. Despite the enemy's numbers, the fifteen Hoosiers of Bierce's group chased the Georgians back up the hill. Two of the Union riflemen—Bierce of Company C and Corporal Dyson Boothroyd of Company A—actually got within fifteen paces of the Rebel entrenchments near the top of the hill. Before he realized it, however, Bierce became an army of one: Boothroyd had been hit in the neck by a Rebel round. It was perhaps at this point that Bierce suddenly became aware that his fellow skirmishers' courage had faltered somewhat farther down the hill, the others failing to follow Boothroyd and Bierce up to the enemy battle line.

With Rebel bullets whizzing past his ears like angry bees, Bierce stooped down, took Boothroyd in his arms, scooped up the corporal's musket and his own, and carried his injured comrade and their weapons some twenty rods back down out of harm's way.[23]

There may have been others of the Ninth as brash as young Bierce, but none so brave—at least on that day. He and the other skirmishers had operated without orders, advancing forward, "from log to tree, and from tree to bush," rushing across the road into the woods. The Hoosiers did not completely retreat after this first repulse, however. When the Georgian fire proved too hot, or the Ohio battery was about to open fire, they would shout out orders to themselves—"Rally to your logs!"—and then follow their own orders and scoot back to a sheltering tree, log, or blackberry bush. Colonel Milroy was still with the artillery, some two to three hundred yards behind them on the opposite hill. Although he tried to call his men back, they largely ignored him. At one point Milroy jumped up on top of one of the logs sheltering the field pieces and waved his hat, yelling at Bierce and the others, "Fall back boys! We're going to fire another shell!"

Instead of retreating, however, Bierce and his comrades began to yell back corrections for the shellfire: "Fire more to the right!"[24] And so it went all afternoon until darkness put a halt to the action. While one correspondent

Bad Boys Make Good Soldiers

The Battle of Laurel Hill (or Belington) was Bierce and the Ninth's first real taste of combat, in which Bierce distinguished himself, leading a charge and carrying a wounded comrade to safety. Sketch shows the situation at 5 p.m. on July 8. *Leslie's Illustrated Weekly*, based on field sketch by Henry Lovie.

characterized the battle as "Indian bush-fighting," another characterized the fray as more akin to "squirrel hunting."

That night, Milroy and the other commanders restrained their men with difficulty. Another column, under General McClellan, was supposed to be advancing from the north to cut off General Garnett and his Georgians and keep them from escaping. However, as would prove typical later in the war, McClellan was slow to move but quick to take credit for others' success. McClellan's column did not, in fact, come up in time; as a result, Garnett and his men got wind of what was afoot behind them. The morning light revealed that the Confederates had escaped in the darkness. General Morris sent his forces forward to make contact with the enemy, but when they reached the main Rebel defenses on the central summit of Laurel Hill, they only encountered a frightened mountain woman in a lone house. When asked about the whereabouts of the "Secesh" troops, she shrugged and replied, "They's done gone."

So ended the battle—such as it was—at Laurel Hills.

3

On a Mountain

> **PRIVATE**, *n*. A military gentleman with a field marshal's baton in his knapsack and an impediment in his hope.

After the action at Laurel Hills, Bierce and the Ninth attempted to pursue the fleeing Rebels, chasing them as far as Carrick's Ford. Here a brief dust-up between the two forces ensued. General McClellan, in charge of another column, was supposed to have come up on the opposite side of Laurel Hill to block the Confederate's escape. Typically McClellan was tardy to arrive, so the Secesh column escaped largely unscathed—save for its commander, who was killed in the rear-guard action at Carrick's.

By the time they had finished with the pursuit, the Ninth Indiana's term of service was close to expiring. In short order, the regiment returned to Indianapolis, where, on July 29, it was officially mustered out of service—Private Bierce was a civilian once more. However, the end of July was neither the end of the Ninth Indiana nor the last of good soldier Bierce.

Years later, one veteran characterized the Ninth's ninety-day term of service as a kind of "preparatory school." In reviewing these three "uncommonly long months," it was observed that Bierce and his comrades had "more than a taste of hard tack and salt horse, had tried the numerous and various kinds of sleeping arrangements . . . had found that scouting, foraging, picket duty, fatigue duty, drill, cooking such food as you could get and the thousand peculiarities of the military in war time" were far more commonplace than any heroics in battle.[1]

No sooner were the three-month men mustered out than Colonel Milroy started to reorganize his command as a three-year regiment. Using LaPorte, Indiana, as his recruiting base, the Grey Eagle gathered together the best of his former command and actively sought out fresh recruits. For some of the former Swamp Devils, three months' military service was quite enough. They had returned from the war hometown heroes, they had done their duty, and they were now content to rest on their laurels (in some cases quite literally). Other ninety-day veterans re-enlisted for active service but for various reasons chose to serve in other regiments. Then there were those like 'Brose, men who had gone "looking for the elephant" in April and still had a hankering for action and were eager to rejoin the Ninth under Colonel Milroy's banner. As his early military service has been poorly researched and even more poorly chronicled, some accounts assert that Bierce "quit" the regiment at the end of July and then had a change of heart.[2] The truth is simply that his original term of enlistment had expired and, as with the rest of his comrades, the state of Indiana was obliged to discharge Bierce back on home soil. It seems clear, however, that Bierce still possessed a taste for war and for service with the Ninth Indiana and that his youthful idealism was as yet untarnished.

As with his initial enlistment, Bierce was among the first to "re-up" for three years of service with the Ninth. Official records, reflecting the rather confused state of military record-keeping, are less than lucid about the exact date of his membership in the reconstituted C Company. For example, the Official Muster of the Ninth Indiana Volunteer Infantry (three years) dates to September 5, 1861. However, the Muster-in Roll for Company C lists Bierce as "joined for duty and enrolled" as of August 27. Bierce's own personal service record notes him as having "joined for duty and enrolled as of August fifteenth."[3]

Based on the documentary record, we can see that Bierce tolerated his new civilian status for little more than two weeks. The reason for the discrepancy of dates between individual, company, and regimental muster-in dates lies less with Bierce's willingness (or unwillingness) to re-up than in the fact that he had to wait for Colonel Milroy to enlist enough veterans and new recruits to make up the minimum quota needed for a new volunteer infantry regiment. Only then could the Ninth Indiana be reborn as a three-year organization. The official records do tell us that when Brady mustered in as a three-year volunteer he was no longer a "military gentleman with . . . an impediment in his hope"—a private—but had re-entered as full sergeant in rank. Although no explanation was given for his promotion, it is likely that Bierce's bravery in battle was noted and duly rewarded. Sergeant Bierce was just the sort of soldier Colonel Milroy needed.

It is apparent that the new three-year regiment was regarded as a veteran organization because after reorganization it trained for a shorter period of time at Camp Colfax in LaPorte before being sent back to western Virginia. The day Bierce and his comrades received their marching orders, the good folk of LaPorte turned out in droves, lining the streets of downtown and shouting out words of encouragement as the regiment marched past on the way to the railroad depot. Despite their recently acquired military bearing, some of the local boys—including an officer or two—would break ranks temporarily to kiss a sweetheart goodbye. Similarly, during the long train ride through Ohio, "splendid Buckeye girls" in the "very fullness of their patriotic devotion" would come up to the soldiers and spontaneously kiss them at the occasional fuel, food, and water stops. Young Ambrose, blue-eyed, fair-haired, and with an erect military bearing and fresh blue uniform, likely did not escape these young ladies' patriotic fervor. In these early days of the war it was still a thrill to be a soldier.[4]

Crossing over the Ohio, the Ninth Indiana arrived at the town of Webster and from there marched under the hot sun to Philippi. Veterans like Bierce regaled the newer recruits with heroic tales (mostly false) of their famous victory there. In any case, Philippi was just a temporary rest stop on the way to the front; after Philippi they marched on to Huttonsville, at the foot of Cheat Mountain. Cheat Mountain rose majestically in the same region of western Virginia where they had fought in July, and Bierce and his fellow "flatlanders" once again reveled in the "savage beauties" of the mountainous "enchanted land" of northwestern Virginia. Even in his cynical old age Bierce was wistfully poetic when describing this region: "With what pure delight we inhaled fragrances of spruce and pine! How we stared with something like awe at its clumps of laurel!" In their spare time, Bierce tells us, he and his messmates gathered spruce-gum and sent it home to their sweethearts in letters. When not on active duty, Bierce tells us that they "ascended every hill within our picket-lines and called it a 'peak.'"[5]

Nonetheless, not all was rustic idyll at Huttonsville and the men's nearby encampment at Elkwater. In fact, several soldiers of the Ninth, unused to the "savage beauties" of the region, fell gravely ill. No sooner had the regiment pitched camp at Elkwater than they suddenly received orders to go forthwith up to the summit of Cheat Mountain; the men were not even given enough time to pack up blankets, overcoats, and other belongings—much less tents. Shortly after making the arduous ascent to the top of Cheat Mountain, the regiment was battered by a "terrible cold rain." On October 26 and 27, Bierce and his comrades had to endure the raw elements on the mountaintop without even their rubber-coated blankets to protect them. The storm was so severe that their horses died from exposure and many of the men who took sick as a result of it never fully recovered. Bierce would later meet some of them again—on visiting the Federal cemetery at Grafton in 1903.[6]

Cheat Mountain, the forlorn peak where they lay chilled, wet and feverish, straddled a strategic highway—the Staunton-Parkersburg Pike—and twelve miles down that same road, the enemy was encamped overlooking the road and well supported by artillery. The Confederates called it Camp Bartow. It was decided by Federal authorities that the enemy should be dislodged from Camp Bartow. Brigadier Joseph J. Reynolds was put in charge of the expedition and, along with other units, the Ninth Indiana was assigned to attack the Rebel camp, giving them a welcome reprieve from their inhospitable mountaintop. Shortly after midnight on October 3, the Ninth Indiana advanced through the darkness, marching behind the Thirty-Second Ohio for some six miles until the pike joined with Gum Road. It was here that the Buckeye regiment halted around six a.m. while the Ninth kept on marching, taking the lead in the Union column. As the Ninth got within about five miles of the enemy camp, Colonel Milroy deployed companies F and K as skirmishers. When they reached the bridge over the Greenbrier River, the Hoosiers ran into a group of Rebel pickets. In the brief firefight that ensued, one man was wounded while another—Sergeant Smith Company H—was shot dead through the head.

Advancing in column, the regiment drove the Rebel pickets to within a mile of their fortified camp. As Bierce puts it, he and his comrades "felt the enemy . . . and the enemy did a little feeling, too."[7] After a brief firefight, the Ninth advanced across the "smooth meadow" in front of the Confederate entrenchments, halting about 1,900 yards from the enemy defenses. "Our commander," Bierce explains, "had the forethought to see that we lay well out of range of the small-arms of the period. A disadvantage of this arrangement was that the enemy was out of reach of us as well, for our rifles were no better than his. Unfortunately—one might almost say unfairly—he had a few pieces of artillery very well protected, and with those he mauled us to the eminent satisfaction of his mind and heart."[8]

In fact, the Federals had some artillery too—Howe's Battery, US Regulars, whose six guns took up position on the Ninth's right and began a healthy counter-fire, arousing the wrath of their opposite numbers. Fortunately, although the "enemy at once returned the fire of our battery from nine guns, throwing shot and shell," the regimental diarist tells us that it was "badly aimed."[9]

Colonel Milroy, observing an attempt to flank their position, moved Bierce and the other men to the left, where they took up position on a wooded hill, all the while exposed to the enmity of enemy artillery fire. It was during this maneuver that one of Bierce's comrades in Company C—Private James Abbott—was killed. The regimental diary simply states that Abbott was "killed by a round shot." Bierce elaborates on the manner of his messmate's demise: "He was lying flat on his stomach and was killed by being struck in the side by a nearly spent cannon-shot that came rolling in among us. The shot remained in him until removed. It was a solid round-shot, evidently cast in some foundry, whose proprietor, setting the laws of thrift above ballistics, had put his 'imprint' upon it." The round-shot, in slightly sunken lettering, bore the name of the foundry: "Abbott."[10]

The Ninth remained in this situation for close to an hour before Milroy ordered them to march by flank along the side of the hill "in line of battle to charge the enemy." What happened next is a little obscure; the regimental diary tells us cryptically that they "awaited in line forty minutes when the regiment began retiring from the field and waited until the regiment retired." Exactly which "regiment" did the retiring is not stated, but it does not seem to have been the Ninth: apparently "the retrograde movement having been made without orders," the Ninth finally "fell back upon the retiring column." Since the Ninth also "halted on the field three-fourths of an hour to carry away the wounded and collect stragglers from the field," it was apparently not the Bloody Ninth who had shown the white feather and skedaddled.[11] Tellingly, the regimental diarist also informs us that "the Twenty-Fifth Ohio awaited our return; formed the rear guard, *by order*" (emphasis added). Unfortunately, in all the confusion, poor Abbott of C Company was forgotten about and left on the battlefield, presumably with the cannon ball still in him.[12] By six p.m. that same day the entire column was back at Cheat Mountain Summit; the next day the Ninth returned to their original encampment of Elkwater.

After the fact, as Bierce informs us, the abortive assault on Camp Bartow was given the official designation of a "reconnaissance in force" to disguise the failed Federal attack. This was but the first of many instances that Bierce would encounter a failure in the field covered up by senior commanders in the official record.

On October 8, Colonel Milroy was promoted to brigadier and placed in charge of the Cheat Mountain brigade, replacing General Reynolds. As a result, Milroy's second in command, Lt. Col. Gideon Moody, stepped up to full colonel of the Ninth Indiana. Not long after, the regiment was ordered back up to the summit of Cheat Mountain "to guard the pass through which nobody wanted to go."[13] This time, the Bloody Ninth was allowed to take their baggage train with them; the transfer from Elkwater was intended to be permanent. Back on top of the mountain, Bierce and his comrades were at pains to construct secure and comfortable winter quarters. After their previous unfortunate experience at the summit, the men of the Ninth undertook to build a series of massive blockhouse-like barracks to endure the winter months. "We slew the forest," Bierce tells us, "and built us giant habitations . . . commodius to lodge an army and fifty loopholed for discomfiture of the adversary." The boys of the work details used massive old growth logs that were not only proof against rifle-fire but also guaranteed to keep out the ill, chill winds that swept the mountaintop. "Cyclopean doors" of equally massive size secured the threshold of each company barracks hall.[14] These mountaintop masterpieces were built along the southeast side of the pike; likely the sight of them alone would have been enough to scare off any attempt to seize the heights.

Then one day a Regular Army officer appeared in camp. After issuing Colonel Moody some peremptory orders, the Regular—Bierce calls him a "marplot"—departed.[15] The men of the Ninth soon found out what orders the staff officer had issued to the Colonel. The Twelfth Ohio also on duty atop the summit, but without such grand accommodations, had been ordered down from the mountain peak and had vacated the earthen redoubt that was their assigned post. The Ninth was ordered to move over to the earthen fort in their stead. After all their efforts to build comfortable winter quarters, the Ninth's rank and file were now condemned to endure the wintry weather atop the mountain pass in flimsy canvas tents.[16] Due to the uneven nature of the ground atop Cheat Mountain, the regiment had no space to carry out drills. In between vain efforts at keeping warm, the troops went out on scouting patrols—called "spy" missions—or hunted wild game, which was abundant. "We were the original game preservers of the Cheat Mountain region," Bierce tells us; "for although we hunted in season and out of season over as wide an area as we dared to cover we took less game, probably, than would have been taken by a certain single hunter of disloyal views we scared away." For his part Bierce, on "many a winter day," would stalk bears to their lair through the deep snow. But the crusty veteran reveals that even as a youth he had a soft heart underneath; for, he confesses, he commonly did not have the desire to slay the giant beast.[17]

Insofar as stalking any enemy, Bierce and his comrades seem to have been as reluctant to kill as Brady was with the bruin. "We had a bit of war now and again," Bierce informs his postwar readers, "sometimes a hazardous scout into the enemy's country, ordered, I fear, more to keep up the appearance of doing something than with a hope of accomplishing a military result."[18] Sergeant Bierce did not provide any details about such scouts, but one of his comrades, William H. Peck, wrote home about a seemingly typical two-day mission: "In the morning before day brake [sic], I started out to reexamin [sic] their encampment, situation of their guns, entrenchments and a place to put ours . . . and I found a very favorable position within about a quarter of a mile of their entrenchments . . . I went so near the camp that I could hear them talk, sing, and whistle, play the violin, [and] count their . . . regiments."[19] Even as Bierce and his fellow Hoosiers stood guard on the high mountain road over Cheat Mountain, at the other end of the pike, through the meandering valleys intervening, the Rebels were doing likewise atop Buffalo Mountain. The mountain—also known as "Top of the Alleghenies," as it was the highest summit of the entire mountain range—was close to twenty-five miles distant, and Bierce tells us, "In those winter days of '61 we used to watch the blue smoke of the Confederate camp with intense interest."[20]

At the beginning of December someone in the upper echelons of Federal command, well to the rear of the Ninth, decided to move against the Rebel garrison ensconced atop Buffalo Mountain, a post which the Johnnies—or Confederate soldiers—called Camp Baldwin. Detachments of the Ninth Indiana and the Second Virginia (Union) made up one Union column, commanded by General Milroy, while General Reynolds was in charge of the main attacking column. The plan was to march down the Staunton-Parkersburg Pike up to where the former enemy camp at Greenbrier, Camp Bartow lay abandoned. At that point the force would divide: General Reynolds would lead the main column straight down the pike to make a frontal assault on Camp Baldwin, and Milroy's column would maneuver around the enemy flanks by a side road, approaching the position from behind. As with most such plans, it seemed good on paper. "All one bright wintry day we marched down from our eyrie . . . all one bright night we climbed the great wooded ridge opposite. How romantic it all was; the sunset valleys full of visible sleep; the glades suffused and interpenetrated with moonlight; the long valley of the Greenbrier stretching away to we knew not what silent cities; the river itself unseen under its 'astral body' of mist."[21]

So it was that six hundred men of the Ninth and two hundred of the Second Virginia marched down from Cheat Mountain and into the valley, accompanied by the three regiments of General Reynolds's command. Even before they reached the scene of their October "reconnaissance in force," the advance guard was fired on by a Rebel patrol that had been lying in wait: "We heard the shots in front; then a long wait. As we trudged on we passed something—some things—lying by the wayside." During a brief rest stop Bierce and his comrades took the opportunity to go over and examine the roadside curiosity. "Lifting the blankets from their yellow-clay faces," Bierce stared with morbid curiosity at the losers of the recent skirmish. The sight both fascinated and repelled him: "How repulsive they looked with their blood-smears, their blank, staring eyes, their teeth uncovered by contraction of the lips! The frost had begun already to whiten their deranged clothing. We were as patriotic as ever, but we did not wish to be that way. For an hour afterward the injunction of silence in the ranks was needless."[22] Arriving at the Camp Bartow location, the force halted to take supper, after which they rested for a time beside the empty enemy position. Resuming their march, the Federals split in two, Reynolds's column advancing on the Rebel stronghold by the more direct route and Milroy's boys taking the backcountry road so as to approach from the opposite side. It was decided that both columns would attack the ridge-top encampment simultaneously at four A.M.

Camp Baldwin, whose blue smoke Bierce and his comrades had so often observed in the remote distance, was the Federal objective. Located astride a steep ridgeline, and commanding the pike that meandered below it, the Rebel fortification had been well sited for defense. Brady was unable to fully appreciate the Rebels' construction skills in 1861. When he revisited the spot in 1903, however, he was able to inspect the defenses at close quarters: "The works are skillfully constructed and nearly a half mile in length, with emplacements for several batteries. They are built on a narrow ridge and are hardly more than one hundred and fifty yards wide at any point."[23]

Early on December 13 Milroy's column trudged along Greenbush Road, expecting to take the enemy by surprise well before the sun came up. However, "led over unknown roads by untrusty guides, encountering obstacles not forseen," Bierce and his comrades failed to arrive on the backside of Buffalo Mountain at the appointed time. In fact, it was closer to eight a.m. when the Hoosiers and loyal Virginians arrived at their destination.[24] In the meantime, General Reynolds's force—despite taking the direct route—fared little better in arriving on time. It was close to seven a.m. when they approached the enemy camp. Enemy pickets had warned of their approach, so the element of surprise was completely lost; worse still, the Federals were now attacking in broad daylight. Nonetheless, the Yankees attempted to storm the summit. The Rebels repeatedly repulsed the Union men, and at times the fighting became hand-to-hand.

Reynolds's column had two batteries of artillery firing in support, but apparently their fire benefited the enemy more than it benefited their own troops. One Southern participant reported that Reynolds's troops were "shelled not by our own batteries, and forced to make a rapid retreat."[25] So by the time Milroy's column had worked their way around the flanks of the Rebel camp, the Secesh garrison "had got good and ready for us to 'surprise' them," as Bierce sarcastically notes. Worse still, from the direction in which they were attacking Camp Baldwin, there was but one avenue of approach—a narrow, winding mountain road that passed through acres of jagged fallen trees. Whether felled on purpose or by some act of nature, the broken and slashed fallen timbers were "impenetrable to a cat," and kept the Bloody Ninth and Second Virginia from attacking in a broad line of battle. Nonetheless, as one Virginia Yankee reported, "Away we went whooping like devils," charging with bayonets fixed.[26] Bierce and his battle-mates reached within two hundred yards of the Rebel position when the fire became too intense to advance any farther.

Company C was in the vanguard—what the British military called "The Forlorn Hope"—with Captain Madden leading his men up the slope in hopes of taking the rear entrance to the camp in one bold rush. But this hope proved even more forlorn than was usual in such attempts: blocking the opening was a large head-log, behind and to either side of which the

Confederates poured a deadly fire down on them. Leading his men at the forefront, Captain Madden presented an excellent target to the Rebel sharpshooters; he crumpled to the ground, mortally wounded. Quickly, the rest of C Company took cover behind the large logs and splintered trees, seeking shelter from the storm of lead aimed in their direction. For four hours the firefight continued "Indian style" as both sides sniped at each other from the protection of trees, timber and earthen embankment.

As Bierce notes, the same "slashed timber" that hindered Company C from rushing the backside of the Rebel stronghold also saved their lives—"most of them"—by shielding them from the increasingly intense enemy fire. As the morning wore on, the Confederate fire increased in both intensity and accuracy. Bierce and his comrades finally realized that the frontal assault by Reynolds's column had failed and that the enemy was "good and ready" to deal with their column, although no messages saying such were ever received from Reynolds. After some six hours of fruitless effort, Milroy ordered his men to withdraw back down the mountain. Extricating his Hoosiers and the loyal Virginians from an increasingly precarious position, Milroy managed to withdraw in good order. Apparently the Rebels had taken enough casualties of their own and chose not to pursue the Federals, who they had just "most gloriously thrashed." Bierce and his comrades were in no mood to appreciate their good fortune, however. As he relates, the retreating Federal column was "in a frame of mind that would have done credit to an imp of Satan."[27]

Milroy's column made it back to the starting point the same day. On the return journey, they passed the field where lay the dead from the previous day's skirmish. Despite their being, "a beaten, dispirited and exhausted force, feeble from fatigue and savage from defeat," Bierce relates, "some of us had life enough left . . . to observe that these bodies had altered their position." The corpses had not only moved themselves during the night, but "appeared also to have thrown off some of their clothing, which lay near by, in disorder. Their expressions, too, had an added blankness—they had no faces."[28] As he would do throughout the war, Bierce exhibited a morbid curiosity regarding these unburied casualties, going into some detail. He later incorporated details of this incident into one of his short stories, "A Coup de Grâce":

> His clothing was deranged; it seemed to have been violently torn apart, exposing the abdomen. Some of the buttons of his jacket had been pulled off and lay on the ground beside him and fragments of his other garments were strewn about. His leather belt was parted and had apparently been dragged

> from beneath him as he lay. There had been no great effusion of blood. The only visible wound was a wide, ragged opening in the abdomen. It was defiled with earth and dead leaves. Protruding from it was a loop of small intestine . . . Fifty yards away, on the crest of a low, thinly wooded hill, he saw several dark objects moving about among the fallen men—a herd of swine. One stood with its back to him, its shoulders sharply elevated. Its forefeet were upon a human body, its head was depressed and invisible. The bristly ridge of its chine showed black against the red west.[29]

In his memoir of the incident, Bierce gives us the denouement of this incident: "As soon as the head of our straggling column had reached the spot, a desultory firing had begun. One might have thought the living paid honors to the dead. No; the firing was a military execution; the condemned, a herd of galloping swine. They had eaten our fallen, but—touching magnanimity!—we did not eat theirs."[30]

Back once more on the summit of Cheat Mountain, Bierce and his messmates passed the rest of December in quiet discomfort. Their foes at the far end of the Staunton-Parkersburg Pike largely left them alone, content to suffer the remainder of the month in equal discomfiture on their own forlorn mountain peak. Finally, at the beginning of January 1862, the Ninth Indiana received orders to vacate their inhospitable outpost. The Hoosiers marched down from the mountain—those still capable of marching—and made a difficult passage to Philippi. From there most of the regiment made their way to Fetterman, West Virginia, where the majority of the regiment passed the next few weeks. In his later years Bierce, despite his well-earned reputation for cynicism, was positively nostalgic when revisiting the scenes of his first military campaign. However, it is doubtful that at the time Bierce and his comrades left Cheat Mountain they had such bucolic affection for the "wild and grand" land that he later held. It is also unlikely that his former messmates would have harbored "a haunting envy of those of his comrades whose fall and burial in that enchanted land he once bewailed," as the mature Bierce seems to have had.[31]

In the voluminous annals of the great War of the Rebellion, the Western Virginia Campaign is generally ranked as a minor sideshow of little import. Certainly in terms of bloodletting, it pales in comparison to what would soon follow. But this is not to say that Bierce and the Ninth's work was all for naught—nor lightly bought. While discussing the campaign during one of their many reunions after the war, one veteran noted that these "petty skirmishes . . . were speedily followed by large political and military results." The effort in western Virginia dispersed a Rebel Army, secured the Ohio River Valley for the North, and kept a vital rail link to Washington, D.C., open. It also recovered a loyal section of the South for the Union—soon to become the state of West Virginia.[32]

During their stay at Fetterman awaiting further deployment, "a large number of our soldiers died from the measles," one veteran remembered in later years.[33] En route to Indiana from West Virginia, an Ohio newspaperman took note of the Ninth's passage through the state, indicating just how much the regiment had had to endure: "This regiment has suffered severely. Originally, the regiment number 1080, but had been reduced, by disease and nineteen killed in battle, to 850—2 having died just before the train reached our depot. We were informed that over two hundred are sick."[34] In his own account, Bierce minimizes the degree of sickness that visited the regiment that winter and fails to mention whether he himself fell ill himself during this period. In later years, however, we know that Bierce suffered terribly from respiratory disease—generally ascribed to chronic asthma. One early biographer of Bierce identified his respiratory ailment with its frequent choking bouts as the source of his seemingly compulsive concern with death—"death and death's music were with him always."[35] The fact that so many of his comrades suffered permanent disability and even died from the severe conditions atop Cheat Mountain in late 1861 and early 1862 leads one to wonder whether young Ambrose Bierce too was a casualty of General Winter's unremitting campaign against both sides.

When Bierce made his 1903 pilgrimage to West Virginia, visiting the battlefields and campgrounds of his youth, one of his stops was the "bivouac of the dead" in Grafton. There he took note of the many graves of his comrades—more of whom had died of disease than of wounds in battle. He also visited the "campos santos" of his foes and noted that their graves also indicated that most had died of disease. In contrast to the well-tended Federal graves at Grafton, Bierce observed that these forlorn Rebel graveyards were neglected and nearly forgotten. The sight of his old enemies' weed-covered resting places inspired certain sentiments in Bierce—not bitter, but more inspired by the "better angels" of his nature: "Is there a man, North or South, who would begrudge the expense of giving to these fallen brothers the tribute of green graves?"[36] Thoughts of the grave, however, would have been far removed from young Brady Bierce's mind during the winter of 1861–1862. These, after all, were still his "green and salad days." In the few short months since he enlisted, Ambrose had made the acquaintance of many young men like himself. Yet there was one acquaintanceship that he first made during this period and that would endure long past the war's ending: his acquaintance with death.

4

Unfamiliar Landscapes

> "O days when all the world was beautiful and strange:
> When unfamiliar constellations burned in the Southern midnight."[1]

Departing the "dim valleys of Wonderland" and leaving behind the sick still in quarantine, 'Brose Bierce and all those of the Ninth Indiana fit for active duty entrained at Fetterman on February 19. By the twenty-second they had left the Department of Western Virginia for good, heading, they thought, for a well-earned respite in Indianapolis.[2] While they may have hoped for time to rest and visit loved ones, it was not to be; instead, the Ninth was transferred to the Department of the Cumberland. Rather than going to Indianapolis, they were shipped to the bustling river port of Cincinnati. Sitting beside the broad Ohio, the Bloody Ninth boarded two steamboats, the *Poland* and *Champion*, with a destination somewhere to their south. The Ninth was now officially part of General Don Carlos Buell's Army of the Ohio. As the Ninth Indiana languished on their frigid mountaintop in western Virginia, the situation on that front remained relatively quiet throughout the winter. Elsewhere in the Western Theater, however, military affairs changed drastically. At Mill Springs, Kentucky, General George Thomas became the first Union commander to pierce the Confederate lines in the west, compelling a Rebel withdrawal southward toward the Tennessee state line.

Then in January 1862, General Henry Halleck—now commander of the Department of Missouri—authorized Brigadier Ulysses S. Grant to undertake an amphibious assault against Forts Donelson and Henry, the twin bastions on the Cumberland and Tennessee Rivers guarding Secessionist Tennessee's long border with "neutral" Kentucky. Grant's stunning victory there in early February shattered the Rebel defenses in the west and forced open the way into Tennessee, leaving that Rebel state's capital of Nashville defenseless. It fell to General Don Carlos Buell's Army of the Ohio, however, rather than to Grant's victorious force, to occupy the Secessionist capital. By prior arrangement, Nashville lay within the sphere of operations of Buell's command. Poised as they were in the Pennyrile region of central Kentucky, Buell's troops easily swooped down upon the helpless enemy capital by road, rail, and river. Panic gripped the populace as the battered remnants of the Provisional Army of Tennessee retreated and formerly defiant Secessionists fled the city in any way possible.[3] On February 25, 1862, Buell's troops were the first Union forces in the war to occupy a Confederate state capital. Before the day was out, Old Glory was waving over Tennessee's lofty statehouse.[4] One of the first units to arrive in the city was General William Babcock Hazen's Nineteenth Brigade. Marching up the acclivity on which the city stood, Hazen arrived at the corner of what is now Fifth and Church Streets. "I halted at the St. Cloud Hotel, and was met by the Hospitable and well-remembered host, Mr. Carter, who invited me and my staff, his first Union guests, to his scanty bar. He tasted everything first himself, in order, as he said, to assure us." At the time the only other guest in the hotel was a drunken Rebel soldier, sound asleep, who was duly taken into custody.[5]

The Ninth Indiana arrived in the city on March 2. Unlike their receptions in Indiana, Ohio, and West Virginia, however, there were no cheering crowds filled with buxom maidens to greet them upon their arrival. Indeed, the sullen crowd that had watched the first troops land on the twenty-fifth seemed more like a crowd of mourners watching a funeral procession. After arriving in the city, the Ninth immediately bivouacked at Camp Jackson, within view of the Nashville skyline. Only a mile or so away from what is now downtown Nashville, this new camp sat astride the Murfreesboro Pike and was described by one German-American volunteer of the Sixth Kentucky as "the prettiest, healthiest and most comfortable camp that we have had until now."[6] After the bitter winter atop Cheat Mountain, there is little doubt that the "unfamiliar landscape" of Camp Jackson was a welcome change of scene for Brady and his platoon as well. Settling into camp, the Ninth Indiana found itself brigaded with two other regiments: the Sixth Kentucky Volunteer Infantry and the Forty-First Ohio. The three together formed the Nineteenth Brigade, the brigade itself freshly created on January 7, at Camp Wyckliffe in Kentucky, only a few weeks prior to Buell's occupation of Nashville.

General Don Carlos Buell, Bierce informs us, "was regarded as the ablest soldier of the Civil War."[7] The previous November, Buell had been placed in command of the new Military Department of the Ohio. Inheriting the remnants of William T. Sherman's Department of the Cumberland—Sherman having had a nervous breakdown—General Buell proceeded to raise, train, and organize an army, mostly from scratch, drawing on the state levies of Indiana, Ohio, and Kentucky. The Army of the Ohio by Civil War standards was a massive force, numbering upwards of 100,000 men.[8] As the Department of the Ohio's commander, Buell was equal in rank to Henry W. Halleck, the commandant of the Department of Missouri. The latter, however, apparently regarded Buell as more of a competitor than an associate. It was actually General Buell who was the first to propose an expedition against the Confederate forts guarding the Tennessee and Cumberland Rivers, but Halleck had initially rejected the joint expedition.

Then, at the beginning of 1862, Halleck dispatched a force under Brigadier Grant to assault Forts Henry and Donelson without consulting Buell—assuring that Halleck would receive sole credit with the Lincoln administration.

Learning of Grant's foray against Donelson and Henry, General Buell was gravely concerned that Grant's force was insufficient to accomplish its mission. Worrying that Grant would be overwhelmed by the large Rebel army guarding the strategic isthmus at Land Between the Rivers, where the Rebel forts had been placed, Buell offered Halleck troops from his own command to support Grant. Again, General Halleck spurned Buell's offer. Of his own accord, however, Buell dispatched a brigade under Colonel Croft plus eight newly raised regiments to assist Grant. This scratch force would become the nucleus of General Lew Wallace's new division, which in the end did yeoman service at the siege of Fort Donelson. After the fall of Fort Henry, Grant boldly pushed overland to besiege Fort Donelson, even though he was greatly outnumbered by the Confederates there. Only then, when the potential for defeat seemed looming, did a worried Halleck call on Buell for help. Fortunately, Buell had ignored Halleck's earlier snub and—still concerned about Grant's precarious position—had dispatched an additional three divisions to Grant's aid. Although Fort Donelson fell before these latter units could arrive to succor Grant, the timely arrival of Wallace's division did in fact play a decisive role in Grant's victory at Fort Donelson in February 1862: General Lew Wallace's newly transferred troops blunted a dangerous Confederate counterattack, thereby assuring Grant's triumph.[9]

While all these events were transpiring to the south, Sgt. Bierce and the Ninth had languished in western Virginia. Now, however, Bierce and his comrades were part of General Buell's new force, encamped at Camp Jackson. They were part of a new army, in a new brigade, and under a new brigade commander—Colonel William Babcock Hazen. Under Colonel Hazen —brevetted to brigadier—the Ninth Indiana soon experienced true military discipline. Colonel Hazen was not just some civilian in uniform holding a state commission, but a combat-tested officer of the Regular Army—and an officer who, moreover, knew what drill and discipline were all about. Indeed, just before the war Hazen was tactics instructor at West Point. Despite the Ninth being combat-tried, when Hazen inspected these Hoosiers he found them wanting: "I naturally expected more of it in the way of accurate soldiership than from my other regiments. On the contrary, it was not only far

Unfamiliar Landscapes

General William B. Hazen. When the Ninth Indiana was assigned to Hazen's brigade in Nashville in late February 1862, Hazen found it wanting and set about instilling regular army discipline in them. Bierce, unlike many of his comrades, took to Hazen's spit-and-polish command style. Library of Congress.

behind the others, but seemed fixed in many vicious habits, acquired while in the three months' service in western Virginia. To correct this, some severity was indispensable."[10] General Hazen quickly instituted an intensive program of instruction to remedy the deficiencies he observed. For the first time since their mustering in, the Hoosier boys of the Ninth began to experience Regular Army discipline and Regular Army drill under a Regular Army officer. It was not well received by many. Bierce described Hazen as "the best hated man that I ever knew, and his very memory is a terror to every unworthy soul in the service."[11] Both during and after the war, General Hazen spent almost as much time fighting his brother officers as he did fighting the enemy.

Hazen was born in Vermont, but as with the Bierce clan, his family had moved westward from New England to the Midwest when he was still young. After graduating from West Point, he spent most of his early military career on the frontier fighting Apaches, Comanches, and other tribes. When the war broke out, Hazen was given command of the Forty-First Ohio. Then, in January 1862, he was put in charge of the newly formed Nineteenth Brigade.[12] Although many in the Ninth's ranks regarded Hazen as an unflinching martinet, 'Brose took an immediate liking to his new brigade commander. Bierce seems to have regarded this new regime of military efficiency a much-needed tonic for his regiment. It may be that Hazen's by-the-book attitude stirred a certain degree of nostalgia for Bierce's old military school days at KMI. That a rebellious youth should warm to the strictures of military discipline seems incongruous; yet we know that Bierce admired his uncle, "General" Lucius, and it may be that he considered the discipline of military life to be far less onerous than the austere discipline of religious fundamentalism and farm life. This appears, at least, to have been the case both at KMI and under Hazen. What is certain is that as the war progressed, Bierce's admiration for Hazen grew, and the two became fast friends.

Most of the enlisted men of the Ninth, however, did not hold such a high opinion of their new brigade commander, at least at first. An indication of the attitude of some of the men may be divined from the fact that one of the regiment's companies earned the nickname, "the Shenanigans." What antics earned that company their sobriquet has not been recorded; we may assume it was well deserved, however. In any case, under Hazen, soldier shenanigans would not be tolerated. This initial clash between the Hoosiers of the Ninth and the harsh realities of military discipline is closely reflected in one of Bierce's classic pieces of short fiction, "Two Military Executions." In his short story, an unlucky soldier was court-martialed and shot for striking a shavetail lieutenant with whom he had roughhoused in the schoolyard as an equal less than a year before. The story opens "in the spring of the year 1862" as "General Buell's big army lay in camp, licking itself into shape for the campaign which resulted in the victory at Shiloh."[13] As Bierce notes, "It was a raw, untrained army, although some of its fractions had seen hard enough service, with a good deal of fighting, in the mountains of Western Virginia . . . The war was young and soldiering a new industry, imperfectly understood by the young American of the period, who found some features of it not altogether to his liking. Chief among these was that essential part of discipline, subordination."[14]

In the United States Army during this period there were many infractions that could put a new recruit on the wrong side of a firing squad—striking an officer being not the least of them. In fact, we know that while Bierce's brigade lay "licking itself into shape" at Camp Jackson in Nashville, Bierce did indeed witness one such military execution. A private of the Twenty-Fourth Ohio—Michael O. Chonwel—had attempted to desert and tried to kill a corporal in the process. Whether Chonwel was convicted for desertion, attempting to kill a superior, or simply being a poor marksman (he shot at the corporal four times and missed), the result was the same—he was sentenced to death. A comrade of Bierce's in the Ninth, William H. Peck, wrote home on March 8, describing the event: "They marched him around in front of the brigade twice as it was drawn up in close order, so all could see at the same time, playing the death march with his coffin in front of him. He was a brave fellow. He eaven kept time with ther music when he was shot. He stood by the side of his coffin when he fell partially lengthways and then rolled off on the ground. The blood can be seen there yet."[15]

After ten days of experiencing Hazen's intense regime of drill and discipline, the Ninth was dispatched on a reconnaissance along the Lebanon Pike eastward toward the nearby town of Lebanon, marching a distance of twelve miles. As there were no enemy troops in that direction at the time, the purpose was likely to simply show the flag and perhaps, as well, Hazen wished to see how well his freshly drilled command performed on the line of march. The brigade halted at The Hermitage, the home of President Andrew Jackson, best remembered for his pugnacious spirit and his staunch defense of the Federal Union against proponents of states' rights and disunion. Upon arrival at The Hermitage, the brigade stacked arms and went to Jackson's grave, where the regimental bands serenaded them with patriotic and mournful music and cannon fired off salutes to the late president. The men arrived back at Camp Jackson "very tired, hungry and dusty."[16]

The bivouac in this warmer clime of Nashville by Bierce and his messmates proved all too brief. Less than a month of retraining at Camp Jackson, Sergeant Bierce and the Ninth Indiana were on the march again. After detaching a number of units to garrison strategic spots in Nashville and the Cumberland region, the bulk of Buell's field army set out overland to rendezvous with General Grant's force, which was currently in the process of assembling far to the southwest along the banks of the Tennessee River near Savannah, Tennessee. After the spectacular Union triumph at Fort Donelson, the surviving Rebel forces had retreated in disarray, abandoning not only Nashville but also a broad swath of the Mid-South. This left Federals in control of a strategic nexus of road, rail, and river transportation, while at the same time abandoning the considerable industrial and agricultural resources badly needed by the Confederacy.

Using Grant's spectacular victory as leverage, General Halleck pressured the Lincoln administration into unifying all Federal military departments in the west into one command, with himself as generalissimo. In consequence, Buell's Department of the Ohio was eliminated and all his forces were placed under Halleck's exalted dominion.[17]

Some indication of Halleck's intense jealousy of Buell may be gleaned from an incident shortly following the fall of Fort Donelson, when Grant traveled to Nashville to confer with General Buell. That two senior field commanders with overlapping zones of operation should confer to coordinate their activities is perfectly understandable and appropriate; at this point, relations between Grant and Buell were generally amicable—perhaps too much so to suit Halleck. Halleck reacted to his subordinate's courtesy visit by having Grant relieved of command. Halleck intimated to General McClellan

General Ulysses S. Grant. As commander of the force that captured Forts Donelson and Henry, he had earned the praise of the Lincoln Administration—and the jealousy of his superior, General Halleck. Nevertheless he was given joint command of his army and General Buell's Army of the Ohio, to which Bierce's regiment belonged. His handling of the Battle of Shiloh would become the subject of acrimonious debate during and after the war—including on the part of Bierce. Drawing by Alden Brooks, Library of Congress.

in Washington that Grant simply had gone to Nashville to engage in a drunken binge; that Grant was insubordinate; and that his army was in disarray. At Halleck's insistence, therefore, Grant was relieved of his command and brought up on charges of dereliction of duty.[18] The accusations against Grant were groundless.

Grant may well have downed a few shots of Tennessee whisky in the saloon that lay on the ground floor of the St. Cloud Hotel, which was Buell's temporary headquarters in Nashville; but if so it is likely that most of Buell's staff were also sharing the brass foot-rail with him at the time. Regardless, that was not the reason for Grant's sojourn to the Rock City. At any rate, because of this incident, General Grant was not present in West Tennessee to direct the initial deployment of his army when it gathered to prepare for a planned advance against the strategic rail junction at Corinth, Mississippi. In his classic essay on this campaign, Bierce notes, "The question has been asked, Why did General Grant occupy the enemy's side of the river in the face of a superior force before the arrival of Buell?"[19] While Bierce gives a facetious answer to his readers, that was indeed a key question and a leading criticism of Grant's generalship by Buell, Hazen, and others after the war. Even Grant's many defenders have been hard put to justify this fundamental blunder. While much blame can be laid at Grant's feet for his generalship in this campaign, he was less culpable on this point than on others.

The original rendezvous point designated for the combined Federal forces of Grant and Buell had, in fact, been planned to be in the vicinity of Savannah, Tennessee, a key river port safely located on the east bank of the Tennessee River. Instead, due to Halleck's jealousy and without General Grant's supervision—and by no one's particular decision—the temporary encampment at Pittsburg Landing, on the west bank of the river, became the main staging area for Grant's rapidly growing field force. When the trumped-up charges against Grant were finally dropped, the larger part of Grant's command was already encamped at the wrong spot. At the time it appeared to be only a minor inconvenience to the overconfident Grant; moreover, to correct the mistake would have wasted much time and effort—seemingly to little purpose. However, this oversight would prove to have fatal consequences for Grant's army.[20]

Perhaps to further gall his rival, Halleck made Major General Buell subordinate to Brigadier General Grant for the Corinth campaign, rather than have Buell and his large army directly under departmental command. If Buell was upset at the arrangement, he did not display any rancor toward Grant. Up until the two engagements of April 6 and 7, relations between the two generals remained cordial. Ordered by Halleck to link up with Grant, Buell chose to move his army overland rather than deploy it by steamboat as Grant urged. In many ways, Grant's amphibious "leapfrog" strategy was far ahead of its time—foreshadowing as it did General Douglas MacArthur's amphibious "island hopping" strategy of World War II.[21] However, the downside of Grant's amphibious strategy was that it left a vast territory between the Mississippi and the mountains unoccupied. Buell, in opting for an overland advance with his Army of the Ohio, was able to "show the flag" to the rebellious populace while also securing the lines of communication radiating from Tennessee's capital. Since there was no perceived urgency in linking up with Grant, Buell decided this to be his wisest course of action.[22] As they began their march, Bierce's brigade formed part of the Fourth Division, commanded by General William Nelson. Ironically, Nelson had begun the war as a lieutenant in the Navy, but his singular service in helping to keep Kentucky in the Union during the early days of the war had led the Lincoln administration to appoint him a general in the army. Weighing in at over three hundred pounds and six feet in height, Nelson had a commanding physical presence and an overbearing personality to match—earning him the epithet "Bull."[23]

The Army of the Ohio's advance proved largely uneventful insofar as contact with the enemy was concerned. Nature, however, proved to be a far more formidable foe than the retreating Confederates. The bountiful spring rains so typical of Tennessee created numerous hindrances to the army's ad-

The Army of the Ohio crossing the Duck River. General Buell chose to march overland to rendezvous with Grant on the Tennessee River. Buell would later become a scapegoat for Grant's blunders at Shiloh—a subject which remained a sore point for Bierce for many years. Sketch by Henry Mosler, Harper's Weekly.

vance. Even small creeks could become swollen and often difficult to cross. As Buell's troops approached the Duck River, the leading troops arrived to find the bridge over the river already in flames. Retreating Rebel cavalry had done their job well. With the Duck River in full flood, the army's advance came to a halt. During this early stage of the war, Federal troops lacked pontoons and even the most basic bridging supplies. Finding the Duck River a raging torrent in places forty feet deep, it seemed impassable for the Ninth Indiana or any other unit of Buell's force. Buell ordered his leading troops to stack arms and construct a new bridge to replace the one burned. This setback did not overly disturb either Buell or Halleck; Grant at Savannah was blandly reassuring them both that his camps were secure and that there was scant sign of any enemy activity.[24]

However, word came down belatedly that the Army of the Tennessee (as Grant's army would come to be called) had bivouacked not on the safe eastern bank of the Tennessee River at Savannah, but upstream on the western side, within easy reach of the enemy operating out of Corinth. Lulled by Grant's bland assurances, however, Buell was not disturbed by this intelligence; only Bull Nelson among Buell's divisional commanders took alarm at this news.

Unfamiliar Landscapes

    Tactical intuition is not a quality that can be taught in any military school, but it is a characteristic that all great captains possess. General Nelson had an uneasy feeling—a presentiment—that Grant's army was vulnerable and open to attack. Bull surveyed the Duck River crossing in person. By the time his division had come up, the river had gone down enough that his wagons could cross it drawing only a few inches of water. Bull Nelson would not wait for the bridge to be rebuilt, and acting on his gut feelings he prevailed upon General Buell to allow his division to press on. Nelson was determined to brave the torrent and ford the Duck River ahead of the rest of the army and link up with Grant as rapidly as possible.[25] The Ninth and the other units of Nelson's division successfully forded the flooded river, but it was not an easy task. Captain Suman, in charge of Company H, "got the chills" and came down with a fever so severe he had to be transported by ambulance for the rest of the journey. Ironically, it was not long after Nelson got the last of his drenched troops across the river that Buell's engineers finally finished bridging the Duck.

    Thanks to Nelson's bull-headedness, his division went from being ranked third in the line of march to assuming the vanguard of the army. Not content with simply taking the lead, however, Bull Nelson continually pushed his men to march as fast and as far as they could. Between March 29 and April 5, General Nelson amply earned his nickname, bullying, cajoling, and prodding his regiments forward. During this march, the Bloody Ninth apparently incurred the enmity of General Nelson—an apparently easy thing to do—by their unauthorized foraging endeavors. While the boys of the Ninth encountered no regular Confederate troops on the line of march, they were confronted by a succession of militant Secessionist chickens, ducks, and geese who allegedly attacked them and who, on numerous occasions, they were forced to capture in self defense. That Bierce and his comrades gave these enemy fowl no quarter apparently angered Nelson, who averred that "men who would do such things would not fight."[26]

    When Nelson's division reached Waynesboro, Tennessee—where Buell had planned to rest his army for a few days—Bull Nelson gave his men no respite, pushing them on without waiting for the rest of the army to catch up. Nelson's sense of urgency soon became infectious, not just among his own troops, but with the army as a whole. The entire Army of the Ohio began to speed up its rate of march toward Savannah. When Hazen's brigade was two days out of Savannah, the general came upon a Union work detail that was constructing a telegraph line eastward. "We met the construction party of the telegraph line, and received at the same time a dispatch from General Grant, directed to the 'Officer in Command of the Advance of General Buell's Army,' stating: 'There is no need of haste; come on by easy marches.'

This dispatch was handed me and read, and then sent to General Nelson."[27] Nelson read the dispatch, passed it on to Buell, and then promptly ignored it; he did not slow his rate of march.

By the time the Ninth Indiana finally reached the banks of the Tennessee River, Sergeant Bierce and his messmates were footsore and very weary. They stacked arms and set up camp for the evening, looking toward light duty the next day—April 6—Easter Sunday.

5

What He Saw of Shiloh

ABRUPT, *adj.* Sudden, without ceremony, like the arrival of a cannon-shot and the departure of the soldier whose interests are most affected by it.

"Nothing can deceive like a document."
—Captain Sir Basil Liddell Hart

Easter morn dawned bright and warm as men of the Ninth Indiana rose later than usual, weary from the exertions of their long march to Savannah and expecting a well-earned day of rest. At General Nelson's headquarters all was quiet. Suddenly, a breeze bore a distant sound to the division's camps "like the heavy breathing of some great animal below the horizon."[1] No official orders alerted Sergeant Bierce and his messmates to what was afoot—none were needed. The veterans of the Ninth Indiana knew too well the sounds of battle, even from a distance. The other regiments of the brigade, new to war, took longer to grasp the meaning of those distant sounds coming from afar. Within a short time, however, all the regiments of the Fourth Division realized what was happening. Bugles calling "assembly" resounded from bivouac to bivouac, and soon all the languid camps under Nelson's command transformed into beehives of activity. General Nelson's presentiment of danger—if that is indeed what it was—had proven true.[2]

The companies of the Ninth Indiana were all astir now, girding for war and mustering their ranks: preparing for battle was one thing, but actually arriving on the scene of battle was quite another. The soldiers were instructed to be ready to march at once and to await further orders. Around one p.m., the regiments of the division finally received orders to move out.

The bivouacs in and around Savannah were some eight to ten miles downstream from Pittsburg Landing—a short distance by modern standards, but in those times the better part of a days' march for a column of infantry laden with arms and knapsacks and trekking through land sodden by spring rains—even leaving the cumbersome artillery train behind. As it turns out, the vanguard of Nelson's command—Ammen's brigade—did not reach the battle until late in the afternoon, and it was already dusk when Bierce's brigade finally arrived opposite Pittsburg Landing.

The Ninth Indiana marched, Bierce informs us, "through a country presenting nothing but interminable swamps and pathless 'bottom lands' with rank overgrowth of jungle." The spring rains affected the broad flood plains of the Tennessee Valley as they had the Duck River farther east, turning low-lying roads near the river into sodden marshland. During their forced march—Bierce describes it as a "terrible race"—north to Pittsburg Landing, the regiments of the brigade lost nearly one-third of their number from fatigue: "Men dropping from the ranks as if shot and left to recover or die at their leisure." At last the "terrible race" was over, and thoughts about what lay on the other side of the river filled Bierce's mind. In the growing dark, he and his comrades strained to make sense of what was happening on the far bank as they waited their turn to cross. The year before, they had naively joined the army, some out of patriotism, some for a noble cause, many simply "looking for the elephant." Now all would find "the elephant" with a vengeance.[3]

When Sergeant Bierce's platoon finally arrived opposite Pittsburg Landing, the scene that greeted them hardly inspired confidence. In the growing darkness the swollen river flowed rapidly, "vexed" periodically by plunging shells and shrouded with blue sheets of gun smoke. Then from out of the darkness two "toy steamers" suddenly appeared to embark Nelson's troops. A line of broken men on stretchers were brought off, followed by others hobbling down the narrow board that connected the boat to shore. In the deepening dark, blue-coated men walked up the narrow gangplank single file. Company after company boarded the side-wheeler until it was filled to overflowing, and then the steamer and its companion boat disappeared from sight back into the gloom.

The western bank of the river could not be seen from the near shore, but the heights opposite burned brightly with thousands of points of light that flared and died second by second, punctuated by broad flashings in the sky that silhouetted the branches of trees between. Occasionally, flames streaked fleetingly over toward the Ninth Indiana "by way of welcome." As the regiment approached the river's edge, bellicose sounds greeted the Hoosier's ears. To the right and left, Bierce heard the sound of Springfield rifles rattling "smartly and petulantly," while to his immediate front the sounds of battle seemed more distant, as though they "sighed and growled." To Bierce, the varied sounds informed him that "the death-line was an arc of which the river was the chord." The experienced ears of Bierce and the other combat-wise veterans of the Ninth could dissect this cacophony into its deadly components, identifying everything from the "deep, shaking explosions and smart shocks" of artillery to the "whisper of stray bullets" from muskets, and distinguishing between "the hurtle of conical shells" and the "rush of round shot."

After watching regiment after regiment crowd aboard the boats and disappear into the night, at last it was the Ninth Indiana's turn to board the 'toy steamer.' The Ninth trooped single file up the narrow gangplank and onto the boat until every inch of deck space was crammed with blue-clad infantry and the top-heavy little steamer seemed on the verge of capsizing. As the side-wheeler slowly churned its way toward the other side, Bierce kept his eyes ahead of him on the plateau above the shore. There he could occasionally glimpse dark figures moving about behind a band of trees, silhouetted by the glow of exploding ordinance. Stray shells occasionally made their way beyond the plateau and plunged into the river perilously close to the steamer, giving Bierce and his comrades some anxious moments.

Until now, all Sergeant Bierce and his squad knew was that a great battle was in progress across the river and that their presence was urgently requested. As to the exact course of the battle, how Grant's army was faring, or what they would find on the far shore, they had scarcely any idea. As the steamer neared the western shore, however, some inkling of the scope of the calamity that had befallen Grant's army began to dawn on Bierce and his comrades.

The actual landing at Pittsburg Landing was simply a strip of open shoreline lying between a steep bluff and the water's edge. As the steamboat pulled close, Bierce could see that the sloping stretch of dirt was packed to capacity with a "confused mass of humanity"—thousands upon thousands of them. "They were mostly unarmed; many were wounded; some dead," Bierce recalls. "Not one of them knew where his regiment was, nor if he had a regiment. Many had not. These were defeated, beaten, cowed. They were deaf to duty and dead to shame. A more demented crew never drifted to the rear of broken battalions."[4] Brigadier Hazen confirmed Bierce's assessment of the scene, providing more details of the chaos that greeted the brigade: "On our arrival, and until dark, a great number of dispersed men of the Army of the Tennessee were congested about the landing, occupying a cleared space of twenty or thirty acres; while a continuous stream of men, a rod or more in breadth, was pressing rapidly down that bank of the river and under its shelter."[5] The stark reality that the Ninth Indiana now confronted was that the panicked masses of Grant's broken army posed a far greater barrier to their advance than any Confederate cannon or musket fire. Even as the steamer attempted to land Bierce and his comrades, a leaderless mob rushed the boat, desperate to get aboard and escape to the opposite bank. Bierce relates that they had to fend the men off at bayonet point.

Once the Ninth debarked and the critically wounded were piled on board the steamer for the return trip, this same mob thronged back, trying to leap aboard—only to be pushed off by the score, "to drown one another in their own way." As they disembarked, Buell's troops insulted Grant's men for their cowardice, shoved them out of the way, and even struck them—all to little effect. Grant's demoralized troops shouted warnings to the newly arrived troops about the "certainty" of their destruction at the hands of the enemy. Bierce hints darkly that the officers of Nelson's division did far more than just shove or hit the panicked survivors to goad them back into returning to battle. With that sardonic irony typical of him, Bierce observes that "an army's bravest men are its cowards. The death which they would not meet at the hands of the enemy they will meet at the hands of their officers, with never a flinching."[6] General "Bull" Nelson, in his dispatch, is more blunt: "They were insensible to shame or sarcasm—for I tried both on them—and, indignant at such poltroonery, I asked permission to open fire on the knaves."[7] Nelson does not report the answer to his request—and one can only speculate as to what action officers under him may have taken of their own accord at Pittsburg Landing that terrible evening.

As the leading elements of Nelson's command reached the front lines, the scene they encountered was no more encouraging than what they had seen at the landing. "I found a semicircle of artillery," reports Nelson, "totally unsupported by infantry, whose fire was the only check to the audacious approach of the enemy." No sooner did the first two regiments of Nelson's division get into the line of battle than a Confederate attack caused the Union left battery and gunners to flee hastily, abandoning their field pieces.[8] General Buell encountered another "artillery park" of unmanned guns, apparently also abandoned by their crews; he initially ordered a quartermaster to move the guns out of the way of the rapidly advancing enemy, but later he used them to repel the final Rebel attack on the Union left.[9]

The repulse of these final Confederate assaults on the Federal left flank on April 6 are often attributed to Grant's much-vaunted "massed artillery" fire from his "big guns." Many modern military historians have put great stock in this myth. Aside from the fact that Grant had only one battery of heavy ordinance available on the field of battle, the real problem with this thesis is that Grant's supposed massed artillery would have been useless if there were no gunners present to man them. Moreover, how many of Grant's cannon listed on the official roster of artillery that were actually still in Union hands by the end of the day's fighting on April 6 is also problematic. The net number of cannon that were actually still manned before Buell's arrival, as alleged, remains a moot—but important—question. Grant's official returns for the two days' battle were cumulative, so it is impossible to actually determine how many guns were overrun by the enemy or simply abandoned by fleeing crews on the first day and then recaptured the next.[10]

By the time the Ninth Indiana debarked, forced its way through the leaderless mob, and reached the field of battle, night had fallen, halting Rebel

Defeat and Retreat. General McClerndon's headquarters was one of the many such undefended camps in Grant's army taken by surprise early on April 6. Thousands of soldiers fled in panic, with whole regiments melting away in the face of the enemy attack without firing a shot. Drawing by Henry Lovie, *Leslie's Illustrated Weekly*.

assaults. Aside from desultory gunfire along the defensive perimeter, the fighting had ended for the day. The Hoosiers of the Ninth wound their way past what little remained of Grant's army, that thin blue line of brave souls who had remained on the firing line, and like the horde of deserters at the landing, these few shaken survivors "recounted the depressing incidents of the day" to the arriving troops. Bierce's company also passed a group of tents huddled in a hollow behind some thickets—a field hospital filled with an unending mass of wounded soldiers waiting to go under the surgeon's knife.

That night a drenching rain fell, making conditions even more miserable for soldiers on both sides. Through the pouring rain Bierce's platoon inched forward; the men advanced in close order, walking heel to toe to avoid becoming lost in the inky blackness: "Through the wreck of battle the division moved, inch by inch, in the direction of the enemy, who had withdrawn a little to reform its lines. But for the lightning the darkness was absolute. Never for a moment did it cease to rain, and never when the thunder did not crack and roar were unheard the moans of the wounded among whom the men felt their way with their feet, and upon whom they stumbled in the gloom. The dead were there too—oh, there were dead a-plenty."[11]

What He Saw of Shiloh

As the glimmer of morning finally crept in through the trees, Sergeant Bierce and his men discovered that they had ended up in open countryside. Neither Bierce nor the men of his squad had any inkling where they were— or whether any other units of Nelson's division had advanced this far. There were no signs of Grant's men anywhere and at first no signs of the enemy either. During the night the Ninth Indiana filed slowly onto the left of the Union line along with the other regiments of Nelson's division and replaced whatever tattered vestiges of Grant's men may have remained. Hazen's brigade occupied the center of the division's battlefront on the left.

At the opposite end of the Union perimeter at Pittsburg Landing, General Lew Wallace's division, some six thousand strong, had also come late to the fight on the sixth and in preparation for the next day's fight took over the far right of the Pittsburg Landing perimeter. In theory, the survivors of Grant's force from the first day's battle—those who hadn't fled, been wounded, or died—had closed ranks and filled in the center between these two new forces along the semi-circular battle line.

As with the issue of Grant's alleged "massed artillery," the question of exactly how many of Grant's infantry were still fit for combat and present on the battle line by the end of April 6 remains highly problematic. Most modern historians have largely accepted Grant and his supporters' "spin" on his battle strength at the end of the first day's battle, dismissing Buell and all the other dissenting accounts as "sour grapes." Clearly, Sergeant Bierce and General Hazen, as well as others in Buell's army, perceived the condition of Grant's army very differently. Writing after the war, General Buell expressed the opinion that Grant's surviving force that evening was far smaller and far more badly disorganized than he had originally assumed upon first arriving at the front. One fact is undeniable, however: early on the morning of April 7, the remnant of Grant's original force was alleged to be occupying the center of this Union battle line. Yet by the afternoon of the April 7 battle, the extreme right elements of Buell's army were protecting the open left flank of General Wallace's division. Where, then, was the rest of Grant's army on the second day?[12] Regardless of the arguments mustered by either side in this debate, in truth, the precise number of Grant's troops still remaining on the front lines the evening of April 6 cannot now be determined with any accuracy by historians—still less can their willingness to fight. Bierce's first-hand observations about the mental state of Grant's troops graphically portray a force utterly demoralized. In the eyes of Bierce and his comrades, Grant's surviving troops were a mob, not an army. While Bierce's testimony may be an impressionistic one, it should not be disregarded out of hand.

The long trek from Nashville to Savannah, the forced march on Easter Day, the drenching rain, the lack of sleep, and an uneasy anticipation of battle on the morrow all combined to make Bierce and his comrades deeply

Pittsburg Landing. As the battle progressed on April 6, thousands upon thousands of leaderless soldiers, panicked, demoralized and leaderless, fled down to the riverside in a desperate attempt to escape. Bierce vividly describes the scene of chaos at the landing when he arrived there that evening, commenting "a more demented crew never drifted to the rear of broken battalions." *Leslie's Illustrated Weekly*, Library of Congress..

fatigued by first light. Yet the distant sound of a bugle calling "assembly" from somewhere before them electrified all ranks—pain and fatigue were erased in a moment as the men made ready to engage the enemy. Buell had instructed General Nelson the night before to "attack the enemy at the earliest dawn." Around five A.M., all of Nelson's division began to advance "in perfect order, as if on drill."

A thin line of skirmishers from the Ninth pushed forward ahead of the main body of the regiment. Directly behind the skirmishers followed a half-company commanded by Sergeant Bierce acting as a reserve. Within half an hour, the Fourth Division made first contact with the enemy. In a short time the regiment moved through the debris-free "oasis" where they had passed the night and encountered abundant evidence of the previous day's battle: trees shredded by shrapnel or studded with Minie balls; knapsacks, bread bags, and canteens hastily discarded in flight; dead horses, wrecked supply wagons, plus the wrack and ruin of an abandoned Union artillery battery. Above all, there were the numerous dead—and those to whom a swift death would have been a mercy.

The progress of the Ninth Indiana and Nelson's other regiments against the enemy line was so rapid that they advanced well ahead of the other

Federal units to their right. Buell ordered Nelson to halt his men so that the rest of the army could catch up. Likewise, Bierce halted his half-company to wait for the main battle line of the Ninth. During the pause, Bierce and his men took note of a grievously wounded Federal soldier close by. The top of the man's skull had been blown away, exposing his brain, which slowly oozed out of the gaping hole: "He lay face upward, taking in his breath in convulsive, rattling snorts, and blowing it out in sputters of froth which crawled creamily down his cheeks, piling itself alongside his neck and ears. A bullet had clipped a groove in his skull, above the temple; from this the brain protruded in bosses, dropping off in flakes and strings. I had not previously known one could get on, even in this unsatisfactory fashion, with so little brain."[13]

One of Bierce's men volunteered to put the stricken sergeant out of his suffering. Bierce dissuaded him: "It was unusual, and too many were looking."

Bierce's graphic description of the sergeant's head wound demonstrates two themes common in Bierce's postwar writings. Many of his works reflect a morbid fascination with mutilated bodies—living or dead. More than once in his postwar writings Bierce explores the subject of euthanasia and suicide. In "Coup de Grâce," for example, a soldier runs a sword through his badly wounded comrade on the battlefield rather than allow him to suffer any further. Additionally, in his essay "On the Right to Kill the Sick," Bierce attempts to make a moral case for this practice.[14]

The pause allowed the Federal battle line to regain its cohesion. Yet it also provided the Confederates time to bring forward their own reinforcements. After seven A.M., as the advance resumed, Bierce's platoon quickly encountered heavy resistance. At the crown of a rise where some furtive horsemen in grey were spotted observing them, Bierce's men came upon a flat open field about a quarter of a mile wide, beyond which was a wooded hillside. First the skirmish line and then Bierce's support platoon pushed out into the open field. The main line halted well behind them at field's edge. The reserve platoon was supposed to halt as well, but following his martial instincts Bierce made them advance at the run with trailed arms to reinforce the skirmish line. At this point, the skirmishers were just some thirty yards from the edge of the woods at the far end of the open field.

The forest erupted in flame with a loud crash, followed by the familiar sound of hissing hot lead as a flood of bullets raced toward the skirmishers. A dozen or more of Bierce's men went down instantly, and more fell in the firefight that followed.

At first, Bierce supposed that they were simply a line of skirmishers like his own, screening the Rebel retreat. Rather, his men were up against the main Confederate battle line. In the face of a withering fire there was little the skirmishers could do besides retreat hastily back across the field. Hazen's brigade had run smack into a large Confederate force of Texans and Alabamans under Lt. Col. John C. Moore. In his own account of this skirmish, Bierce is circumspect as to his role in this fight. In the engagement occurring between nine and ten A.M., Bierce merely says the Ninth Indiana had a "tough tussle." In fact, along with the Sixth Kentucky, the Ninth Indiana drove Rebel gunners from several artillery pieces, capturing their ordinance intact. The victory proved fleeting, however. A fierce Rebel counterattack was quickly mounted and for a time the fighting was hand-to-hand. Outnumbered, Bierce and rest of the Ninth Indiana finally fell back. As part of the Ninth Indiana's advance guard, Bierce and his detachment were likely at the forefront throughout all this carnage.[15]

For hours the two sides traded volleys across the open meadow, neither side willing to risk certain death in the open field. While only two of Hazen's regiments occupied this segment of the battle line at any time, beyond the thick woods on either flank they could hear the uncertain progress of the

A fight for the cannon at Shiloh. This depicts one of the several desperate engagements during the April 7 battle (called by many in the Army of the Ohio "Buell's Battle") where Buell's troops fought to retake artillery captured by the Rebels from Grant's men the day before. Bierce was in the thick of at least one such bloody fight, but chose not to write about it, simply referring to the hand-to-hand fighting as "a tough tussle." Drawing by Alonzo Chapel.

other brigades of the division, also heavily engaged. The Confederates brought up several more batteries of artillery and they now had a telling effect on the Union line. In his haste to reach Grant's army the day before, Nelson had been compelled to leave his entire artillery train behind near Savannah—a decision that put Hazen's men at a serious disadvantage, now confronting a strong infantry force well supported by artillery. To remedy this deficiency, General Buell dispatched Mendenhall's battery, Fourth US Artillery, to support Hazen's brigade. Equipped with four smooth-bore bronze muzzle-loading twelve-pounders and two rifled iron breach-loading ten-pounder Parrott guns, Mendenhall's regulars proved of singular service in the raging struggle. For some time an artillery duel ensued between the two forces.[16]

The presence of Union artillery decidedly stirred mixed emotions in Bierce: "The infantry soldier feels a confidence in this cumbrous arm quite unwarranted by its actual achievement in thinning out the opposition," he observes. The thick woods on either flank limited the artillery of both sides to the opposing edges of the open field directly facing one another. Interspersed among the troops of the Ninth Indiana, Mendenhall's cannon thundered away at the enemy, and the Confederate artillery returned the compliment. "By lying flat on our faces between the guns we were screened from view by a straggling row of brambles . . . but the enemy's grape were sharper than his eyes, and it was poor consolation to know that his gunners could not see what they were doing, so long as they did it." The close proximity of Bierce's platoon to the battery assures that they received the brunt of Rebel return fire. The Union artillery's salvo served as an aiming point for their opposite numbers: "They seemed to raise their 'cloud by day' solely to direct aright the streaming procession of Confederate missiles. They no longer inspired confidence, but begot apprehension."[17]

While details of Bierce's own role in this heavy fighting are lacking, he does relate one incident that occurred within earshot of him that day that illustrates the intensity of fire they received. Years later, apropos of an incident in the Boer War, Bierce related it in connection with the issue of the propriety of officers taking cover in combat:

> During a pause in the fight of Hazen's brigade, the enemy's fire being sharp and incessant, a young lieutenant, as witty and as brave a man as the brigade contained, was standing behind a tree. A fat and fussy field officer passing by roared out:
>
> "Lieutenant, what are you doing behind that tree? Behind that tree, sir?"
>
> The offender left his cover, walked coolly up to his irascible superior, and, respectfully, saluting, replied:

> "Sir, I have the honor to report that I was engaged in wishing that it grew in my father's pasture."

One would be tempted to assume that the anonymous lieutenant was Bierce himself, save for the fact that he was still a sergeant at this point; as for the "fat and fussy" irascible superior, there is a strong suspicion he may be referring to none other than General Bull Nelson.[18]

After being posted some while to this exposed position, the Ninth Indiana was relieved from the front and transferred to a height overlooking a burned-out ravine. The ravine had been the site of a massacre of one of Grant's retreating Illinois regiments on Sunday. The temporary lull in combat allowed Bierce to indulge his morbid curiosity. Bierce went over to inspect in detail the horribly charred bodies at the bottom of the ravine—a "ravine of the dead." The scene would be burned into Bierce's memory:

> I remember a deep ravine a little to the left and rear of the field I have described, in which, by some mad freak of heroic incompetence, a part of an Illinois regiment had been surrounded, and refusing to surrender was destroyed, as it very well deserved. My regiment having at last been relieved at the guns and moved over to the heights above this ravine for no obvious purpose, I obtained leave to go down into the valley of death and gratify a reprehensible curiosity.
>
> Forbidding enough it was in every way. The fire had swept every superficial foot of it, and at every step I sank into ashes to the ankle. It had contained a thick undergrowth of young saplings, every one of which had been severed by a bullet, the foliage of the prostrate tops being afterward burnt and the stumps charred. Death had put his sickle into this thicket and fire had gleaned the field. Along a line which was not that of extreme depression, but was at every point significantly equidistant from the heights on either hand, lay the bodies, half buried in ashes; some in the unlovely looseness of attitude denoting sudden death by the bullet, but by far the greater number in postures of agony that told of the tormenting flame. Their clothing was half burnt away—their hair and beard entirely; the rain had come too late to save their nails. Some were swollen to double girth; others shriveled to manikins. According to degree of exposure, their faces were bloated and black or yellow and shrunken. The contraction of muscles which had given them claws for hands had cursed

each countenance with a hideous grin. Faugh! I cannot catalogue the charms of these gallant gentlemen who had got what they enlisted for.[19]

By three o'clock in the afternoon, the Ninth Indiana was back in its former position near the open field. By this point in the battle, the artillery duel had subsided. In its stead, the Confederates resolved to mount one last major effort to break Buell's advance and retrieve the day—and in so doing consolidate their victory of Easter Sunday. From the forest to the right emerged three lines of Confederate infantry, each a half mile in length. Mendenhall and Terrell's Union batteries immediately opened up on the gray ranks that sprung out of the forest. The Confederates pressed on toward the waiting Union battle line, charging with bayonets fixed. The first wave fell before the Rebels could bring their triangular steel bayonets to bear, their ranks withering before the rifle volleys of Hazen's troops. The second wave of Rebels loosed volleys of their own against Hazen's brigade to telling effect. Reserves rushed forward to stiffen the Union line, and this assault also failed.

Finally, the third wave of gray and butternut closed in on the Federal line, their war cry resounding. At this point a drummer beat "advance," and Sergeant Bierce and his men moved forward to counter the looming threat. Within an area of three hundred by fifty yards, six regiments struggled for supremacy. The fighting was hand-to-hand, bayonet-to-bayonet.

The contest of arms was finally decided when a Union detachment worked around the Confederate left and turned the Johnnies' flank, forcing them to retreat. The Ninth Indiana and the other regiments of Hazen's command pursued, recapturing one of the Union camps overrun the day before. The Ninth Indiana's successful attack, however, was stopped by the arrival of fresh Confederate battalions. Now it was the Federals' turn to be pursued, until at last a reserve brigade of Federals came forward to stabilize the front. Soon even more Union regiments came up from the rear as Buell's forces pushed the enemy assaults back by sheer weight of numbers. Bierce and his men expected to hear the sound of still more Rebel counterattacks and to see the advancing Union ranks ahead of them come back at a run at any moment: "We still our breathing to catch the full grandeur of the volleys that are to tear them to shreds. Minute after minute passes and the sound does not come. Then for the first time we note that the silence of the whole region is not comparative, but absolute."[20] Soon Bierce and his half-company saw stretcher-bearers darting about, followed by a Union surgeon, then a chaplain. It was only then that Bierce realized the battle was over.

Captain D. B. McConnell recalled the end to that afternoon's fighting somewhat differently than Bierce. After repulsing the Confederate attack along with their brigade's sister regiments, the Ninth was sent over to the left to support Ammen's brigade and again came into close contact with the enemy. After helping out there, the colonel was ordered to take his regiment back, where they encountered fresh troops marching to the front and the Ninth joined this column.

General Nelson galloped up and asked, "What regiment is this?" To which the troops replied, "Nineteenth Ohio."

"Nineteenth Ohio, forward, double quick, march!" and away they went.

To the next regiment Nelson said, "What regiment?" "Tenth Indiana" was the reply. Again Nelson said, "Tenth Indiana, forward, double quick, march!" To the next formation again Nelson asked, "What regiment is this?" "Fourth Kentucky" was the answer. "Fourth Kentucky, forward, double quick, march!" and they too joined the battle line.

Finally Bull Nelson, whose opinion of the Ninth had not hitherto been too favorable, rode up to them and asked "What regiment is this?" "Ninth Indiana" was the reply. Nelson quickly replied, "The Ninth Indiana has done enough: Colonel, march your men back." After witnessing their performance at Shiloh, Nelson held the Bloody Ninth in high regard.[21]

There is little doubt that the ordeal of Shiloh had a profound effect on young Ambrose Bierce. Even though he and his comrades were already inured to combat, nothing could have prepared them for the unprecedented

The gallant charge of the Nineteenth Brigade. Although somewhat romanticized in this print, Bierce's brigade did indeed do hard fighting on April 7, and his regiment amply earned their nickname "The Bloody Ninth" that day. Lithograph by Henry Mosler (Library of Congress).

carnage of Shiloh. Bierce's experiences in this battle would be amply reflected in his later literary efforts. Certainly the best-known expression of Bierce's experiences at Pittsburg Landing is his memoir, "What I Saw at Shiloh." It first appeared in 1874, but Bierce revised and reprinted it several times during his lifetime. It has since gone on to become a classic of war literature—indeed, of American literature in general. One biographer described it as the finest single work that Ambrose ever penned. The grim, graphic realism of "What I Saw at Shiloh" strikes a distinctly modern tone; however, to nineteenth-century readers used to more comforting, romantic tales of heroism that conveniently ignore the horror and gore of war, Bierce's account must have seemed quite startling, if not positively offensive.

Famed literary critic Edmund Wilson also connects Shiloh with one of Bierce's most acclaimed fictional pieces, "An Occurrence at Owl Creek Bridge." Wilson and other literary students of Bierce have vested a great deal of symbolism, largely unjustified, in the name of the eponymous creek. Bierce's short story is widely regarded as a masterpiece, and many feel it is his best single work of short fiction. The impulse to find meaning in every nuance of the story is thus very strong.

It is true that Bierce witnessed several military executions; it is also true that one of the streams meandering through the Shiloh battlefield is in fact called "Owl Creek." The connection between "Occurrence at Owl Creek Bridge" and Shiloh, however, is a tenuous one at best. In fact, there is also an Owl Creek in northern Alabama—the locale of Bierce's story—although neither it nor the one in Tennessee traverses any rail lines. Truth be told, a diligent search of the eastern United States would doubtless turn up many similar toponyms, none of which could be proven to have inspired the title of Bierce's short story. Rather, the context of the events behind Bierce's famous short story are far more closely connected with Bierce's subsequent experiences in 1862, while on duty in northern Alabama guarding the Memphis and Charleston Railroad, rather than with his earlier traumatic combat experiences at Shiloh.[22]

Far more relevant to Bierce's experience at Pittsburg Landing is his story "Two Military Executions." As noted previously, in this story a shavetail lieutenant orders the execution of one of his men while stationed in Nashville. At Shiloh, the lieutenant is shot dead in the dark before the second day's battle while calling the roll. At first glance, the story seems to be one of Bierce's macabre fictional tales with a supernatural twist. A different interpretation of the story is possible, however. In his memoir of the battle, Bierce hints at the summary execution of deserters by officers of Nelson's division arriving at Pittsburg Landing. This—plus the fact that General Nelson himself would later be shot and killed by a disgruntled subordinate—suggests an alternate explanation: that "Two Military Executions" is really an account of Civil War "fragging"—the murder of an unpopular officer in the field by one of his own enlisted men.[23]

In addition to the two consecutive encounters at Shiloh that ended on the afternoon of April 7, a third conflict ensued immediately in the wake of the first two: a bitter battle of words. It was a running conflict that would continue on long after the war ended—one in which Bierce never hesitated to fire off salvos with his pen. In unrelated stories and articles, Bierce often inserted comments about the battle, its leadership or its outcome, even when they seemed unrelated to the subject at hand. In one story, for example, Bierce injects this bit of editorializing: "On the morning of the memorable sixth of April, at Shiloh, many of Grant's men when spitted on Confederate bayonets were as naked as civilians; but it should not be allowed that this was not because of any defect in their picket line. Their error was of another sort: they had no pickets."[24] The sometimes acrimonious debate over the battle remained a sore point for Bierce throughout the rest of his life.

There would be other battles for Ambrose Bierce and other generals that he would serve under. But Shiloh was young Bierce's initiation into the true horrors of war, one that would leave an indelible impression on him. After Shiloh the war—and Bierce—would never be quite the same again.

6

Excursions and Alarums
Corinth, Owl Creek, and Perryville

> "It was a campaign of 'excursions and alarums,'
> of reconnaissances and counter-marches, of cross-
> purposes and countermanded orders."[1]

Neglected in the many discussions of the two successive battles of April 6 and 7, 1862, is the fact that the original goal of that campaign was neither Pittsburg Landing nor nearby Shiloh Church. Rather, the true objective was possession of the key railroad junction of Corinth, Mississippi. As Bierce tells us, "The town of Corinth was a wretched place—the capital of a swamp. It is a two days' march west of the Tennessee River . . . got to . . . by a road worn through a thickly wooded country seamed with ravines and bayous, rising nobody knows where and running . . . under sylvan arches heavily draped with Spanish moss. In some places they were obstructed by fallen trees."[2] In 1862, this town was a strategic transportation hub for the Confederacy and the reason that General Halleck had dispatched both Grant and Buell's armies thither westward. Had all gone according to Halleck's grand strategy, the great climactic battle of the Western Theater—and perhaps of the war—would have happened at Corinth, not among Grant's undefended temporary Federal camps sprawling beside the Tennessee River.

As it was, Grant's demoralized army needed several weeks to recover from its devastating defeat at Shiloh. While Buell's victorious Army of the Ohio was sound and able to advance, Halleck nevertheless halted all offensive operations until he could arrive to take command in person, and he then waited yet another week for General Pope's small army to also arrive. In fact, it was not until April 29 that Halleck's amalgamated force of three armies began to move from their bivouacs around Shiloh.

In all the voluminous literature on the Civil War, there are few studies of the Corinth campaign proper.[3] The reason for this is simple: what should have been Halleck's finest hour as a military commander ended up being his most ignominious. Halleck resolved to utilize a policy of "gradual

Excursions and Alarums

The advance on Corinth. Bierce characterized General Halleck's Corinth campaign as "a campaign of 'excursions and alarums,' of reconnaissances and counter-marches, of cross-purposes and countermanded orders." Library of Congress.

approaches by parallels"—short advances interspersed with entrenching in hopes that the enemy would cooperate and leave the soldiers alone. It was only some twenty-five miles to Corinth, but admittedly the terrain had numerous small creeks and much boggy ground, with poor dirt roads connecting them. Nonetheless, in the first two days of the advance, the massive army actually covered over fifteen miles of ground toward the rail junction. But then, when they were only six miles outside of Corinth, General "Old Brains" Halleck ordered his huge force to erect siege lines all around the enemy perimeter. Whenever the army, or part of it, advanced a few paces, they again heavily entrenched themselves and awaited attack by an army half their size. A member of Bierce's sister regiment, the Sixth Kentucky, recalls that the brigade had to stand in the line of battle daily from morning until night awaiting attacks that never came and then go back to camp and drill until dark, often being called out at two a.m. to do it all over again.[4] As the days turned into weeks, criticism in the ranks and among reporters began to grow. Halleck could exile the newspapermen back to Pittsburg Landing, but not the soldiers.

Unspoken, but obvious in hindsight, was the psychological effect that Grant's thorough whipping during the April 6 battle had had on Halleck. Because he was a rear echelon planner by nature and not a man of action, one may well understand how the surprise attack on Grant and his unpreparedness for it had made Halleck overly cautious. He could not very well fire

The occupation of Corinth proved anti-climactic, with General Beauregard evacuating the town before Halleck attacked. Bierce described Corinth as, "a wretched place—the capital of a swamp." Library of Congress.

Grant—that would be tantamount to admitting that "Old Brains" himself had erred—so instead he kicked Grant upstairs and made him second in command, but without any real duties. Above all, Halleck wanted to avoid another bloody debacle such as Shiloh. His strategy was aimed not so much at winning as it was at not losing.

To be sure, there was a series of short sharp affairs: Farmington, Russell House, Widow Surratt Farm, Double Log House, Surratt's Hill, Bridge Creek, and lesser "excursions and alarums." But when Halleck's massive force finally entered Corinth at the end of May, all they found were exploded military stores, smoldering campfires devoid of men, derisive graffiti, and "Quaker guns" where cannon ought to have been. General Beauregard had extricated his army unscathed from certain destruction by a magnificent bluff.[5]

Bierce's short story, "An Affair of Outposts," employs this frustrating post-Shiloh period and the advance on Corinth as its backdrop. In his introduction, Bierce leaves readers little doubt about his views on both Shiloh and Corinth and on the respective merits of the main Union commanders involved:

> For manifest incompetence Grant, whose beaten army had been saved from destruction and capture by Buell's soldierly activity and skill, had been relieved of his command, which

nevertheless had not been given to Buell, but to Halleck, a man of unproved powers, a theorist, sluggish, irresolute. Foot by foot his troops, always deployed in line-of-battle to resist the enemy's entrenching against the columns that never came, advanced across the thirty miles of forest and swamp toward an antagonist prepared to vanish at contact, like a ghost at cock-crow.[6]

At first glance, "An Affair of Outposts" seems to be one of Bierce's typical misogynistic anti-romances, inspired more by his unhappy postwar marriage than any Civil War experience. Bierce spins the yarn of a young man who petitions for commission as a Union officer from an unnamed northern governor so that he may seek an "honorable" death in combat. The reason for the young man's death wish: the unfaithfulness of his wife. During the many alarms and excursions of the plodding advance toward Corinth, the young officer unwittingly dies saving the life of the man who seduced his wife—the governor.

"An Affair of Outposts" is in fact thinly disguised as fiction. At the time of the Corinth campaign it was the subject of widespread gossip between both Buell and Grant's armies. For modern readers, however, the leading subjects of the story remain obscure. One of Bierce's modern biographers theorized that the unnamed governor in this story was Governor Oliver P. Morton of Indiana—who did indeed visit his state's troops at Pittsburg Landing after Shiloh. However, contemporary sources provide us with the actual prototype, as well as hint at some of the lurid details about the real "affair."[7] After Shiloh, Governor Richard Yates of Illinois likewise graced the front-line troops with his august presence, doing so in a manner that irritated many there in the field. Chicago newspapers at the time chronicled Yates's grand tour of the front in detail within their pages, including some details that His Excellency Governor Yates no doubt would have preferred not to have had publicized.[8]

For all his personal failings (and they were many), Governor Richard Yates was nonetheless an important figure in the early phases of the Civil War in the West. As chief executive of President Lincoln's home state, Yates felt obliged to raise a large number of regiments for service in response to Lincoln's call for troops, and in fact, Yates sent to the front more than double the state's quota. It was also Governor Yates who originally gave Ulysses Grant his officer's commission in the Illinois volunteers after Regular Army brass snubbed Grant's offer of his services. Furthermore, Yates was the first to grant officer's commissions to female nurses—a tradition that continues in the American armed services to this day. As Bierce anonymously described him in his short story, Yates was "already famous for the intelligence and zeal with which he directed all the powers and resources of his state to the services of the Union."[9]

Governor Yates's zeal for the Union cause was indeed great, but it was not his only passion. The zealous governor also had a passion for wine, women, and song—not necessarily in that order. In fact, Yates had chartered his own steamboat to visit the front, well stocked with liquor, fine food and pleasant company—including a large female contingent. As *The Chicago Times* made abundantly clear, Governor Yates rarely missed an opportunity to indulge his passions.

In the aftermath of Shiloh, the northern papers picked up on many human-interest stories generated by the battle. One of the more notable stories reported in the popular press was that regarding the bravery of a Union officer's wife at the front. The story instantly caught the fancy of the public. Arabella—Belle—Reynolds had followed her husband to the front, and when fighting broke out on April 6, she heroically stayed to tend to the wounded. After nearly a week of almost continual exertion on behalf of the sick and injured, and with the knowledge that her husband had come through the battle unscathed, Belle finally boarded a steamer to return to Peoria for a well-deserved rest. While aboard the steamboat, Belle's heroic efforts came to the attention of Governor Yates, who had come to the front to see his Illinois troops. In recognition of Arabella's heroic service, Yates gave the young wife a field commission as a major in the Illinois state volunteers.[10]

After sharing the many privations of military campaigning with equanimity, the heady atmosphere of Governor Yates's pleasure craft was an entirely new experience for young Arabella—a woman far from family, peers, and her husband's companionship. All this accolade and attention could not have failed to turn young Arabella's head. Ensuing newspapers reports had Belle keeping close company with Governor Yates and hinted at a relationship far more than platonic: "She is said to be on the Governor's *staff*, which is likely enough from all appearances. The Admirable Executive was drunk, as usual, the most of the time while he was here."[11]

Even an army as massive as the combined force approaching Corinth can be a small place indeed when a juicy piece of scandal is in the wind. The modern reader, of course, unaware of the original context of Bierce's story, would have little inkling as to who he may have been referring to. In 1887, however, among the many thousands of veterans of Grant, Buell, and Pope's forces who were part of Halleck's *Grande Armée* the references in "An Affair of Outposts" would have been all too obvious.

In the end, General Halleck's plodding investment of Corinth proved anticlimactic. The Confederate commander, General Beauregard, escaped unscathed with his entire army intact at the last minute and left General

Halleck and his combined *Grande Armée* with a hollow victory that seemed more like a defeat.

In the aftermath of Corinth, both sides wrought changes in the Western Theater of operations.[12] In the Confederate camp, although he had failed to attain the South's strategic objectives at Shiloh, General Beauregard could nonetheless fairly claim to have delivered a bloody nose to Federal forces and halted their rapid conquest of the Confederate heartland. His withdrawal from Corinth, while hardly a Confederate triumph, nonetheless demonstrated superior tactical skill in the face of overwhelming odds. In the end, Beauregard had preserved operational mobility for the western Confederate forces and had renewed their ability to go over to the offensive.

Halleck, by contrast, had shown himself to be a commander of "masterly inactivity," in Bierce's words. In allowing an enemy far inferior in strength to escape unscathed, Halleck's generalship disgusted many soldiers under his command—not least among them Ambrose Bierce. General Halleck's nickname, "Old Brains," now began to take on a wholly different meaning among the troops, being transformed from compliment to insult.For his efforts on behalf of the Confederacy, General Beauregard was relieved of command, while General Halleck—whose command decisions at Shiloh and Corinth had been unerringly wrong—was rewarded, retaining overall command of Federal forces in the west.

Given the changed strategic realities after Corinth, Halleck deconstructed his *Grande Armée* back into its component parts and each segment was soon dispatched on new missions. General Grant regained operational control of his Army of the Tennessee in July and was assigned the Mississippi and Tennessee River Valleys as his sphere of operations. Meanwhile, Halleck gave General Don Carlos Buell the mission of capturing Chattanooga.

Assessing the situation, Buell concluded that it would be best to advance on Chattanooga from Nashville, using that as his supply base and moving southeastward from there. This route, he judged, would be far less vulnerable to enemy attack and would possess a more secure supply route. "Old Brains," however, overruled Buell and insisted on an eastward movement directly from Corinth, following the line of the Memphis and Charleston Railroad, which ran through northern Mississippi and Alabama.[13] By advancing along the line of the Memphis and Charleston Railroad, Old Brains reasoned that the Army of the Ohio could accomplish two goals at the same time: the occupation and repair of a vital east-west line of communication, plus the capture of the strategic city of Chattanooga, the gateway to the Deep South.

Buell objected to Halleck's proposed line of advance. His main problem with that route was that it exposed his army's prolonged right flank to attacks from Confederate forces, which had by now deployed south of the railway line as they passed through northern Mississippi and Alabama. Events soon demonstrated that Buell's assessment of the situation was, indeed, the correct one.

The Army of the Ohio advanced slowly eastward along the Memphis and Charleston, rebuilding the line and constructing blockhouses and small stockades for protection as they went. However, as they did so, Buell's troops became increasingly subject to raids by Confederate cavalry and local guerillas. No sooner would Buell's troops occupy and repair one section of the railway than the enemy sabotaged the section behind them. Raids by insurgents in civilian garb proved particularly galling to the frustrated Federals. Guerillas and individual saboteurs captured by the Union army were dealt with harshly by Northern troops. Inevitably, the Army of the Ohio became progressively bogged down, frittering away companies, regiments, and brigades on isolated garrisons that needed to be placed along an ever-elongating line of communications, guarding an extended and increasingly vulnerable front. With each mile the army advanced, it became more susceptible to enemy raids. This frustrating period of galling guerilla warfare all along the Memphis and Charleston Railway was the inspiration for Ambrose Bierce's classic tale, "An Occurrence at Owl Creek Bridge."[14]

In this tale, one of Bierce's most acclaimed short stories, a local planter—Peyton Farquhar—is captured by Federal troops while trying to burn one of the many wooden trestles along the route of the Memphis and Charleston. After a drumhead court-martial, the civilian saboteur is condemned to be hung from the very bridge he was trying to destroy. While the story itself is fictional, unquestionably Bierce drew on the very real situation that he observed firsthand in northern Alabama in 1862.[15]

The only seemingly anachronistic element in Bierce's story is the motif of the Union *agent provocateur* tempting Farquhar to burn the railroad bridge over Owl Creek. At this early stage of the war, the Federals had not yet developed their secret police, counter-intelligence, and guerilla suppression operations to the degree they would attain later in the war. Union "police" would develop an odious reputation among the civilian populace of the Mid-South and their violation of civil and human rights were many and varied.[16] However, John Fitch, an early annalist of the Army of the Cumberland and the war in the Western Theater, does mention one Southern loyalist, who he calls John Morford and who was indeed working as a Union operative in the area in early 1862. Whether Bierce was aware of this particular Southern loyalist and his friends, however, is doubtful.[17]

Insofar as the toponym of the story is concerned, not surprisingly, a thorough search of the extant records reveals that there was no "Owl Creek

Excursions and Alarums

Bridge" along the route of the Memphis and Charleston or its branch lines in 1862. As noted previously, much has been made of the fact that there was an Owl Creek located at Shiloh. Coincidence aside, there is nothing to connect the story to that particular creek. In any case, whence Bierce may have derived the story's toponym is largely irrelevant from both a historical and a literary point of view.[18]

Beyond the occasional gentleman saboteur such as Bierce's fictional Peyton Farquhar, or the more plebian and far more numerous real bushwhackers taking random potshots at Federal work gangs, a far more serious threat was posed by the growth of large guerilla bands operating against the overextended Union lines of communication. Roaming bands of guerillas frequently engaged in vicious attacks against isolated Federal detachments. On July 27, for example, Brigadier General Robert L. McCook, prostrated by illness, was traveling in an ambulance along the road toward Winchester, Tennessee, when Rebel guerillas fell upon his party. Not only did the irregulars kill all the unarmed teamsters and medical orderlies, they murdered McCook in cold blood as he lay helpless on his sickbed.[19]

Union train destroyed by guerillas. These and similar incidents caused Federal troops to take reprisals against civilians in the area, such as the "Rape of Athens." Bierce's regiment was not involved in that incident, but occupied the town of Athens just prior to it. The drumhead court-martials and summary executions of civilian saboteurs during this period formed the inspiration for his short story, "Incident at Owl Creek Bridge." Sketch by Alfred Waud. Library of Congress.

The culmination of the Federals' frustration with these widespread guerilla attacks came with an incident called "The Rape of Athens." Bierce and the Ninth Indiana had, in fact, occupied Athens, Alabama from June 30 through July 17. While Sergeant Bierce's regiment was not directly involved in this affair, he was certainly aware of it. Soon after the Ninth Indiana's tour of duty in Athens, their successor garrison suffered attacks by armed parties dressed in civilian garb. The Federal garrison then at Athens, under Colonel John Basil Turchin, blamed the residents of the city for those unprovoked attacks.

The Nineteenth Illinois Volunteer Infantry, venting their frustration and rage on the town of Athens, went on a rampage, looting the stores of local merchants and vandalizing private property. While the incident shocked many in both the North and South, it seems that contemporary accounts exaggerated the incident. The term "rape" was largely applied figuratively. No sexual molestation of the white female population occurred at all and even the town's buildings suffered no permanent damage. Certainly, compared to the vicious scorched earth policy that Sherman's army visited on Georgia later in the war, the treatment of the town of Athens was mild.[20]

Soon after Corinth, Bierce and the Ninth had moved some thirty miles south in support of General John Pope's little army, now near Baldwin, Mississippi. Pope's force of 10,000 had successfully captured Island No. 10 in the Mississippi before being sent to join Halleck's *Grande Armée* for the slow processional to Corinth. Now Halleck had dispatched Pope's 10,000 on an Anabasis to pacify the irate farmers around Baldwin who, not surprisingly, resented the presence of chicken-stealing Yankees in their midst. The Ninth reached Pope's force in three days, covering approximately the same distance it had taken Halleck a month to march to Corinth in May. Bierce and his comrades then spent the rest of June marching and counter-marching through a good portion of northern Mississippi and Alabama—seemingly to no good purpose. Finally, at the end of June, Bierce and the Ninth arrived at Athens to take up garrison duties there.

As the summer wore on, Buell's command encountered even greater difficulties. Large columns of mounted raiders began to rampage deep behind Federal lines, overrunning isolated Union garrisons, disrupting communications, and severing supply lines. Cavalry columns under Colonel John Hunt Morgan and General Nathan Bedford Forrest roamed almost at will, cutting a wide swath through Middle Tennessee and Kentucky and even at times threatening major urban centers. With more than a third of Buell's field army tied down in small static garrisons or occupied with repair duty, and with Rebel raiders becoming daily bolder, the "rapid advance" on

Excursions and Alarums

Confederate raiders attacking Union supply wagons, near Jasper, Tennessee. As the Army of the Ohio inched eastward toward Chattanooga, such attacks became commonplace, slowing the Union advance to a crawl. All along the line of communications of the army Buell's troops became vulnerable to ambushes and raids. Engraving based on sketch by J. F. E. Hillen, Leslie's, *The Soldier in Our Civil War*.

Chattanooga became a vain hope. The advance on Chattanooga was finally abandoned entirely when it became apparent that the Confederates were planning to mount a major new offensive.

Beauregard's replacement, General Braxton Bragg, now assumed command of the western forces of the Confederacy with a sweeping promise to regain the initiative for the South: "to assume the offensive from western Virginia to Corinth."[21] The new Confederate commander soon tried to fulfill his promise, massing his forces in southeast Tennessee. On July 29, Bragg moved his headquarters to Chattanooga. Along with Bragg's movement, further raids and demonstrations were launched by Confederate cavalry throughout Tennessee and the west, not just to keep the Federals guessing as to the goal of the main Confederate army's advance, but also to forestall Grant reinforcing Buell.

On leaving Athens, Alabama, Bierce and his regiment marched northward, stopping at Camp Turner near Reynold's Station for a few days. From there they entrained for the Cumberland Valley and disembarked at a spot along the Little Harpeth River (Little Harper's Creek) somewhere near Franklin. Bierce and his comrades then marched eastward to Murfreesboro, where Buell was reassembling his scattered army. Here the regiment reunited with its sister regiments of Hazen's Nineteenth Brigade. While at Murfreesboro, some Yankee soldiers, frustrated by the fruitless summer campaigning and equally unhappy over the retrograde movement toward Kentucky, decided to hold a bonfire to buoy up their spirits. They apparently thought that the Rutherford County Courthouse would make an ideal subject for their incendiary celebrations. The local citizenry did not appreciate their efforts. The locals approached General Hazen, protesting Yankee arson, whereupon the general called out a detachment of his own men to put the blaze out. Whether Bierce was among the firemen is unknown; hopefully he was not among the arsonists.[22]

Toward the latter part of August, Bierce and the Ninth were detailed to escort their old divisional commander, General Nelson, from Nashville to Bowling Green, Kentucky. The roads and rail line north of Nashville were so infested by Rebel cavalry and guerillas that the general needed a full regiment as escort to make his way safely into Kentucky. Nelson was on his way north to raise fresh troops and organize the defenses of Louisville against the threat of Rebel attack. General Kirby Smith's Confederate army was already making its way into Kentucky by way of the Cumberland Gap. Meanwhile, the intentions of the main Confederate army under General Bragg remained a deep mystery to Federals. From his base at Chattanooga, Bragg not only threatened Nashville and the Cumberland Basin; by traveling through East Tennessee, he could also link up with Rebel forces already present there and easily invade Kentucky by that route. Buell needed to be prepared for either eventuality.

On returning from escorting their old divisional commander, the Ninth encamped along Mansker's Creek, a stream that straddled the border between the county in which Nashville lay and neighboring Sumner County. For the next several weeks the Ninth was assigned to guard the rail line that headed northeastward toward Gallatin, Tennessee and to protect work parties repairing that route. Several detachments of the Ninth Indiana were sent further up the line to Drake's Creek and Pilot Knob in Sumner County. Doubtless Bierce took part in at least some of these missions during this period. What is more certain is that on September 12, Sergeant Bierce was promoted to sergeant major, making him senior non-commissioned officer in the regiment.[23]

By the middle of September, General Bragg's real intentions were becoming all too clear. General Nelson's hastily raised scratch force to defend Louisville had been defeated by the Rebel army already in Kentucky, while Bragg's Army of Tennessee was reported crossing the Cumberland at Carthage and was well on its way toward Kentucky. The race was on to see who would reach Louisville first. The Ninth and all the other scattered units of the Army of the Ohio were put in motion toward the Kentucky border. Bragg's goal was not just to conquer the state of Kentucky for the Confederacy but to seize Louisville and sack Cincinnati. The entire Ohio Valley was under imminent threat of Confederate invasion. Although the Ninth Indiana took an active part in the Kentucky Campaign, the operation does not seem to have inspired any of Bierce's postwar prose—at least not directly. Regardless of Bierce's silence on the subject, Bierce and the Ninth endured some hard campaigning for the next month.

From their main encampment on Mansker's Creek, the Ninth marched northward some forty-seven miles to Bowling Green, Kentucky. By the seventeenth of September the regiment had caught up with the rest of Hazen's brigade and the Fourth Division. Marching in company with the rest of Buell's army, by the twenty-ninth they had marched over one hundred ten miles to Louisville, although to keep up their fast pace, the regiment had had to leave behind their "camp equipage."

Merging his army with the remnant of Nelson's scratch force, Buell sallied forth to do battle with Bragg's command, which had now combined with Kirby Smith's force. The two reinforced armies met in battle on October 8 at Perryville. Referred to by one historian as "a grand havoc of a battle," Perryville was a battle noted for its confusion, lack of communications, and a peculiar phenomenon known as "acoustic shadow." Although Bierce did not write about Perryville, he saw fit to include reference to acoustic shadow in his short story "A Resumed Identity." In that story, which takes place during the Battle of Stones River, the narrator (with a background suspiciously similar to Bierce's) tells us that "if you stand in an acoustic shadow there is one direction from which you will hear nothing." It is more or less the acoustic equivalent of a solar eclipse. The narrator then goes on to cite several examples of battles where this odd phenomenon occurred; strangely, however, Bierce does not mention the one battle in which he experienced it himself—Perryville.[24]

During the Battle of Perryville, the Union left was heavily engaged throughout most of the battle and came close to being overrun by Bragg. Yet despite the intensity of the fighting, Buell's headquarters and the entire Union right wing remained totally oblivious to the danger on their left. The din of musketry and roar of cannon fire went entirely unnoticed by the rest of the Federal army, as the general in charge of the Union left flank struggled all day to keep from being overwhelmed by the Rebels. Certainly poor communication had a part in all this, but the bizarre phenomenon of acoustic shadow played a key role in Buell's failure to respond to the danger against his army's left.[25] By the time Buell finally learned of the dire threat to his left wing, the day's battle was largely over.[26] Buell, assuming the successful Confederates would resume the fight on the following day, awoke sur-

Corinth, Owl Creek, and Perryville

prised to find the Rebels gone on the morrow. General Bragg, on the verge of complete victory, had managed to turn Perryville into a Southern defeat. It would not be the last time Bragg accomplished this remarkable feat.

In truth, neither Buell nor Bragg merit any praise for their conduct at Perryville or the Kentucky campaign in general. For his part, Buell's pursuit of the retreating Rebels was hardly the model of aggressiveness. General Buell had no interest in pursuing the combined Confederate forces deep into the rough mountainous terrain of East Tennessee—a terrain amply suited to defense. Moreover, Buell was concerned—with some justification—for the safety of the strategic transportation hub of Nashville.

Nonetheless, the Ninth Indiana did take an active role in chasing Bragg's boys out of Kentucky. Bierce and Company C engaged in skirmishes at Danville, Kentucky, at Camp Wild Cat, near Rockcastle River, as well as Pitman's Ferry, near London, Kentucky. As Bierce and the Ninth chased the retreating Rebels through Danville—500 Hoosiers chasing some 3,500 Johnnies through the streets of the town—the "Loyal and devoted women" of Danville came to their doors and cheered Bierce and his comrades on. As one

The Ninth Indiana advancing through Danville, Kentucky. Although Bierce chose not to write about the Kentucky Campaign, he and his regiment took an active part in it and fought a running skirmish with retreating Rebels in Danville. Lithograph by H. Mosler, *Harper's Weekly*.

company commander recalled, "How handsomely we were entertained by those brave ladies when we returned to town. How they appeared in their doors waving Union flags, and how they feasted us . . . and how they talked about the handsome manner in which we rid the town of their enemies."[27] In all, the Bloody Ninth skirmished and pursued the Johnnies of Bragg's army 136 miles by the time they reached Glasgow, Kentucky. At Glasgow, the Federals finally called a halt to the chase and the Ninth returned to Nashville by way of Gallatin, Tennessee.

While the Federal army's performance in Kentucky had been less than stellar, in the end the Confederate threat to Kentucky had been repulsed. Even more importantly, the campaign finally shattered Southern illusions that thousands of ardent Secessionists were waiting in Kentucky to rise up and drive out the hated Yankees. No surge of volunteers flocked to the Rebel flag when Bragg's army marched through the state. In contrast, although initially his men were green and ill prepared for combat, General Nelson had raised a substantial number of new recruits to defend Louisville in a short amount of time.

Ironically, in the end Bull Nelson did not die in combat at Confederate hands. Rather, a bullet from one of his own officers killed him: in the lobby of the Gault Hotel in Louisville, General Jefferson Davis—a Union officer—murdered his superior before stunned hotel goers. General Hazen was in the hotel at the time to meet Nelson for dinner. Strangely, General Davis was never prosecuted for his crime by Federal authorities. Before returning to Tennessee, Bierce and his regiment served as honor guard at Nelson's funeral in Louisville.[28]

In the end, the Lincoln administration viewed the Kentucky campaign not as a strategic success, but rather as a series of lost opportunities. Lincoln, Stanton, and Halleck were decidedly unhappy with Buell. For one thing, although Bragg's invasion had been blunted, his army withdrew unscathed to fight another day. Washington had hoped for its complete annihilation. Then too, for pressing political reasons, Washington desired the immediate occupation of East Tennessee. The calculations of the Lincoln administration had not accounted for the fact that there were no less than two undefeated Confederate armies still roaming the mountains of East Tennessee virtually at will. Moreover, General Halleck—no friend of Buell's—needed little encouragement to portray his subordinate's performance in the worst possible light to Lincoln and Stanton.[29]

On October 30, 1862, therefore, General Buell was relieved of command of the Army of the Ohio. Only a few days previously, on October 24, Major General W. S. Rosecrans had been appointed chief of a newly recreated Department of the Cumberland. With the dismissal of Buell, Rosecrans took over not only Nelson's ad hoc Army of Kentucky, but Buell's army as well, redesignating the combined entity "The Army of the Cumberland." For all intents and purposes, however, Rosecrans's new force was much the same army Buell had led.

Sergeant Major Bierce and his regiment returned to Nashville to encounter a new commander, a new army, and a new mission.

7

Stones River

> **EPAULET**, *n*. An ornamented badge, serving to distinguish a military officer from the enemy—that is to say, from the officer of lower rank to whom his death would give promotion.

On October 24, 1862, the War Department appointed Major General W. S. Rosecrans chief of a new Department of the Cumberland. With the dismissal of Buell, Rosecrans also took over Buell's Army of the Ohio, redesignating the combined command "The Army of the Cumberland." For all intents and purposes, however, Rosecrans's new command was essentially the same army that Buell had led. Ambrose Bierce's opinion of his new army commander was somewhat complex; on the one hand Bierce describes General Rosecrans as "many kinds of a brilliant crank" and does not hesitate criticizing him. On the other hand, in Bierce's writings, Rosecrans never receives the sort of venomous invective that Bierce reserves for commanders such as Grant, Sherman, or the notorious "Oh-Oh!" Howard. Overall, Bierce's postwar assessment of "Old Rosey" seems a positive one, defending Rosecrans against charges of cowardice and affirming the general's overall popularity among his troops.[1]

No sooner had Rosecrans taken charge of his new command, however, than the Lincoln administration began dunning the new army commander to pursue the same course of action they had urged on Buell—an immediate campaign to conquer East Tennessee. While the liberation of the largely Unionist population of East Tennessee was indeed a desirable political end, Rosecrans faced the same military realities that had confronted Buell. The invasion of a mountainous region composed of steep sinuous defiles and narrow passes, one that was easily defended by small numbers of enemy troops—coupled with the enormous logistical problems such an invasion entailed—required a major commitment of men and resources. At best it would be a hazardous military undertaking if the Rebels held the region in force.

Invading East Tennessee at this point also meant leaving Nashville virtually undefended. It was doubtful that even General Bragg could fail to resist such a tempting target. In fact, a Confederate force under General

General William S. Rosecrans. Replaced Don Carlos Buell as commander of the army, now renamed The Army of The Cumberland. Bierce describes him as "many kinds of a brilliant crank" but Rosecrans was popular with his troops and Bierce's overall assessment of "Old Rosey" was positive. Library of Congress.

Breckenridge had already threatened Nashville during Buell's absence in early autumn. In addition, two separate Confederate columns of Rebel cavalry raided within sight of the city. By the beginning of November, moreover, intelligence reports indicated that General Bragg was rapidly concentrating his army near Murfreesboro, only a short march southeast of Nashville.[2] In light of all these factors, Rosecrans had little choice but to order the bulk of his new command back to Nashville. Political goals had to take a back seat to military realities.

According to the regimental diary, after a brief stint as train guards near Mitchellville, Tennessee, the Ninth returned to Nashville, where they went into camp, "during which time we went out foraging five different times."[3] They again encamped a few miles from what is now downtown Nashville, along the Murfreesboro Pike. A return to the Cumberland Valley was no doubt a welcome respite from weeks of hard marching and fruitless campaigning. Regular lodging and hot meals were also a decided improvement over sleeping wrapped in a blanket on hard ground and eating stale hardtack. Other pleasures of the flesh beckoned to troops bivouacked near Nashville as well.[4]

In reality, Bivouacking near Nashville in the fall of 1862 would not turn out to be quite the life of leisure that Bierce and his messmates might have imagined a return to the fleshpots of Nashville would be. The urgency of protecting Kentucky from Rebel invasion had also required the Federals to hastily recruit a host of new regiments, most of them lacking proper organization or training. Moreover, the dispersion of the veteran units on isolated garrison duty, followed by months of march and counter-march, had dulled their sharpness. Even in the more experienced units, discipline and military preparedness had slacked off considerably. General Rosecrans's first task, therefore, was to set about rectifying these deficiencies and whipping his army into shape.

Under Rosecrans, military discipline was made uniform across all the regiments of the army so that infractions received the same degree of severity regardless of the officers in charge. A daily regimen of drill and training was also instituted throughout the army, bringing all troops up to the same level of military readiness. Last but not least, Rosecrans summarily—and publicly—dismissed unfit, cowardly, or incompetent officers from their commands, replacing them with men who had proven themselves in combat.

On December 1, 1862, Ambrose Bierce, by now a platoon commander and the senior non-commissioned officer of the regiment, was promoted to Second Lieutenant.[5] Given Ambrose Bierce's conspicuous bravery during the previous year and a half, his battlefield commission was certainly merited. Nonetheless, Bierce's promotion to officer was not well received in some quarters—notably within his own Company C. In letters to their hometown newspaper during December and January, several of the enlisted men of Company C complained bitterly about Bierce's elevation over them. They characterized Bierce as "an individual very obnoxious to the company" and identified his promotion as "a great Injustice."[6] When Bierce learned of this adverse correspondence with the hometown paper, he was quick to respond to the accusations. Unfortunately, the *Elkhart Review* did not directly quote Bierce, but simply printed "he complains of the great injustice done him by a correspondent of the *Review*."[7] The precise cause of such ill feeling is not certain, but the fact that most of the men in his company would have known Bierce since the old days when he ran errands and cleaned spittoons in a saloon may have caused some of them to have difficulty accepting him as their new superior.

Moreover, the election of volunteer and militia officers had a long-standing tradition in America, especially in the west. In such cases, social ranking and peer popularity had far more to do with officer selection than any military aptitude. On the regimental command level and above, political influence or wealth far more heavily influenced state governors' appointments than training, ability, or courage. As a result, the dearth of competent officers at all levels had often proved disastrous to the Union during the early battles of the Civil War. General Rosecrans's dismissal of "dead wood" from the officer corps as well as the attrition from casualties in combat had opened up numerous vacancies in the commissioned ranks. Bierce's promotion to Second Lieutenant, while richly deserved, was a consequence of Rosecrans's reorganization. That Bierce's appointment came from above rather than through election may well have been a cause of resentment within Company C.

Of some significance as well may be the fact that Bierce's promotion to the commissioned ranks coincided with Rosecrans's tightening of military discipline throughout the army. Ambrose Bierce was already an admirer of Hazen's spit-and-polish approach to command. Rosecrans's new regime—calling as it did for five roll calls per day and constant drilling from morning until night—likely did not go over well with many enlisted men. Second Lieutenant Bierce, as the newest and lowest ranking officer in the regiment, would naturally have drawn the least pleasant tasks among the officers of the regiment. With shavetail Bierce overseeing the daily drudgery of drill and discipline, resentment among his comrades in Company C would have magnified accordingly.[8]

Even as General Rosecrans was carrying out his reorganization, he was also coming under increasing pressure from Washington to take action—any action—against the Confederate army before winter set in. Farther west, Grant wisely mollified the Lincoln administration by marching back and forth across northern Mississippi, while back east General Burnside was very vocal about taking the offensive against Lee. In the end, Grant's maneuvering accomplished nothing in practical terms, while in the Eastern Theater Burnside's campaign resulted in the disastrous Union defeat at Fredericksburg.

By late December, ready or not, Rosecrans could no longer delay taking the offensive. Although he would have preferred more time to prepare, in truth, the Army of the Cumberland was in far better condition than it had been just after Perryville. Broken supply lines had been re-established, massive quantities of military stores were stockpiled in and around Nashville, the reorganization and re-equipment of the army was largely complete, and the morale and combat readiness of the troops were greatly improved.

In contrast, the respite following the Battle of Perryville had caused General Bragg and the Confederate government in Richmond to grow complacent. Bragg was well situated to stage an assault on Nashville in November, yet failed to do so. By mid-December, in fact, Confederate forces began settling into winter bivouac around Murfreesboro and its neighboring communities. Richmond even saw fit to dispatch one of Bragg's infantry divisions west to help fend off Grant's maneuvers in Mississippi, while Bragg himself dispatched the bulk of his elite cavalry off on long-range raids to the north and west. If Rosecrans intended to move against Bragg, there was no better time to try.

Thus on December 26, to the relief of the Lincoln administration, Rosecrans began his offensive. On the eve of his advance, he melodramatically exhorted his generals to "Fight them! Fight them! Fight them, I say!"[9] Soon, long sinuous blue-clad columns filled the pikes leading south out of the city.

Hazen's brigade was now part of General John Palmer's division and formed a segment of the left wing of the Federal advance. The serried ranks of Palmer's command lined the Murfreesboro Pike as far as the eye could see. During the advance southward, Union columns repeatedly skirmished with enemy pickets. In truth, however, the Federals found rain, sleet, and mud to be far more formidable foes than the Confederates. The early hours of December 31 found the two armies lined up for battle, facing one other along the serpentine banks of Stones River, only a short distance north of the town of Murfreesboro.

Although lengthy tomes have been written about the Battle of Stones River, Bierce's own observations of the battle are surprisingly succinct: "The history of that action is exceedingly simple. The two armies, nearly equal in strength, confronted one another on level ground at daybreak. As the Federal left was preparing to attack the Confederate right the Confederate left took the initiative and attacked the Federal right. By nightfall, which put an end to the engagement, the whole Federal line had been turned upon its left, as upon a hinge, till it lay at a right angle to its first direction . . . Two days later Bragg made a feeble attempt with six thousand men upon our left and rear."[10]

Judging solely by Bierce's terse postwar pronouncements, one might assume that he and his comrades were only lightly engaged on December 31. Such, however, was not the case. Ironically, Bragg and Rosecrans drew up battle plans that were in essence mirror images of one another: each called for a crushing blow against their foe's left flank. As fate would have it, however, Bragg instructed his troops to attack "at first light"; Rosecrans, instead, issued a specific time for his generals to launch their assault. The Rebels were able to land the first blow by the space of only a half hour—but that was just enough for Bragg to gain the advantage in the day's fight. Although one could hardly characterize the Rebel assault as a surprise attack, it nonetheless caught the Federal right wing completely off guard. Union encampments were overrun, commanders hastily scrambled to form battle lines, and even whole regiments melted away in the face of the initial Rebel onslaught. In the initial stages, it was embarrassingly similar to what had happened to Grant's men at Shiloh.

As the battle progressed that morning, the Union lines, although battered and forced continually backwards, never broke entirely. By the afternoon, Confederate efforts to outflank the Union army had lost momentum and General Rosecrans was finally able to stabilize his battle line. From their original positions extending in a general east-west axis along Stone's River that morning, Rosecrans's Army of the Cumberland had now re-formed along a north-south axis, facing the Rebels at a diagonal and with their backs jutted up against their only two escape routes: the Nashville Pike and the Nashville and Chattanooga Railroad.

In order to steady the nerves of his troops—and perhaps his own—Rosecrans rode along the length of the battle line with his staff, exhorting the soldiers by showing them that he was as exposed to danger as they. Unfortunately, Rosecrans's display of martial virtue did not quite convey the impression intended. According to Bierce, Rosecrans and his staff rode at a "wild gallop" rather than a steady trot, conveying a sense of unease or nervousness. Worse still, the silhouette of this mounted party, traveling just behind the firing line, made an ideal aiming point for Confederate artillerymen. Sure enough, a rebel shell came whistling across the field aimed right at Rosecrans and his party. The shot missed Rosecrans by inches, only to hit his chief of staff, Julius Garesché. Garesché's head exploded in the blink of an eye, splattering Rosecrans with his gore. The headless horseman rode on for some distance before the lifeless corpse finally tumbled off the panicked mount. Bierce could not help noting with his typically macabre humor that "it was not the only head of that group lost that day, but it was the best one."[11]

As the Federal right was forced back under pressure from successive Confederate attacks, the left wing of the army came to play a decisive role in the outcome of the battle. On the left, the Ninth Indiana and the other regiments of Hazen's brigade came under increasing enemy pressure as their position served to anchor the rest of the Union line, which was being forced back. In essence Hazen's brigade became the "hinge" upon which the rest of the battle line pivoted. Should the Confederates have overrun this vital segment of Rosecrans's left, they could then "roll-up" the entire Federal battle line with ease and destroy the entire army.

After the war, Ambrose Bierce often declaimed against the "save the day-ers" who made inflated claims to have won Stones River single-handedly. This may account for Bierce's reticence about his and his regiment's own efforts at Stones River—for while Bierce may have resented other officers' inflated boasts of averting disaster, the Ninth Indiana—and Hazen's command in general—could have fairly laid claim to just such an honor.[12] Captain Amasa Johnson, describing the Ninth's stand that day, was more forthcoming as to the role that the regiment played: "At night we were the only regiment that held the same position that we did on entering the battle. Never in any battle did our regiment occupy so important and strong a position and inflict such heavy losses upon the enemy."[13]

The morning of December 31, 1862, Hazen's brigade had been one of several units on the Union left detailed to attack Bragg's right wing. No sooner had the lead elements of the brigade begun to move against the Confederate right before them, however, than the sound of intense firing on the far right of the line warned that something had gone terribly awry. Almost before anyone realized it, the Rebels were behind them, which the Union right should have been covering. Hurriedly, the Federals on the left shifted from offense to defense. As they did so, however, a gap opened up in the line—a small copse of oak and cedar that jutted out from the Union front—a position that came to be called "the Round Forest." Hazen's command was ordered to defend it. From shortly after eight a.m. until darkness fell, the Ninth Indiana and its sister regiments withstood charge after charge by Bragg's brigades. Long waves of Butternuts hurled themselves against Hazen's command like breakers crashing against a rocky shore. As ammunition became short, Hazen advised his regimental commanders to "rely on the bayonet."

At one point, the divisional commander, General Palmer, came to Hazen and said, "Hazen, you'll have to fall back!"

"I'd like to know where in hell I'll fall back to!" replied General Hazen.

Hazen may have been insubordinate, but his logic was flawless. The brigade held the Round Forest against all comers.[14]

Battle of Stone's River, showing Palmer's division, which included Hazen's brigade. In the far distance is the "Round Forest" where Bierce and his comrades kept the Union line from collapsing for most of the day. Library of Congress.

Amid it all, Bierce's regiment held its ground and where today the Hazen Monument stands, at least 113 men of the Bloody Ninth fell defending the Round Forest. They are still there where they fell that day, resting with others of the brigade.

As he had on earlier occasions, Bierce distinguished himself in combat. During one intense firefight, Lieutenant James Braden was struck down by enemy fire. Bierce, exposing himself to a heavy enemy fusillade, ran up to help the stricken Braden. In later life Bierce adopted the public persona of a callous cynic; that was not his attitude on this day. According to Braden, Bierce "knelt beside me and gripped my hand in what we both thought was a last goodbye . . . I tell you he was crying like a little girl."[15] Sergeant Brower, of Company I, saw Braden struck just under the left eye and relates how the men thought it was all up for the wounded officer, but how Bierce, despite the hail of bullets, caught him up in his arms and carried Braden to safety.[16]

In writing about Stones River, Bierce noted that it was only nightfall that ended the days' bloodletting. In truth, both sides had fought themselves to the point of exhaustion. As the sun set on the carnage, moreover, the armies confronted an equally deadly foe—the bitter winter weather.

Before the battle, Confederate cavalry had done a good job of attacking the Yankee supply trains traveling in support of the Army of the Cumberland. While Rosecrans still had ample ammunition, he was woefully short of just about everything else. Moreover, in the chaotic ebb and flow of the day's fighting, most of the Federals had dropped their backpacks and blankets to fight and were unable to retrieve them by day's end. The troops were without food or even rudimentary protection from the elements. Adding further to their misery, Rosecrans also forbade campfires, lest the Rebel snipers use the open flames as targets. All in all, the Federal troops passed a most miserable night on the battlefield. In particular, the wounded lying all about in open field and forest suffered intensely from the bitter cold and exposure.[17] While historians often record all the minutiae of a battle, the aftermath of combat often escapes their attention. Not so with Bierce, who suffered through it. The wicked winter weather that cold New Year's Eve inspired his macabre short tale "A Cold Night."

One of Bierce's lesser-known pieces with overtones of the supernatural, "A Cold Night" is nonetheless a story that has the ring of truth to it. Exposed to the elements a chilled squad of Union troops huddle in the darkness, more concerned about the cold than any enemy lurking in the dark. Nearby, the body of a fallen soldier is laid out, covered by a blanket. Suffering intensely from the bitter chill, one of their number is finally emboldened to inspect the corpse. The head of the dead soldier has a single bullet wound to the forehead, as neat as a drill-hole. Reassured that the slain soldier will not miss it, the living soldier expropriates the blanket for his own use. The next morning the soldier and his comrades awake to find their deceased neighbor has been uneasy during the night. Instead of resting in peace in the prone position where they left him, the blanket thief and his messmates now find the dead man all curled up—as if during the night he had awoken from the dead to find himself lacking his woolen shroud and had doubled up to ward off the cold!

Had the stricken warrior somehow survived a bullet to the brain only to freeze to death? Was it some bizarre form of rigor mortis? Did the dead man come back to life? Or can the dead catch a chill too? Bierce leaves us wondering.[18]

That any man may take a bullet directly to the middle of his forehead and still live may seem to defy nature, common sense, and science alike. Yet this did in fact happen to a fellow member of Bierce's regiment. Jacob Miller, from Logansport, Indiana, was a member of Company K, Ninth Indiana, having joined the regiment about the same time as Bierce. He was in the first line at

Burial of Colonel Garesche, Rosecran's chief of staff, by General Hazen after the first day's battle. Beheaded by a cannonball, Garesche, as Bierce observed, "was not the only head of that group lost that day, but it was the best one." *Leslie's Illustrated Weekly*, February 26, 1863.

Stones River

Searching for wounded by torchlight. After the first day's fight at Stone's River, men of the Ninth Indiana combed the battlefield that night searching of fallen comrades. Lacking tents and blankets, and forbidden to light fires for warmth, the troops spent a miserable night in the bitter cold; many of the wounded died of exposure. *Harper's Weekly,* March 8, 1862.

Chickamauga, when suddenly a musket ball struck him squarely in the center of his forehead, entering just above the eyebrows. Left for dead on the battlefield, he somehow managed to crawl and then walk to safety. Thirty years later Miller still had the open wound in the center of his head.[19] Bierce may have known of his comrade's weird plight and incorporated it into his tale, or it may be that another casualty at Stone's River suffered a similar fate and simply didn't survive the night. We shall never know for sure. Nevertheless, Miller's fate affirms the reality—however bizarre—of Bierce's uncanny tale.

What is known is that search parties from the Ninth wandered among the many ranks of the dead that night in search of any still living; they encountered corpses in all manner of contorted positions.[20] General Hazen himself supervised the burial of Colonel Garesche's headless corpse into a shallow grave.

Far better known than "A Cold Night" is Bierce's short story, "A Resumed Identity,"[21] also inspired by Stone's River. Like "A Cold Night," Bierce's classic short story is less about the battle itself than it is about how the aftermath of battle affects men. In "A Resumed Identity," a bewildered Union officer suffering from a head wound at Stone's River watches as a phantom army silently glides northward along the old pike leading toward Nashville. He looks away for a moment, and when he glances back the noiseless column of troops has mysteriously vanished.

The soldier accosts a passing stranger—a doctor—and identifies himself as a lieutenant in the Federal army, "of the staff of General Hazen." The lieutenant had been struck by a bullet and had fallen unconscious, he explains, and now he is keen to locate the army he just witnessed passing by. The lieutenant's bewilderment increases as the doctor points out the lieutenant's civilian attire, and the fact that he appears far older than the twenty-three years he claims. The soldier storms away from the unhelpful doctor and comes across a "square, solid monument of hewn stone"—the Hazen Monument—marking the spot where Hazen's brigade made its stand on December 31, 1862. Slowly it dawns on the bewildered lieutenant that he has been unconscious for far more than the span of a day or two. It is now summer, for one thing, not winter; for another, the stone monument before his bewildered eyes has obviously been there for some time.

The soldier looks at his withered hands; then, glancing at a shallow pool of rainwater, he sees his face is now old and wrinkled. With full force the soldier finally realizes that decades—not hours or months—have passed since the battle. The shock of realization that he has lost forty years literally in the blink of an eye is too much for the old soldier. With that realization he collapses, "and yielded up the life that spanned another life."

The Hazen Monument. Stone's River battlefield. One of the earliest memorials erected by Union troops, it figures largely in Bierce's story, "A Resumed Identity," about a wounded veteran (like Bierce) who suddenly wakens to find fifty years has passed. Library of Congress.

While the battlefield of Stone's River and the Hazen Monument do figure prominently in the story—one of Bierce's more acclaimed works—as we have seen previously in regard to Perrysville, this same story contains elements that reflect wartime experiences drawn from elsewhere than Stones River. The protagonist describes himself as a lieutenant on the staff of General Hazen—a position Bierce held, but not until the spring of 1863. Likewise, the protagonist suffered a wound to the head—as did Bierce—although not until the Battle of Kennesaw Mountain in 1864. Whether Bierce suffered temporary amnesia from his head wound is not known, but it would not have been unusual if he had.[22] Finally, the motif of a veteran returning to a scene of battle from his youth is one that certainly reflects Ambrose Bierce's own later life experience as well. Bierce is known to have made several sojourns back to the Southern battlefields of his youth in his later years, including at least one visit to Stone's River.

The December 31 fight proved a trying experience for soldiers on both sides. Rosecrans had managed to blunt the Rebel onslaught by day's end—but only just. In truth, Rosecrans was very fortunate that he had General Bragg as his opponent. Bragg was a Confederate commander who had an unerring knack for snatching defeat from the jaws of victory.

On New Year's Eve the Union army was short of food, shelter, and other necessities, and General Rosecrans seriously contemplated retreat. At a conference of war with his commanders, Rosecrans sought their advice about whether to hold his ground or retreat. While the Federals' line had held, they clearly had been bested in the day's fight and there were several voices urging him to fall back. Just then, old "Pap" Thomas, half slumbering through the discussion, spoke up and gave Rosecrans his view of the situation: "No better place to die, sir, no better place to die!" Thomas's words stiffened Rosey's resolve: the army would hold its ground.

It was indeed fortunate that Rosecrans listened to old Pap, for instead of pushing his advantage the next day, General Bragg obligingly gave Rosecrans a day's grace to rest and resupply before resuming his attack.

After creating yet more Southern widows in a futile charge on the second of January, Bragg withdrew southward, allowing Rosecrans to claim victory—pyrrhic as it was. During the desperate assault on the Federal left on January 2, the Bloody Ninth poured a deadly fire into the Confederate ranks as they splashed across chilly Stone's River. Within minutes, the river ran red and then the Yankees pressed their advantage, with the Ninth as always in the forefront of the fight.

As Bragg withdrew his army southward, the Federals too began moving—although not so silently as the phantom army in Bierce's story. The Army of the Cumberland moved into winter's quarters in and around Murfreesboro, establishing a sprawling supply dump—Fortress Rosecrans—on part of the battlefield. Having satisfied the Lincoln administration's need for action—but accomplishing little else—Old Rosey methodically began to plan his next move. The dawning year would bring with it fresh challenges and new opportunities for the Army of the Cumberland. At the beginning of January 1863, however, the only certainty was that Second Lieutenant Bierce would still be present to confront them.

8

Sitzkrieg to Blitzkrieg

> **DRAGOON**, *n*. A soldier who combines dash and steadiness in so equal measure that he makes his advances on foot and his retreats on horseback.

Following the bloody clash at Stone's River, the armies of Generals Bragg and Rosecrans separated, like two punch-drunk prizefighters, to their respective corners to rest for the next round. By leaving Rosecrans in possession of the battlefield, Bragg enabled him to lay a nominal claim to victory. Fortunately for the commander of the Army of the Cumberland, President Lincoln was perfectly content to accept his claim of victory, nominal or not. While Grant would later disparage Rosey's efforts at Stones River, it was clear that for Lincoln, schooled in frontier brawls where the last man standing won, to be in possession of the battlefield was sufficient for the President to claim victory. After his self-inflicted defeat at Stone's River, Bragg fell back to a defensive line north of the Duck River and extending up to the Barrens, a line of rugged foothills shielding the Rebel army from the Yankees. With the Federals firmly in possession of Murfreesboro and the surrounding countryside, the two armies' outposts continued to spar with one another through the interlude that followed.

In January 1863, the Army of Tennessee hunkered down and began to dig in, expecting Rosecrans to assault them straightaway. Some twenty-five miles south of Murfreesboro, General Leonidas Polk's corps constructed strong entrenchments around Shelbyville; twenty miles east of Polk, Bragg fortified his headquarters and supply base at Tullahoma, where road and rail connected him to Chattanooga and the Deep South. In advance of these two main bastions, General Hardee held down the Confederate right at Wartrace, also sitting astride the Nashville and Chattanooga railroad, and then dispersed the rest of his corps to cover the strategic passes of Liberty, Hoover, and Guy gaps.

From these secure defensive positions, General Bragg could easily sally forth at any time to challenge the Army of the Cumberland at Murfreesboro. Rather than attacking General Rosecrans, however, Bragg sat behind his defenses and battled with his own commanders instead.

Sitzkrieg to Blitzkrieg

General Rosecrans for his part showed an equal reluctance to take offensive action. Before Stone's River, Rosecrans had been badgered by Washington to take action before he felt he was ready. Rightly or wrongly, Rosecrans believed that had he not taken the offensive prematurely, the results at Stone's River would have been more decisive. Rosecrans therefore resolved not to take action again until he felt assured of victory. In response to repeated goading from General Halleck and the Lincoln administration, Old Rosey promised to take action—but wouldn't say when. What ensued during the first part of 1863, therefore, was a period that in the twentieth century would have been labeled a "phoney war" or "sitzkrieg"—a period of strategic inaction in which neither side was willing to take the offensive. It is against this background that this period of Lieutenant Bierce's career should be understood.[1]

Because of the general inaction, this phase of the Army of the Cumberland's history has been largely passed over by historians as well as by Bierce's biographers. Certainly elsewhere there were far more dramatic events transpiring that made for more compelling copy. The United States Navy, bringing to bear a large fleet and massive firepower, was repulsed at the important Rebel port of Charleston, South Carolina in April. In Virginia, Generals Lee and Jackson met and defeated the Army of the Potomac again, this time at Chancellorsville—perhaps Lee's greatest victory. To the west, although he was no more successful in practical terms than Rosecrans, Grant at least knew how to mollify Stanton and Lincoln with the appearance of activity. In truth, one scheme after another of Grant's to reduce the Confederate fortress of Vicksburg proved fruitless.

Although the first half of 1863 was seemingly blank insofar as the Army of the Cumberland was concerned, such was not the case in regard to Bierce's own writings and military career. Following Stone's River, Hazen's brigade was detailed to occupy an outlying town on the left flank of the main Union bivouac. Their mission was to keep an eye on Bragg's troops in the unlikely eventuality that Bragg might take decisive action.

A few days after the battle, therefore, Bierce and his comrades marched from Murfreesboro to Readyville. Readyville in 1863 was "a hamlet of about a dozen houses," which lay some ten miles east of Murfreesboro and served to guard the left flank of the army. With cavalry and artillery support, Hazen's brigade established camp on the tenth of January. The brigade stayed there for close to six months—longer than at any other post—and spent much of the time drilling, foraging, and skirmishing.[2]

Hazen's command at Readyville had its Rebel counterpart nearby at Woodbury. As Bierce tells us, "Connecting Readyville and Woodbury was a good, hard turnpike nine or ten miles long. Readyville was an outpost of the

Federal army Murfreesboro, Woodbury had the same relation to the Confederate army at Tullahoma. For months after the big battle at Stone's River these outposts were in constant quarrel, most of the trouble occurring, naturally, on the turnpike mentioned, between detachments of cavalry. Sometimes the infantry and artillery took a hand in the game by way of showing their goodwill."[3]

This tactical situation served as the background for Bierce's short story, "A Baffled Ambuscade." In it Bierce relates a weird tale of a nighttime cavalry patrol along the Readyville-Woodbury turnpike. In the story, a trooper by the name of Dunning is posted as part of a vidette (advance guard) ahead on the road, awaiting the arrival of a patrol under Major Seidel. When the squadron catches up with the vidette, it turns out that Dunning has gone ahead to investigate. Two or three miles into the patrol the major halts the column. He sees a shadowy figure at the edge of a thick cedar forest. Advancing closer, Seidel can make out in the dim starlight that the figure is Dunning and he seems to be standing over a dead man and horse. Dunning waves off the major, silently warning of an enemy ambush in the nearby cedar glade. Returning to his men, Major Seidel waits for the scout's return. Some time passes and toward dawn the major, irritated that Dunning isn't coming back, finally advances the patrol with caution.

As they approach the spot where Dunning had been sighted by Seidel, they find the dead man and his horse, but no Dunning. On closer inspection, however, the major realizes the dead man slain in the road *is* Dunning—long dead—and the surrounding woods show recent signs of enemy activity.

Besides belying the old saw that dead men tell no tales, "A Baffled Ambuscade" is notable as an early example of a Civil War ghost story. Bierce penned several, but this particular tale is unusual: in it, he uses a real name and actual unit. In the majority of his short stories—including those based on fact—Bierce substitutes fictitious names or no names at all. Checking the official records reveals that there was indeed a Major Charles Seidel, that he commanded a cavalry unit, and that his unit was indeed stationed at Readyville along with Hazen's brigade during the first half of 1863.

Major Seidel commanded the Second Battalion, Third Ohio Volunteer Cavalry during the spring of 1863. Like the Ninth, the Third Ohio was part of the garrison at Readyville. Not surprisingly, however, a search of official records reveals no report of ghostly encounters—only a number of nighttime patrol actions along the Readyville-Woodbury pike, as Bierce describes in his tale.[4] Ambrose Bierce thus leaves us to ponder whether his curious little tale is fiction or uncanny fact.

No sooner was the brigade established in their new bivouac than Hazen established a "general school of instruction" for the entire unit. None of the officers were exempt; from second lieutenant to colonel, they were required to "recite" from *Hardee's Tactics*. In addition, Hazen obliged them to diligently study Jomini's *Art of War* and a history of the Napoleonic Wars. All this was on top of daily drills. It was not all military drudgery for Bierce and other soldiers of the brigade at Readyville, however. A marketplace was set up at the fore-post of the camp, and two days a week a market was held where the local populace could come and sell produce and other goods to the soldiers, whose regular payrolls had no other convenient place to be spent.

The populace may have secretly harbored Secessionist sympathies, but Federal dollars were far more spendable than Rebel paper "shinplasters." Hazen also set up a pavilion and dance floor where both soldiers and civilians were serenaded by a military band, which Hazen assures us was "excellent." Even in peacetime there was not much to do out in the country, and the prospect of market day was a powerful lure to the female population of the region. Hazen tells us that "girls from all the country round came regularly, some to sell their marketing, others to dance."

Winter in Middle Tennessee is wet but generally mild, and the area is often favored by a spring of long duration and moderate temperatures. The season and climate of their stay at Readyville was "perfection" and despite the heavy round of military duties he levied on his men, Hazen describes the period as a "continued picnic."[5] Although the crusty brigadier is discreet about the details, it is clear that numerous wartime romances blossomed between soldier and civilian while at Readyville. Whether Lieutenant Bierce was struck by cupid's arrow is unknown, but it would have been remarkable if he had not at least been tempted. Of greater consequence than camp life or any military actions during Bierce's stay at Readyville, however, is the fact that during this period he was promoted in rank and given far greater responsibilities. Initially it may seem that his promotion from second lieutenant to first lieutenant was due to bravery in action at Stone's River. While Bierce was certainly deserving of promotion, such was not the case; as his personnel record indicates, Bierce was advanced in rank "to fill vacancy . . . in same co."[6] How that vacancy came about is indicative of the nature of military service during this period of "phony war."

In addition to daily drill and occasional clashes with the Butternuts down the road at Woodbury, one other necessary military activity was to forage the countryside in search of food and fodder for man and beast. Not long after establishing bivouac at Readyville, one such foraging expedition was returning to camp. The lead wagons were in fact already passing the picket line when the leader of the expedition, Captain Risley of Company C, spied a nearby corncrib and resolved to take a few men and wagons and gather up the crib's copious contents. They were so close to camp that Risley felt there was nothing to risk and something tasty to gain. Leaving one vidette outside the crude log hut to keep watch, Risley and his squad stacked arms and went inside. As they were busy inside gathering up the golden bounty, a Rebel cavalry patrol suddenly swooped down on them outside. The lone watchman failed to fire his rifle or give the alarm, and within minutes Risley and his men were surrounded and surrendered, virtually within sight of camp.[7]

Captain Risley's misfortune was Second Lieutenant Bierce's opportunity. The resulting gap in command of Company C meant that the next officer in line became company commander, and Bierce was advanced in rank one grade. Although Bierce was actually promoted on February 14, his official commission papers did not come through until April 28.

Within only a few weeks of his promotion in Company C, First Lieutenant Bierce was tapped to serve on General Hazen's staff at brigade headquarters. The brigade return for April describes Bierce's staff duty for the month as "Provost Marshal."[8] A provost marshal played an important role during the Civil War, but his duties were often as odious as they were necessary. During this era there was no such thing as military police per se. Specific officers and detachments were detailed as needed to carry out varied police functions for the army. Provost duties might be temporary or an officer might be assigned as provost marshal more or less on a permanent basis. Similarly a squad, a company, or even a whole regiment might be designated as provost guard. In the Army of the Potomac, for example, toward the latter part of the war, Collis's Zouaves (114th Pennsylvania Volunteer Infantry) were made the army's provost guard. A wayward soldier didn't need to see any armband saying "M. P." to know they were in hot water; the Zouaves' colorful turbans and bright red baggy pants—backed up by bayoneted muskets—were sufficient to inform a Union soldier in that army that they were in trouble with the law.

In First Lieutenant Bierce's case, there were no colorful costumes to wear. We know from his own words, however, that Bierce ensured that military discipline was carried out. In the old army it did not take much to incur the wrath of military justice. Even minor infractions of the rules could incur severe and painful punishment. The provost marshal was the person who would see that such punishment was meted out.

Ambrose Bierce describes Hazen's dedication to duty as virtually religious in nature. While Hazen's "missionary" efforts were mainly directed against "spiritual darkness" on the part of his superiors, we are also told that "he would turn aside from pursuit of his erring commander to set a chicken-thieving orderly astride a wooden horse, with a heavy stone attached to each foot."[9] An article in *Chambers's Journal* some years after the war on the brutalities of the eighteenth century English army set Bierce reminiscing about the American version of the "wooden horse." While the British apparently

Bound and gagged. One of several types of corporal punishment inflicted on soldiers who disobeyed orders. On promotion to first lieutenant, Bierce was briefly made provost marshal and put in charge of discipline. Sketch by Charles Reed. Library of Congress.

outlawed the practice sometime after 1760, Bierce testifies to the continued use of *"Equus penalis Hobarti"* in the American army "as lately as 1863."[10] "In the land of light and law," Bierce informs his readers, "the spectacle of a wooden horse carrying double or even triple was for weeks a familiar one to this present writer. Indeed, I have seen the animal serving as charger to as many as a half-dozen American warriors, the two legs of each thoughtfully provided with ballast of rocks." Bierce specifically tells us he was witness to such in the "little Tennessee village of Readyville." As provost marshal, Hazen would have charged Bierce with overseeing such corporal punishments.[11]

Overseeing discipline for minor infractions may not have been the limit of Bierce's duties as provost marshal. About this same time Lieutenant Bierce was also present for several military executions. Although he is not specific, Bierce tells of one cavalryman condemned by a court-martial for desertion. One may speculate that the deserter in question was from the Third Ohio Cavalry also at Readyville: "He was seated astride his coffin, a black bandage about his eyes, his arms bound behind his back. The officer in charge of the firing squad gave the command, 'ready—aim!' and a dozen loaded carbines were leveled at his breast."

At this point the condemned called out at the very last second. The officer stepped forward to hear his final request. Then the officer repeated the commands, "and a second later the poor fellow was a thing of shreds and patches." Bierce inquired of the cavalryman's last wish—it turned out he had wanted to die astride a saddle![12]

On another occasion, almost certainly during this same period, Bierce watched an execution held at nearby Murfreesboro, performed on a "brace of miscreants." Bierce tells us, "The fellows were hanged by the military for a murder of revolting atrocity, committed without orders." Just before the trap door of the gallows was pulled, one of the murderers began spouting self-righteous assertions that he "was going home to Jesus." As the criminal uttered his hypocritical pronouncements, a nearby steam-engine let loose with a loud "hoot-hoot!" The soldiers gathered to witness the proceedings began to guffaw at the irony of the mocking train whistle, even as the men dropped from the scaffold. Bierce asserts that "the ropes about their necks were actually kept slack for some seconds by the gusts of laughter ascending from below."[13]

Given that Journalist Bierce carefully groomed his cynical persona in his postwar newspaper columns, it is difficult to divine Provost Marshal Bierce's actual feelings toward observing and carrying out the often-brutal military discipline. While his comments on the wooden horse seem to indicate a certain disdain toward such punishments, his sardonic "gallows humor" regarding the executions seems to contradict that. Moreover, in later years Bierce is known to have penned an entire essay in defense of capital punishment. Whether Lieutenant Bierce requested a different posting on the staff or whether Hazen perceived that his new staff officer's talents lay in other areas is not known; what we do know is that the next brigade return indicates that Bierce's talents were redirected to a position more suited to his temperament and perhaps his military school training: topographical engineer. During the Civil War, staff officers were not the specialized, technical experts one finds in today's armies, who often sit in sealed rooms remote from the battlefront. The staffs, even of divisions or corps, were generally small, and while assigned specific duties, they could be detailed for any task their commander wished done. In battle, the staff were the eyes, ears and voice of their general.

In one of his fiction pieces, Bierce gives a succinct description of the Civil War staff officer's routine in combat: "From a position of that comparative security from which a civilian would ascribe his escape to a 'miracle,' he may be dispatched with an order to some commander of a prone regiment in the front line—a person for the moment inconspicuous and not always easy to find without a deal of search among men somewhat preoccupied, and in a din in which question and answer alike must be imparted in the sign language. It is customary in such cases to duck the head and scuttle away on a keen run, an object of lively interest to some thousands of admiring marksmen."[14]

The Army of the Cumberland under General Rosecrans, and later General Thomas, put great faith in maps and mapmaking. Earlier in the war, in western Virginia and again at Shiloh, unfamiliarity with the landscape had greatly hindered successful Union operations. Outdated or inaccurate maps, information derived from unreliable local residents, or similar flaws in tactical intelligence often led to loss of surprise, late arrival of reinforcements, and the delay or cancellation of attacks. One modern expert on the subject has described the Army of the Cumberland as "the most map-conscious army in the war."[15] General Rosecrans wanted no confusion or mistakes when he finally resolved to take action. As he planned his upcoming campaign, he envisioned complex maneuvering, surprise, and precise timing—all of which would require reliable topographical engineers. Lieutenant A. G. Bierce was one such candidate.

Although Bierce tells us little directly of his activities as topographical officer, in one of his short stories set during the Atlanta Campaign, he gives us greater insight into his activities:

> My duties as topographical engineer kept me working like a beaver—all day in the saddle and half the night at my drawing-table, platting my surveys. It was hazardous work; the nearer to the enemy lines I could penetrate, the more valuable were my field notes and the resulting maps. It was a business in which the lives of men counted as nothing against the chance of defining a road or sketching a bridge. Whole squadrons of cavalry escort had sometimes to be sent thundering against a powerful infantry outpost in order that the brief time between the charge and the inevitable retreat might be utilized in sounding a ford or determining the point of intersection of two roads.[16]

After his brief service in April as provost marshal, Bierce was noted in the Company Muster Roll for May–June as having been "detached on Sp. Service as Topograp. Eng. of 3d Brig 2d Dv. 21 ac."[17] There is a hint in the records regarding what specifically Hazen had Bierce doing during this period. On another War Department document entitled "Appears on Returns," which was a postwar collation of various wartime returns on Bierce, is the notation, "June 1863 Absent on Detached Service as Chief of Scouts Brig. Hdqs." During this period, the terms "scout" and "spy" were interchangeable. A scout was generally responsible for penetrating behind enemy lines to learn dispositions, defenses, troop strength, and the like. Whether called scout or spy, his fate would be much the same as the Federal sergeant in Bierce's story "Parker Addison, Philosopher": a speedy death at the hands of the enemy. Bierce's designation as "Chief of Scouts" indicates he was charged by Hazen with command of an important mission behind enemy lines. What such mission was, Bierce never shared with readers, but during the Spanish American he did ruminate once on his brief service as spymaster:

> I once had command of about a dozen spies for some months—gave them their assignments, received and collated their reports and tried as hard as I could to believe them. I must say that they were about as scurvy a lot of imposters as could be found on Uncle Sam's payroll (that was before the pension era) and I should have experienced a secret joy if they had been caught and hanged. But they were in an honorable calling—a calling in which the proportion of intelligent and conscientious workers is probably about the same as in other trades and professions.[18]

If his brief stint as spymaster was indeed in June 1863, it is not hard to deduce what Bierce and his "scurvy lot of imposters" were up to. The brigade return for June, completed at the end of that month, no longer lists Bierce's post as Readyville, but rather lists him at Manchester, Tennessee. He and his spies were engaged in scouting missions behind enemy lines preparatory to the series of broader tactical maneuvers begun in late June which came to be known as the Tullahoma Campaign.

As we have seen, following the winter dust-up at Stones River, Bragg had withdrawn his army southward, setting up his defensive line along the Duck River and its branches; he had posted strong pickets to guard all the passes leading southward and had also constructed major strong-points in depth. Bragg was confident that any Yankee attempt to take on the Army of Tennessee would meet with bloody defeat.[19] Unfortunately for Bragg, when General Rosecrans finally did take the offensive, he declined to accommodate Bragg. Instead of acting as Bragg expected, Rosey used his cavalry and a small force of infantry to make a demonstration toward the Rebel fortress of Shelbyville. Then Rosecrans, through a series of complex but rapid marches and counter-marches, proceeded to go around and behind Bragg's carefully constructed defensive line. Those few military historians who have studied the Tullahoma Campaign in depth have generally given Rosecrans high marks. One professional soldier described it as "strategically more important than Gettysburg and tactically superior to Vicksburg."[20]

The crucial part of Rosecrans's strategy involved the quick seizure of the three strategic passes through The Barrens, the line of foothills that shielded the Confederates from surprise attack. His plan involved dividing his army and attacking all three passes simultaneously. Once through, the Union columns had to combine and recombine with precise timing before the Rebels could react.

Beginning on June 23, the Army of the Cumberland started what was surely one of the most complicated and risky operations of the war. Separate columns simultaneously captured Hoover's, Liberty, and Guy's Gaps. Once these gates had been opened, the bulk of the army flooded through. Despite heavy rains that impeded their progress, the Union army succeeded in outflanking the Confederates and working behind their main defensive lines. By the time Bragg realized what had happened, he was outmaneuvered, outnumbered, and in danger of being surrounded. He thus ordered a hasty retreat over the Cumberland Mountains toward Chattanooga. As newspapers reported at the time, Bragg was "bumfuzzled" by Rosecrans. By July 4, the campaign was all over. General Rosecrans and the Army of the Cumberland had driven eighty miles through heavily defended territory at a cost of only 560 men; the Confederates had lost some 2,000. Although overshadowed in the news by the Union's costly siege of Vicksburg and its bloody draw at Gettysburg, both of which ended on the same day, in truth Rosecrans's Tullahoma Campaign was a greater tactical and strategic victory than either. It was a classic example of "lightning warfare," or *blitzkrieg*.[21]

Behind this brilliant strategy and stunning success lay a less heralded factor: Rosecrans's firm knowledge of the terrain and the disposition of the enemy forces. Underlying Rosey's victory was competent work by the topographical engineers and the scouts who, at great personal risk, provided the tactical intelligence necessary for the Union columns to execute those complex maneuvers. Bierce was one of several such officers who hazarded much to bring back the needed information.

Days later, on July 14, Lieutenant Bierce received an order from divisional headquarters to conduct a survey of a section of the Big Duck River. He was instructed to show "as to depth width and approach and nature of fords. Also route from Manchester to Shelbyville down Duck River."[22] In the several "quick maps" prepared in June and early July for the Tullahoma Campaign, there were numerous blank areas where only a question mark lay. Most of these quick maps have the notation, "All the Topl. Engineers are asked to send such as soon as possible to these headquarters."[23] Although the army had already occupied this large swath of territory, transportation routes, fords and the like were still poorly known. Rosecrans clearly needed better topographical information to plan the logistics of his next advance.

Bierce and the other topographical engineers of the army played a crucial role in that planning.

Ironically, despite Rosecrans's spectacular success, Washington acted as if he had accomplished nothing. Of course, as overall commander, General Halleck hated nothing more than to be proved wrong—and Rosecrans was not the sort of man to smooth ruffled feathers. Halleck and Stanton soon began barraging Rosecrans with telegrams, badgering him to pursue Bragg immediately. Rosecrans, however, knew that traversing the Cumberland Mountains, crossing the broad Tennessee River, and then seizing the strategic transportation nexus of Chattanooga was no easy task. It was a difficult mission fraught with even more potential danger than the Tullahoma advance. Not surprisingly, the cautious Rosecrans resolved to follow up his carefully planned first victory with an even more carefully planned second. General Hazen doubted the necessity of such a long delay before advancing on Chattanooga: "It was alleged this was to repair the railroads necessary for our further march."[24] Hazen spent the following month in Manchester drilling his brigade and further instructing his officers.

After a month of inaction on Rosecrans's part, Halleck ordered him to move, ready or not. Fortunately, Rosecrans was almost ready. Again consulting his maps and mapmakers, Rosecrans set the Army of the Cumberland in motion over the mountains. Once again Rosecrans put his faith in a flanking maneuver coupled with a diversionary action to outwit Bragg—this time a feint to the southeast. The diversion played a key role in Rosecrans's strategy. A small force, composed of Hazen's brigade, Wilder's "Lighting Brigade" of mounted infantry, armed with repeating rifles and Minty's cavalry brigade, plus two batteries of artillery, all under the command of General Hazen, were to be sent over Walden Ridge to distract Bragg.[25] Hazen's command set up camp at Poe's Tavern, ten miles above Chattanooga on the north bank of the Tennessee River, and from there detachments were sent out to watch all the crossings and distract the enemy as much as possible. For a distance of fifty miles, infantry, cavalry, and artillery lightly occupied the riverbank. On the twenty-first of August, Hazen's force began shelling Chattanooga, which did little damage but caused much alarm among the Butternuts occupying the town.

Hazen also instituted a systematic program of foraging, but contrary to common practice, the iron brigadier made sure that the local populace was not randomly pillaged by his troops. Only one foraging patrol per regiment was sent out at a time, and the farmers and merchants were duly compensated. In the Sequatchie and Tennessee Valleys, the local population was far different in attitude than those they had encountered in West Tennessee, Alabama, or Mississippi. Hazen describes them as "rather primitive and strongly Union" people, who treated his troops hospitably.[26] For several weeks Hazen and his command made merry mischief, confusing the enemy and causing Bragg to withdraw forces from his left flank to strengthen the threatened right. Bands played loudly and often, and the scattered regiments of Hazen's force raised all the chatter and noise of a large army. The ruse worked perfectly, and Hazen's command managed to convince Bragg that the Yankees would be attacking the city from the north and east rather than from the west.

When the Army of the Cumberland's main force finally crossed the Tennessee at Bridgeport, Alabama and other points, the landings there met only slight resistance. Once again, Bragg was "bumfuzzled." As before, he chose flight over fight and abandoned Chattanooga, the strategic prize that had been Rosecrans's primary goal. Throughout all this jockeying back and forth along the meandering banks of the Tennessee, Hazen's command played a crucial role with its strategic deception. During all these maneuvers, staff officer Bierce was at the forefront of action, running errands, acting as his commander's eyes, scouting out potential fords and back country tracks, and serving as an integral member of Hazen's team carrying out the general's will to the letter.

Bierce glosses over the operations that led the Federals to capture the city of Chattanooga, and unfortunately he is not alone in doing so. The Tullahoma Campaign and the successive forced crossing of the Tennessee were far and away the most successful Union operations of the war, and the two operations together constitute classic examples of strategic deception and a war of movement—examples that have been studiously ignored by historians ever since. Even in 1863, the magnitude of the Army of the Cumberland's accomplishment was not given full recognition. General Rosecrans was seriously miffed at the Lincoln administration's lack of appreciation of his great victory. Writing to Secretary of War Stanton, he expressed the hope that the Department of War "may not overlook so great an event because it is not written in letters of blood." In this hope, the good general would be sorely disappointed.

9

Chickamauga

> **VALOR**, *n*. A soldierly compound of vanity, duty and the gambler's hope.
>
> "Why have you halted?" roared the commander of a division at Chickamauga, who had ordered a charge; "move forward, sir, at once."
> "General," said the commander of the delinquent brigade, "I am persuaded that any further display of valor by my troops will bring them into collision with the enemy."

Like the battle at Shiloh, the Battle of Chickamauga was a great and bloody clash of arms that should have—but didn't—decide the war in the West. While in the case of Chickamauga there is no doubt about who won the battle, just about everything else has been the subject of contention, debate, and blame—a situation made all the more complex by the inability of eyewitnesses and official reports on either side to agree as to what happened where, to whom, by whom, and when. After 150 years of debate, historians and Civil War enthusiasts have more or less arrived at a general consensus of sorts; however, that does not necessarily mean they have plumbed the truth of the matter.

First, it is important to understand that—contrary to most popular accounts—the name Chickamauga does not and has never meant "River of Death."[1] However, after the events of September 19 and 20, 1863, Chickamauga did indeed seem to be synonymous with death in the minds of all the participants in that battle. Just a few miles south of Chattanooga on the far side of Missionary Ridge, West Chickamauga Creek meanders through a valley and, as is common in the South, a small country road follows the line of that creek, running generally northward into the Tennessee River near Chattanooga. It was an integral part of what the paramount chief of the Chickamauga Indians dubbed "The Dark and Bloody Ground."[2]

The area in question was, by itself, of no strategic value and not even particularly useful as farmland, consisting mostly of thick scrub, tangled vines, and wasteland, interspersed with an occasional pasture or cornfield. It was here in the early fall that the armies of Generals Rosecrans and Bragg clashed; it was here that much blood was shed and cost both sides many dead. Here too reputations were both lost and bolstered.

In 1898, Ambrose Bierce penned a memoir of the Battle of Chickamauga for readers of his newspaper columns.[3] Bierce informs us that his intent in writing his memoir was not to render a complete history of the battle, "but only relate some parts of what I saw of it." Although the memoir goes by various titles, it is generally referred to as "A Little of Chickamauga." As Bierce notes, although Rosecrans had "maneuvered [Bragg] out of Chattanooga," he "had not maneuvered . . . [the] entire army into it . . . By the time that Rosecrans had got his three scattered corps together we were a long way from Chattanooga."[4] Rosecrans, in seeking to pursue Bragg, had allowed the Army of the Cumberland's line of communications back toward Chattanooga to become attenuated and vulnerable. As it advanced into Georgia, the army's whole supply line became dependent on the single country road that paralleled Chickamauga Creek. As Bierce succinctly notes, "Chickamauga was a fight for possession of a road."[5]

Had General Rosecrans been content with the capture of Chattanooga and halted there to consolidate his gains, likely history would have hailed him as one of the great captains of the war. It may even be that he, not Grant, would have become the general who Lincoln would choose to lead all the Union armies to victory. But goaded by the slights of Halleck and Stanton, and seeing his nemesis on the run, Rosecrans kept up the pursuit. If the Army of the Cumberland could run Bragg to ground and destroy his army, then the whole of the Deep South would be vulnerable and open to easy conquest. With all of the states of the Confederacy between the Appalachians and the Mississippi virtually defenseless, Rosecrans would be hailed as a great victor. It was a prize too tempting for Rosecrans to resist.

Yet, whatever his faults (and they were many), Braxton Bragg was no fool. Seeing an opportunity, Bragg turned around, hoping to cut off Rosecrans's line of retreat and destroy him. Bierce, as a staff officer, had an inkling as to what was about to transpire. As he put it, "We knew well enough that there was to be a fight: the fact that we did not want one could have told us that, for Bragg always retired when we wanted to fight and fought when we most desired peace."[6]

After crossing the Tennessee River on the tenth of September, Hazen's brigade had encountered some occasional skirmishing, but nothing of any consequence. About a week after crossing the river, a sharp skirmish ensued for a bridge over Chickamauga Creek—Reed's Bridge. It is generally portrayed as a cavalry action involving Minty's Federals and some Georgia cavalry units, but with one or another infantry unit also mentioned. By some chronicler's accounting, the skirmishes for Reed's Bridge on the seventeenth and eighteenth marked the beginning of the Battle of Chickamauga.[7] As they were maneuvering, the horsemen of Minty's brigade cautioned Mrs. Reed, whose home was dangerously close to the looming clash of arms, to save herself and her family. The woman, an unrepentant Secessionist, gave them a rude answer. Soon thereafter, Mrs. Reed was shredded by Rebel artillery. It is thought that this incident was the inspiration for a similar event portrayed in Bierce's short story, "Chickamauga."[8]

If the memories of veterans of the Ninth Indiana are to be trusted, at least some members of the Ninth's Company C also participated in this preliminary action on the seventeenth and eighteenth.[9] That night the brigade moved to a position one mile north of Gordon's Mill, where they formed a battle line near La Fayette and Rossville Road. The brigade lay there until about eleven a.m. the next day, when they moved about one and a half miles to their left, in front of General Thomas's troops. It was at this point that the fighting became severe. Upon reaching the McNamara House on LaFayette and Rossville Road, the brigade, along with the rest of the Second Division, formed two lines facing east and then advanced about three quarters of a mile where they almost immediately clashed with the main line of the Rebel army. An intense firefight ensued, the Federal units to their left having already been hotly engaged for some time.[10] After twice exhausting their ammunition, Hazen's brigade was replaced in the line by another unit and fell back to the road to resupply and clean their fouled guns. Until they could do so, the brigade's usefulness in the front lines was limited. Watching the regiments falling back was Lt. Bierce, standing next to General Hazen, who at the time was with the divisional artillery train. At that moment the guns were parked on an acclivity overlooking the road and were lacking any infantry support.

Lt. Bierce provides a vivid description of what happened next: "Before our weary and virtually drained men had actually reached the guns the line in front gave way, fell back behind the guns and went on, the Lord knows whither. A moment later the field was gray with Confederates in pursuit." In the blink of an eye, Hazen and Bierce went from being well behind the front to being well in advance of it, without support on either side and directly in the path of the onrushing enemy. Amid the artillery, Bierce was witness to the ensuing affair. As the only general officer above bird colonel in sight, Hazen took charge of every soldier in sight not already in full flight: "I hastily gathered and placed in position all the artillery then in reach, including portions of Standart's, Cockerill's, Cushing's and Russell's batteries, in all about twenty pieces."[11] The enemy advance was so swift, there was no time even for Hazen's own men to be formed into a line, "there being but about two minutes to make dispositions before the blow came."[12]

"The guns opened fire with grape and canister;" Bierce continues, "and for perhaps four minutes—it seemed an hour—nothing could be heard but the infernal din of the discharge and nothing seen through the smoke but a great ascension of dust from the smitten soil. When all was over, and the dust cloud had lifted, the spectacle was too dreadful to describe. The Confederates were still there—all of them, it seemed—some almost under the muzzle of the guns. But not a man of all these brave fellows was on his feet, and so thickly were all covered with dust that they looked as if they had been reclothed in yellow." Standing next to one of the gunners observing his handiwork, Lieutenant Bierce heard him remark with grim humor, "We bury our dead!"[13]

The evening of the nineteenth passed without any other major clash of arms, but all during the night both sides maneuvered in preparation for the morrow's fight. In the dark the Confederates continued to stretch their line northward in an attempt to flank the Union positions posted in advance of the road. "We neither saw nor heard his movement, but any man with half a head would have known that he was making it, and we met it by a parallel movement to our left."[14] During the night General Thomas had assumed command of all Federal troops on the left, including the Second Division. Beginning shortly after daybreak, Hazen and all the other brigade commanders of the Second set their men to building stout breastworks of log and rail (Bierce calls them "rude intrenchments") a short distance from the road facing the expected enemy attacks. Around eight o'clock, according to Hazen, Confederate attacks began on the far left of the Federals and then swept along the line, hitting Hazen's position about fifteen minutes later. The Rebel assaults had little effect on the Union defenses until they passed beyond General Reynolds's position on the right of Hazen's brigade.

Hazen tells us the enemy attacks kept up "without intermission" until about eleven o'clock, with "a fury never witnessed upon the field either of Shiloh or Stone's River." As Bierce describes it, "When repulsed, the enemy came again and again—his persistence was dispiriting."[15] The intensity of the fighting that morning seriously depleted the brigade's ammunition supplies. Although Hazen's men more than held their own behind the log barricades, General Hazen was constantly concerned that his command would run out of ammunition. Throughout the morning, he tells us, he repeatedly sent his aides—"couriers"—to bring up fresh stores of munitions.

Who, when, and how many of Hazen's staff were engaged running back and forth to secure shot, shell, cartridges, and powder we are not told, and doubtless in the heat of action not even the general knew. By his own account, Lieutenant Bierce was one such "courier" that morning: "I had been sent by my chief, General Hazen, to order up some artillery ammunition and rode away to the right and rear in search of it." Attached to the brigade was Battery F, First Ohio Volunteer Artillery—Cockerill's battery—and like the infantry, they had expended a great deal of munitions that morn, largely canister and grape, doing horrific damage to the surging lines of gray that sought to overrun the Union lines.

Finding an ordnance train, Bierce tells us, "I obtained from the officer in charge a few wagons loaded with what I wanted, but he seemed in doubt as to the occupancy of the region across which I proposed to guide them. Although assured that I had just traversed it, and that it lay immediately behind Wood's division, he insisted on riding to the top of the ridge behind where his train lay and overlooking the ground." Riding with the quartermaster, Lt. Bierce was astonished at the sight that lay before him: "The very earth seemed to be moving toward us! They came on in thousands, and so rapidly that we barely had time to turn back and gallop down the hill and away."[16]

In their frantic efforts to turn the wagons about and escape, the teamsters ended up tipping over a good number of the ordnance wagons. Panicked teamsters cut teams loose and then mounted the first animal they could, riding as fast as the still-harnessed beasts could go. He did not realize it at the time, but Topographical Officer Bierce was smack in the middle of one of the worst Union debacles of the war. Some distance further north, General Hazen was beginning to fret about the fate of the staffers he had sent in search of munitions. "At about 10 a.m. our couriers for ammunition, previously prompt to return, failed to come back, and it soon came to be believed that our trains had been captured." [17] Although on their front things had actually begun to quiet down, Hazen cautioned his commanders to instruct their men to observe a strict fire discipline. In his report, Hazen says that from about eleven a.m. until about three p.m., a lull fell upon their sector of the line. Hazen notes, "The stillness that now hung over the battle-field was ominous."[18]

It was after three p.m., Hazen states, when "a fearful onslaught was made upon this line." The firefight, "with apparently varying fortunes," served to deplete the stock of ammunition in all of the brigades holding the line; but a flanking attack on what had been their rear areas now threatened to encircle them all. Several brigadiers expressed the need for one of the units to "move over and strike the deciding blow." Hazen, after having his colonels survey their units' available supply of cartridges, found they still had some forty rounds per man left.

Hazen immediately moved his men at the double-quick to the threatened quarter with a frontage of two regiments, the two weaker regiments forming their support. Firing by volleys, with one lining stepping forward while the other reloaded, Hazen's brigade was able to deliver a nearly continuous wall of fire at the charging Rebel ranks. Longstreet's men, the pride of the Army of Northern Virginia, fell in droves. Although to those in the front ranks it seemed an eternity, within but a few minutes the brigade had blunted the enemy onslaught.[19]

In his report Colonel Suman of the Ninth indicates how confused the fighting was at this point, recalling that after this incident, the regiment was relocated still further to the right, taking position "on a high hill." "It was while in this position that my attention was drawn to my right by an unnecessary amount of talking." Going over to see what the matter was, Suman was suddenly surprised to find himself staring down the barrel of a revolver belonging to a Rebel officer, demanding his surrender.

Thinking quickly, Colonel Suman told the Johnny that he had already surrendered; when the officer's attention was distracted, Suman slipped away, brought up two of his rifle companies, and dispersed the Rebels, members of a Virginia regiment that had arrived only a few hours before. After the war, veterans of the Ninth had animated discussions with their former enemies about the incident, the latter claiming that the Hoosiers had cheated, that the men of the regiment were their prisoners and should have behaved as such. Needless to say, Colonel Suman's views on the incident differed substantially from that of his foes.[20]

While Bierce was elsewhere, Colonel Suman and the Ninth had been detached from the brigade and sent to the extreme right flank as sacrificial goats to cover General Brannon's retreat. Brannon also abandoned three other regiments on the left, already out of ammunition, to the same purpose. The Ninth escaped, but General Brannon falsified his report, and adding insult to injury, his lies deprived the regiment of full credit for their desperate stand. After the war, in the process of erecting regimental monuments in the battlefield park, a heated argument arose between the Ninth's survivors and the monument commission over the right location for their memorial, the commission preferring a general's lies to the soldiers' truth.[21] In any case, Hazen's timely action had stopped the Confederates from outflanking and overwhelming General Thomas's command. That crisis averted, Hazen claims, "There was no more fighting." Toward dark, Hazen received orders from General Thomas to withdraw toward Rossville.

In the heat of action that day and in the dark march from the battlefield after, few on the Federal side knew exactly why things had gone so terribly awry. All understood, however, that a calamity of the first magnitude had befallen the army. What exactly had gone wrong? All through the morning fight, the Federal line, although heavily challenged, had managed to stave off a determined and persistent threat with few casualties. This was partly due to the hastily constructed breastworks the Federals used, but even more was their success due to Bragg's tactics of attacking the Union line piecemeal. Hazen obliquely criticizes Bragg's tactics in his report: "The effect of sending in fractions to battle with an entire army is to waste our strength without perceptibly weakening the enemy."[22]

Even Braxton Bragg, however, eventually had to face reality. After General Polk's corps spent the morning "wasting our strength" by attacking the Union left "in echelon," the irascible Confederate army commander was persuaded to mount a full-strength assault against the right-center of the Federal line, using the whole of General Peter Longstreet's Corps, arrived by train from Virginia only hours before. It was at this point that the gods of war smiled on the undeserving Rebel commander of the Army of Tennessee.

As he had done during the previous day's fighting, on the morning of the twentieth General Rosecrans was shifting units about to meet each threat as it arose along the front. At one point after the war, Bierce responded to a reader's comments about his essay on Chickamauga and gave his perspective on the catastrophe: "Wood was directed to close on the right of another division, which was supposed to be next to him on the left. It was not, and in order to reach it he left the front line to move behind the troops intervening. Rosecrans had forgotten his own dispositions."[23]

Some historians have suggested that Wood's literal obedience of Rosecrans's order may not have been accidental—that Wood may have been motivated by spite. Earlier in the battle, an agitated Rosecrans had berated Wood publicly for not carrying out an order speedily enough. So, in full knowledge of the folly of this present order from Rosecrans, Wood carried it out without bothering to question or verify it, thereby deliberately bringing about disaster.[24] While the precise language of Rosecrans's curt reproof of his subordinate is unknown, it was likely something to the effect of, "It is not permitted to you to know anything. It is sufficient that you obey my order." Although General Wood was no lowly artillery officer, like the fictional character in "One Kind of Officer," he too obeyed an order he knew was certainly in error.[25]

As fate would have it, at the very same time that Wood began his abrupt withdrawal from the front line, Longstreet's Corps, fresh off the trains from Virginia, plus General Buckner's also recently arrived corps came barreling through the newly opened gap in the lines, nearly 23,000 men strong. Longstreet's divisions were originally to wheel to their left (the Union right) and roll up that wing after breaking through the center. However, the Union right had collapsed like a house of cards and the Butternuts (actually some of Longstreet's men were dressed in blue, adding to Union confusion) met such little resistance that they simply kept on going forward, penetrating deeply into the Union center. General Rosecrans's own headquarters was located in the center, directly in Longstreet's path. The Confederate attack effectively kept the Union commander from knowing what was happening to the rest of the army.

While Bierce would later defend Rosecrans against accusations of cowardice—which apparently originated from Jefferson C. Davis (the homicidal Union general, not the Secessionist president) and his staff—Bierce's defense of his former commander in chief was typically a left-handed one. "Rosecrans's retirement from the field was not cowardly: he was caught in the rout of the right and naturally supposed that the entire army had given way. His error lay in accepting that view of the disaster without inquiring . . . There is no doubt that he acted on his best judgment, which, however, was never very good."[26]

General Rosecrans and his staff were caught up in the panic of the right and swept away, where whole divisions disintegrated into mobs of men crazy to get away from the enemy. Charles Dana—Secretary of War Stanton's resident spy with Rosecrans—described the event: "I was awakened by the most infernal noise I ever heard. Never in any battle I had witnessed was there such a discharge of cannon and musketry. I sat up on the grass, and the first thing I saw was General Rosecrans crossing himself—he was a very devout Catholic. 'Hello!' I said to myself, 'if the general is crossing himself, we are in a desperate situation.'"[27]

The lone member of General Rosecrans's staff who did bother to make it back to the battlefield that afternoon was his chief of staff, General James A. Garfield, a political appointee, whose postwar political career was assured by this one heroic act.[28] Typically, Bierce, while acknowledging the act, disdains any great merit in it: "A good deal of nonsense used to be talked about the heroism of General Garfield. . . . There was no great heroism in it; that is what every man should have done, including the commander of the army. We could hear Thomas's guns going—those of us who had ears for them— and all that was needed was to make a sufficiently wide detour and then move toward the sound. I did so myself, and have never felt it ought to make me President."[29]

A "sufficiently wide detour" indeed. Somewhere to the right rear of where Wood's division ought to have been but wasn't, Lt. Bierce parted ways with the querulous quartermaster and his skittish teamsters. Suddenly, Bierce found himself alone on a rapidly changing battlefield, like a shipwrecked sailor in a sea of angry sharks. The one saving grace Bierce possessed was that, as topographical engineer, he had a better-than-average notion of the lay of the land and knew how to get back to his command. As he slowly made his way around the enemy force, Bierce ran into General Negley. As a first-class mapmaker, Bierce says he volunteered his services to Negley "to pilot him back to glory or the grave." Negley rejected Bierce's offer "a little uncivilly." Bierce attributes Negley's rudeness to "the general's obvious absence of mind," speculating that "his mind, I think, was in Nashville, behind a breastwork."[30] Actually, Bierce did not know the half of it. Negley not only did not wish to come to Thomas's aid, he had lately left the field of battle, even though specifically directed to support Thomas by Rosecrans. Worse still, General Negley took with him most of the artillery and all the remaining ammunition trains. Thomas, ever the Southern gentleman, does not mention names in his report, but merely says that "someone" had removed the ammunition from the front.

By the time Bierce finally found his way back to the brigade's original position, he was unable to find Hazen or any of the regiments of the brigade. So Bierce reported to General Thomas, who "directed me to remain with him." Thomas and the left wing by now had gained some idea of the magnitude of the disaster that had befallen the right wing of the army. Assuming command, Thomas attempted to gather together all the fragments of the army that had made their way to his end of the battlefield and organize a resistance to the growing Confederate onslaught. Meanwhile, Longstreet's divisions after the successful breakthrough eventually wheeled to their right, heading toward Thomas's positions. As the afternoon wore on, the Rebels pressed their attacks with greater and greater intensity: "The battle was fierce and continuous," Bierce relates, "the enemy extending his lines farther and farther around our right, toward our line of retreat. We could not meet the extension otherwise than by "refusing" our right flank and letting him inclose us, which but for gallant Gordon Granger, he would have done."[31] Even as the Rebels began to close the noose around Thomas's command, according to Bierce, "looking across the fields in our rear . . . I had the happy distinction of a discoverer. What I saw was the shimmer of sunlight on metal: lines of troops were coming in behind us! The distance was too great, the atmosphere too hazy to distinguish the color of their uniform, even with a glass."

Bierce says he reported this discovery to General Thomas, who directed him to go and see whether they were friend or foe. Bierce says he galloped near enough toward them "to see they were of our kidney" and then hastened back to Thomas on Snodgrass Hill with the "glad tidings," at which point Thomas sent him back to guide the column to their position. Bierce closed on the Federal column to find that it was General Granger with "two strong brigades of the reserve" who, hearing the firing, had come "soldierlike" to join the fray. Bierce says he directed Granger and his staff to General Thomas and then went "visiting."[32]

Chickamauga

General Steedman's men rushing to the aid of Thomas on Snodgrass Hill. Bierce, along with his brother Albert, was with the vanguard of General Granger's relief force just as the defending Federals under Thomas were about to be overrun. Field sketch by Alfred Waud, Library of Congress.

It so happened that Bierce's brother Albert was also in Granger's column, part of the Eighteenth Ohio Light Artillery Battery (also known as Aleshire's Battery), which by chance was near the head of the column. "As we moved forward we had a comfortable chat among such of the enemy's bullets as had inconsiderably been fired too high."[33] In short order, Granger's force went into action on the Union right, which was at that moment in imminent danger of being overrun. After this, Lt. Bierce finally located his brigade, "or what remained of it." This he found "had made a half-mile march to add itself to the unrouted at the memorable Snodgrass Hill." Bierce says that when he rejoined Hazen, the general's first words were not ones of welcome but to inquire about the artillery ammunition he'd been sent to get—and failed to return with. Bierce remained with the brigade for the remainder of the day.

Even with Granger's timely arrival, it was still a very near thing for the men of Thomas's command. All except Granger's brigades were extremely low on ammo. Fortunately, the Rebels too had suffered heavily and their attacks began slacking off toward late in the day. As evening approached, Thomas gave orders for the various units to quietly retire from the field, with Hazen's brigade being one of the last to retreat. Away to the far left and rear, some of Bragg's troops sent up a Rebel yell. To Bierce and his comrades it was "the ugliest sound that any mortal ever heard . . . it was taken up successively and passed round to our front, along our right and in behind us again, until it seemed almost to have got to the point whence it started." In the gathering gloom there was still a small space behind them where the yell did not prolong itself, and it was through that gap that Thomas's weary regiments finally retired "in profound silence and dejection."[34]

Although he would return to the topic of Chickamauga on other occasions, Bierce's essay chronicling the "little bit" he saw of the battle nonetheless tells quite a lot. There is only one problem with his narrative: according to several modern historians, the whole episode he relates about the twentieth of September is a fabrication—a tissue of lies and false claims.

Peter Cozzens, the highly respected military historian and a leading expert on the Battle of Chickamauga, has stated that "the few comments Bierce made about Chickamauga were largely false."[35] More recently, Gordon Berg, another well-qualified and well-respected Civil War author, while more cautious in his accusations, has characterized Bierce's account of the battle as a "tall tale."[36] The modern experts aver that Bierce "was continually by Hazen's side, according to Hazen," and not wandering the battlefield in search of artillery ammunition.[37] By this reading of the sources, Bierce's whole odyssey that afternoon, including his heroic encounter with Granger's column, was simply egotistic fantasy masquerading as fact. Cozzens cites General Thomas's own report, where credit for recognizing and guiding the rescue column is specifically given to a certain Captain G. M. I. Johnson.

Additionally, Cozzens argues that Bierce's short story, also called "Chickamauga," could not possibly be an account of Bierce's observations. There was indeed an incident on September 18 of a civilian woman's death similar to the one related in the short story. The incident, Cozzens insists, was actually observed by Federal cavalry near the Reed House, and neither Bierce nor his brigade was anywhere near the Reed House at the time.[38]

These accusations made against Bierce are serious. It is more than simply a matter of "poetic license." For one thing, Bierce prided himself on never making false or inflated claims regarding his war record. Quite the contrary, although others noted his heroism on multiple occasions, Bierce was generally circumspect about his war record in his own nonfiction essays. Moreover, he frequently bristled at the "save the dayers"— those boastful officers who after the war made inflated claims of their heroics. He particularly resented that rather large group of generals who lied to cover up their wartime mistakes. He once commented, "I would rather be a dead dog among buzzards than a dead hero among admirers."[39] Such accusations by modern historians cut to the very heart of Bierce's integrity as an eyewitness to the war. If he lied about this, what more regarding the war did he lie about?

Of these criticisms of Bierce's accounts of Chickamauga, the last noted is the one most easily disposed of. The short story called "Chickamauga" is explicitly presented by Bierce as a work of fiction and ought to be judged on those merits alone. Although we have already demonstrated that many of his fictional pieces are fact-based and relate to actual incidents he experienced, there is no compelling reason that they should be—nor does that in any way diminish their value, literary or otherwise. In this case, it is strongly believed that an incident that occurred just before the main battle was indeed the inspiration for the similar motif in Bierce's short story. We do not know whether Bierce actually witnessed the incident at the Reed House; he may well have heard about the defiant Mrs. Reed being shredded by Confederate cannon fire from other soldiers even if he wasn't there to see it with his own eyes. Then too, there were numerous times during the war when civilians were caught in the crossfire of disputing armies and killed, and surely Bierce saw more than one civilian corpse caught in the crossfire of contending armies. Any one or all such incidents may have inspired the motif in this story.

Even so, one of Bierce's comrades in Company C attests to the fact that, whatever the rest of the brigade was doing at that moment, at least one detachment of the Ninth may have been involved in that cavalry skirmish near Reed House that occurred before the main battle began on the nineteenth and that is generally credited with being the opening action of the Battle of Chickamauga. In one of the many reunions held by veterans of the Ninth during the postwar era, Sam Kessler of Company C relates an anecdote to his comrades about meeting an old Rebel cavalryman who was there on the seventeenth when the "first shot" of the battle was fired. The old Johnny Reb's commander, Captain Helmenstien of the Sixth Georgia Cavalry, received the unfortunate honor of being the battle's first fatality. Kessler, who was also there, remembered seeing the Johnny officer fall, the fatal bullet coming from someone in Company C. Even if Bierce was not present in person for the engagement, he would surely have heard the soldier's tale from others of Company C who were.[40]

In the same short story, Bierce also gives us a graphic description of masses of grotesquely wounded men crawling on the ground. The men are so horribly mangled they do not even seem human anymore, and a deaf and dumb child, thinking it all a game, rides them in play. The story may be fiction, but the details are not. Not only Bierce, but also any soldier who served in the front lines would have witnessed similar horrors, be it at Chickamauga or elsewhere. While we cannot be certain Lieutenant Bierce actually witnessed such a grotesque scene at Chickamauga, others most certainly did. Bierce's scene of the mutilated men trying to escape the battle is chillingly accurate; no one can dispute that. In fact, Confederate Private Sam Watkins, whose homespun memoirs of the war from the Rebel side is itself regarded as a classic of war literature, relates a scene uncannily similar to Bierce's that he himself observed at Chickamauga:

> The Confederate and Federal dead, wounded, and dying were everywhere scattered over the battlefield. Men were lying where they fell, shot in every conceivable part of the body.

> Some with their entrails torn out and still hanging to them and piled up on the ground beside them, and they still alive. Some with their under jaw torn off, and hanging by a fragment of skin to their cheeks, with their tongues lolling from their mouth, and they trying to talk. Some with both eyes shot out, with one eye hanging down on their cheek. In fact, you might walk over the battlefield and find men shot from the crown of the head to the tip end of the toe. And then to see all those dead, wounded and dying horses, their heads and tails drooping, and they seeming to be so intelligent as if they comprehended everything. I felt like shedding a tear for those innocent dumb brutes.[41]

In regard to Bierce's account of the twentieth of September as he relates it in "A Little of Chickamauga," the issue of veracity is more complex than with his overtly fictional piece. Although Bierce advises his audience at the outset that his purpose is "not instruction but entertainment," his essay is presented to readers as factual and must be judged as such.

That being said, however, determining what the truth is with regards to battlefield accounts is never as simple as it may seem to the layman. Winston Churchill once observed "in war, truth is the first casualty." We have the official reports, of course, written soon after the event. Sometimes such official reports are taken as gospel, as if every word therein should be accepted as infallible. In truth, when their careers were at stake, military commanders often put the best face on their behavior—particularly if such behavior included dereliction and cowardice. Other commanders may report what they experienced to the best of their ability, but their recollections may be flawed in part or all, even though written shortly after the event. Postwar memoirs can also be subject to such motivations and, in addition, time plays tricks on the memory of even the most honest of men. Then too, there is what is referred to as "the fog of war." It is not uncommon for men from the same unit to have very clear yet vastly different recollections of an event. Their veracity is unquestionable; their perceptions are not. Different units in the same battle will often have wildly different experiences of the same event; still more so their former foes. All this must be taken into account, not only in evaluating Bierce's memoirs of Chickamauga, but in evaluating others' accounts as well.

After the debacle of September 20, General Rosecrans's continued command of the army was seriously in question. His departure was further hastened by the presence on the battlefield of Charles Dana, one-time Socialist, sometime Spiritualist, former editor of the New York Tribune, and at the time of the battle, the War Department's observer and administration spy. Dana's highly colored reports of the twentieth and its aftermath virtually sealed Rosecrans's doom. Besides Rosecrans, however, there were a number of subordinates—many of whom held greater blame for the defeat—whose fates were not yet sealed. How they presented their actions in their reports to Washington had a great deal to do with their continuing in command. For example, General Sheridan did not obey when Rosecrans ordered him to Thomas's support; nevertheless, in his report he successfully justified his actions in Washington's eyes.[42] General Negley, as Bierce noted in his essay, did likewise, but was not as fortunate as Sheridan in excusing his actions. He too had been requested to come to Thomas's aid and instead advanced in the opposite direction. In Negley's case, his behavior earned him a Court of Inquiry and he was relieved of command.

General Hazen's after-action dispatch, fortunately, lacks such personal agendas and in general is a straightforward report; that does not mean, however, that it is necessarily free of error. In his report Hazen commends his entire staff for their role during the action and mentions Bierce in this context saying, "Commissary of subsistence, Lieut. F. D. Cobb, Forty-First Ohio and my topographical officer, Lieut. A. G. Bierce, Ninth Indiana, were with me at all times, doing valuable service."[43] Taking Hazen's comment out of context, it would seem to confirm the accusations that Bierce never went on his odyssey behind the lines. However, one may well question exactly what Hazen meant by the phrase, "with me at all times." Did the general literally mean that his two staff officers, Cobb and Bierce, stood by his shoulder constantly like two bookends throughout the fight? If so, how could they possibly have been doing "valuable service?"

As we noted previously, the role of a Civil War staff officer was not static, whatever his official title. While Bierce's normal role was mapmaker, in the heat of battle he was often called upon to perform many tasks at the behest of his commander, as were all the members of Hazen's staff. It would not have been at all unusual for Hazen to have Bierce seek out and obtain several wagons of artillery munitions for his attached field pieces. Is there any corroboration for Bierce's account of having done so?

In fact there is. In addition to his published essays on the war, Bierce also corresponded with other veterans and those interested in the war. One such person was an erstwhile historian by the name of Archibald Gracie who was writing a book about Chickamauga. Colonel Archibald Gracie's father had been a Confederate officer who fought at Chickamauga, although Gracie himself grew up in the North. Having heard his father tell of his Civil War experiences as a boy, Gracie as an adult decided to write about it and spent seven years writing his book, *The Truth About Chickamauga*. As part of his research, Gracie contacted various veterans, including Ambrose Bierce. Toward the end of his research, Gracie asked Bierce if he could prevail on his brother Albert to provide information on the battle. Bierce apparently obliged Gracie and Albert did in fact write a memoir of the battle, a copy of which also survived in Bierce's papers.[44]

Albert's memoir is of his own experiences in the battle and is independent of his brother's. It has hitherto remained unpublished. Albert's battery, the Eighteenth Ohio, was part of General Granger's Reserve Corps, the sole Union column that came to Thomas's aid on September 20. Since Ambrose specifically references meeting Albert at the head of the relief column, Albert's own recollections constitute a crucial piece of evidence.

Albert's letter to his brother is dated March 23, 1911, is addressed "My Dear Brother," and is headed, "This is my story of Chickamauga all of which is true to the best of my recollections."[45] In the letter, Albert records the activities of Aleshire's Battery (Eighteenth Ohio Light Artillery Battery) during the battle in some detail. Albert recalled being near General Granger when Granger received General Rosecrans's order to fall back, "which order he promptly sent and which was promptly disregarded by Granger." Instead, Granger followed Napoleon's dictum to "ride to the sound of the guns." At that point Albert estimated they were about three miles from Thomas, and it was, "to my best recollection, about 12 noon."

Granger's column marched to "the Snodgrass" with but a short halt of twenty minutes to deal with some Rebel cavalry and artillery to their left. Albert remembered the enemy artillery fire broke the pole of one of his cannon, which he repaired by splicing a sapling onto it. "This happened but a short-time before you met me," Albert tells his brother. Albert goes on to say, "I remember your saying to me that Hazen had left his position that he held when you left him to go for the ammunition train and as you did not know where he was at the time you would stay with the battery." Albert reminds his brother that Granger reported to Thomas "not far from the Snodgrass house and then went into position at the edge of a cornfield." Albert also recalls that they were both "agreeably surprised" that the battery's position was among Hazen's troops; he remembers the Rebels attacking through the cornfield and "harvesting the corn with canister."

Apparently even in 1911 there was some disagreement with Hazen's account of the afternoon battle, for Albert mentions, "I think that this whole muddle of placing the battery at the Kelley farm comes about by the mistake of Hazen putting the time of his arrival at the Snodgrass farm about two hours too late."

Albert Bierce's hitherto unpublished eyewitness account is crucial in vindicating his brother's published version of events. Curiously, in his article

Thomas's command defends Snodgrass Hill. Bierce, rejoining Hazen's command on "The Snodgrass," participated in some of the most desperate fighting of the war that afternoon. One of the few Federal units with any rounds left, Hazen's force poured volley after volley into the massed ranks of attacking Rebels. *Harper's Weekly*.

impugning Ambrose Bierce's veracity, Gordon Berg mentions Albert's account in passing; but either Berg did not read Albert's narrative fully or he failed to understand its full import. Clearly, Ambrose Bierce *was* sent to obtain artillery ammunition by Hazen; he *did* meet Granger's column before they reached Thomas; and he *did* accompany his brother Albert back to the front lines, where he then rejoined his brigade for the remainder of the day. Regarding Bierce's claim to have been with Thomas before he met his brother and before his ride to guide Granger back, the evidence is less clear. However, there is nothing in Albert's narrative that would preclude Ambrose from having done so.

Certainly, we have General Thomas's report that credits Captain Johnson of the Second Indiana Cavalry, a staff officer of Negley's division, as being dispatched "with orders to push [Granger] forward and take position on Brannon's right."[46] This is all Thomas has to say on the subject. Other officers on Snodgrass Hill may have also spotted the approaching column at the same time and sought to verify whether they were "of our kidney," but they were either not the first or they escaped Thomas's notice. It may be that Bierce was one of a number to do so; we cannot know. In any case, if Bierce's narrative, written in 1898, was off in some details, there is no evidence that there was conscious fabrication. His memoir overall is truthful and as accurate as one can reasonably expect, allowing for "time and General Bragg."

As the sun went down, Thomas gave orders for an orderly withdrawal. In the growing darkness Hazen's brigade was among the very last to leave the field and at one point even had to form a "hollow square" to ward off a potential Rebel attack.

Chickamauga was one of the bloodiest and hardest-fought battles Bierce and his comrades had ever seen—and for many it would be the last they would ever see.

10

Besieged

> **ABATIS**, *n.* Rubbish in front of a fort, to prevent the rubbish outside from molesting the rubbish inside.

One early chronicler of the Army of the Cumberland, John Fitch, described the Battle of Chickamauga as "the price of Chattanooga." General Rosecrans, in his report, tried to justify the battle in somewhat similar terms. Truth be known, had Rosecrans simply consolidated his hold on the city, he would have been hailed as a brilliant strategist and a great military hero. No doubt Bragg would have eventually besieged the city, but under far more unfavorable conditions, with the Yankees instead of the Rebels in control of the commanding heights.[1] Rosecrans's defeat and retreat at Chickamauga, as bad as it was, would have been far worse save for two factors. The first, of course, was General Thomas's valiant stand with the Union left at Snodgrass Hill. The second factor—which Bierce was less aware of at the time—was General Braxton Bragg's unerring knack for blunting even this, his most spectacular victory.

Nathan Bedford Forrest, the contentious Confederate cavalry commander, had it right: "Every hour is worth a thousand men."[2] General Longstreet, whose assault had decimated the Union right and center, pressed General Bragg for a close pursuit of the defeated Yankees into Chattanooga; even that pious clergyman turned indifferent general, Leonidas Polk, urged for a speedy and forceful follow-up. General Bragg, however, ignored his corps commanders and true to his contrary nature, hesitated, still unsure of victory. One Rebel soldier, who had observed the Yankee rout firsthand, was presented to Bragg to convince him of the Federal defeat. The incredulous Bragg asked him, "Do you know what a retreat looks like?" "I ought to general," was the soldier's reply, "I've been with you during your whole campaign."[3]

Incredibly, it was fully two and a half days before Bragg would allow his commanders to advance the twelve miles from Chickamauga to the outskirts of Chattanooga. That was just the breathing space Rosecrans needed to shore up his defense of the city. The day after the battle, General Thomas was already establishing an outer defense perimeter to guard the approaches

Besieged

to the city. The Ninth and the rest of Hazen's troops were thus kept busy constructing defenses on the twenty-first. Rosecrans, however, after weighing his options, chose to contract the Federal defenses closer in to the city and prepared for a desperate siege until reinforcements could arrive.

Eventually Bragg's men drew up siege lines overlooking the city on the commanding heights surrounding it, forming a rough semicircle. By the time Bragg finished his leisurely investment of the city, only a rough, winding, and narrow wagon trail connected Chattanooga to the outside world. The trail meandered up and over Walden Ridge, a rugged spine of the Cumberland Mountains' southern outlier on the north side of the river. Besides rough terrain and wintry weather, Rebel cavalry played hell with this vulnerable supply line. Hundreds of mules died hauling supplies over this sixty mile-long trail. Soon, the Federals found their meager fare was in increasingly short supply and the Army of the Cumberland faced lean times—although not so lean as some of General Grant's boosters would later characterize it.

In the aftermath of Chickamauga, a number of changes were made to the army inside the besieged city. Generals were brought before courts of inquiry: some were relieved of duty, others exonerated. Many units decimated by the battle were reorganized as well, including Hazen's brigade. On October 10, the Ninth Indiana was transferred out of Hazen's Second Brigade, Second Division, Twenty-First Corps and moved to the Third Brigade of the

Union encampments, Chattanooga. Following Chickamauga, Hazen's brigade kept busy with building defense lines, while Bierce's duties as topographical engineer also kept him active outside the lines. Library of Congress.

First Division, Fourth Corps. Lieutenant Bierce, although nominally still part of the regiment, did not go with them. General Hazen regarded Bierce's service highly enough that he specifically requested his topographical officer remain on his staff. Despite Bierce's failure to obtain the requested artillery munitions on the twentieth, the general still apparently valued his service.[4] Although Bierce's own testimony is lacking, the documentary evidence indicates that during this crucial period Bierce was of stellar service to the besieged army.

Rosecrans and his Chief of Engineers, Major General William F. "Baldy" Smith, devised a plan to relieve the severe supply problems that beset the army. Before he could devote any efforts to breaking the siege, Rosecrans first needed to feed his army and bring in enough supplies to maintain it in the field. Rosey and Baldy devised a bold plan: two brigades—Hazen's and Turchin's—would descend on the vital crossing at Brown's Ferry, lying on the far side of Confederate-held Lookout Mountain. Part of Hazen's men would descend the river by pontoon boats in the dark of night under the very noses of Confederate artillery, while General Turchin—the "Russian Thunderbolt"—would make a forced march overland across the narrow neck of Moccasin Bend on the north bank of the Tennessee River. By seizing the Confederate-held crossing and its environs, the Federals could add a second supply route and considerably shorten the distance into the city. In effect the

Chattanooga during the siege. Viewed from across the river from the north bank of the Tennessee River. Rebel held Lookout Mountain looms ominously to the right; Brown's Landing is out of sight further to the right. *Harper's Pictorial History of the Civil War.*

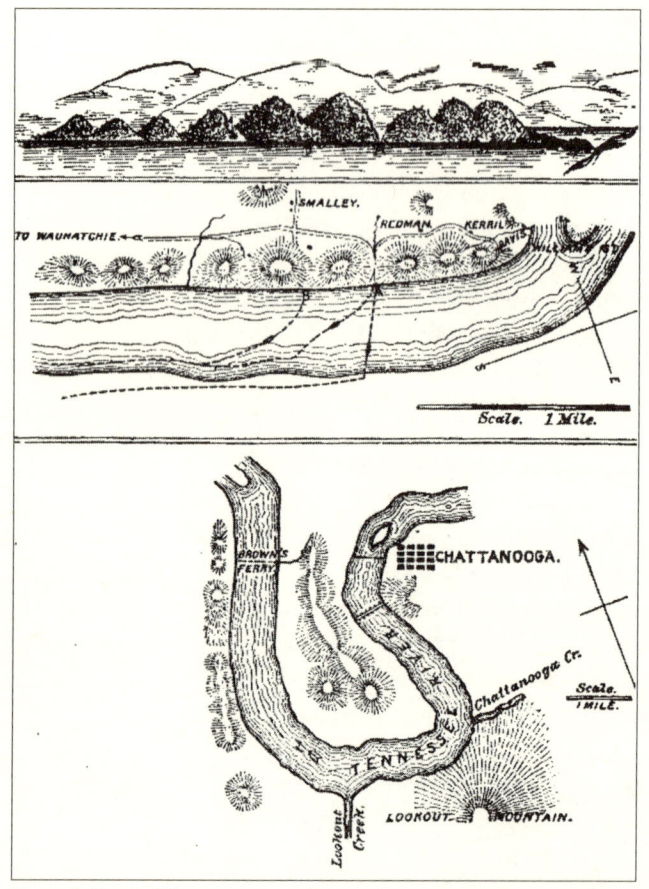

Brown's Ferry. These maps and the others are from the *The War of the Rebellion Official Records of the Union and Confederate Armies*, a multi-volume tome which Bierce described as "a book that is more than a book." Hazen's reports in the Official Records are unique in that they are illustrated; as a rule maps and other illustrations were relegated to a separate atlas volume. That these maps closely resemble the ones attributed to Bierce in Hazen's memoirs suggest that they were done by Bierce himself. From OR Ser. 1, Vol. 31, Pt. 1, p. 83.

siege would be broken. For such a hazardous operation, however, accurate maps were essential.

On October 18, the Superintendent of Topographical Engineers, Army of the Cumberland ordered Lieutenant Bierce to report to headquarters forthwith.[5] The reason for the summons is not disclosed in the orders, but other sources indicate what the mission was. As topographical engineer,

Bierce's primary duty was to conduct surveys and make maps. Dating to this period is a "Military Map of Brown's Ferry—Tenn." In clear lettering it is labeled, "Drawn by Lieut. A. G. Bierce at the command of Gen. Hazen."[6]

The map is precisely drawn, with each hill, acclivity, and mountain bordering Brown's Ferry rendered with exact elevation lines, plus creeks and streams, as well as farmhouses, mills, and other landmarks, all placed exactly. While parts of the map are missing, it was clearly intended for use by military commanders in the field. In addition, in the *Official Record*, General Hazen's report is illustrated with a sketch of the embankment and another map of Brown's Ferry and Moccasin Bend. It is highly unusual for such action reports in the OR to have accompanying sketches or maps integral to the report: his report seems unique in this regard. Such sketches and maps as a rule are found in the Atlas volume to the *Official Record*. It is very likely that Bierce rendered these sketches at the time also. Such topographical renderings would necessarily have required Bierce to penetrate behind enemy lines, with a high risk of death or capture. Such a scout by Topographical Engineer Bierce would certainly have been regarded by the enemy as an act of espionage and earned him a summary execution if caught.

On October 23, General Ulysses S. Grant arrived in Chattanooga. He was now in overall command of Union forces in the west and charged by the Lincoln administration with retrieving the situation at Chattanooga. Although Grant relieved Rosecrans of command, he also recognized the soundness of Rosecrans's plan to seize Brown's Ferry and immediately made the plan his own.[7] At three a.m. on October 27, over one thousand of General Hazen's men were to load onto fifty-two flat-bottomed boats, twenty-five men and one officer to each boat. The boats were to row downriver in the dark, cruising under the very muzzles of Rebel guns for some nine miles in the dark. Then, just before daybreak they were to land on the left bank of the river and seize the southern shore of Brown's Ferry. Simultaneously, on the north bank of the river Turchin's men, along with the remainder of Hazen's brigade and some artillery support, were to traverse the hilly neck of Moccasin Bend. They were to mass in the woods above the landing, out of sight of Rebel pickets, and as soon as the flotilla appeared on the far shore, Turchin's command was to seize the northern bank.

All involved knew this was an extremely hazardous maneuver. Hazen's boats, descending the river at night, must land at exactly the right spot before daybreak. Turchin's force needed to cross overland in the dark and arrive at a precise point at the precise time to rendezvous with the flotilla. Each unit, each man, must follow orders precisely. The plan easily could have gone awry if either force arrived at the wrong spot, or if their timing was off. To this end, accurate maps of the terrain were essential.

Around midnight on the twenty-sixth of October, the chosen men were awakened. By two a.m. the men were marching down to the riverbank to embark. The detachments had been kept in ignorance of what they were to do beforehand; they were simply told to show up with their cartridge boxes filled with sixty rounds each and to be ready to go on a march without blankets. As time edged closer to embarkation, rumor informed the men that a boat expedition is afoot. "Tried and distinguished" officers were chosen to lead the four commands of the mission. They were fully informed as to the part they were to do and were given details as to the terrain and features of the embankment and the landings they were to assault. Just before dark on the twenty-sixth, the officers summoned their squad-leaders and clearly instructed them as to their duties. It was in the nature of the mission that each squad must operate independently yet act in strict accord with instructions. At the riverbank Hazen's men found fifty-two pontoon boats ready to launch. Each boat was thirty feet long by about seven feet wide and of shallow draft. Each held twenty-five men, with five rowers and a helmsman, and had two axes on hand. At precisely three A.M., the flotilla shoved noiselessly off into the dark river.

It was a moonlit night, but fortunately it was also cloudy and there was a fog on the river, cloaking the flotilla's progress. The men soon found that oars were unnecessary as the current was sufficient to carry them where they needed to go in time. After about three miles, the flotilla came under the enemy's guns, and the men tried to hug the far bank to avoid discovery. One of the boats hit a snag on the shore and a man was caught by the collar of his blouse and yanked into the river. A sharp cry for help arises from the boat and other flat-bottom vessels came over to assist. The man scrambled to shore and hissed from the shadows, "Go along with your old boat, I'm not half drowned yet."

"All right," was the hoarse response, and with muffled oars the boat pulled back into the current. General Hazen was in the van of the flotilla, directing it in a barely intelligible voice and calling out clear and low, "Close up! Close up!" The boats were moving at different speeds as they descended the river, and it was imperative that they all reach Brown's Ferry at the same time lest the Rebels pick them off one at a time. During the descent some of the men fell asleep as they made their long, quiet voyage in the dark.

Suddenly they were awakened to the sound of bullets whizzing over their heads and on either side, some plunking into the water beside the boat.

"Push for shore! Push for shore!" was the command, and the oarsmen pulled heavily on their oars. Fortunately the flotilla was almost at the landing now, although the current had carried them slightly below their desired spot. The boats ground with a crunch on the sloping shore and the soldiers

Besieged

hastily leapt over the side, splashing quickly to shore and rapidly forming into companies. In the waning dusk the bluecoats quickly overwhelmed the Rebel pickets along the shore, establishing a toehold on the southern bank. Charging across a flat space of land the troops rushed for a steep hill overlooking the landing, where a firefight broke out with the retreating Rebel guards. Other detachments seized the road, while still others began felling trees to build emplacements and skirmishers pushed farther inland.

Meanwhile, the pontoon flatboats were turned about and each paddled to the opposite bank of the river where Turchin's men waited to be ferried across from the far shore. Once these troops were all safely across and joining the firefight, the flatboats were once again repurposed. Yankee engineers set to work transforming the boats into a pontoon bridge, even as the two brigades of infantry secured the landing and began felling logs to form barricades and an abatis. By the time the Confederates were able to react to this amphibious assault and bring up reinforcements, the Federals had not only established a fortified foothold on both banks but had built a bridge as well. Confederate counterattacks proved fruitless.

The operation came off perfectly, a virtual textbook example of an amphibious assault. As General Hazen observed, it was "complete to the

Amphibious assault on Brown's Landing. Although Bierce is silent about his role in this key operation, but he was with Hazen during the night attack and played an important role in accurately mapping the area prior to the assault. *Harper's Weekly*.

Besieged

minutest detail." Even the Richmond Press described it as an "admirably conceived and brilliantly executed coup."⁸ Bierce tells us nothing of his role in the whole operation, but as Hazen's staff officer and mapmaker it would have been significant. Bierce would have been at Hazen's service throughout most of the whole Brown's Ferry landing. Doubtless other topographical officers were also detailed for the preliminary work leading up to this operation. Nonetheless, Bierce's contribution was undeniably a key element in its success.

Interestingly enough, another military action that happened nearby a few days later received far more attention from Bierce, even though he had no hand it. This was the night fight near Wauhatchie Depot, which went down in Union army lore as "The Charge of the Mule Brigade."⁹ To understand that fight it is essential to go back a few weeks, to soon after the debacle at Chickamauga. In the wake of the defeat, Secretary of War Stanton quickly set in motion massive reinforcements to retrieve the situation. In addition to appointing Grant as overall commander in the West, he also dispatched 20,000 men of Grant's Army of the Tennessee, now under General Sherman, from Memphis to Rosecrans's relief. Unfortunately, as Halleck had done to Buell the year before, "Old Brains"—still in overall military command—ordered Sherman to repair the rail lines as he advanced, effectively slowing down his relief column to a snail's pace. Fortunately, Stanton had detailed two corps from the listless Army of the Potomac westward as well, placing General Hooker in command. Within seven days' time, Hooker's corps had reached Nashville by rail; only a few days later they began unloading at the railhead near Bridgeport, Alabama.

From the Federal base at Bridgeport, Hooker's Eleventh and Twelfth corps began marching overland with plans to force open a route to Brown's Ferry. As it so happened, it was only a few days after the successful amphibious operation by Hazen that Hooker's men came marching up Lookout Valley. With Hooker's arrival, the Union army now had two new supply routes leading into Chattanooga. Supplies soon started flowing into the besieged city in large quantities. Three miles or so up the valley from Brown's Ferry, Hooker had left Geary's division of the Twelfth Corps at Wauhatchie Depot as a rearguard. While today Wauhatchie is a major rail yard where freight is transshipped throughout the South, back then it was a small country rail depot. In fact, at the time mules were more in evidence there than locomotives. Hundreds of mules had died in hauling the supply wagons over Walden Ridge during the siege, while others starved to death from lack of fodder. The rear of Hooker's relief column therefore had a large herd of these beasts as partial replacement.

Meanwhile, the Confederates were not content to simply sit idly by and watch the Yankees break the siege. From the commanding heights of Lookout Mountain General Longstreet observed the arrival of Hooker's column with dismay, but he also saw an opportunity. He could see that Geary's rearguard was isolated from the rest of the force and therefore vulnerable. So Longstreet devised a plan, with Bragg's approval. According to the original plan, the Rebels would attack the men of Geary's division at night, wipe them out, and sever the Union land route. To do this, two full divisions were designated: General Micah Jenkins's Division would deliver the attack, while General McLaws's Division would hold the ford at Lookout Creek and keep Hooker from reinforcing his rearguard.

Longstreet's plan, as conceived, probably would have succeeded. However, General Longstreet did not count on Bragg's ability to hinder it. Without informing Longstreet, Bragg decided not to commit McLaws's Division to the night attack. It was about midnight on the twenty-eighth when Longstreet realized something was awry and arrived at the jumping-off point to find McLaws's Division nowhere in sight. When he sorted it all out, Longstreet assumed that Jenkins would not go ahead with the attack unsupported, but failed to issue positive orders to that effect.

Initially Jenkins's night attack went well. Geary and his men were caught by surprise and the Rebel regiments came on swiftly and aggressively, causing pandemonium in the dark. Finally, however, the New York and Pennsylvania regiments of Geary's command recovered from the initial shock and began to put up a stiff resistance. As one might expect in a night fight, the struggle was at times confused, with battle lines defined only by the flashes from muzzle-blasts. Not surprisingly, Union and Confederate accounts vary quite a bit as to what happened that night.

All agree that General Bratton's South Carolina brigade stormed the Federal camp with élan, capturing wagons and trains, overrunning the enemy tents, and creating chaos. General Jenkins contended later that instead of Geary's 1,500 or so men, they ran fully into 5,000 of Hooker's main force and were forced back up the slopes of Lookout Mountain. The Yankees had a different tale to tell—and so did Bierce.

While it is true that Hooker eventually did send a relief column to rescue Geary's men, that is not what defeated the Butternuts at Wauhatchie Depot. When the Rebels descended like howling demons in the dark on the Federal camp, the teamsters in the camp panicked and fled, abandoning their beasts of burden—the mules. The mules too panicked and fled. Between the flashes of musket and cannon fire, the loud report of the guns, and the yelling and chaos in the dark, the mules stampeded. As fate would have it, this large herd of jackasses headed straight toward the Rebel lines. What the Rebels heard—or thought they heard—was the sound of the thundering hooves of hundreds of Yankee cavalry rapidly bearing down on them in the dark. Surely, they thought, it was a whole division of bluecoat cavalry, with sabers flashing and slashing at them in the night. With all those Yankee cavalrymen ready to slice them up and send them to kingdom come, the boys in gray retreated every which way they could in the dark, scampering back up the steep slopes of Lookout Mountain faster than they'd come down.

No doubt the ghost of old Chief Wauhatchie looked down and laughed at the scene that night—the Federals certainly did the next day. The incident became the subject of much mirth among Hooker's easterners and the westerners of the Army of the Cumberland, and the story grew in the telling. Even General Grant affirmed the story in his memoirs.[10] According to General Horace Porter, after the battle, the officer in charge of the mules filed a recommendation that the mules, "for their gallantry in this action, may have conferred upon them the brevet rank of horses."[11] Some unnamed wit went so far as to compose a mock-heroic poem about the famous victory. Patterned on Tennyson's "Charge of the Light Brigade," the parody was entitled, "The Charge of the Mule Brigade":

> When can their glory fade?
> O the wild charge they made!
> All the world wondered.
> Honor the charge they made!
> Honor the Mule Brigade.
> Long-eared two hundred![12]

It perhaps goes without saying that Confederate accounts vehemently deny this incident, while Federal ones affirm its veracity. While Bierce was not present for that legendary battle, he was only a few miles up the road with Hazen's brigade. The absurdity of the incident could not have failed to impress him as it did his comrades, all sorely in need of some levity after the many trials they had been through in the preceding weeks.

After the war this incident inspired Bierce to pen the short story entitled "Jupiter Doke, Brigadier General." While "Jupiter Doke" preserves the essentially absurd nature of the incident, Bierce also manages to make a few serious points in between the mirth.[13] Like his classic ghost story, "The Moonlit Road," "Jupiter Doke" is told from the perspective of multiple eyewitnesses. In this case, Bierce tells the tale through a series of military dispatches, an editorial, and a resolution of Congress; the real truth of the matter is only revealed, however, in the statement of an old Negro from "Jayhawk, Kentucky."

Jupiter Doke, as it becomes clear through his correspondence, is a political creature, corrupt and full of nostrums but short of either courage or common sense. Union Brigadier General Doke is given command of a division and is regarded as entirely expendable by his superior commander, "Major-General Blount Wardog." For their part, the Confederates find Doke and his "small brigade of undisciplined troops, apparently without a commander" also useful. By leaving them alone, the Rebels hope to convey an illusion of weakness in that sector, when in fact they have amassed a force of 25,000 men and thirty-two cannon, with plans to conquer northern Kentucky, capture Cincinnati, and occupy the whole Ohio Valley.

However, as revealed through the perspectives of different Confederate commanders, their plans are foiled. One Rebel general attributes it to a tornado passing along the entire length of his army; another to a surprise attack by "fifty thousand cavalry" who attack in the darkness. A third Confederate—a "General Schneddeker Baumshank, C.S.A." of foreign extraction—is even more bewildered than the others. General Baumshank's report read in part: 'Yost den somdings occur, I know nod vot if vos . . . und I finds meinselluf, afder leedle vides, in dis place, midout a hors und no men und goons." The foreign general abruptly resigns, resolving to leave a country "vere I gets vipped and knows nod how it vos done."[14] Doke is quick to take undeserved credit for the mysterious victory and his friends in Congress promote him to major general. In a statement by "Mr. Hannibal Alcazar Peyton, of Jayhawk, Kentucky," the reader learns the truth. In his haste to flee the Confederates, Doke accidentally stampedes a large herd of mules grazing in a nearby field that in turn stampede the Rebel army.

In rendering the actual incident into fictional form, Bierce obviously allowed himself considerable literary license. The scene of action is transferred from Chattanooga in 1863 to northern Kentucky; moreover, the multiple perspectives allow for both North and South to be equally guilty of rewriting the facts to suit their purposes and save face. Bierce in his burlesque spares no one. The addition of the German officer writing in dialect is an added touch, partly based on fact. Hooker's Eleventh Corps was known to be made up of large numbers of German-Americans who had volunteered for the Union cause in droves. Bierce, present with his unit at Brown's landing to meet the Eleventh Corps when they arrived, would have been familiar with both these "Dutchmen" and their mules.

Some literary critics see the target of Bierce's "Jupiter Doke" satire as none other than General Grant himself. Although a West Point graduate, at the beginning of the war Grant had been passed over for commissioning as an officer by the Regular Army and only owed his appointment and initial promotion to the good offices of Governor Yates of Illinois—Grant therefore *was* a political appointee. Certainly Bierce makes no secret of his belief in Grant's ability to write action reports that partook more of creative fiction than fact and of his belief that Grant's ability to gloss over his mistakes was a major factor in his advancement. On these two points, then, Jupiter Doke certainly does resemble Bierce's perception of Grant. However, Bierce's target here is broader than just General Grant. In the course of his war literature Bierce inveighs against a number of other Union generals to varying degrees, including Sherman and Howard. His critique of mendacity on the part of Union commanders is therefore more general than just one general.

In some of his writings, moreover, Bierce at times even comes to Grant's defense. In what passes for an obituary of Grant, Bierce's target is not so much the general himself as it is those sycophants who would deify him and, in so doing, strip him of his humanity. Bierce, citing General James Wilson, observes of Grant "that the great strategist was a poor tactician."[15] In another context, Bierce defends Grant against detractors and says he was "really an admirable soldier."[16] Clearly, Bierce's tar and feathers are applied to more than just Grant.

There is another aspect to "Jupitor Doke" underneath the burlesque. Bierce, through his use of multiple perspectives, reveals the difficulty for participants in a battle to truly know what is happening to them. Only the foreigner admits his bewilderment; yet all the others are equally in the dark as to the truth, save the untutored Negro farmer. Chaos is inherent in the nature of combat, even for senior commanders. Rosecrans gave orders at Chickamauga thinking the situation was one thing when it was another, then mistakenly retreated when he could have retrieved the situation instead. Bragg, by sheer dumb luck, did the right thing at the right time and then confounded himself and frittered away his victory. The fog of war obscured the true nature of the battle to both commanders. No one is blameless.

Although Hooker's easterners and the Army of the Cumberland had effectively broken the siege, Grant still held an equally low opinion of both forces. Before he could begin his big counter-offensive, therefore, Grant felt that he needed Sherman and his trusty Army of the Tennessee. As the Federals grew stronger by the day, General Bragg dispatched General Longstreet and his corps from the Army of Northern Virginia to lay siege to Knoxville, where a Union army under General Burnside was in control. Bragg's motive for this maneuver was not out of any grand strategy; he simply wished to be shed of a general who was too blunt in his criticisms. Bragg's folly was Grant's opportunity. When Sherman's troops finally arrived, Grant began to put in motion his plans to break Bragg and the siege. On the twenty-third of November, Grant ordered a "reconnaissance in force" against Orchard Knob. Orchard Knob was an isolated hill that lay well in advance of the first line of Rebel rifle pits extending along the foot of Missionary Ridge, and it was an enemy outpost uncomfortably close to the Union lines. The Rebels had fortified the prominence and both sides regarded it as a tough nut to crack.

Besieged

The capture of Orchard Knob by Hazen and Willich's brigades, in which Bierce took part. Grant had not expected much the Army of the Cumberland, but Hazen and Willich's men surprised him with their success and élan. Library of Congress.

In assigning the Army of the Cumberland to assault it, Grant did not have any high hopes for their success. His main goal was simply to test the Rebel defenses. The Army of the Cumberland, after its humiliating defeat, was eager for an opportunity at redemption. Advancing against heavy initial fire, they rapidly overwhelmed the Rebel defenders—much to Grant's surprise.

Then on the twenty-fourth, Grant launched a one-two punch against Bragg's besieging army. From his positions at Brown's Ferry and Lookout Valley, General Hooker launched an attack to take the far left of the Confederate lines running along the lower slopes of Lookout Mountain. It was a damp, overcast day and a misty rain obscured the slopes of the mountain. Due to the low rain clouds on the slopes, the fight was dubbed "the Battle above the Clouds." At the same time, General Sherman crossed the Tennessee River east of the city with plans to attack the Rebels' extreme right and capture the northern end of Missionary Ridge by surprise. Sherman's men attempted to seize what they thought was the tip of this precipitous ridgeline. In fact, what Sherman's men attacked—but did not seize—was not even the ridgeline proper, but merely an outlier of it, Tunnel Hill. The main part of Missionary Ridge was separated from Tunnel Hill by a declivity. Grant had intended Sherman's assault to be the main event of the battle; yet with two full corps from the Army of the Tennessee, the Army of the Potomac's Eleventh Corps, and two divisions borrowed from the Army of the Cumberland, Sherman was fought to a standstill by Patrick Cleburne's lone division of Arkansans, with just two brigades in support. In the process of his failed attack, Sherman lost the key element of surprise against a hill that was not even the main objective of his attack. Historians have characterized Sherman's attacks of the twenty-fourth and twenty-fifth as hampered by "poor reconnaissance." This is true enough; more accurately however, Sherman's singular failure was a case of poor mapmaking and inaccurate maps. Perhaps if topographical engineers like Lieutenant Ambrose Bierce had served Sherman's troops, the outcome of his operation might have been more successful—certainly it would have been less bloody.

After Brown's Ferry, the Army of the Cumberland had adopted a passive role—by Grant's design. This changed with the assault on Orchard Knob, in which Wood's division played a leading role. In the division's attack on that hill, Hazen's brigade formed the division's right flank. Knowing Hazen's pro-active nature as a commander, it is likely that he had Bierce in the forefront of this action, conveying orders and reporting on the troop's progress. Hooker and Sherman's commands played the leading roles on the twenty-forth, while the Army of the Cumberland again stood idle. General Thomas's army now formed Grant's center, facing the length of Missionary Ridge.

The next day, Grant had planned the Army of the Cumberland to play a passive role yet again. Sherman's troops were supposed to gain all the glory of defeating Bragg's army by seizing the northern end of Missionary Ridge and thus turning the Confederate's right flank. Things did not quite go according to plan, however. For one thing, Sherman's troops spent a good part of the day getting another bloody nose from Cleburne's men. With the element of surprise already lost, the Rebels were well prepared to repel every assault, despite overwhelming Yankee numbers. On the morning of the twenty-fifth, despite repeated attempts and every resource at his command, Sherman could not even capture Tunnel Hill. In order to "relieve the pressure" on Sherman, therefore, Grant ordered Thomas to have his army mount a diversionary attack against the Confederate center, stretching southward along Missionary Ridge. The Cumberlanders were to assault the Rebel picket lines and take the rifle pits at the foot of this formidable ridgeline—nothing more.

Watching the proceedings the morning of the twenty-fifth from atop Orchard Knob were General Grant, his staff, and a "variable group of other general and staff officers." Among the multitude were Generals Thomas, Granger, Sheridan, Wood, and Hazen—and Lieutenant Bierce. Lying almost directly in the center of the broad battlefield facing the ridge, Orchard Knob

Grant and officers on Orchard Knob, observing the battle for Missionary Ridge. Bierce was with Hazen there for several hours and observed that Grant and others, "they looked upon the wine when it was red, these tall fellow—they bit the glass. The poisoned chalice went about and about." Painting by Thure de Thulstrup. Library of Congress.

was an excellent spot from which to watch the day's battle unfold. Bierce tells us that he was on Orchard Knob for some "six or seven hours" that day, in close proximity to Grant and the other commanders. While Bierce's remarks on what transpired there are not as detailed as one would wish, such observations as he did commit to paper are quite enlightening, even if they have not made it into the standard histories.

A long-standing controversy regarding Grant and his generalship has been the issue of his drinking and to what extent it impaired his ability to command. Defenders of the general, such as Bruce Catton and Kenneth Williams, seriously question or deny Grant's weakness for liquor. Other historians, such as William McFeely and Shelby Foote, accept it as fact. Ambrose Bierce's own perspective on the Grant alcoholism controversy is interesting, particularly because of his firsthand observations and the fact that he was certainly no unquestioning cheerleader of the general. On this issue, Bierce rises to Grant's defense—although in a singularly left-handed manner. According to Bierce's own observations on Orchard Knob during the Battle of Missionary Ridge, General Grant did indeed "kiss the dragon" that afternoon. But, Bierce avers, Grant was not alone in doing so. The whole confraternity of generals on the knob also partook: "They looked upon the wine when it was red, these tall fellow—they bit the glass. The poisoned chalice went about and about . . . my recollection is that Grant commonly did."[17]

Bierce, despite affirming Grant's tippling, denies that it impaired his ability to command. Indeed, Bierce makes a case for the virtues of alcohol and leadership: "I know of nothing in great military or civic abilities incompatible with a love of strong drink . . . Alexander the Great was a drunkard . . . Webster was as often drunk as sober."[18] That Bierce himself was a lifelong imbiber of strong drink may have somewhat colored his viewpoint on the issue of Grant and alcohol. Toward the end of his essay on the subject, Bierce confesses, "I don't think that he took enough to comfort the enemy . . . but I was all the time afraid he would, which was ungenerous, for he did not appear at all afraid I would."[19] From other sources we learn that Grant and his senior commanders were not the only tipplers on the Union side that day. After repulsing Sherman's troops on Tunnel Hill, Cleburne's men found that their prisoner's canteens were full of whiskey—as were many of the canteens belonging to the Union dead and wounded.[20] Moreover, Charles Dana cites the case of General Sheridan who, as he led his men up Missionary Ridge, offered a silent toast from his silver whisky flask to a Confederate officer at the top of the ridgeline.[21]

As was the case two days before during the capture Orchard Knob, Wood's division would play a prominent part in the attack on Missionary Ridge. Once again Hazen's brigade was to be placed on the right of the divisional battle line, with Sheridan's division next in line on Hazen's right. All told, four divisions from the Army of the Cumberland were detailed for the attack late that Wednesday afternoon. Besides partaking of fermented beverages that day, Bierce was also detailed for more prosaic tasks as the brigade made ready for their "diversionary" attack. Bierce was instructed by Hazen to convey the order for the attack to Colonel James C. Foy, commander of the Twenty-Third Kentucky Infantry, and see to it that the regiment found its proper place in the battle line. Bierce describes Foy as "a good fellow and a brave man but not a very clear thinker." By Bierce's account, Colonel Foy had a habit of getting himself and his regiment lost while maneuvering in battle.[22]

Just before four o'clock in the afternoon, six black cannon boomed out from Orchard Knob, signaling the Army of the Cumberland to advance against the Rebel rifle pits at the foot of the ridge. The movement unfolded across an almost level valley from 1,200 to 1,400 yards wide, with only about the first four hundred yards of that timbered. The remainder of the battleground was open space in full view of the enemy on the ridge. Broad lines of bluecoats marched toward the ridgeline in the slanting rays of the bright

Colonel Foy, commander of the Twenty-Third Kentucky of Hazen's brigade. Bierce thought him "a good fellow and a brave man but not a very clear thinker." As staff officer, Bierce led Foy's regiment to the start line for the attack on Missionary Ridge. Hazen, *Narrative of Military Service*.

autumn afternoon. As they made their way across about a quarter of the wooded ground, the Rebels opened up with a furious cannonade from atop the ridge. The curvature of the ridge-crest allowed the Rebels to concentrate their fire on the advancing Federals. On clearing the timber, the bluecoats quickly became easy targets for the fifty or so Rebel canon while the rattle of Rebel small arms added to the din of battle. In the face of this increasing fire the Federals advanced, first at a walk, then quick time, then double-quick time and finally charging at a full run.

Undeterred by gunfire from the rifle pits ahead or volleys of shot and shell plunging from the ridgeline above, the bluecoats surged into the first Rebel line. A few intense minutes of hand-to-hand fighting and the Federals were masters of the rifle pits. The surviving Rebels retreated up the slope. The Army of the Cumberland's objective had been achieved; however, this was only the beginning of their danger.

Two Confederate corps held the ridgeline, occupying two more lines of defense further up the slope. The next Rebel line was midway up the acclivity, while the artillery and the remainder of the infantry firmly held the crest. Both enemy lines now let loose their full fury of fire at the Federals below at the base of the ridge. After only a few minutes of plunging fire, one thing became clear to the Army of the Cumberland: they could not stay where they were. The Yankees must either retreat or advance on up the hill. Given their original orders, the logical thing would simply have been to fall back. But the soldiers of the Army of the Cumberland knew that both Hooker's

Besieged

Attack on Mission Ridge. During the attack Bierce was in the forefront throughout, at one point leading one of the brigade's regiments to redirect their assault. Combat Sketch by Alfred Waud. Library of Congress.

and Sherman's troops already held a low opinion of them after the debacle of Chickamauga. If they fell back now, it would only confirm their already tarnished reputation. That left but one alternative: advance or die.

No official order was ever issued to charge up this steep acclivity. By all the rules of war it was certain death to ascend these slopes. Nevertheless, almost as if by instinct, groups of soldiers began advancing up the slopes of the ridge. They advanced partly to escape the deadly fire from above, partly in pursuit of the retreating Rebels, and partly to redeem their honor.

In a few cases, the oral instructions to the troops may have been muddled: some assumed they were supposed to go up the slope. In other cases officers, seeing some men going on ahead, ordered the rest to follow. General Hazen, for his part, says that "giving the men five minutes to breathe, and receiving no orders, I gave the word forward, which was eagerly obeyed." Hazen adds that "necessity . . . was apparent to every soldier of the command." Somewhere in all this confusion, Lieutenant Bierce was also advancing up the ridge.[23] One noted historian of the battle describes this charge up Missionary Ridge as "born of desperation, anger, and the instinct of war-wise combat veterans."[24] From Orchard Hill, the scene unfolded before the incredulous eyes of General Grant as he watched the ragged lines of blue claw their way up the steep slopes. Grant turned to his subordinates and angrily demanded to know who issued the orders to ascend. No one knew. Consternation gave way to jubilation, however, as first one, and then another, and then another regimental banner could be seen waving along the crest of Missionary Ridge.

Hazen's troops were among the first to reach the summit. To their left and right other units encountered resistance from Rebels still holding the crest, retarding their upward progress. Hazen therefore "hastened" his men to the left and right along the ridgeline to take the enemy in the flank. Hazen sent Lt. Bierce over to Major Whitaker, who was commanding the Sixth Kentucky on the extreme left of the brigade and also atop the crest, and instructed him to tell Whitaker to dispatch some of his men to help the right, which mission Bierce promptly carried out.[25] On Hazen's right, Sheridan's division was about ten minutes behind, still only some two-thirds of the way up the steep slope, with the Rebels continuing to pour a heavy fire down on them. Spreading out to the right along the ridge, Bierce and the rest of Hazen's troops chased the Butternuts off the crest. This assist enabled Sheridan's men to reach the top with less loss than otherwise would have been the case. Sheridan rewarded this timely help by maligning Hazen's achievement and falsifying his reports.[26]

Capture of Rebel guns on Missionary Ridge. Hazen's brigade overran the Rebel guns about ten minutes before Sheridan's men, but Sheridan tried to take credit for their capture. This was but one of the many self-serving prevarications by Union commanders that Bierce encountered during war. *Harper's Weekly.*

Besieged

As the November sun set on the victorious troops atop Missionary Ridge, General Bragg's career was in shambles; General Grant's career was on the ascent; the gray-clad Army of Tennessee was in full retreat; and the Army of the Cumberland's pride and honor were at last redeemed. And somewhere amid that jubilant crowd atop Missionary Ridge stood Lieutenant Ambrose Bierce.

11

Lieb und Krieg

> Not quite forgotten, though the years endeavor
> To fling a veil between thy soul and mine;
> Deep in my heart thy memory livest ever;
> By tears and smiles unalter'd is thy shrine.
> —Ambrose Bierce[1]

After enduring defeat, privation, siege, and then victory, the Ninth Indiana had amply earned respite from battle. More importantly for the army, their three-year term of enlistment was up. However, such was their esprit de corps that the men of the Ninth chose to re-enlist for the remainder of the war. By re-enlisting "as veterans," by the terms of General Order 291, they were granted a full thirty-day furlough back home. Although Lieutenant Bierce was on detached service with another brigade, he too earned a spell back home in Indiana.[2] Arriving in Indianapolis on January 9, 1864 from Chattanooga, the regiment was given a warm greeting, with a plentitude of speeches and celebrations. Governor Morton himself delivered a welcome address, comparing the Ninth favorably to Napoleon Bonaparte's Old Guard and similar encomiums. Once the accolades were finished, the men dispersed to their various hometowns to reconnect with family and friends, husbands to their wives and beaus to their sweethearts. The officers were also detailed to scour their hometowns for new recruits to replace the many gaps that had opened in the regiment's ranks.

Topographic Engineer Bierce also returned home, visiting both Warsaw and nearby Elkhart. He too reconnected with family and friends—and one special friend in particular. Because of Bierce's virtually obsessive privacy regarding his personal life, very little is known for certain about his early love life. His earliest and one of his best biographers, Carey McWilliams, pieced together most of what little we know.[3] For example, McWilliams found that before the war Ambrose was romantically involved with a local Warsaw girl that he went to school with, Bernice Wright. From what he gleaned, Bierce had a crush on her when they went to school together, although she seems not to have been aware of it at the time.

Upon his joining the service in 1861, Brady Bierce wrote Miss Wright a love poem expressing his feelings for her and sent it to her anonymously.

According to one version of the incident, in the poem he addressed her by his personal pet name for her—"Fatima"—instead of by her given name Bernice, and he presumed she therefore would know who sent it. That, at least, is what his previous biographers all relate. When Bierce arrived back in Warsaw on furlough in early January, he professed his love for her and asked whether she had ever gotten the secret love poem. To this she replied, "Oh, was it you?"[4]

Information that seeks to illumine this, his first relationship, and the young Miss Wright in general, however, raises more questions about Bierce's prewar relationship than it answers. The 1860 census records verify that the Wright family resided in Warsaw, Indiana, having moved there from Ohio. The father, Benjamin Wright, was listed as "hotelkeeper," with real estate valued at $5,000 and a personal estate listed at $8,000. The entire family is listed in this census schedule: besides father Benjamin and his wife Sarah are Oliver, 19; Clarissa 17; Fatima, 15; plus younger siblings Sarah, Mary, and Rolla.[5] By all the standards of the day, the Wrights were a prosperous and respectable family.

From a family genealogy and a local history based on contemporary newspapers, we can glean a few more details about the Wrights. Benjamin Wright built "Wright House," a hotel in Warsaw, at a cost of $50,000 (apparently the patriarch of the family seriously undervalued his estate to the government census-taker); it was located on the northeast corner of Center and Buffalo Streets, and at the time when Bierce lived in Warsaw it would have been a sturdy wood frame building. Later, in 1867, the hotel burned and it was rebuilt as a four-story brick building. In its day the hotel was well regarded in that part of Indiana. James Whitcomb Riley, the "Hoosier Poet," stayed there in his earlier days.[6] In time, Benjamin also owned a general store in Warsaw. Fatima's father apparently had a knack for being an ad man as well as an entrepreneur. His advertising slogan was "The right man in the right place." The family genealogy also tells us that in later years, family members referred to Fatima as "Aunt Bennie." We learn as well that parents Benjamin and Sarah had four other children who all died in infancy—a common occurrence in those days.[7]

What is glaring from the official records is that Miss Wright's given name was Fatima, *not* Bernice. Fatima was not some secret pet name that Brady had given her. The 1850 census confirms the fact that she was known from childhood as Fatima and not Bernice. The other striking piece of information is Fatima's age. While it is not inconceivable that nineteen-year-old Brady would have had a crush on a sixteen-year-old girl when he marched off to war in 1861, biographers have long asserted that they were grade school sweethearts in the early 1850s, long before Bierce left home. In 1850, the

Wrights were still residing in Ohio, and Fatima was only five; even in 1857 she would have only been twelve or thirteen. The later tales of Bierce's teenage romance seem to have been greatly exaggerated. When he marched off to war, Brady may well have had a secret crush on Fatima Wright. From old photos of her, she indeed seems to have been a pretty young lady. Her family genealogy confirms her age: she was born on January 25, 1845. About the time when Brady was working as apprentice at the town newspaper, she would have been only thirteen; when he marched off to war, she would have just turned sixteen. In contrast, her sister Clarissa (Clara) was far closer in age to Brady, having also been born in 1842.

Although assertions of a prewar liaison between Ambrose Bierce and Fatima Wright raise a number of questions, we are on firmer ground regarding their wartime relationship. Apparently Lieutenant Bierce did conduct a whirlwind romance while home on leave for the first time in the war. After Carey McWilliams had published his groundbreaking biography of Bierce, he managed to track down Fatima, still alive at the time. However Fatima was in her eighties when he contacted her and while she did confirm and amplify what was previously known, some details of her recollections seem to have been conflated or confused—not at all surprising given the number of years that had passed since she had known Bierce. Fatima verified the poem sent to her in April 1861 and gave McWilliams the complete poem, the earliest literary piece we have of Bierce's to survive. The poem was flowery and romantic; it was certainly not the work of a cynic, but rather the product of an idealistic youth quite smitten with love—or at least with the idea of love.

Fatima's brother Oliver was also a member of the Ninth Indiana and in a letter told of Brady's heroism, relating to his sisters Bierce's bravery in western Virginia and urging them to "entertain him royally," should he return to town. When Bierce did come home on the "veteran's furlough," he made a beeline for the Wright residence and apparently the two sisters obliged brother Oliver's injunction to them. Fatima amplified the details to McWilliams of the anecdote about the anonymous poem. When she claimed ignorance as to its authorship, she says Bierce asked her, "If you knew the man that wrote the poem would you love him?" She claims that "I said certainly I would love him; how could I help but love any one who loved me so much?" That was apparently exactly what Bierce wished to hear.

Lieutenant Bierce paid court to Fatima Wright, with sister Clara accompanying them as chaperone. Bierce by all accounts was an earnest suitor—perhaps too earnest at times. One time Tima (her real nickname) played a practical joke on him by putting an elegant veil over a beat-up old straw hat and sashayed down the walk to where Brady was waiting in a carriage to take them for a ride in the country. The proper young officer was not amused at the absurd sight, and ordered the two girls to go back in and dress appropriately.

One of the few pieces of Bierce's wartime correspondence to survive verifies this courtship. Curiously though, Bierce addressed this letter to sister Clara, not to his beloved Tima. Dated June 8, 1864, only a few months after this furlough, the letter confirms that Fatima and Ambrose did indeed do some "sparking" while he was on leave. In it, Bierce refers to a romantic carriage ride out to Eagle Lake—albeit with Clarissa in tow. Bierce in his letter also makes vague reference to perhaps having "written something as heartless and cruel as I used to say to her" and the possibility that it offended Tima. Apparently Bierce's acid tongue—and his inability to control it—dates back to the war years and even before.[8]

Almost every day during his leave, Bierce would take Fatima and Clara to a rustic cabin at the verge of a forest just outside of town, and there Bierce would read aloud to them from one or another of his favorite books. Fatima for her part would weave a garland of wild rosebuds. Only once, on January 27, did Bierce cancel his date with the sisters twain; he was attacked by "giddiness" followed by a severe headache and sent a note to Clara (*not* Tima) apologizing for not being able to take them to a concert that night. Overall, the evidence definitely points to young Lieutenant Bierce being wounded by Cupid's arrow while visiting Warsaw. How deeply enamored Tima Wright was of this handsome young officer is, however, open to question.

If we are short on specifics, at least a general picture emerges of the couple. Brady and Tima came from similar backgrounds and would have had much in common. They went to the same school (or schools), even if several years apart. Although Fatima's father was a townsman and a merchant, Brady's father was also a respectable and well-established resident—Lord knows he was God-fearing. While it is more likely that the adolescent Brady spent more time teasing little Tima and pulling her pigtails than romancing her, they did know one another as children. By January 1864, however, Fatima was a beautiful young woman, and the high-spirited young boy had grown into a handsome and dashing young officer. We may not doubt that during his leave Bierce turned her head with his newly acquired manners, charm, and military bearing. With most of the other young men away at war, Fatima may well have entered into an engagement—or serious understanding of some sort—with the dashing young lieutenant.

The Ninth Indiana's "veteran's leave" ended in the middle of February, although they were allowed the end of the month to return to Nashville, Tennessee to muster in. As a staff officer, Lieutenant Bierce seems to have been granted an extended furlough, since his service record indicates he was still on leave throughout March and did not officially return to Hazen's brigade until April 18. During his leave, the golden-haired young lion wooed and won the young maid of his daydreams before returning to the front. Winning her heart was done; keeping her heart would prove more difficult, however.

By late April our young hero had once more resumed his profession, leaving behind his beloved—and leaving us an enduring enigma.

12

Crimes and Misdemeanors
The Atlanta Campaign

> **REBEL**, *n.* A proponent of a new misrule who has failed to establish it.

Lieutenant Bierce returned from his extended leave just in time to participate in his brigade's next great campaign: the advance against Atlanta.[1] As reward for his great victory at Chattanooga, General Grant had been promoted General in Chief of all Union armies and had gone east to directly supervise the Eastern Theater of the war. In turn, Grant appointed his close associate General Sherman (called "Uncle Billy" by his men) as commander of the Western Theater. Whether Sherman's appointment was deserved remains a matter of some dispute. Under Sherman's immediate control were three Union field armies, totaling upwards of 100,000 men.

Arrayed against Sherman's combined forces was the Confederate Army of Tennessee, which could field 50,000 men. Jefferson Davis's favorite, General Bragg, was finally gone—although Davis still found Bragg a place of trust in his administration to continue to making mischief. Besides Bragg's dismissal, the Confederates had but two other positive factors to counterbalance Sherman's vast advantages in men and materiel: the terrain of northern Georgia and General Joseph P. Johnston—or as the soldiers of the Army of Tennessee called him, "Uncle Joe." General Johnston had been in command back east early in the war, but President Davis did not think him aggressive enough. In the spring of 1864, Joe Johnston was still not aggressive enough to suit the Confederate president, but by now Davis had few other choices to head the Confederacy's main western army.

There is no question that Joe Johnston preferred the defensive over the offensive. However, given what faced the western Confederacy in the person of "Uncle Billy" Sherman and his vast military resources, Joe Johnston was by far their best hope. So, in the spring of 1864, a contest of wits was begun between Uncle Joe and Uncle Billy.

May 3 found Hazen's brigade at McDonald's Station, some thirty miles outside of Chattanooga and sitting astride the Chattanooga and East

Tennessee Railroad. While General Hazen now counted eight regiments in his command, the whole brigade numbered only 2,312 men and 131 officers effective strength. At noon that day the brigade broke camp and began their march southward as Sherman launched his campaign to seize the "Richmond of the West"—Atlanta. Between Chattanooga and Atlanta lay a series of steep and craggy mountains, interspersed with rapid rivers and streams. It was a country ideal for defense and the Confederates under General Johnston made maximum use of it, entrenching and building emplacements whenever and wherever they could. Johnston virtually dared Sherman to attack these defenses. In the face of such a series of formidable defenses, manned by an army with the skill and experience to use them to maximum effect, Sherman resolved to outmaneuver his rival rather than to attack directly. Whatever Sherman's faults, stupidity was not one of them. With more than ample manpower at his disposal, Sherman continually sought to outflank Johnston and to try to get behind him to sever his supply lines.

For Hazen's brigade, therefore, the following weeks consisted mostly of marching and skirmishing, interspersed with occasional big bloody battles. In the first two weeks of the campaign, the brigade fought for or occupied positions at Rocky Face Ridge, Buzzard Roost, and an array of lesser locations. By the thirteenth, the brigade was passing though Dalton, Georgia.

Although the Yankees fully expected a fight near Dalton, the Rebels refused to oblige, retreating in the night—and so the next day Hazen's men advanced again. Around ten a.m. the brigade ran into Rebel cavalry four miles before Resaca. After repulsing the Rebel horsemen, the brigade formed two lines and began advancing in battle formation. The brigade kept this up for about two miles, at which point they came up in line with the left wing of the Federal Twenty-Third Corps, who were already engaging the enemy. Hazen's brigade relieved them and then resumed the advance, pushing back the Johnnies until they occupied a hill some one hundred yards from a salient of the Confederate's main line of defense.[2]

We learn more of Bierce's experience at Resaca through his fiction than through his nonfiction; Bierce describes his brigade's dispositions that day succinctly: "In front of our brigade the enemy's line of earthworks was through open fields along a slight crest. At each end of the open ground we were close up to him in the woods, but the clear ground we could not hope to occupy. . . . roughly, we formed a semicircle, the enemy's fortified line being the chord of the arc."[3]

The next day an assault was ordered against these enemy works, to be carried out in conjunction with General Hooker's maneuvering to flank the Confederates elsewhere. At the given signal, Hazen's men climbed over their works and advanced into the open ground toward the enemy lines. The at-

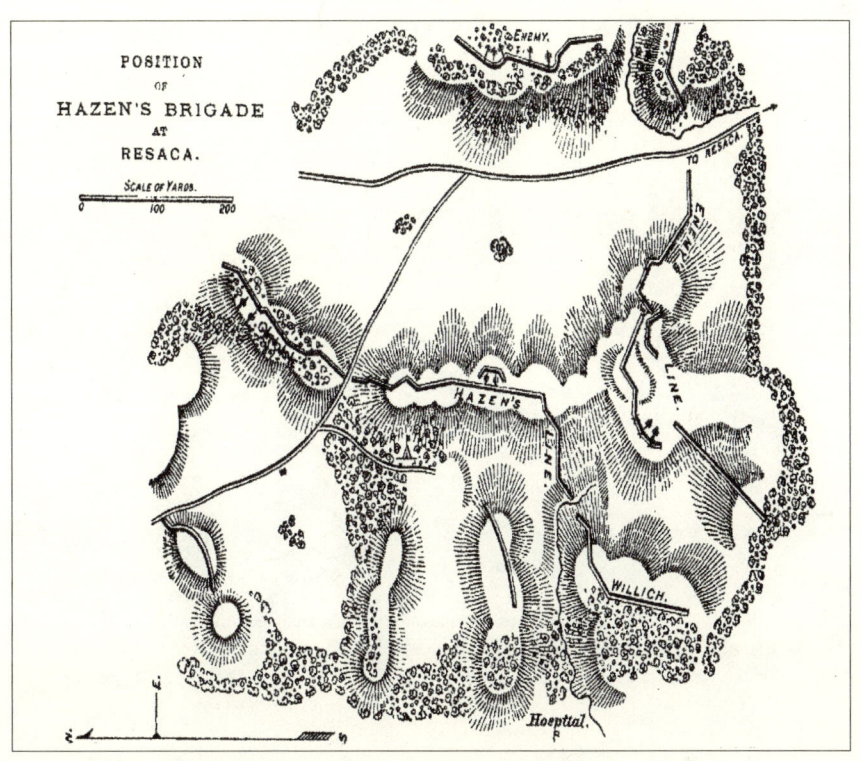

Battle of Resaca. Left unsupported by other Federal troops, Hazen's men took heavy casualties in this attack. Map attributed to Bierce. From OR, Ser. 1, Vol. 38, Pt. 1, p. 426.

tack was to be carried out in concert with brigades on either side of them. However, those brigades to either side failed to move forward at all, so the whole of the Rebel battle line was able to concentrate their fire solely on Hazen's men. In the space of thirty seconds, 120 men of the brigade fell before the withering fire. In the face of such intense fire—and total lack of support by the other Federal units—Hazen had no choice but to order his men back. That night, around ten p.m., the Butternuts opened a "noisy fire" at the Yankee lines and retired in the dark under cover of the diversion. The next morning, Hazen sent a regiment forward to investigate. The detachment met no opposition.[4]

The sole positive result of the action at Resaca came many years later, in the form of Bierce's short story. In "Killed at Resaca," Bierce tells the tale of a young officer who is "vain of courage" and repeatedly exposes himself to danger unnecessarily. Finally at Resaca the odds catch up with "Lieutenant Henry Brayle." After the war, the narrator—coincidentally a topographical officer—is entrusted with returning a letter to a young lady who had written

Crimes and Misdemeanors

The Battle of Resaca, as portrayed by Alfred Waud. Bierce participated in the attack and incorporated his experience into one of his short stories, "Killed at Resaca." Library of Congress.

impugning Brayle's courage, causing his unnecessary death. Repulsed at seeing blood on the letter, she thoughtlessly flings the missive into the fireplace. When she casually asks the cause of Brayle's death, the officer sarcastically replies, "He was killed by a snake."

The short story accurately reflects the day's fight at Resaca, and the romantic relationship in the story was also no doubt a common situation during the war. Undoubtedly, there were many such thoughtless young girls back home whose callousness or vanity caused some young soldier's needless demise through his trying to prove his valor to her. Unfortunately, some Bierce biographers have assumed this particular tale to be literally true. While doubtless Bierce knew about instances of naïve young officers being "killed by a snake," there is no proof that it happened at Resaca. The snakes that killed Hazen's men on this day were the Union brigadiers on either flank who failed to do their duty as ordered.

After Resaca, the Federals chased the Rebels through Adairsville, Kingston, and Cassville, Georgia. Occasional skirmishes alternated with hard marching as the two sides maneuvered for positions of advantage against one another. At Cassville it seemed at one point that the Johnnies would make a stand, but the next day found the Rebels had retreated back across

Allatoona Mountain. It was near Allatoona (or Altoona) that an old association was renewed. Reuben Williams, Bierce's old publisher, was by now colonel of the regiment of Indiana volunteers and his command had been halted, expecting to assault the Rebel defenses there. "A young man rode up to us, shook hands, and called us by name. It was no wonder that we did not recognize the youth of sixteen that had commenced learning the printing business four years previously, in the tall, good-looking and bearded young man that stood before us." After the cordial reunion, they parted ways, never to meet again.[5]

The military game of cat and mouse continued over the next several days. As Hazen's brigade approached Dallas, Georgia, however, the skirmishing became more intense. Finally the Federals came upon a firmly entrenched enemy position. It was clear that Uncle Joe was going to make Uncle Billy pay dearly if he wanted to move forward. Unfortunately for his men, Sherman's subordinate commanders were only too willing to oblige the Confederates. Due to the criminal incompetence demonstrated during the ensuing fight on the part of the senior Union commanders present, and because Hazen's brigade bore the brunt of the bloodletting, this particular action earned a considerably detailed description in one of Bierce's postwar memoirs.

Once again Bierce gives a succinct description of what was a complex series of tactical maneuvers leading up to the battle: "For three weeks we had been pushing the Confederates southward . . . Each army offered battle everywhere, but would accept it only on its own terms. At Dallas Johnston made another stand and Sherman, facing the hostile line, began his customary maneuvering for advantage."[6]

General Wood's division, of which Hazen's brigade formed a part, was in the Fourth Corps and under the command of General Oliver O. Howard. This fact alone should have given the soldiers of the corps some cause for concern; although called the "Christian General" by the press, as commander of the Eleventh Corps back east, Howard had earned the dubious epithet of "Oh-Oh!" Howard for his unerring knack of getting those serving under his command unnecessarily slaughtered. Bierce calls him a "consummate master of the art of needless defeat."[7] During the Battle of Chancellorsville, Howard had been in command of the Eleventh Corps when Stonewall Jackson launched his famous attack against the Army of the Potomac's flank—the very flank that General Howard was supposed to be defending. By dint of Howard's sterling leadership ability, the Eleventh Corps disintegrated under the onslaught of Stonewall's corps-strength assault.

After Chancellorsville, the Eleventh gained a reputation as a "hard luck" outfit. This is why, when the Secretary of War called upon General Meade for troops to send west, Meade readily dispatched Howard's corps instead of a more highly regarded outfit; he was glad to be shed of both Howard and his corps. By May 1864, among all the changes wrought by Sherman's reorganization of his forces, Wood's division came under the control of "Oh-Oh!" Howard.

All of this was known by Bierce but was not in the forefront of his thoughts on the morning of May 27. About nine that morning, the division had been pulled out of line and was ordered to move four miles to the left through thick forest. By around two in the afternoon they marched to the point where General Howard thought he had reached the end of the Rebel lines and could get behind them. The idea was to deliver a crushing blow against Johnston's left flank and roll up his line—much as Stonewall Jackson had done at Chancellorsville. Only General Howard was no Stonewall Jackson. The assault on the Confederate flank at Pickett's Mill was intended to be a surprise attack and was supposed to be carried out in columns of brigades, with Hazen's brigade taking the point and the other brigades of the division following in close support to exploit the breach in the enemy line. Such, at least, was General Hazen's understanding; such, indeed, was what any marginally competent senior commander would have done. However, as Bierce tells us, "after a march of less than a mile an hour and a further delay of three hours at the end of it to acquaint the enemy of our intentions to surprise him," only Hazen's lone brigade was to be sent in to achieve the goals of the assault.[8]

Standing within earshot of both the corps and the divisional commanders, Bierce heard the words that condemned his comrades to a needless death. General Wood turned to the "Christian General" Howard and said, "We will put in Hazen and see what success he has." The corps commander concurred with his divisional commander. Bierce glanced at Hazen and then realized what was in store for the brigade: "Only by a look which I knew how to read did he betray his sense of the criminal blunder."[9] During those several hours of apparently needless delay, the enemy did indeed become well acquainted with the Federal's intentions and acted quickly to deal with the threat. Johnston extended his line to the right with one of the best units in the army: Cleburne's Division. In addition, a division of 'Fighting Joe' Wheeler's elite cavalry was also dispatched to that flank to support Cleburne. Two of the South's best divisions, led by two of its best commanders, were to do battle against a weak Union brigade sent in without support. At full initial complement, the eight regiments of Hazen's brigade would have had rifle strength of close to eight thousand men. Now, as they advanced in full view of the enemy, Hazen's brigade could field fewer than fifteen hundred men.

Cleburne's division, it may be recalled, was the Rebel unit that had repulsed Sherman's attack on Tunnel Hill. At that time, Sherman had thrown two full corps and additional divisions against the feisty Irishman and his Arkansas sharpshooters, only to fail miserably in the attempt. Grant had intended to make Sherman and his army the heroes of the Missionary Ridge battle and have them garner all the glory, but instead General Thomas and the disgraced Army of the Cumberland had won fame there as the victors. Cleburne and his men had foiled Grant's scheme that day. This was the nature of the foe that Hazen's men now faced at Pickett's Mill on May 27.[10] In theory, as Hazen's troops advanced, there were brigades available as support. Thanks to Wood and Howard's orders, however, they stood by idly, in the nature of spectators at a show, or more precisely, mourners at a funeral.

As the brigade's topographical engineer, Bierce pushed forward ahead of the rest, making a hasty inspection of the ground before them. He advanced "a quarter-mile uphill through almost impassable tangles of underwood, along and across precipitous ravines," beyond which lay the well-prepared breastworks of the two crack Confederate divisions. Lieutenant Bierce scouted far enough forward through the undergrowth that he could distinctly hear the murmur of the Rebels awaiting them, and then he returned to Hazen and reported his findings. The advance continued: "After skirmishing about 800 yards," Hazen reported to his superiors, "the front line came upon and immediately engaged the enemy." In the first line were four regiments (or remnants thereof) organized into two battalions: on the right, the Forty-First Ohio and the First Ohio; on the left, the One Twenty-Fourth Ohio and the Ninety-Third Ohio. Under Hazen's personal supervision the first line advanced to within ten yards of Cleburne's defenses. A slight irregularity in the ground gave Hazen's men partial cover from the withering enemy fire.[11]

Following behind the first, Hazen's second line was also formed into two battalions of four weak regiments: the Fifth Kentucky and Sixth Ohio in one and Colonel Foy's Twenty-Third and Sixth Kentucky in the other. The second line moved forward as the first advanced through the woods. Due to the thick underbrush, however, the second line changed direction to the left, coming into position immediately to the first line's left flank. This was actually fortunate, as the second line encountered no enemy breastworks and found only slight resistance. As they progressed further, however, the second line received heavy fire from the side, which effectively stopped their advance.[12]

Bierce, who was with Hazen in the first line, gives a vivid description of their tribulations: "We moved forward. In less than one minute the twin battalions had become simply a swarm of men struggling through the undergrowth . . . the front was irregularly serrated, the strongest and bravest in advance, the others followers in fan-like formation, variable and inconstant, ever defining themselves anew."[13]

Crimes and Misdemeanors

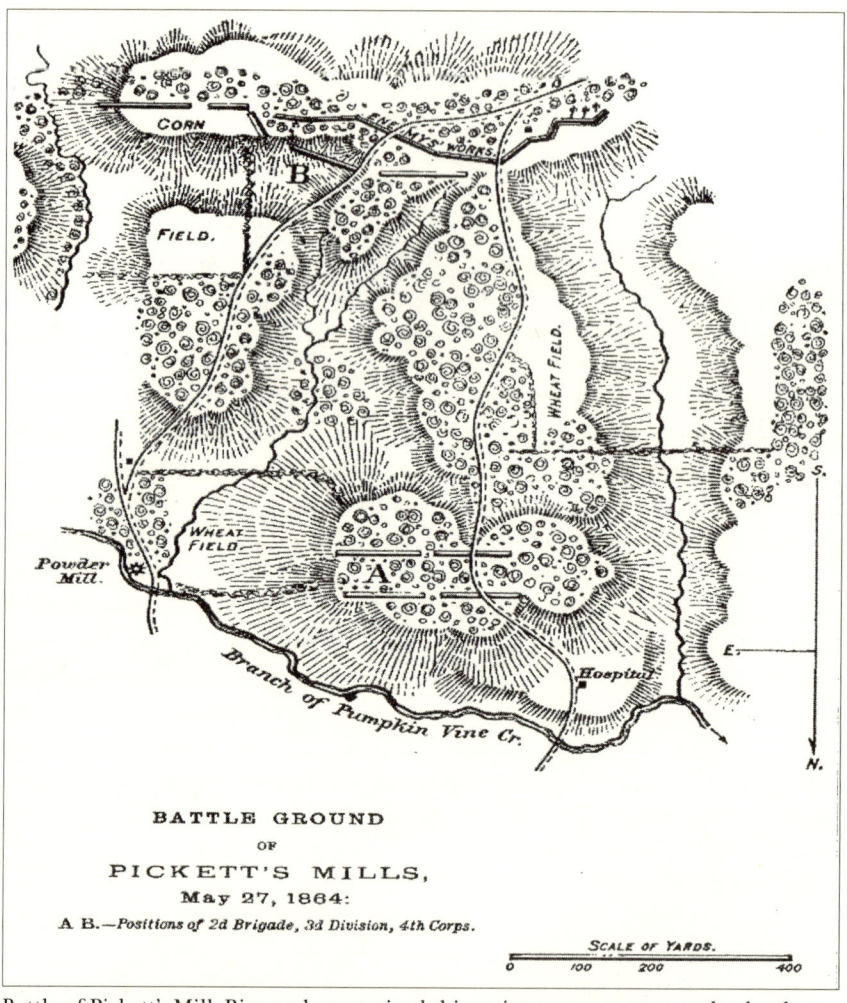

BATTLE GROUND OF PICKETT'S MILLS, May 27, 1864:
A B.—*Positions of 2d Brigade, 3d Division, 4th Corps.*

Battle of Pickett's Mill. Bierce characterized this action not as not so much a battle as a crime and blamed both Sherman and corps commander "Oh-Oh" Howard. Hazen's brigade, badly depleted in previous battles, was sent in unsupported to attack two of the Rebel's best divisions. After Hazen's men had been severely mauled, other brigades were sent in piecemeal to also get chewed up to no purpose. From OR, Ser. 1, Vol. 38, Pt. 1, p. 427.

Initially, the path of the first line's left battalion followed the left side of a small creek in a deep ravine until it came to a fork in the gulley. Some of the men of the two battalions crossed above the fork, others below, passing over both branches; in the process, the two frontline battalions became mixed. Hazen and his staff, including Bierce, struggled to keep up with the front ranks as best they could. All of a sudden came the "ringing rattle" of heavy musket fire, quickly followed by the familiar hissing of bullets. The fire halted the forward edge of the advancing brigade and the rest of the men soon came up beside them, forming themselves into something resembling a line of battle. On the right of the line stood Bierce, where they occupied the edge of an open space. The enemy had cleared a space in front of their breastworks to make their task of execution easier. Bierce saw the regimental colors unfurl, counting no less than six color-bearers out in front. The life expectancy of a standard bearer that day could be counted in minutes.

Offering an idea of how fiercely Hazen's men fought that day, Bierce cites General Johnston's report. Uncle Joe thought the entire Fourth Corps had mounted an assault against his flank. Johnston states that Hazen's men actually came within fifteen paces of his breastworks. The brigade could advance no farther. As they stood firing at point-blank range and the Rebels did likewise, a "dead-line" developed, marked by an accumulating mass of Union corpses. On the left, the brigade's second line had somewhat better success. After falling back they fought from the corner of a cornfield with a bordering fence, which allowed them some nominal protection. Along that fence, parts of both the first and second lines made a stand as the Johnnies mounted a counterattack. Hazen had sent Bierce over to that flank on an errand, and the lieutenant witnessed the fight: "The apparently slight advantage of the imperfect cover and the open range worked its customary miracle: the assault, a singularly spiritless one, considering the advantages it promised and that it was made by an organized and victorious force against a broken and retreating one, was checked. The assailants actually retired, and if they afterward renewed the movement they encountered none but our dead and wounded."[14]

Had the brigade been given any support at this point by the abundant forces at Howard's command, Hazen's men might well have turned the tables on the Rebel defenders. Hazen tells us, "Believing our work well commenced . . . I sent all my staff in succession to bring forward the other lines of the column. In addition to them several members of the regimental staffs were sent for the same purpose, some of whom were wounded while carrying the message."[15] It was now more than forty minutes into the attack. Even without Lt. Bierce and every other staff officer in the brigade being sent back to bring forward the reserves, any competent divisional or corps commander should have quickly done so already. It was not done. Instead, it was only after Hazen's attack was fully spent and his men out of ammunition that the rear brigades were sent in piecemeal. Belatedly, Wood sent in Gibson's brigade. They met Hazen's battered troops in the woods, but without additional support their task was hopeless. Finally, a third brigade, Knefler's, was also ordered forward. By now it was close to sunset. Knefler's men were mainly employed to cover the removal of the wounded. While the slaughter among Gibson's and Knefler's brigades was not nearly so severe as Hazen's, their losses were simply more needless additions to the casualty lists. Two hours too late, orders came down from Sherman calling off the attack.[16]

It would at least be comprehensible if the folly of Pickett's Mill could be blamed on drunkenness of the senior officer in the field—Howard. But General Howard was one of the few Union generals known to be a teetotaler. When General Wood sent in Hazen's men unsupported, all that was required was a word from Howard to correct the mistake. For that matter, with all the delays in even mounting the attack, both Howard and Wood should have known the element of surprise was lost and that any effort that day would be futile. Neither commander intervened to prevent the inevitable slaughter. Bierce was well justified in calling it a crime.

As for General Wood, it should be remembered that he was the same military genius who, in literal compliance to General Rosecrans's erroneous order, had pulled his division completely out of the firing line at Chickamauga. Wood knew full well this would create a wide gap in the Federal lines yet did so regardless of the consequences. It was through this breach that Longstreet's corps charged on September 20, 1863, bringing disaster to the army and disgrace to Rosecrans. At Pickett's Mill, Wood was still "one kind of officer." Rosecrans was removed for his unwitting error; Wood, for his deliberate act, was not.

The defeat at Pickett's Mill having given the enemy encouragement, the Confederates remained holding this line until the beginning of June. Hazen's brigade—or rather what was left of it—remained near the scene of the crime until the morning of June 5, when they found that the Rebels had vanished in the night. Again there ensued the "zigzag advance," characterized by hard marching and small but bloody actions, as Johnston's Army of Tennessee continued to pursue their successful Fabian strategy. As Hazen describes it, "The command moved forward at short intervals, taking up new positions and fortifying them as the enemy would take up new lines, losing a few men each day."[17]

It was on June 8, a little over a week after Pickett's Mill, that Bierce wrote a letter home to Warsaw, to his fiancée's sister, Clarissa. Although Bierce was mainly concerned over his lover's failure to write, one can also sense a growing disillusionment with the war: "I am getting very tired of my present life and weary of the profession of arms," Bierce wrote Clara. Ambrose hastens to explain it is because he wishes to be with Clara and her sister Fatima: "The pleasant weeks with you, so like a dream, have nearly spoiled the soldier to make me the—pensive individual."[18] This letter, inquiring about his fiancée Fatima—whom he had not heard from since May 11—was directed to

Clarissa. Clara was the same age as Ambrose—and her more mature temperament may well have made her a better match for the soldier than her younger sister was. Whether caused by war weariness or love sickness, in either case Bierce's letter is a curious one. Unfortunately, Bierce's letter of early June is the lone surviving example of what undoubtedly was a more extensive correspondence between him and the Wright sisters.

The next two weeks were taken up with still more maneuvering, each army jockeying for position so they might gain advantage over the other and each countering to deny that advantage. By the twenty-second of June, Hazen's brigade had reached the environs of Kennesaw Mountain, only to find Uncle Joe and his boys already firmly entrenched along its craggy heights. General Sherman reported to Washington that "the whole country is one vast fort, and Johnston must have at least 50 miles of connected trenches with abates and finished batteries . . . Kennesaw . . . is the key to the whole country."[19]

On June 27, Sherman, frustrated by Johnston's cat and mouse game, finally resolved to make a full-out frontal assault against Johnston's army. Ambrose Bierce, however, would not be present to see it.

13

Casualties of War

> Fate—whose edict oft hath wrung
> Anguish—drops from hearts unstrung—
> Tears of hopeless prayerless pain
> I now defy thee. Free again,
> My soul though darkened still by thee,
> And 'bittered still, spurns thy decree.
> —Ambrose Bierce, 1864[1]

The orders come down from the divisional commander: advance your skirmish line. The massive acclivity where the Rebels lie in wait looms ominously above the blue-coated ranks. Where exactly the foe's advanced rifle pits are placed is not known. The general in charge of the division wishes to know; the brigadier is to find out. The brigadier turns to one of his aides. The Lieutenant steps forward, gives a sharp salute, then attends to his commander's orders. The Lieutenant is fair-haired, with a drooping mustache and piercing blue eyes. One might take him for a regular to judge by his martial bearing. He is not. Like most of the brigade, he spent his youth with the sights, sounds, and smells of rural life in his senses. Unlike family and friends though, the Lieutenant hated his bucolic life. When war finally comes, he is eager for adventure and the excitement of war. Too, the Lieutenant's uncle is a quixotic adventurer with a veneer of military polish—everything the Lieutenant's father was not. So, to emulate his uncle as well as serve a noble cause, the handsome young officer enlisted in the volunteer infantry. Now, after three years of war, the Lieutenant is in a position of trust. To be appointed to a general's staff is a rare honor—and often times a fatal one. The Lieutenant is cited by the brigadier for his efforts in official dispatches. In one report, the brigadier calls him "a fearless and trusty man." The general knows he can count on the Lieutenant to carry out an order—or die trying.

"Advance the skirmish line . . . direct it and cause it to be done." That is the brigadier's order to the Lieutenant. Somewhere across the field, a man in dun-colored clothes lies flat on a piece of high ground, looking over the valley below. He is observing a group of blue-clad men gathered in the near distance. At one time his homespun uniform may have been some shade of gray, but the vegetable dyes, fading from sun and aided by rain and mud, have gradually turned to a hue called butternut. The man in butternut is observing the blue-clad soldiers with intense interest; he is observing

Casualties of War

them over the sight of his rifled musket. The figures occupying his interest seem to be gathering with some object in mind. As a duly sworn member of the opposing side, it is the Butternut's boundin duty to dissuade them of their goal.

It is not difficult. The Butternut is now a soldier of several summers; even before, as a youth, he would hunt game of all shapes and sizes in these same hills and mountains. Compared to wary woodland game, the blue-hued game presently in his sights are easy targets.

The man in dust-brown clothes soon selects a target of particular interest. One of the bluecoats is directing the others to some purpose. Even at this range it is easy to see he is an officer. The glint of the metal bars on his shoulders confirms it. The Butternut pulls back the hammer of his Enfield musket. He puts a fresh cap on the tip of the firing nipple. The Butternut makes sure of his aim. He holds his breath; he gently pulls the trigger. The bluecoat officer, standing one second, slumps to the ground the next. There is a commotion among the other blue men in the open field. Then another man, with silver bars on his shoulders, comes up to the first man on the ground. Another easy target for the Butternut.

He reloads his musket, biting off the end of the paper cartridge, pouring its contents down the muzzle of his Enfield, and ramming a ball down the muzzle. He replaces the ramrod. He calmly puts another cap in place on top of the lock and then sights down the barrel.

The Butternut takes aim; he pauses a second. The shot is more difficult this time. The second officer is kneeling over the first now. No mind; he presses the trigger. A loud report, a flash, a puff of grey smoke, then-nothing. For a moment the Butternut thinks he misses. But no; suddenly the second man also falls to the ground. It is a good day for hunting Yankees.

After receiving his orders from General Hazen, Lieutenant Bierce went straightaway to the double regiment detailed for picket duty that day: the Fifth Kentucky and the Ninety-Third Ohio Volunteer Infantry. By now both bodies of men were regiments in name only. The Ninety-Third Ohio had begun the war with 968 men; when they began the Atlanta Campaign on May 3 they had less than two hundred men; by June 22 they had lost close to ninety more. The Fifth Kentucky had suffered similar attrition. In theory, advancing the picket line should have been a simple task. The Confederates, however, could easily observe every Federal movement from their well-entrenched aeries atop Kennesaw Mountain. Well in advance of the main defenses enemy pickets and sharpshooters lay in wait, ready to fire on anything that moved. Officers were a particular favorite of Rebel snipers. Bierce, who obeyed his orders to the letter, did not simply transmit the command to the officers in charge of the two regiments. He was enjoined "to direct it and cause it to be done."

One of the officers of the Ninety-Third Ohio was a man in his early thirties named Captain John Eastman. Formerly a lieutenant, Eastman had been promoted to captain of Company "H" the previous October and then appointed quartermaster of the regiment. Under normal circumstances, the regimental quartermaster would not have even been in the front lines leading troops. But with the regiment so greatly reduced in numbers, it had only one wagon to carry all its gear and supplies, and the quartermaster's job simplified accordingly. Moreover, the number of officers in the regiment had become as diminished as the rank and file and every surviving officer was needed to lead the men in battle.

Moving the picket line forward proved to be more than a simple walk in the woods on June 23. The double regiment came under heavy fire shortly after the movement began. By the end of the day, the Ninety-Third Ohio alone had suffered forty casualties, including one officer killed—Captain Eastman. Some thirty-three years later, the son of the slain quartermaster wrote Bierce, inquiring about the circumstances of his father's death. From his correspondence with Bierce we can glean some of what happened that fatal day.[2] When a Confederate sharpshooter struck Eastman, Bierce rushed to his aid, exposing himself to danger as well. Eastman lay dying in Bierce's arms, the staff officer comforting the quartermaster in his final moments. Bierce may have even tried to carry Eastman off the field. It was some time

Captain John Eastman, killed at Kennesaw Mountain; he died in Bierce's arms shortly before Bierce himself was shot. Hazen, *Narrative of Military Science*.

after this act of bravery—or perhaps because of it—that Bierce himself became the target of a Confederate sniper.

The Johnny's bullet hit Bierce in the head, fracturing the left temple and penetrating under the scalp around the back of the head. Less than an inch or so to one side and the shot would have been squarely between the eyes—likely the sharpshooter's intent. Bierce later described how his head was "broken like a walnut." Hazen referred to it as "a very dangerous and complicated wound." The ball remained lodged in Bierce's head and was not removed until some time later; the aid stations and field hospitals at the front had neither the time nor skill to deal with it.

At least Bierce—unlike the protagonist of his short story, which was set during the Battle of Kennesaw Mountain—was not "One of the Missing." Bierce's brother Albert heard of his brother's wounding and immediately came to his assistance. Bierce was carried off the battlefield and sent to an aid station in the rear. He was then passed from "station to station" until finally being evacuated by train northward. One of his early biographers extracted a few details of the wounding from Bierce's daughter Helen, who noted that the sights, sounds, and sensations of Bierce's train ride north remained etched in his mind forever after and she heard him tell of it in later years. The suffering endured during that journey, however, remained too painful a memory for even Bierce to render into written form.

The casualties were loaded onto flatcars, covered with only a tarp for protection. Once loaded, the wounded—moaning, crying, and suffering varying degrees of misery and pain—were forgotten about for hours. Finally, when someone decided they had a full load, the hospital train pulled out on its long ride north. Only the bright light of the rising moon kept Bierce company during the trip. The train rumbled through the night as cloudy overcast skies alternated with a summer Southern moon. The night air was heavy, thick with moisture, and it was difficult to breathe, as it often is in Georgia in June. Sometime in the night the oppressive humidity gave way to a drizzling rain. The train ride seemed interminable to Bierce: "The train cautiously made its way over miles of doubtful tracks; its movement was almost imperceptible."[3] Eventually Bierce, along with all the other wounded from Sherman's army, was offloaded from the train. A certificate issued by the Medical Director Post indicates that he was admitted to Hospital No. 1 in Chattanooga, where he stayed several days.[4] Bierce's muster rolls also indicate that during at least part of July he was in hospital at Nashville, Tennessee, recovering from his wound.[5]

Bierce's short story called "The Other Lodgers" relates to this agonizing period of his service. The story is set in Atlanta just after Sherman captured the city, and while Bierce was not present to witness Atlanta's fall, the tale clearly describes wartime conditions with which Bierce was all too familiar. The narrator, a "Colonel Leavering," was "worn out by two days and a night of hard railway travel and had not entirely recovered from a gunshot wound in the head." It takes little deductive ability to divine that the colonel and Bierce are, for our purposes, identical.

Taking his rest in a rickety old hotel "in urgent need of repairs," the colonel awakes in the middle of the night to find that he is not the only occupant of the room. The "other lodgers" are the dead, and death's handiwork is all about: "They lay on their backs, disposed orderly along three sides of the room, their feet to the walls—against the other wall, farthest from the door, stood my bed and the chair. All the faces were covered, but under their white cloths the features of the two bodies that lay in the square patch of moonlight near the window showed in sharp profile as to nose and chin." [6] The description is of wartime conditions in a hotel turned military hospital, where the dead and recent dead share space with the living. It could as easily have been Chattanooga in 1863 or 1864 as Atlanta after its fall.

Conditions in the hospitals at Chattanooga may have ameliorated since the siege that occurred during the fall of 1863, but with casualties streaming back from Sherman's campaign, it is likely that the Chattanooga hospitals too were soon overwhelmed in the summer of 1864. With Bierce's head wound throbbing and a bullet still lodged in it, medical authorities at Chattanooga may have deemed it safer to send him to Nashville to recover, where the medical resources were far more comprehensive. The official record is vague on this point, but it was probably in Nashville that army surgeons finally dared to remove the ball from the back of his skull. Given the level of surgical skill at the time, Bierce was fortunate to have survived it.

As the prime logistical center and transportation hub for almost all Federal campaigns in the Western Theater, Nashville at any given time was crowded with thousands of Union soldiers recovering—and dying—in hospitals. How long Lieutenant Bierce remained in Nashville that July is uncertain, as is the time it took for him to recover enough to be discharged from the hospital there. The old University of Nashville's Lindsley Hall on Rutledge Hill, just south of downtown, had been commandeered by the Yankees to serve as the officer's hospital for Union forces. Lieutenant Bierce would most likely have been billeted here for most of his stay in that city.

In Nashville, in addition to the military authorities ministering to the soldier's physical ailments, there was also an abundance of ladies of the evening resident to service the soldier's other physical needs. Known as the "Athens of the South" before the war, Nashville could also offer intellectual stimulation to soldiers should they desire it. The noted actor John Wilkes Booth, for example, once performed at one of the several theaters in the city. Booth

Officer's Hospital in Nashville (Lindsley Hall of the old University of Nashville). Bierce spent at least some time recuperating here after being transferred from the hospital in Chattanooga. Photo by George F. Barnard. Library of Congress.

was on friendly terms with Military Governor Andrew Johnson, whose activities in town extended well beyond throwing local civilians in jail without charges. There were concerts by military bands as well, and the military hospital Bierce stayed in had once been part of a university with a well-stocked library. It was a heady wartime environment for a young man on his own to be thrown into.

Whatever transpired in Nashville, by August 9 Lieutenant Bierce was back home in Indiana. On that date the Indiana Office of the Medical Director certified that Lieutenant Bierce was still "unfit for duty and not able to travel" and advised that he would not be fit for duty for at least forty days from that date.[7] Bierce's leave home at the beginning of the year had been a pleasant idyll and by all accounts romantically successful. Yet we know that by June there had been a pronounced change in the nature of the relationship between Bierce and his hometown sweetheart. Whether they made up in the interim is unknown. All that we know for sure is that sometime after their final breakup, Fatima discreetly destroyed all of Bierce's love letters to her. Even the letter that Bierce sent to Fatima's sister Clara in June seemed as much about his affection for her as for her younger sister Fatima. In the letter written on June 8, Bierce was discouraging Clara's interest in two other young men; his tone sounded almost as though he were jealous of their attentions toward her. Perhaps Fatima understood Lieutenant Bierce's heart better than he did himself.

With Bierce's second furlough in August, the rocky nature of their romance seems to have come to the breaking point. Bierce came home a wounded hero, but there is evidence that the pain from the head injury made him less than pleasant company. McWilliams tells us of a little girl named Piper who would sneak over to the Bierce home to see the wounded hero almost daily. Bierce was often resting on his father's couch covered in a military cape. One time she caught him in a bad mood and "he teased the young girl so unmercifully that she was glad to escape." McWilliams also says the wound "occasioned apologies and broken engagements."[8] Beyond the pain, which certainly could not have helped the young warrior's disposition, there may have been other after effects. Bierce's blow to the head may have seriously altered his personality as well. After two world wars and several other modern conflicts, the medical literature is abundant with studies regarding how severe head trauma can affect wounded patients' personalities, both in the short term and on a permanent basis.

One of Bierce's devoted followers, citing his brother Albert, seems to confirm that the near-fatal head wound did alter Bierce in a profound manner. Years later Albert, who knew Ambrose better than anyone else, said, "He was

Casualty of war. Sent home to Indiana to recuperate, Bierce was still ill in body and spirit during his stay there. While his body would heal, it is debatable whether his spirit ever did; his engagement to Fatima Wright may also have been a casualty of the war. Indianapolis *Star*, February 12, 1928.

never the same after that. Some of the iron of that shell seemed to stick in his brain, and he became bitter and suspicious, especially of his close friends. He would remember each failing and slight, fancied or otherwise, of such person, say nothing of it at the time, and then, many years afterward, release the stored-up poison in a flood."[9] If Bierce was as morose and short of temper to Fatima as he would later be to friends and acquaintances in California, one may not wonder that she broke off their engagement. While we cannot be certain that the relationship ended during Bierce's last leave, all circumstances point to it.

McWilliams, in a brief article on their romance, states that Bierce was later surprised to learn that Fatima had married and "would not credit the report until confirmed by his brother, Albert." Supposedly this happened when he "returned from California to New York on his way back to Warsaw."[10] One may question this particular recollection, since we know that Bierce did not finally end up in California until 1867 and remained in California for several years afterward. Surely Bierce would not have been expecting Fatima to wait for him back home in Indiana all this time?

Certainly we know that Miss Wright was certainly not holding her breath waiting for Bierce to return from the war. Fatima did have a certain weakness for men in uniform, however, and in fact ended up marrying a Union soldier—just not Bierce. On September 3, 1866, Fatima Wright married James Edwin Benham, a soldier about the same age as Ambrose and a member of Company I, Thirty-Third Indiana Volunteers. Her veteran husband lived until 1874. She later remarried, to a man named William J. Fleming, under which surname McWilliams encountered her in 1932.[11]

Details of Bierce's visit to his family during the furlough are also vague. We know he stayed awhile at his parents' home in Elkhart; he also visited other relatives and friends who were still around in either Warsaw or Elkhart. One day Bierce showed up in Elkhart at his brother Andrew's, riding a horse, his head all bandaged up. Unfortunately, by the time a reporter interviewed Bierce's older brother "Dime," he was far advanced in years and neither he nor his wife were able to recall any specifics of the visit.

"When he rode away on his horse again, with that bandage around his head, it was the last we saw of him," Mrs. Bierce told a local reporter.[12] From the 1870 census we know that both of Bierce's parents were still living in 1864 and that sometime before 1870 they had moved from the outskirts of Warsaw to the Elkhart area; Walter Neale's informants narrow the move down to sometime before the war, but clearly after the 1860 census.

In any case, most of Bierce's biographers portray this last furlough home as an unremittingly bleak one for the wounded warrior. "The farms were rundown; the towns were deserted; and even a returned hero had a hard time to find amusement. He scoffed at the place very indignantly and left to spend the rest of his leave in more congenial surroundings."[13] Considering that he was still recovering from a severe head wound, Bierce's mental state could hardly have been settled. Moreover, being rejected—or rejecting—a lover could not have improved his disposition any and certainly made for a less than happy visit home. But the above description of Warsaw and Elkhart in 1864 sounds far more like Georgia after Sherman had passed through it on his way to the sea than the prosperous Midwest in wartime.

Young soldiers like Bierce returning home on leave were often feted and hailed as heroes. If anything, the Midwest in 1864 was a time of prosperity and abundance. True, many young men were away at the war, but the farmers were able to sell everything they grew or raised to feed the Union armies in the field. Factories sprouted up virtually overnight all over the Midwest to provide materiel for the Union war machine. While the war was an unmitigated disaster for the South, it was quite the opposite for the North. By 1864, the northern states' economy alone was greater in size than the entire nation's had been before the war. In farm and city alike it was a golden time insofar as commerce was concerned.[14] Whether Lieutenant Bierce was in any mood to appreciate all this wartime abundance, much less the warm welcome awaiting him at home, is unknown. Perhaps his emotional turmoil and the intense pain he was in colored his perception of everyone and everything around him. We do know that by the end of his furlough Lieutenant Bierce was ready to return to the war. Bierce left the rural life of Indiana behind without regret. Not only was he himself a casualty: his home life and his first love had also become casualties of war.

14

What Happens

The Road to Franklin

DEFENCELESS, *adj.* Unable to attack.

If Ambrose Bierce had found things greatly changed back home in Indiana, on returning to active duty he found circumstances altered at the front as well. Atlanta had finally fallen to Sherman's armies, and between the retreating Confederates and General Sherman's incendiary proclivities, there was precious little of that city that hadn't been put to the torch. Regardless, one campaign had ended and two new ones were about to begin. Sherman was about to launch his famous—or infamous—March to the Sea, and he was busy transferring units and officers about, picking those he thought best suited to his envisioned scorched-earth campaign.

When Lieutenant Bierce at last returned to the Second Brigade of Third Division, Fourth Corps, it was no longer Hazen's brigade. General Hazen, despite his insubordinate inclinations, had proven to be a competent and pugnacious commander and these qualities were recognized and rewarded by Sherman, who promoted him to the command of the Second Division, Fifteenth Corps for the Georgia Campaign.

In the Confederate camp there were changes as well. President Jefferson Davis had tired of General Joseph Johnston's policy of conserving Confederate lives by making Sherman pay for every foot of ground, so Davis appointed General John Bell Hood. John Bell Hood was the former commander of the Texas Brigade and had a well-earned reputation for aggressiveness. Hood was a man who was personally courageous, but when President Davis dunned General Robert E. Lee for a recommendation, he was less than enthusiastic: at first he wired Davis, "Hood is a bold fighter. I am doubtful as to other qualities necessary."

Not satisfied with this tepid response, Davis pressed Lee, who responded with a follow-up telegram, saying, "Hood is a good fighter very industrious on the battle field, careless off & I have had no opportunity of judging of his action, when the whole responsibility rested upon him. I have a high opinion of his gallantry, earnestness & zeal."[1] Even at that, Lee strongly hinted that General Hardee would prove a better army commander. Although competent as a lower echelon battlefield commander, General Lee clearly felt Hood lacked the attributes necessary to make a competent general officer in charge of an independent command. While Hood's record in the Eastern Theater was unblemished, his career with the Army of Tennessee was marked by controversy. All agree, however, that Hood was on a personal level both gallant and brave.

Jefferson Davis, who had acted as Secretary of War in the Federal Government and had served as a volunteer officer in the Mexican War, fancied himself an expert in military affairs. In truth, Davis's actual grasp of strategy reeked far less of Bonaparte than the Confederate chief executive imagined. The Rebel president had been dissatisfied with Johnston's Fabian policy and had decided that the more aggressive General Hood was the man for the job. Davis did not wish to consider any dissenting opinions; Lee was wise enough to defer to his president's will. No sooner was Hood made commander of the army defending Atlanta than he immediately undertook a series of direct counterattacks against Sherman. Quick to put Davis's mandate for action into practice, Hood launched into a series of bloody attacks whose only notable achievement was to create thousands of new Southern widows. Thus Atlanta fell to the Yankees. Sherman's next big push would be to advance farther into the Deep South; this everyone knew. What form or direction this would take was unknown to the Rebels. John Bell Hood was not the sort of man to sit around and wait to find out. Instead of fighting yet another series of defensive battles on home soil in Georgia or Alabama, Hood devised a bold plan for an invasion of his own. He would attack northward.

As General Hood envisioned it, he would strike first at Nashville, seize that vast storehouse of Yankee munitions and supplies, advance on Louisville next and capture that strategic river port, recruit masses of sympathetic Kentuckians, and then advance up the length of the Ohio Valley. From there, who knew where—perhaps he would even strike eastward into the Yankee heartlands. Even if he should succeed only in part, Hood believed Sherman would be forced to turn about and pursue him—Washington would demand it—and deal with the threat to his rear. If Hood were to succeed in this bold gamble, what then? Generations of historians in general have dismissed Hood's plan as hopeless from the start; even after the war Hood characterized his mission as a "Forlorn Hope," a military term implying a suicidal mission. Regardless, the Lincoln administration certainly did not regard Hood's invasion as hopeless or in vain; Lincoln, Stanton, Halleck, and Grant all took the threat quite seriously. Who is to say that Hood's strategy was not the best one available to the Confederacy at the time?

When Lieutenant Bierce resumed his duties with the Army of the Cumberland, Sherman and Hood's respective plans remained still a gleam in the eyes of both generals. As Bierce tells us, he arrived back at the front during a period of "surprising and resultless series of marches and counter-marches since the fall of Atlanta."[2] Bierce rode into the camp of Second Brigade's headquarters resplendent in a newly tailored officer's uniform—in "full fig," as he puts it. Whether he obtained the new uniform in Indiana or at Nashville on the way back to the front is not known. The fresh colors and crisp creases of his uniform stood out among the campaign-faded blue togs of his fellow staff officers at brigade headquarters.

According to the official returns, the Second Brigade was posted at this time "near Atlanta, Georgia"—which was probably as close as the camp scribe at the time could reckon where in the Georgia backcountry they were. In fact, throughout most of September, Sherman's troops were kept busy doing the Georgia two-step with Hood, traversing country they had already fought and won in the summer. The beginning of October found Wood's division camped along the Coosa River near Gaylesville, in northern Alabama, glowering across the water at the Rebels. Bierce describes it as "an interregnum of expectancy between two regimes of activity." For the moment, Colonel Henry K. McConnell was acting as temporary commander of Second Brigade, while Brigadier General Philip Sidney Post was absent from camp. As Bierce notes, Colonel McConnell, normally commander of the Seventy-First Ohio Volunteers, did not keep an overly watchful eye on his sometimes-wayward young staff officers.

The Coosa, although the formal line separating the two armies, was not heavily defended—nor was it an impassible barrier. One Sunday morning, Bierce and a fellow staff officer, Lieutenant Cobb, were out riding. On a lark, the two men decided to race across a small tributary of the Coosa. Lieutenant Cobb managed to splash across it in relatively dry condition. Lieutenant Bierce was not so lucky; no Moses, he became soaked to the skin as the waters failed to part for him. Bierce's new blue uniform was no longer pristine. He spent half an hour drying his clothes, and it was another half hour before he reached the Coosa. While the far side was enemy territory, "the charm of the unknown" lured the two officers to explore the undiscovered country there. Although no enemy was in sight, Bierce and Cobb knew they must be about somewhere. Nonetheless the two officers and some privates detailed as pickets who were of similar inclination all ventured across the river by boat. Having successfully invaded enemy territory, the two officers and three enlisted men ventured down an old road bounded by rows of corn. Unfortunately, the adventurers wandered too far and soon found themselves face to face with Rebel cavalry. Cobb dived into a patch of woods

Rebel "Guerilla/Deserter" as portrayed by Waud. Bierce had a close encounter with murderous guerillas similar to this one in northern Alabama, just before the start of the Autumn Campaign. Library of Congress.

and escaped, while Bierce and the rest made for a swamp. In attempting to make his way back to safety, Bierce was taken prisoner.

After being displayed like a prize hog by a home guard, Bierce was taken in tow by two armed escorts. They warned Bierce about a local guerilla chief—Jeff Gatewood—who would have hung him outright. "Jeff Gatewood," Bierce tells us, "was a 'guerilla' chief of local notoriety, who was a greater terror to his friends than to his other foes." It was Gatewood's camp that Bierce had blundered into the first day of his adventure. After traveling some fifteen miles, Bierce and his captors bedded down in a local cabin for the night. While everyone slumbered, Bierce made good his escape, evading the hounds and eventually finding his way back across the river. When he saw "two patriots in blue" carrying a stolen pig on a pole, Bierce felt safe at last. Bierce finally staggered back into camp and collapsed, his uniform in rags and barely recognizable.

While Bierce was away on his great adventure across the Coosa, General Sherman had resolved that he would only pursue Hood as far as Gaylesville. As long as Sherman was tethered to his long supply line from Atlanta backwards toward Chattanooga, he knew he would be vulnerable to attacks on his rear and forced to defend it. Instead, Sherman now resolved to cut loose from this long tether and take the offensive, following through with his long contemplated "great raid." Then, when it became apparent that Hood was moving north to invade Tennessee, General Sherman became virtually jubilant. "Damn him! if he will go to the Ohio River I'll give him rations!" Upon learning of Hood's movement toward Middle Tennessee, Sherman is also reported to have said, "Let him go North, my business is down South!"[3]

Sherman sent General George Thomas—"The Rock"— to Nashville (in those days known as "the rock city") to organize its defense. Union detachments were ordered from as far away as Missouri to reinforce Thomas and the Army of the Cumberland. Sherman also detached the Fourth and Twenty-Third Corps from his own command (what at one point had been named the reconstituted "Army of the Ohio") to bolster the city's garrison, and Uncle Billy placed General John Schofield in command. Wiley Sword, the noted historian, says that Schofield "looked the part of perhaps a rogue banker with the ghost of evil in his eye."[4] Schofield proved to be a competent army commander, but he had a tendency to play politics on the sly—a trait he may have picked up from serving under Grant.

Bierce, as a member of the Fourth Corps, was now under the overall command of Major General David S. Stanley. "Oh-Oh!" Howard, for reasons known only to Sherman, was chosen to participate in Uncle Billy's Georgia campaign. Soon Bierce was involved in a far greater enterprise than dodging murderous guerillas or hapless home guards.

Fortunately for the Federals, Hood's invasion of Tennessee was delayed for more than a month due to rain, lack of supplies, and poor planning. Thinking he would lead Sherman on a merry chase through Tennessee, Hood was shocked and angered when Sherman refused to play his game. Sherman had set out from Atlanta on November 15, after destroying what little was left of the city: his March to the Sea had begun. It was not until November 21 that Hood finally left Florence, Alabama on his own much-delayed invasion. Despite Hood's tardiness, the reinforcements that Sherman intended for Thomas were too dispersed to go straight to Nashville—and General Thomas did not wish them to do so. Initially, Bierce's brigade and the remainder of Fourth Corps regrouped and moved toward Pulaski, Tennessee to rendezvous with the Twenty-Third Corps. Gathering together his widely scattered command at Pulaski by November 14, General Schofield had moved his "little army" thirty miles north toward Columbia "in hot haste," arriving just barely ahead of Hood's army.

Although Bierce describes their movement as a retreat, Schofield and Hood's respective movements were more akin to a foot race, with Schofield attempting to stay between Hood's Rebels and fortress Nashville. Aware of the two Yankee corps at Pulaski, Hood had hoped to get to Columbia first and keep the Federals trapped south of the Duck River. Bierce notes, "Had he succeeded, he would indubitably have bagged the whole bunch of us. As it was, he simply took position in front of us and gave us plenty of employment, but did not attack."[5] Schofield had gathered most of his forces at Columbia by the twenty-fifth, where he hunkered down and continued to fortify both banks of the river. Bierce observed, "For several days, in snow and rain, General Schofield's little army had crouched in its hastily constructed defenses."

Bierce was unaware of it, but General Thomas had in fact given Schofield a twofold mission. While Thomas needed Schofield's two army corps intact to complete his army at Nashville, he also wished Schofield to delay Hood's progress as long as possible to allow time for the other far-flung Union forces to concentrate at Nashville as well. The two goals were, to put it mildly, contradictory.

Although the two corps had made it safely to Columbia ahead of Hood, Rebel cavalry had been snapping at their heels all along the way. Now, with their back against the river and Hood's main force surrounding them, Schofield knew he must make a move soon or be trapped. On the night of the twenty-seventh, "we pulled up stakes and crossed to the north bank to continue our retreat to Nashville . . . It was high time too, for before noon the next day Forrest's cavalry forded the river a few miles above us and began pushing back on our own horse toward Spring Hill, ten miles in our rear, on our only good road."[6] Bierce in his memoir wonders "why our infantry was not immediately put in motion toward the threatened point, so vital to our safety," observing, "General Schofield could have told better than I. Howbeit, we lay inactive all day."[7] General Schofield did know why—General Thomas still wanted him to hold onto Columbia and the bridges across the Duck River.

Although the weak Union cavalry tried to halt Forrest's mounted warriors, they were unable to prevent the Rebel raiders from crossing the Duck on the twenty-eighth. General Wilson, Schofield's cavalry chief, advised him that Hood's infantry would soon be crossing as well and that he had best withdraw toward Franklin. Before sunrise on the twenty-ninth, the Confederates of Cheatham's Corps, led by General Patrick Cleburne's troops, were crossing at Davis's Ford, five miles east and upstream of Columbia. Notified of the Rebel maneuvers, Schofield dispatched Post's brigade over to the ford for a look-see while at the same time putting most of Fourth Corps on the road northward. "As a member of Colonel Post's staff, I was naturally favored with a good view of the performance." Bierce saw the head of Hood's army crossing over the recently created pontoon bridge, "a right pretty spectacle it would have been to one whom it did not concern." Unfortunately, it concerned Bierce and Second Brigade quite a bit.

"We formed in line of battle at a distance of perhaps a half-mile from the bridge-head, but the unending column of gray and steel gave us no more attention than if we had been a crowd of farmer-folk." Cheatham's Corps had more urgent business on hand than to brush aside "a small brigade whose only offense was curiosity."[8] All day long Bierce watched the seemingly endless line of infantry march over the bridge and off yonder toward the rear of the Yankee army. "It was an unnerving spectacle," Bierce says. Watching, Bierce and the others also knew that they would be among the very last in the army to be put on the road north. The race was on again. Following up in the rear, Bierce was not present to witness the next act of the drama; nonetheless, he knew of the dispute surrounding it.

Schofield had thrown General Stanley's lead division, "four thousand weak," ahead of the rest of the column to secure Spring Hill and forestall Hood's move to cut off the Federal column. "Why Stanley was not immediately effaced is still a matter of controversy," Bierce tells us. "Hood, who was early on the ground, declared that he gave the needful orders and tried vainly to enforce them; Cheatham, in command of his leading corps, that he did not."[9]

In fact it was a very near thing. Even as the rear elements of Schofield's force continued to resist on the north bank of the Duck River, Wilson's cavalrymen were trying to keep Rebel cavalry from cutting off the Federal escape route. General Wagner's infantry barely came up in time to repulse the Rebel cavalry at Spring Hill. Then, as Cleburne's foot-soldiers came up to support the Rebel horse, they were met with such hot fire from musket and artillery that it made them think the Federals were there in greater numbers than was actually the case. In truth, part of the problem lay in the fact that Hood had held back a large part of his infantry to protect his flanks, fearing a surprise attack from the Yankees. It was not an unreasonable precaution. Apparently Post's lone brigade, observing him cross the Duck River, had worried Hood enough to reserve troops to guard his left flank to prevent a potential Yankee attack. As a result, the Rebels were not "fustest with the mostest" at Spring Hill that day as they should have been.[10]

Confusion reigned among the Confederate high command at Spring Hill, with missed opportunities and confused orders foiling Hood's plans and compounding each error. The dispute over who was to blame for failing to destroy the Federals that afternoon continued on until well after the war. Bierce comments, "Doubtless the dispute is still being carried on between these chieftains from their beds of asphodel and moly in Elysium."[11] After the day's battle ended Hood, while frustrated, was still confident that he would crush his old West Point colleague Schofield on the morrow. He drew up the bulk of his army on an eminence just north of the Federal positions at Spring Hill, believing firmly that Schofield must either surrender or be annihilated. Schofield, however, had other ideas.

The day's fighting had ended with the Union troops still holding the village of Spring Hill and the Rebel army gathered in full strength just above it, ready to do battle the next day. That battle did not happen; the Yankees neither surrendered, nor were they crushed. What happened next is not in dispute, but how it was accomplished is. Bierce, who witnessed it all, simply explains that "fools are God's peculiar care, and one of his protective methods is the stupidity of other fools."[12] Other Union veterans who were there referred to it as "The Miracle of Spring Hill."

At his headquarters, General Hood was fully confident of success on the morrow. Although the day's fighting had made no decision, by all the rules of war Schofield was checkmated; there were Confederates before and behind him; he was surrounded and the closing noose around his little army would soon get even tighter. The next morning was bound to be a stunning victory for Hood, so he retired for the evening looking forward to a brighter day. Having been in the saddle all day and with a lame arm and only one leg, Hood had to have been in quite a bit of pain. It has been suggested by historians that Hood medicated himself with alcohol and perhaps with a good quantity of Laudanum (opium) to dull the pain; other than local gossip, however, no evidence of such has ever surfaced.[13] More likely, Hood was simply overcome with fatigue, as was much of his army. In any case, it was not unreasonable, whatever the general's mental and physical state, to expect his subordinate commanders to do their duty and be on guard against possible Federal maneuvers while he slept.

As Hood slumbered, Schofield resolved on a desperate gamble. Every man in his army was ordered to muffle his equipment and maintain a strict silence. Upon learning that the Franklin Pike was not blocked, rather than stand and fight the next day, Schofield would try to walk past the Rebels in the night.

It was a moonless night and the Rebels had their campfires burning bright, heightening the dark all around them. In truth, most of the Butternuts were dog-tired from marching and fighting, and they were hungry to boot—hardly at their best. Looking forward to a big fight the next day, most of the soldiers no doubt wanted to rest up before the battle. Along with the rest of Post's brigade, Bierce marched by the Johnnies in anticipatory silence:

> That night the entire Confederate army lay within a half mile of our road, while we all sneaked by, infantry, artillery, and trains. The enemy's camp-fires shone redly—miles of them—seemingly a stone's throw from our hurrying column. His men were plainly visible about them, cooking their suppers . . . At intervals of a few hundred yards we passed dim figures

on horseback by the roadside, enjoying the silence. Needless precaution; we could not have spoken if we had tried, for our hearts were in our throats . . . By daybreak our last man and last wagon had passed the fateful spot unchallenged, and our first were entering Franklin, ten miles away.[14]

When Hood awoke from his deep slumber he was, as one Rebel general described it, "wrathy as a rattlesnake, striking at everything."[15] In Hood's mind, everyone was to blame for Schofield's escape but himself, and he was in no mood to be gainsaid. In an even more belligerent mood than normal, Hood led the Army of Tennessee after the Yankees, resolved to do battle with them before they reached Nashville.

During the Battle of Franklin, Ambrose Bierce's division was with the rear echelon guarding the army's supply train. By the time the Battle of Franklin actually began, the supply train had already made it across the Harpeth River. General Wood and his staff were stationed on a bluff overlooking both river and town and for the duration of the battle had the benefit of a box seat to view the entire clash of arms. From his panoramic vantage point Bierce was well situated to observe the events unfolding down below. From his point of view, Bierce regarded the Union lines as none too secure: "Our line, with its reserve brigades, was about a mile and a half long, both flanks on the river, above and below the town—a mere bridgehead. It did not look a very formidable obstacle to the march of an army of more than forty thousand men. In a more tranquil temper than his failure at Spring Hill had put him into Hood would probably have passed around our left and turned us out with ease."[16]

Fortunately for Schofield, Hood was not "tranquil." Unfortunately, however, one particular divisional commander, General Wagner, had taken it into his head to post his men in a hastily built redoubt well ahead of the main Union line of defense. Bierce sharply criticizes the futility of Wagner having "foolishly posted" two weak brigades a half mile in front of the main line where—he observed—they were "needless for appraisal and powerless for resistance."

Bierce did not know the half of it. According to one observer on the scene, Wagner was drunk when he ordered the weak redoubt constructed and ordered two thirds of his division into it. A third brigade commander of Wagner's—General Opdycke—was insubordinate and outright refused to participate in what he rightly regarded as criminal folly. About the middle of the afternoon, Bierce and the other officers watching on the bluffs north of town spied the head of the Confederate column through their field glasses emerging from the range of hills two miles below Franklin. For the next few hours Bierce watched the Rebels change from marching columns into lines of battle, "impudently deploying on the level ground with a spectacular display of flags and glitter of arms." The parade-ground precision of the Confederate army's deployment gave a false air of serenity to the whole scene, further enhanced in Bierce's mind by the mild weather: "The sun burned crimson in a gray-blue sky through a delicate Indian-summer haze, as beautiful as a daydream in paradise."[17]

Finally, "with atoning rapidity," the Confederate Army of Tennessee moved forward and struck first at the exposed brigades of General Wagner's division. Bierce notes that the two vulnerable brigades, posted in an isolated redoubt well out in front of the main Federal trenches sitting astride the Columbia Pike, "had not stayed the advance for a moment, and as might have been foreseen were now a peril to the main line, which could protect itself only by the slaughter of its friends."[18]

Soon Federal soldiers were paying the price in blood for Wagner's mistake:

> Wagner's conquerors were pouring across the breastwork like water over a dam. The guns that had spared the fugitives had now no time to fire; their infantry supports gave way and for a space of more than two hundred yards in the very center of our line the assailants, mad with exultation, had everything their own way. From the right and the left their gray masses converged into the gap, pushed through, and then, spreading, turned our men out of the works so hardly held against the attack on their front. From our viewpoint on the bluff we could mark the constant widening of the gap, the steady encroachment of that blazing and smoking mass against its disordered opposition.[19]

At that moment it seemed from their vantage in the rear that "it is all up," as a fellow member of the staff confided to Bierce. Just then, however,

> a new tumult of musketry had broken loose. Colonel Emerson Opdycke had rushed his reserve brigade into the melee and was bitterly disputing the Confederate advantage. Other fresh regiments joined the countercharge, commanderless groups of retreating men returned to their work, and there ensued a hand-to-hand contest of incredible fury ... Such devil's work does not last long, and we had the great joy to see it ending, not as it began, but "more nearly to the heart's

desire" . . . The retaken guns in the embrasures pushed up towering clouds of white smoke; to east and to west along the reoccupied parapet ran a line of misty red till the spitfire crest was without a break from flank to flank.[20]

While this lively work had been doing in the center, there had been no lack of diligence elsewhere, and now all were as busy as bees. I have read of many "successive attacks" —"charge after charge"—but I think the only assaults after the first were those of the second Confederate lines and possibly some of the reserves; certainly there were no visible abatement and renewal of effort anywhere except where men who had been pushed out of the works backward tried to re-enter. And all the time there was fighting . . . Along the line of fire we could see, dimly in the smoke, mounted officers, singly and in small groups, attempting to force their horses across the slight parapet, but all went down . . . It was a great day for Confederates in the line for promotion.[21]

Bierce tells us that there was no general retreat: "At many points the fight continued, with lessening ferocity and lengthening range, well into the night. It became an affair of twinkling musketry and broad flares of artillery; then it sank to silence in the dark." As the Butternuts became exhausted and the attacks abated, Schofield quietly withdrew his rear-guard and continued his march north unmolested: "As at Spring Hill, daybreak found us on the road with all our impedimenta, except some of our wounded, and that night we encamped under the protecting guns of Thomas, at Nashville."[22]

15

A Son of the Gods
The Battle of Nashville and After

> **BATTLE**, *n*. A method of untying with the teeth of a political knot that would not yield to the tongue.

Lieutenant A. G. Bierce and the rest of "Schofield's little army" were safely under the protecting guns of General Thomas at Nashville. Soon, very soon, Hood's shattered legions also arrived on the outskirts of Nashville and encamped within sight of the city. The siege of Nashville had begun.[1]

Bierce had been in and out of Nashville throughout the war—first as sergeant, then as a shavetail lieutenant, and now as a seasoned staff officer. He had seen the city soon after its fall, had walked its streets when it was a bustling Federal supply base and garrison town, recovered from a near fatal wound here, and now he was back again as it was transformed into a bristling fortress, bursting to the seams with troops. How much intercourse Bierce had with the local populace of the city during the war remains something of a quandary. Although the native citizenry of Nashville resented the Yankee occupiers with a passion, the Yankees nevertheless succeeded in arousing other passions among the female population on occasion. For example, one officer described his future wife when first they met as a "Secesh scratch-cat"; their courtship was tempestuous, to say the least. It is estimated that some 187 Union officers married local women during or after the war, with many settling in the city when the guns went quiet. There were, of course, less respectable liaisons with the resident female population as well, for with the advent of the Federal army, an army of prostitutes also descended on the city.

Whether Bierce spent the largely idle first few weeks of December 1864 in such diversions is not known. Typically, he is silent on the subject. We do know that Bierce does express a certain amount of empathy for the enemy without and an ambivalence of the city's population within: "I sometimes wondered what were the feelings of those fellows, gazing over our heads at their own dwellings, where wives and children or their aged parents were perhaps suffering for the necessaries of life, and certainly . . . cowering under the tyranny and power of the barbarous Yankees."[2]

Within a few days of his arriving in Nashville, Lieutenant Bierce was notified of a new assignment. Special Order 119, dated December sixth, but effective from the first, reassigned him from the Second Brigade to the headquarters of the Third Division, now under the command of Brigadier General Samuel Beatty.[3] General Stanley, the former commander of Fourth Corps, had been wounded at Franklin and was replaced by the Third Division's commander, General Wood. General Beatty, in turn, stepped up to command the division. Bierce was certainly familiar with "General Sam" as a brigade commander, and the general apparently thought highly enough of Bierce to specifically request his services for his divisional staff.

When the Fourth Corps arrived, General Thomas assigned it to a sector of the defenses along the southwestern edge of the city. The Third Division's segment ran between the Granny White Pike (now Twelfth Avenue South) and the Hillsboro Pike (modern Twenty-first Avenue South). Where today academics and musicians brush shoulders in a sedate urban setting, in those days it was pleasant countryside graced by occasional antebellum villas and estates. General Wood took the opulent Belmont Mansion for his corps headquarters, while a short distance away General Sam and his staff settled down in the less grandiose but still spacious Lawrence Mansion, which lay on a ridge overlooking Granny White. Not far beyond, Hood's men also settled in. However, instead of comfortable mansions and well-stocked larders, the Johnnies bivouacked in damp and cold trenches, short of food and often shoeless. Regardless of hardships, Rebel artillery began plugging away at the two Yankee-held mansions, whose prominent locations made them excellent aiming marks.[4]

Meanwhile, as General Thomas set about methodically preparing his crushing blow against Hood's decimated army—and Washington waxed hysterical over the specter of Confederate hordes overrunning the Ohio Valley—Bierce and his fellow staffers at General Sam's headquarters generally had light duty and whiled away their idle hours playing practical jokes on one another. One such prank was aimed at a fellow member of their staff who fancied himself a ladies man. Bierce later enshrined the incident in a short piece entitled "The Major's Tale."[5] While Bierce fictionalized the tale, there is reason to believe it is based on actual circumstance.

The officer—to whom Bierce assigns the pseudonym of "Lt. Haberton"—constantly recounts his amorous conquests to his fellow staffers during their off hours. The self-styled Don Juan's bragging soon began to wear on the nerves of Beatty's other staffers, so the headquarters personnel devised a plan to put "Lt. Haberton" in his place.

In the story, Bierce describes General Beatty's headquarters as "a large dwelling which stood just behind our line of works . . . hastily abandoned by its civilian occupants, and who had left everything,"[6] including closets full of elegant clothing. Recalling that women's garb is still gracing a closet upstairs in the Lawrence mansion, the conspirators resolve to dress a teenage orderly in female attire to lure the lothario lieutenant into their snare. The orderly, barely seventeen, plays the part of a coquette to the tee, and "Lt. Haberton" is completely taken in. Chivalrously comforting the distraught Southern belle, Haberton moves closer to her on the drawing-room couch as he listens to her petition with sympathy. The other staff members pretend to go about their business, but in fact are striving mightily to suppress their laughter. As the lieutenant moves in on the object of his affection, suddenly there is "the distant boom of a heavy gun, followed by the approaching rush of the shot." Although Rebel guns lob shells periodically in their direction, on this occasion the shell finds its mark with a "boom, *whiz*, BANG!" The staffers spring to their feet with a start, realizing the shell has crashed into the house and exploded in an upper room above them. At the same time the terrified orderly hurriedly sheds pieces of his feminine attire left and right, literally not wishing to be caught dead in women's clothing. Everyone but Lt. Haberton bursts into raucous laughter.

In his story, Bierce declaims against men who boast of their amorous conquests to their peers, citing a number of reasons, then concluding: "There are, in short, no circumstances under which a man, even from the best of motives, or no motive at all, can relate his feats of love without distinctly lowering himself in the esteem of his male auditor; and herein lies a just punishment for such as kiss and tell. In my younger days I was myself not entirely out of favor with the ladies, and have a memory stored with much concerning them which doubtless I might put into acceptable narrative."[7]

Bierce unfortunately never composed that "acceptable narrative," but his attitude as expressed in this story goes far toward explaining the void we have regarding details his early love life. While it is possible (but unlikely) that the handsome and dashing young lieutenant remained wholly celibate for the entire four years of war, it would not have been due to lack of opportunity. Moreover, if Bierce did abstain from such pleasures of the flesh, he would have been the exception—not the rule—among soldiers of the Army of the Cumberland.

On December 15, The Rock of Chickamauga finally unleashed the full might of the Army of the Cumberland against Hood's decimated, ill-clad, and starving force. Lieutenant Bierce provides us a panoramic view of events as the battle begins:

> Six men are on a hill—a general and his staff. Below, in the gray fog of a winter morning, an army, which has left its

A Son of the Gods

entrenchments, is moving upon those of the enemy—creeping silently into position. In an hour the whole wide valley for miles to left and right will be all aroar with musketry stricken to seeming silence now and again by thunder claps of big guns. In the meantime the risen sun has burned a way through the fog, splendoring a part of the beleaguered city.

"Look at that, General," says an aide; "it is like enchantment."

"Go and enchant Colonel Post," said the general, without taking his field-glass from his eyes, "and tell him to pitch in as soon as he hears Smith's guns."[8]

The heavy fog that morning delayed the start of the Union offensive, but when it began at last, it progressed with an overwhelming inertia against the Rebel lines, crushing all before it like an inexorable tide. Thomas's cavalry corps first rode westward along the Harding Pike and then, supported by masses of infantry, wheeled south against the Rebels' far left flank. Fourth Corps, under General Wood, advanced southwestward on either side of the Hillsboro Pike against the Confederates facing them. Around two p.m. Beatty's

Officers on a hill observing the Battle of Nashville. Bierce wrote in "Sole Surviver": "Six men are on horseback on a hill—a general and his staff. Below, in the gray fog of a winter morning, an army, which has left its intrenchments, is moving upon those of the enemy." Photo by George F. Barnard, Library of Congress.

division assaulted Montgomery Hill, a commanding eminence held by the enemy, and easily carried the position. While Federal divisions on their right assaulted Hood's earthen redoubts and trench-works farther west along the Hillsboro Pike, late in the afternoon General Sam's troops again moved forward, assaulting the main Rebel line to their front and carrying it. Then the division wheeled eastward, advancing toward fortified enemy positions astride the Franklin Pike.

On the sixteenth, Beatty's men confronted the enemy "strongly posted" on Overton Knob, described as a "double ridge" that bracketed the Franklin Pike. This position was held in force and protected by a strong abatis, which successfully kept the Federals from getting close to the enemy entrenchments in any strength. Post's brigade was repulsed in its initial assault on the position. Bierce was present on the sixteenth to witness the struggle for this key eminence:

> During the two days of that memorable engagement the only reverse sustained by our arms was in the assault upon Overton Hill, a fortified salient of the Confederate line on the second day . . . I was serving on Gen. Beatty's staff, but

"Hurry Up and Wait," the Battle of Nashville. Union defensive line just before the beginning of the battle; a thick morning mist has delayed the start of the attack as men lounge about seemingly unconcerned. Photo by George F. Barnard, Library of Congress.

A Son of the Gods

The Battle of Nashville, looking westward from Fort Negley towards the sector held by Bierce's division. Photo by George F. Barnard, Library of Congress.

> was not doing duty that day, being disabled by a wound—just sitting in the saddle and looking on . . . The front of the enemy's earthworks was protected by an intricate abatis of felled trees denuded of their foliage and twigs. Through this obstacle a cat would have made slow progress, its passage by troops under fire was hopeless from the first.[9]

In addition to Post's veteran brigade, a brigade of relatively green Negro troops was also flung against the Rebel stronghold. Both brigades were chewed up in the initial attack. In a postwar article Bierce awards high praise to the United States Colored Volunteers in this battle, doing so at the expense of his own reputation.

The efforts of Post's brigade and the USCV were not in vain. In his haste at reinforcing Overton Hill, Hood stripped Shy's Hill, a key Confederate strongpoint, of sufficient troops to hold on to it. In so doing, Hood caused his entire left flank, already badly battered, to completely collapse. Uncharacteristically, the Army of Tennessee, bled dry at Franklin, demoralized by two weeks of cold and hunger, and finally defeated by the Yankees, fled in panic, with men dropping arms and equipment in their haste to escape. Some simply preferred Yankee captivity to more pointless suffering and sur-

The Battle of Nashville and After

rendered. Meanwhile, the Third Division was in the thick of it all throughout the Battle of Nashville. As a member of Beatty's staff, Bierce was kept busy conveying messages back and forth, making sure units hit their starting mark, observing, and then reporting back to General Sam on the brigades' and regiments' success as the battle progressed.

While in retrospect the outcome of the battle may seem to have been a foregone conclusion, it did not appear so at the time—certainly not to the high command in Washington. Ulysses S. Grant, whose ultimate victories at both Vicksburg and Petersburg dragged on for months, was impatient regarding the two weeks Thomas used to prepare his overwhelming victory at Nashville. When news arrived in Washington of Thomas's spectacular triumph, General Grant was in fact on the verge of coming to Nashville and eager to relieve Thomas in person for "not attacking in a timely manner." The Confederate army had resisted valiantly given its limited resources. Outnumbered and outgunned, the proud Army of Tennessee finally disintegrated under the crushing onslaught of General Thomas's relentless attacks. By the end of the battle, General Thomas, "The Rock of Chickamauga," had added another epithet—the Sledge of Nashville—to his laurels.

In the ensuing pursuit, Lieutenant Bierce continued to play an important role. One incident in particular proved memorable enough for him not only to pen a short story based on it, but also to comment on it more than once in his journalism. As Beatty's division advanced southward in pursuit of the beaten Butternuts, divisional headquarters received an urgent telegraph from one of the brigade commanders now ten miles distant: "Please relieve me," the dispatch read; "I am suffering from an attack of General Debility." Showing the missive to Lt. Bierce, General Sam sarcastically commented, "The ablest cavalry officer in the Confederate Army . . . I served under him in Mexico."[10]

In truth, at the Gap of Brentwood, Hood had somehow managed to rally the tattered fragments of his broken command and made a stand, which in turn forced his Yankee pursuers to form a line of battle. That this show of resistance was merely a rear guard to allow the bulk of the defeated survivors time to make good their escape southward was something unknown to the pursuers of Forth Corps at the time.[11] As a remedy for his brigadier's unexpected malaise, General Sam promptly prescribed three regiments of infantry and a battery of Rodman guns. He assigned Bierce to pilot the medicine to the suffering brigadier in person.

The precipitous retreat of the beaten Rebel army had caused the pursuing Yankee forces to disperse, and the front had ceased to be continuous. There was in fact a very real danger that large pockets of the enemy lay between headquarters and the front. Then too, Confederate cavalry always

205

A Son of the Gods

had an unpleasant knack of showing up in unexpected places to chastise careless Federal commanders. Nearly four years of battling the regiments of the Army of Tennessee had taught the soldiers of the Army of the Cumberland to have a healthy respect for their foe, even in defeat.

As Bierce later remembered, "I never felt so brave in all my life. I rode a hundred yards in advance, prepared to expostulate single-handed with the victorious enemy at whatever point I might encounter him."[12] Not content just to take the point, Lt. Bierce told the commander of the relief column he need not bother throwing out an advance guard to warn of an ambush—Bierce himself volunteered to draw any enemy fire: "I dashed forward through every open space into every suspicious looking wood and spurred to the crest of every hill, exposing myself recklessly to draw the Confederates' fire and disclose their position."[13] In a short story, "A Son of the Gods," Bierce gives us a detailed description of this incident:

> A breezy day and a sunny landscape. An open country to right and left and forward; behind, a wood. In the edge of this wood, facing the open but not venturing into it, long lines of troops, halted . . . Detached groups of horsemen are well in front—not altogether exposed—many of them intently regarding the crest of a hill a mile away in the direction of the interrupted advance. For this powerful army, moving in battle order through a forest, has met with a formidable obstacle—the open country. The crest of that gentle hill a mile away has a sinister look; it says, Beware! Along it runs a stone wall extending to left and right a great distance. Behind the wall is a hedge; behind the hedge are seen the tops of trees in rather straggling order. Among the trees—what? It is necessary to know . . .
>
> Galloping rapidly along in the edge of the open ground comes a young officer on a snow-white horse. His saddle blanket is scarlet . . . That such colors are fashionable in military life must be accepted as the most astonishing of all the phenomena of human vanity. They would seem to have been devised to increase the death-rate . . . This young officer is in full uniform, as if on parade. He is all agleam with bullion—a blue-and-gold edition of the Poetry of War . . .
>
> If the enemy has not retreated he is in force on that ridge. The investigator will encounter nothing less than a line-of-battle . . . But how ascertain if the enemy is there? There is but one way—somebody must go and see. The natural and

customary thing to do is to send forward a line of skirmishers. But in this case they will answer in the affirmative with all their lives; the enemy, crouching in double ranks behind the stone wall and in cover of the hedge, will wait until it is possible to count each assailant's teeth. At the first volley a half of the questioning line will fall, the other half before it can accomplish the predestined retreat. What a price to pay for gratified curiosity! At what a dear rate an army must sometimes purchase knowledge! "Let me pay all," says this gallant man—this military Christ![14]

In the story, the young staff officer does indeed find the enemy lying in wait and deliberately draws their fire to warn his comrades of the danger lurking, gallantly—if foolishly—dying in the process. Unfortunately his death is in vain, for his final *beau geste* provokes the Union ranks to surge forward to avenge him. In the actual event, the "son of the gods" did not sacrifice himself—vainly or otherwise. Ironically, even in his own day, literary critics castigated Bierce's war stories for not being "realistic" enough and singled out this "poor little battle-yarn" as highly improbable—one presumed expert went so far as to criticize this story and its "stage hero" as "magnificent, but it is not war."[15] Needless to say, this criticism roused Bierce's particular ire and he rejoined that in this case he "saw that thing done, just as related. True, the 'Son' escaped whole, but he 'rode out' all right, and if matters had been as we all believed them to be, and as he thought them himself, he would have been shot to rags."[16] The criticism of Bierce's war stories as unrealistic by persons who had never been to war may be why Bierce once defined Realism as "the art of depicting nature as it is seen by toads."[17]

When Bierce's relief column finally did reach the front, "there was no fighting: the forces of General Debility had conquered nobody but the brigade commander—his troops were holding their ground nobly, reading dime novels and playing draw poker pending the arrival of our succoring command."[18] General Thomas continued to run the tattered remnants of the once-proud Army of Tennessee into the ground. In the end it was not "General Debility" but General Winter that proved too great an adversary for the bluecoats to overcome. Wet winter weather hindered Union pursuit all the way into Alabama. Once the ragged survivors of Hood's ill-fated campaign made their way back across the Tennessee River, the pursuit had largely ended. January 5, 1865 found Bierce and the Third Division in Huntsville, Alabama, where they remained for the rest of the month.

Although General Thomas had accomplished what no other Federal army commander had done during the entire war—destroy a Confederate army in pitched battle and then force the survivors to flee in disarray—the administration denied him full recognition for his achievement. Instead of praise, in Washington, Grant and his devoted acolytes picked up the litany that Thomas was "slow" and repeated this chant over and over to Lincoln, his war cabinet, and the press, working diligently to dim the magnitude of his achievement.

According to official records, First Lieutenant Bierce's last hurrah was the Battle of Nashville. His head wound had continued to plague him, first during his misadventure behind the lines in Alabama and then during the Battle of Nashville, causing headaches, dizziness, and even fainting. Through channels Bierce made an official request for medical discharge. His military service record indicates that on January 16, 1865, Ambrose Bierce was given an honorable discharge from active service—sort of.

All surviving official documents testify that First Lieutenant Bierce was officially discharged on January 16, although the notification did not catch up with him until January 23. At that date, insofar as the United States Government was concerned, Lieutenant Bierce ceased to exist; citizen Bierce, veteran, came into being. Except we now know that that is not what happened.

The first few months of 1865 constitute one of those mysterious periods regarding Ambrose Bierce's life that has never been fully explained or understood. His end in Mexico is, of course, the most famous; we have also seen his immediate prewar life is similarly rife with unresolved contradictions. The events of Bierce's life from late January 1865 to the end of the war have never been fully explored, nor adequately explained.[19] Although Lieutenant Bierce did indeed receive his discharge papers, a diligent search of his widely scattered papers reveals that he continued on in active service—quite active service in fact—until at least late March 1865, if not later. Nowhere in any of his published works—fiction, nonfiction, or verse—does Ambrose Bierce refer to this lost period of military service. It is a blank. Yet moldering away in the archives is a notebook containing a daily log of the Carolina Campaign, written in Bierce's neat, precise, topographical engineer's hand. The journal chronicles his service, not with Thomas's Army of the Cumberland, but rather with Sherman's marauding hordes as they plundered and burned their way through the Carolinas—the ultimate campaign of the war.

While an adequate explanation is lacking for this lost period, there are some hints of what may have happened in the surviving fragments of Bierce's war correspondence. When Bierce returned to duty with the Second Brigade from his sick leave, he had resumed duty with his old unit. Bierce's old commander, General Hazen, was gone and the brigade was now under Philip Sidney Post. Hazen had been hand-picked by Sherman to command the Second Division, Fifteenth Corps for his March to the Sea. General Hazen, however, had specifically requested that Lieutenant Bierce be allowed to serve with him in his new command. In a missive dated September 30, from East Point, Georgia, Hazen states "that Lt. Bierce has served with me for a long time and I believe he will still be of great service to me, and greater service to the Govt. in such capacity than any other."[20]

The request was forwarded to Colonel Suman of the Ninth and approved; it was also forwarded to other commanders throughout the month of October, all of whom approved it and forwarded it on. However, General Wood, General Beatty, and Colonel Post seem never to have seen or signed off on it.

The problem was obvious. At the time, Fourth Corps was on the move and the situation at the front changing daily. It's highly unlikely that Hazen's request ever caught up with the proper authorities before Schofield's little army reached Nashville and merged with Thomas's command. Even if Bierce's commander—whether Post or Beatty—had seen and approved the request, as long as Hood's army lay squatting before Nashville, no one was going anywhere. We do know that Bierce remained with Beatty's division as far as Huntsville, Alabama. It was also at Huntsville that Bierce's discharge papers finally caught up with him. It may be that missives from General Hazen belatedly caught up with him here as well—but they have not been found.

Where the official record ends, Bierce's unpublished war journal picks up. The first entry, undated, is a "Topographical Survey of the Country South of Proctors Creek to East Point and [Tilroy] Creek, bounded East and West by Macon & Western RR and Chattahoochie River."[21] The survey's starting point was in the city of Atlanta on Peach Tree Street near First Methodist Church. The next several pages are taken up with the actual survey, consisting largely of numbers and brief notations, plus assorted scratch calculations. After the survey, Bierce has a summary of pioneering tools issued to three brigades (units not specified) and a Pioneer Corps, and seems dated to the twenty-eighth of January.[22] This seems to relate to the following entries about the Carolinas and not to his survey entries. The next two pages also show sketches of roads, indicating where sections have been corduroyed, and these are dated the twenty-ninth. Clearly, Bierce was still on active duty as of late January. Then, on a separate page, under the heading "Beaufort S. C. Jan. 21st 1865" is the notation "Contrabands in Pioneer Corps For Duty 82, Feb. 8th"[23] It is perhaps of some significance that according to Hazen's diary, from January 16 to 24,[24] his division was in camp at Beaufort, South Carolina, preparing for Sherman's next campaign. Even more to the point, on February 4, Hazen issued the following order: "Brigade commanders are directed to organize into pioneer corps for labor on roads and other purposes all

209

unarmed men and superfluous servants now or that may hereafter be in their commands. They are also directed to gather up able-bodied negroes for this service."[25]

Beginning on January 30, Lieutenant Bierce began keeping a meticulous, detailed daily log, noting distances traveled, character and conditions of road, weather, incidents, and nightly camp locations. Bierce continued entries up until March 24, when he crossed the Nuse River and encamped near Goldsboro, North Carolina. At the end of the daily log, Bierce summarizes the Carolina campaign in technical terms: miles marched, 461.5; days, 56; total amount of corduroying, 17,417 yards; total amount of bridging, 4,850 feet; etc. Unfortunately, nowhere in this meticulous journal—clearly the work of a military engineer of some skill—does Bierce mention which unit or command he was attached to. There are hints in the entries, however: "impeded by Third Division"; "Fourth Division at Maxwells Bridge"; "marched at 1 a.m. to the relief of Slocum"; "take a position inline on left of Right Wing."

Reading General Hazen's somewhat disjointed reports on the Carolina Campaign, the entries in Bierce's engineering log coincide almost exactly with Hazen's progress through the Carolinas in February and March, even down to similar phrases. The entries seem so similar, in fact, that one might suspect someone other than the general may have penned at least one of the reports—someone on his staff who had kept a detailed daily log—namely Lieutenant Bierce. Curiously, Bierce is not mentioned at all in Hazen's Carolina dispatches, although quite a number of staffers and other officers are. Again, we are left with an enigma.[26]

Following the Carolina Campaign log, the next dated entry—in the same neat and legible hand—is Bierce's diary of his vacation in Panama, which began on September 13, 1865. But that entry belongs to the next phase of Bierce's career, when the military campaigns had ceased—and the threat of death increased.

16

In High Cotton
Carpetbaggers, Confederates, and Corruption

> **PLUNDER**, *v.* To take the property of another without observing the decent and customary reticences of theft. To effect a change of ownership with the candid concomitance of a brass band. To wrest the wealth of A from B and leave C lamenting a vanishing opportunity.
>
> **RASCALITY**, *n.* Stupidity militant.

The close of hostilities in 1865 soon found Ambrose Bierce no longer a soldier, at least officially, yet still employed by the Federal government. The period immediately following the Carolina Campaign may have been occupied with conducting the Georgia survey which, though it fills the first section of his notebook, is not dated. While we cannot be certain as to its precise dating, in early January, northern and middle Georgia would have still been a very dangerous place for a lone Yankee surveyor and his pole-carriers if not accompanied by a strong escort.

Bierce's next employment is better documented, although one whose precise chronology also remains vague. In any case, Bierce was still in government employ, although definitely in a civilian capacity: "I was a minor official in the Treasury Department," he tells us, "engaged in performance of duties exceedingly disagreeable not only to the people of the vicinity, but to myself as well."[1] How he acquired this position after his discharge from the army, Bierce never explained. However the fact that his superior was a gentleman by the name of Sherburne Blake Eaton, the Special Treasury Agent for central Alabama, provides a clue as to how he came by this job. Eaton, like Bierce, was a former military man, a captain in the 124th Ohio Volunteer Infantry. Like Bierce, Eaton had served on the staff of General

Hazen. Unlike Bierce, however, Eaton was the scion of privilege; he had attended the prestigious Phillips Academy in Andover, Massachusetts and then attended the Ivy League Brown University. Rather than entering the service as a lowly private, Eaton was appointed First Lieutenant in the 124th OVI in October 1862 and then promoted to captain by June of the following year. However, like Bierce, Eaton was severely wounded during the Atlanta Campaign and resigned his commission in November 1864.[2] So Eaton knew Bierce's worth in a difficult situation and also knew that Bierce was now at loose ends. Captain Eaton needed no persuading to hire Bierce as his assistant in his "disagreeable" but highly lucrative endeavor.

As "agency aide" to Special Agent Eaton in the early postwar South, Bierce's task was to track down "captured and abandoned property." The property in question consisted mostly of abandoned plantations and cotton. With the plantation owners mostly dead or fled and regular agriculture at a standstill, abandoned plantations were less of a problem—and less profitable—than the large quantities of cotton still at large. Hidden throughout the countryside of central Alabama were large stockpiles of cotton in bales, ready to be shipped. Moreover, immediately after the war there was a ready market for this cotton, both up north and overseas. With cotton at a going rate of $500 per bale, there were large and easy profits to be made in 1865.

Even before the guns had fallen silent, treasury agents were descending on the Deep South seeking contraband cotton. Most of the Southern planters had already sold their crops to the Confederate government, who paid them in virtually worthless paper. The Federal government therefore claimed all such cotton sold to Rebel authorities as contraband of war. The penurious Southern planters, however, had a far different view of the situation.

On June 1, 1865, the union commandant in Opalika, east of Selma, published a notice to the civilian subjects of his military district, and similar notices published elsewhere in the state under the heel of occupation by the Yankee's Sixteenth Corps. It read, in part, "all stores of whatever nature will be collected, belonging to the United States, which includes all property in the hands of Confederate States officials or private parties, belonging to the Government of the Confederate State....in compliance with the foregoing instructions, all persons in this vicinity having either Federal or Confederate property in their possession will report at once to the Head Quarters with such property and turn same over to the Commanding Officer at this place." That the colonel publishing the notice was wildly optimistic at its compliance goes without saying. Similarly, his other notice, published on the same day that, "the possession of fire-arm by citizens at this time is unnecessary to good order....it is therefore Ordered that all having fire-arms in this community turn them over at these Head Quarters immediately for safe keeping," was honored more in the breach than the observance. There was no rush by the loyal (or otherwise) citizenry of the state to obey either order.[3]

Bierce describes, "The original owners . . . manifested an unamiable reluctance to give it {cotton} up, for if they could market it for themselves it would more than recoup them for all their losses in the war."[4] The original owners concealed the bales in swamps and other obscure locations, then fabricated forged affidavits of ownership or otherwise sought to obliterate evidence of any sale to the Confederacy. Adding to the difficulty of the situation was the way in which the Treasury Department chose to pay its agents and employees for their sometimes-hazardous work. Rather than receiving a straight salary, the agents were paid out of the proceeds from the sales of the confiscated cotton. The more cotton they seized, the more money the agents made. Of course, if some of that cotton was sold on the sly by the agents themselves, the profits realized would be all the greater. The incentive for dishonesty and official corruption was therefore almost boundless. Secretary of the Treasury McCulloch later said, "I am sure I sent some honest cotton agents South; but it sometimes seems very doubtful whether any of them remained honest very long."[5] While perhaps not among the worst offenders sent South, Captain Eaton—with the First Agency—was also not among the least: in one of his transactions, he reported total receipts of $27,799.48 and total expenses $27,799.48.[6] Later, as a well-heeled corporate lawyer in New York, Eaton declaimed against the very system of commission that proved so lucrative to him.[7]

Complicating matters even more, following the collapse of the Confederate government, virtually all law and order had disappeared in the South, especially in rural areas. Martial law had been enacted to be sure, but Federal authority was effective "only within areas covered by the guns of isolated forts." Beyond these hated Yankee outposts, lawlessness prevailed. Vigilantism—or as Bierce put it, "the immemorial laws of self-preservation and retaliation"—was the order of the day in Alabama and elsewhere in the South. Bierce notes that the retaliation part was "liberally interpreted" against straggling Yankee soldiers and "too zealous government officials."[8]

When Special Agent Eaton first arrived in Selma, "the great cotton centre of the state,"[9] he arrived in time to act as "sole mourner" at the funeral of his predecessor. Only a few days later, two Federal marshals' bodies were found just outside Selma by the roadside with their throats cut. Others in the employ of the United States simply disappeared without a trace. Both Bierce and Eaton had fought in some of the bloodiest battles of the war, but neither had experienced such a sense of personal danger as they did now. In a very real sense, Selma—and most of the Deep South—was still very much a war zone. Despite the danger, Bierce could not find it in him to blame the local populace. The "better class," he claimed, was not a part of the lawlessness; but those who were a party to it, he tells us, were "impoverished and smarting with a sense of defeat."

In April 1865, General Wilson's Yankee cavalry had come through Selma and fought General Forrest's Rebel horsemen there. In the battle and its aftermath, a good part of the city went up in flames—although local Negroes were also blamed for feeding the fires.[10] There was still a great deal of residual bitterness in Selma toward Yankees of any ilk as a result. Although organized resistance had ceased, many Confederate soldiers never formally surrendered; they simply went home. "Men trained in the use of arms did not consider themselves included in the surrender," Biérce explains, "and conscientiously believed it both right and expedient to prolong the struggle by private enterprise."[11]

In truth, what Ambrose Bierce was witness to—although he never uses the name—were the beginnings of the Ku Klux Klan. Bierce's erstwhile former corps commander, the infamous "Oh-Oh!" Howard, was now head of the Freedman's Bureau and had a more general familiarity with it. Unfortunately, General Howard proved even more incompetent in dealing with the problem of the Klan than he had been in dealing with the Confederate army.

The vigilante organization now known as the Ku Klux Klan was begun in Pulaski, Tennessee in December 1865. Eight Confederate veterans originally started it, and supposedly it had neither racial nor political goals to begin with. Prohibited by law from gainful employment, the former Rebels ostensibly formed it as a "social" organization to while away their idle hours and much of its activities were initially dismissed as pranks and drunken hijinks.[12] Throughout the South, similarly embittered groups of veterans arose more or less spontaneously almost as soon as the Rebel armies had ceased to exist, and they soon began taking law into their own hands where none now existed. At first this violence was largely aimed at the Yankee occupiers and the white Southern loyalists among them rather than at indigenous blacks. As these separate vigilante groups grew in strength, they merged into a more coherent underground organization with famed former cavalry leader Nathan Bedford Forrest as its nominal head. Bierce's memoir about his spell as an assistant Treasury agent unwittingly chronicles the first stirrings of this infamous movement.

Fortunately for Bierce not all the locals around Selma were unremittingly hostile to the newly arrived Yankee agents. For one thing, the owners of contraband cotton still needed to get it to market, and to that end bribery was far more effective than violence. For example, Bierce relates one case where he learned of one hidden cache of cotton, some seven hundred bales' worth, but could not locate its hiding place. Two Southern gentlemen hinted to Bierce that they knew its whereabouts, and for several months Bierce played a polite cat-and-mouse game with them. Bierce, suffering from the unfortunate affliction of honesty, could not be bribed. The two men, for their part, did not want to accept a mere twenty-five percent commission for it, hoping to realize a greater profit. While Bierce and the two men maintained a cordial relationship, neither side would compromise and the hidden cotton never came to light.

Freebooters from all over were drawn to the South by the lure of easy money. These individuals descended on Dixie to make a profit any way they could—mainly by dealing in contraband cotton. One such individual, who Bierce named "Jack Harris," was a particularly colorful character. Jack offered a bribe for Bierce if he would simply sign some blank shipping permits, explaining that he knew where a thousand bales were stored. In the dark of night he proposed to seize—steal—them, load them onto a waiting steamboat, and then ship them to Cuba nonstop. Bierce, however, had to disappoint his "California adventurer" friend. Given the nature of his job and his unfortunate proclivity for honesty, in the normal scheme of things, Treasury Aide Bierce should have ended up dead, as so many fellow officials did. Bierce attributes his survival to having made the acquaintance of two young Southern gentlemen, who he simply calls "Charles" and "Frank."

The sons of a wealthy citizen of Selma, Charles and Frank were still persons of considerable influence in the community despite the war's misfortunes. They had both been officers in the Confederate Army, and with these two former foes Bierce felt a great sense of comradeship. Men who have been in war—even on opposing sides—often feel more comradery with one another than with the civilians who did not share their experiences. So it was with Bierce and his two Rebel friends. Because Charles and Frank's family had high social standing in the community, Bierce gained a certain degree of immunity when they befriended him. In addition to their family's status, Charles and Frank were also known to be quick on the trigger and, Bierce tells us, "would rather fight a duel than eat—nay, drink." The two, needless to say, were quite fond of both food and drink.

Although there was never any formal arrangement between Bierce and his friends, Charles and Frank more or less served as unofficial bodyguards during Bierce's sojourn in Selma. Bierce cites one example of the value of their comradeship: one night after an evening of revelry, Bierce, the two brothers, and another drinking companion were walking down the darkened streets of Selma. They became aware that someone was following them. Even after they confronted the man, he continued to shadow them most suspiciously. Then, without a word, Frank grabbed Bierce's gun from out of his pocket (throughout his life, Bierce always went about armed), whirled around and shot the man in the leg. The mysterious man was taken to a nearby hotel, where his leg was amputated. Bierce paid the doctor and hotel bill and even paid the mysterious stranger's fare back to Mobile, Alabama. Curiously, the man never revealed his name or purpose in following them. Neither Bierce nor the brothers were punished for the shooting, although Frank was ultimately fined five dollars for "disorderly conduct."

Bierce's duties as aide to Treasury Agent Eaton involved far more dangerous scrapes than his late-night encounter in Selma. On one occasion, Bierce accompanied Eaton down the Tombigbee River with a large load of six hundred bales of government cotton to market. As a precaution against marauders, Bierce and Eaton picked up a squad of soldiers to act as guard. With bales of cotton piled all about the decks, the steamboat lazily made its way downstream. Late one afternoon, as the boat rounded a bend and the current pulled them close to the left bank of the river, a hail of lead suddenly broke the tranquility as a volley of buckshot and bullets came hurling at them from the nearby shore.

Bierce could see a swarm of men shooting at them from cover. The captain and the pilot abandoned their posts, and only Bierce and one other man returned fire. It turns out that the military guard had come aboard without any ammunition for their guns and were cowering among the bales along with the crew. Besides Bierce's own pocket pistol, he could hear the distinct sound of a "cannon" firing from the front of the boat. Bierce kept firing until his bullets were gone. Then, knowing that capture meant certain death, Bierce seized the cowering pilot, put the empty pistol to his head, and threatened his life if he did not steer the steamboat back into the center of the river and out of harm's way.

As the firing from shore gradually receded, Bierce looked about for the source of the cannon fire he'd heard. On the front deck, lying prone and in the act of sighting his old-fashioned horse pistol at the raiders, was a scruffy-looking individual. The man, "clad in faded butternut," was bareheaded with long unkempt hair. He was a former Confederate soldier who had decided to make common cause with the Yankees on board. The "cannon" Bierce had had heard was the sound of the two-foot-long horse pistol discharging. When Bierce thanked the Johnny Reb for his help, he asked him why he'd joined in the fight. The Rebel drawled in reply, "I hadn't ary a cent, so thought I'd jist kinder work my passage."[13] While Ambrose Bierce carried out the duties of his office with honesty, courage, and diligence, it is clear that among Federal officials in Alabama he was in a distinct minority. Even more than the brutality and senselessness of the war, the rampant corruption and abuse of power that Bierce witnessed in the Reconstruction South disillusioned him. This was not what he'd fought and was almost killed for.

After months facing danger equal to or worse than anything he'd ever experienced during the war, the stress eventually took its toll on Bierce. In September 1865, Bierce decided to take a break and headed down to New Orleans for a vacation.

While enjoying the pleasures of the Crescent City, on an impulse Bierce boarded a ship to the tropics and spent several weeks in Colon ("Aspinwall") Panama.[14] While the change of scene proved salubrious for the young veteran, it also gave him a fresh perspective about his work "in Alabam." While it had not been his original intent, when Bierce returned to the South, it would be a return of limited duration.

17

Phantoms and Presentiments

> **CONTROVERSY**, *n*. A battle in which spittle or ink replaces the injurious cannonball and the inconsiderate bayonet.

After his sojourn to Panama, Ambrose Bierce resolved to shake the Alabama dust from his boots and seek out lands less soiled by the "carnival of corruption." In so doing, it is likely Bierce believed he was shedding the last vestiges of the war and exorcising all its dark memories. However, like so many men who fought in the war and earnestly sought to leave its horrors behind them, Bierce could not keep the vivid memories of this period buried. Throughout the remainder of his life, these "phantoms of the blood stained period" remained with him to haunt his dreams and even bedevil his waking hours. While many veterans returned to hearth and home and successfully resumed their former life, that was not to be for Ambrose Bierce.

Upon returning from Panama in the fall of 1865, by happy circumstance Bierce found a letter from his old commander, General William B. Hazen, awaiting him. Hazen offered him a post as "engineering attaché" on a projected expedition through Indian Territory. Disillusioned with the corruption he saw all around him in the Reconstruction South, Bierce welcomed Hazen's invitation. Bierce had originally sought discharge on the basis of his wounds and thought that civilian life would be less stressful. After experiencing a taste of that life, however, the military life did not seem quite so bad after all. Hazen promised Bierce a commission—a captaincy—and in fact, judging by the correspondence that tried to catch up with him as he ventured west, the War Office did indeed want him in the regular army.

It took awhile before Hazen's expedition was ready, but even so, the military paperwork was still not complete before Bierce set out with Hazen on the western survey. Notice of Bierce's appointment as Second Lieutenant—subject to his approval—followed him about the country: even Washington apparently didn't know where Hazen was at any given point. While the original date of his appointment was May 26, 1866, it doesn't seem to have caught up to Bierce until April 1867—apparently sent care of his brother Albert at the Treasury Department in San Francisco.[1] Regarding his postwar military service (or lack thereof), Bierce was also appointed brevet major in addition to his documented commission as second lieutenant in the Fifth Infantry Regiment. The brevet commission was backdated to March 13, 1865, although the document was not actually signed by President Andrew Johnson until August 3, 1866. The brevet appointment, however, seems to have been purely honorary, "for distinguished service during the war."[2]

It has been suggested that Bierce had originally asked Hazen for a captaincy in the regulars, and when offered only the rank of second lieutenant he felt slighted by the offer and turned it down. However, in the postwar army many who had served several ranks higher reverted to a lower rank once the fighting stopped. Regardless, during his postwar years Bierce was alternately referred to formally as lieutenant, captain, and major, much to the confusion of his modern chroniclers.

In truth, by the time that Ambrose Bierce reached California and the offer of commission had finally caught up with him, the young veteran had had a change of heart yet again regarding a military career. His Boswell and publisher, Walter Neale, averred that Bierce left the choice of a military versus a literary career up to a coin toss.[3] Whether Bierce actually told him this or it is one of Neale's confabulations, we can't be sure. What we know for certain is that rather than accepting the commission, Bierce decided instead to settle in bustling San Francisco and give civilian life another try. After obtaining a position with the Treasury Department—again—Bierce amused himself with his first forays into writing. He quickly developed a local reputation for his sharp wit, and his fame began to spread well beyond the confines of San Francisco. By the time he left for England, Bierce was beginning to develop a national reputation.[4]

Curiously, during this early period of Bierce's journalistic career and as he was establishing his reputation as a writer, his literary output did not include anything relating to the Civil War, still fresh in everyone's memory. Rather, it was his acute observations on contemporary people and events and his satirical pieces that were his initial claim to fame. It was several years before Ambrose Bierce saw fit to write about the Civil War. One theory holds that it was President Garfield's assassination in 1881 that sparked Bierce's writing about the Civil War. As General Rosecrans's chief of staff, Garfield was certainly someone who Bierce was familiar with and would have met on occasion. To what degree this fellow veteran's death itself moved Bierce enough to draw from the deep well of his war memories is hard to say. We do know that Bierce took note of it in an article for his column, but we also know that he began writing about the war well before Garfield's death.

It has been previously assumed that Bierce's writings on the Civil War only began with the publication of his classic, "What I Saw of Shiloh," in

1881. In fact, as we now know, that memoir was originally published in 1874 during his British period, well before the death of Garfield, and it was simply reprinted in the states in 1881. It is also important to note that Bierce made another early foray into the subject of the Civil War in 1878 with his short article, "On Military Executions," after reading an article on the same subject in a British magazine.[5] Bierce's literary and journalistic output on the Civil War gained steam throughout the 1880s and continued on at a steady pace into the 1890s and early 1900s. His prose output on the war is certainly among his best known, with both fiction and nonfiction works earning him laurels. Even in his poetry, Bierce could not refrain from discussions about the war and the polemics surrounding it.

Beginning in the 1880s and continuing on up to the year before his disappearance, Bierce also engaged in a running battle with the government bureaucracy over back pay and pensions. While the documentation is voluminous, it is also incomplete: as we've seen, his official discharge dated to January 16, 1865, yet from his own notebook it is clear he served in Georgia and the Carolinas. Because there is no record of his service there, it may be that he was never paid for that period of service. The only hint of it is a document issued by the Adjutant General of the State of Indiana, dated January 14, 1886; it summarizes his service record, ending with the cryptic notation: "Resigned Jan. 16, 1865—Expiration of term (erroneous)."[6] Eventually Bierce was granted a pension of sorts, but it seems that the issue of back pay was never fully resolved.

As often as not, contemporary postwar events were what inspired Bierce's reminisces about the war. Well after the 1860s, current events and incidents continued to stir passionate debates related to controversial war topics. In the *Century Magazine* war series, later issued in book form as the classic *Battles and Leaders of the Civil War*, former generals fought the old battles all over again. In magazines and newspapers, North and South, old controversies simmered on. The only difference between their wartime and postwar battles, aside from it being ink instead of blood being shed, was that the combatants were usually generals on the same side fighting each other rather than their old enemies. Shiloh, Chickamauga, Spring Hill, and Franklin continued to be fought and refought—as they still are today.

The deaths of prominent personalities such as Grant or Jefferson Davis also could not pass without comment by Bierce. Then too, the appointment of General "Oh-Oh!" Howard—the butcher of Pickett's Mill—to head a historical journal particularly galled him. To Bierce, Howard's pompous piety and military incompetence were bad enough; becoming the arbiter of the historical record and enshrining his lies for posterity was too much for the survivor of the general's butchery. These and other incidents were grist for

Bierce's journalistic mill. Less obvious, but also relevant to A. G.'s preoccupation with his Civil War years, was his predilection for drawing on the South as a backdrop for his fantastic fiction. For example one of his classic ghost stories, "The Moonlit Road," is set in Nashville. Other bizarre tales seem to have been inspired by contemporary news items from the South, even when he changed details: "The Baby Tramp" (1891), for example, is set in the Midwest, but the motif of a rain of blood mentioned in passing was probably based on a real but uncanny news item emanating from Bath, Kentucky.[7]

Similarly, "The Difficulty of Crossing a Field," one of several short pieces dealing with mysterious disappearances, is set in prewar Alabama. We know, however, that it was actually based on an odd news item emanating from postwar Gallatin, Tennessee, a place Bierce had visited during the war. The story originated with a traveling salesman named Mulhattan, whose nom de plume was "Orange Blossom" and who, like Bierce, was a notorious teller of tall tales and drinker of strong drinks. In fact, Mulhattan was even fonder of intoxicating spirits than Bierce was, and when in his cups he would turn local new items into magnificent edifices of imaginative writing. It is believed that Mulhattan heard the story of a farmer's disappearance in Gallatin from locals while staying at the hotel there.

The disappearance tale of a Mr. Williamson (a.k.a. David Lang) emanated from a letter by "Orange Blossom" to the *Cincinnati Inquirer* during the 1880s, whose editors also had a strong affinity for fantastic news pieces (pigmy Indians, sightings of woolly mammoths, ghost stories, etc.). During the era when Bierce was active as an editor and journalist, it was not uncommon for one newspaper to reprint news items from papers elsewhere in the country. The fact that the family of General Hazen's wife owned the *Inquirer* may have been more than mere coincidence in this regard. Regardless, such strange tales appealed to Bierce's offbeat sensibilities and his taste for the bizarre.[8]

While it is best left to academia to register expert opinion regarding the quality of Bierce's poetic output, it should be noted that Bierce's Civil War poetry is not well read even among his devotees. Stylistically, Bierce's poems are somewhat odd. His verse, although impassioned, is not romantic, realist, or abstract. His poetry was thus at odds with both nineteenth- and twentieth-century trends in verse and literature. Bierce's Civil War verse, in fact, more closely resembles argumentative essays than pure poetry. As with his prose, one finds that contemporary events that impinge on memories of the war are often what inspire Bierce to take a turn for the verse. Although readers of his daily columns would doubtless have understood the references in such argumentative verse, a modern reader of such poetry would likely be at a loss to understand their context.

Take for example, "The Confederate Flags."[9] In this piece, Bierce scolds "you veterans and heroes" who are upset at President Chester A. Arthur's return of captured Confederate war banners. Even with the war long over, President Arthur's gracious gesture of returning the captured Rebel flags incurred the wrath of many Northerners. For many years after the war, "waving the bloody shirt" was a surefire way for demagogues to get votes in the North. Bierce wades into this controversy with gusto. At times, "The Confederate Flags" reads more like a religious sermon scolding the unrighteous than a poem appealing to emotions. As with his argumentative prose, Bierce leaves no doubt about his opinion of the controversy:

> Give back the foolish flags whose bearers fell,
> Too valiant to forsake them.
> Is it presumptuous, this counsel? Well,
> I helped to take them.

In another poem, "The Hesitating Veteran" (1901),[10] Bierce makes a rare postwar reference to his youthful idealism that "made my heart beat faster then." While the poem does make a passing nod to the contemporary issue of Negro voting rights, his affirmation of it to modern ears sounds tepid at best. The dominant tone of Bierce's verse here seems more of a nod to the political agnosticism of his older years:

> I know what uniform I wore—
> O, that I knew which side I fought for!

On another occasion, a northern politician's inflammatory Memorial Day speech also drew Bierce's wrath. "To E. S. Salomon" is Bierce's poetic rebuttal to the orator's criticism over the decorating of the graves of Confederate dead.[11] Originally known as "Decoration Day," Memorial Day originated not as a day commemorating America's war dead in general but as a day specifically to commemorate Civil War dead; some have even argued that it was first done to honor just the Confederate dead. As with other postwar polemics, E. S. Salomon's intemperate remarks provoked the full fury of Bierce's not inconsiderable talent for invective:

> The brave respect the brave. The brave
> Respect the dead; but you—you draw
> That ancient blade, the ass's jaw,
> And shake it o'er a hero's grave.

Although Bierce has often been compared to Poe (he hated that comparison) and more appropriately to Rudyard Kipling, the nearest analogy one might draw with regard to his verse is to the poetry of Alexander Pope. While perhaps not close in either meter or rhyme, Bierce's odd mix of sarcasm and rationalism in his verse seems more at home in the eighteenth century than in the nineteenth or twentieth.

While he may have had some spats with members of his regiment during the war, in the postwar era Bierce remained in contact with his fellow veterans of the Ninth Indiana and maintained membership in their veterans association. As it often does, time mellowed the men who had shared privation and risked death together, and whatever their wartime differences may have been, they looked back on their wartime service with pride and wonder at all they had done and survived. On occasion, Bierce also contributed to the regiment's annual reunion proceedings. He also had contacts with individual veterans, some from the Rebel side, and corresponded with the sons of those he had fought with in the war. Even in his extensive personal correspondence with various civilian friends, memories of the war would sometimes well up and intrude into the letters. In a letter to his female friend Harriet Hershburg, for example, Bierce teasingly complains that thoughts of her interrupted his reverie about "the march of a column of troops from Readyville, Tennessee to Woodbury, Tennessee"—an incident from the Tullahoma Campaign.[12] On another occasion, Bierce writes about how the sight of autumn leaves being blown by the wind against a fence reminds him of soldiers huddled against a wall, summoning up courage for another charge at the enemy.

The outbreak of the Spanish-American War could not fail to stir old memories of the former conflict in Bierce. He temporarily changed the name of his column to "War Topics," and while some of the articles dealt solely with contemporary military issues, comparisons with the Late Unpleasantness also inevitably arose. On one occasion, reading some comment pontificating on the virtuous nature of volunteers for the war, Bierce delivered an irascible lecture in his column on the less-than-virtuous nature of him and his fellow soldiers during the Civil War. Bierce was only too aware of the false patriotism that lay behind this new war—a war in large part fomented by his publisher and benefactor, William Randolph Hearst. When Bierce dusted off his old essay, "What I Saw at Shiloh," it was modified and the context in which it appeared in the newspaper in 1898 was far different than when it was originally published.[13]

The Spanish-American War stirred contradictory emotions in Bierce. On the one hand, it rekindled the old warhorse in him with a desire to serve again—as other former Confederate and Union officers were doing. On the other hand, Bierce could easily see through all the jingoism surrounding the war—much of which his own newspaper was the source. Bierce the old soldier continued to coexist with Bierce the cynic, even into his later years. At one point Bierce even delivered a lecture at the US Army's War College in Washington, D.C. On Saturday, October 3, 1908, Bierce delivered a lecture on his "theory and system of giving oral commands" in combat. While a transcript of the speech does not exist—although a phonograph recording of it may have been made—from an incident related by his publisher, we do have a hint of what Bierce's ideas on the subject may have been.

Walter Neale, Bierce's publisher and early chronicler, tells of an incident that occurred while he was visiting Bierce at the Army and Navy Club in Washington, D.C. While there with Neale, one time Bierce got on the subject of delivering commands in battle, telling Neale "that he thought oral commands in the field should be given slowly, in rolling tones, as carrying several times farther than sharp and crisp orders." Apparently some young popinjay of an officer in the club took issue with Bierce's ideas. Neale tells us that Bierce uncharacteristically "subsided" instead of coming back with a sharp verbal retort.[14] Standing on the podium at the War College in 1908 was neither Bierce the cynic, nor Bierce the satirist, nor Bierce the muckraking journalist. Rather it was Major Ambrose Bierce, the combat-tested veteran, delivering a serious military lecture before an audience of professional soldiers. Unlike the supercilious subaltern who gainsaid him at the club, the senior officers present listened respectfully to Bierce and were impressed with his ideas.[15]

It is clear that after the war Bierce made a concerted effort to put memories of the conflict behind him. Between his travels, his business ventures, his marriage, and his witty journalism, Bierce succeeded in burying the "bloodstained" memories for several years. Inevitably, however, the "phantoms" of that period refused to stay buried. They haunted not only his mind but the minds of other contemporaries as well. In issues of the day, the war, like Duncan's ghost, continued to haunt Bierce. The Civil War had affected Bierce profoundly, and in the end there could be no forgetting it. In time, moreover, the past became a prologue for Bierce. Scattered throughout his war literature are strong comments about how he too should have died in battle and about how he envied those who did. Similar to veterans of more modern conflicts, Bierce possessed a sense of survivor's guilt that was revealed in his writing—a guilt that at times almost became a sense of foreboding and perhaps in the end became a self-fulfilling prophecy.

Although we have the benefit of hindsight, many of Bierce's later tales in retrospect do take on an almost prophetic aspect. Stories such as "A Resumed Identity"—in which the protagonist awakens after decades of amnesia and finds himself, like Rip Van Winkle, suddenly an old man, and then dies on the battlefield of his youth—make it difficult to avoid the idea that they foreshadow Bierce's own ending. While the term has fallen into disuse, during the Civil War the phenomenon of the "presentiment" was quite common among combatants of both sides. A presentiment is an overwhelming sense that one's death is imminent. Veterans who wrote about the phenomenon firmly believed in such an intuition, and it invariably proved fatal. Bierce himself may not have used that precise word; however about a year after his disappearance, one of his comrades of the Ninth, Captain Alexander Whitehall, recalled the tone of Bierce's final letter to him and used that term in reference to Bierce's final words. To what extent Bierce's belief in such things influenced his own fate one cannot be sure, but it surely had some influence on his thinking in the period leading up to his own end.[16]

As Bierce aged and his health—impaired in youth and magnified by time—declined, thoughts about his own mortality grew. Then, when another civil war broke out south of the border, close to where his old regiment had spent its last days in service, it could not have failed to stir more thoughts about Bierce's own fate.

As the final act of his life played out, it was apparent that the Civil War continued to occupy his thoughts and actions to the very end. Although it was only four years out of his life, "The Period of Honorable Strife" left an indelible mark on Ambrose Bierce to the end.

Epilogue

The Difficulty of Crossing a Battlefield

> "Death is not the end; there remains the litigation of the estate."
> —Bierce

Although details of Bierce's end will forever remain a mystery, some of the circumstances seem clear. A man whose writings are full of uncanny events, bizarre deaths, mysterious disappearances, and deadly ironies voluntarily puts himself in harm's way. That Bierce would fall prey to a fate similar to what he wrote about seems more than mere chance. By now, however, we may safely presume him dead. There remains but the litigation, as it were.[1]

What was Ambrose Bierce's exact motivation for his sojourn south of the border? Did he really wish to visit South America by way of war-torn Mexico? Did he intend to commit suicide? Or did he use the trip as a cover to disappear from the scene only to start anew elsewhere? The questions are endless. One breathless biographer has even speculated that Bierce didn't go to Mexico at all. Instead, he traveled to the Grand Canyon and shot himself in some obscure valley. Mexico or the Grand Canyon, if Bierce had simply wished to commit suicide he easily could have done so at home. No; something more complex than simple suicide was at play with the elder Bierce, although it led to the same place.

Before his final trip, Ambrose Bierce gave away his collection of books, "save the few volumes which were presented to the University."[2] Only a few years before, Bierce wrote to a friend discussing an infamous murder trial. He mentions the case of Dr. Bowere, who was tried for murdering his wife and "the really serious offense of stealing books from a public library."[3] Obviously, Bierce valued books highly—his own collection even more so. A man does not give away his prized possessions if he is expecting to return. When Bierce left on his final sojourn, clearly it was going to be a one-way trip. While Miss Carrie Christianson, his loyal secretary, consigned much of his personal correspondence to the flames, she did summarize some of his final letters. Other stray pieces of correspondence also survived the secretary's

Epilogue

holocaust, offering a fair idea of his final sojourn—up to a point. In a letter he wrote just prior to embarking on his pilgrimage, Bierce writes of his projected trip in glowing terms: "I shall go; I shall retrace my old routes and lines of march; stand in my old camps, inspect my battlefields to see that all is right and undisturbed. I shall go to the Enchanted Forest."[4] It was not a coincidence that Bierce engaged in a grand tour of the Civil War battlefields of his youth just prior to going to Mexico. While he had made previous nostalgic visits to the old wartime haunts, this tour distinctly took on the aspect of a final farewell.

On October 4, 1913, Bierce arrived in Chattanooga. The next day he visited Chickamauga battlefield, and he is reported to have covered fifteen miles of the battlefield that day. While there, Bierce also made a sketch of the Eighteenth Ohio Battery monument for Albert and sent it to him in Berkeley. Bierce next visited Franklin and its battlefield as well as the Murfreesboro and Stones River battlefields in Middle Tennessee, staying at the Hermitage Hotel in nearby Nashville. The Hazen Monument at Stones River, it should be remembered, was the focus of his tale "A Resumed Identity." One can't help but wonder what went through Bierce's mind when he gazed upon the monument this one last time.

On the twelfth, Bierce left Nashville and "journeyed upriver" by boat to Pittsburg Landing. The river was much lower when he visited in 1913 than it was in that fateful spring of 1862. According to Miss Christianson's summary, he found the steamboat trip there "a long and tedious voyage." On the twentieth an early snowstorm hit, adversely affecting Bierce's health and temperament. He arrived at Corinth from Shiloh after a long ride overland, after which he "fled south" toward New Orleans. After New Orleans, Bierce made his way to San Antonio, Texas, where he arrived on October 27. Although Bierce's own military service had terminated elsewhere in the South, his old regiment had soldiered on, first at New Orleans and then at San Antonio, where they were finally mustered out in September 1865. Bierce's Civil War pilgrimage thus ended virtually at the Mexican border—close to where a new civil war was now hotly raging.

After entering Mexico, Bierce wrote a few letters to family and friends and then the correspondence abruptly stopped. Word came filtering back, more rumor than report, of Bierce alternately fighting with Villa or against Villa. Then rumors arrived of his death—at the hands of Villistas, Federales, or lawless bandits. Or, if one later Hollywood version is to be believed, Bierce fell afoul of voluptuous blood-sucking vampires. Time has only magnified and multiplied tales of his mysterious demise. Still, from some of this late correspondence, it is not too difficult to divine his intent. In one prophetic missive he says: "Good-bye—if you hear of my being stood up against a Mexican stone wall and shot to rags please know that I think that a pretty good way to depart this life. It beats old age, disease, or falling down the cellar stairs. To be a Gringo in Mexico—ah, that is euthanasia!"[5]

The lure of another civil war, where he might find a fate awaiting him that he had dodged many years before and that so many of his comrades had already succumbed to, could have been too strong a temptation for the old soldier to resist. He chose to allow random circumstance to overtake him, although he deliberately put himself in harm's way to do so. Writing to Bierce's daughter Helen in early 1915, Alexander Whitehall, Secretary of the Ninth Indiana Volunteer Veteran Association, also notes Bierce's fatalism in his last letter to his old comrades of the Ninth: "It would seem he had a presentiment he might not get out of Mexico."[6] To paraphrase a soldier of another generation and another war, it is clear that Ambrose Bierce believed he had a "Rendezvous with Death" on some secluded barricade in Mexico—and it is also clear that he meant to keep that rendezvous.

It is not too much of a stretch to say that author Bierce chose to write the final chapter of his own life. Ambrose Bierce could have remained in the states, gradually growing older and more debilitated, progressively losing his vigor, his mental facilities, and his memory. Instead he chose to make his exit in the manner and at the time of his choosing. Helen Bierce believed something of this sort was what her father had in mind: "I was confident that Father had left this world and gone the way he wanted to go. Soldiering in the Civil War, he had seen many shattered bodies, and could never rid himself of the horror of them. When his hour struck he wanted to go quickly and with none of his friends near to look upon his face afterward. That was given him."[7]

Bierce's ultimate fate in Mexico will never be known precisely. One thing is certain, however: so long as Ambrose Bierce's stories continue to be read and reread, the old soldier will never fade away.

Appendix I

What Albert Bierce Saw
A Little Bit More of Chickamauga

Albert Bierce's narrative of his experiences at Chickamauga, to the best of my knowledge, has never been in print before. I believe it was among the contents of a trunk containing most of Bierce's papers that his daughter Helen owned and that Carey McWilliams inveigled her into showing and selling. Since then, different parts of the Bierce papers have made their way to various archives across the country. Albert's account, written at the behest of his brother for another writer, ended up in the University of Virginia's archives, and the university has been kind enough to allow me access to it in researching this book. That it also sheds light on his brother Ambrose's activities during the battle makes it valuable as a corroboration of Bierce's own account, but it has historical value in its own right and I have deemed it well worth seeing the light of day.

Montisano
My Dear Brother
This is my story of Chickamauga all of which is true to the best of my recollection.

On the evening of the 18 of Sept. 1863 Whitaker's brigade to which Allshire's battery was attached was on the Ringgold road, probably about a mile east of McAlpine's church where, just at dusk, we met the enemy and engaged in a sharp but short artillery duel in which infantry took part. After dark the brigade was withdrawn to McAlpine's church where Granger was, with the rest of his command. My section of the battery was left on picket duty about a quarter of a mile in advance of this position with instructions to remain awake all night and take note of any sound which might indicate a movement of the enemy, for, as the staff officer said to me, they will either learn our front tonight or attack us in the morning. In the latter case when I was sure of his advance I was to fire one gun as a signal to prepare to receive the advance and then fall back to the main line near the church. At about daybreak I heard the rumble of his artillery in motion but waited till I saw him coming, fired the one shot and fell back as ordered and reported to Granger. The attack was made and repulsed, renewed about an hour later with the same result. In this attack Lieut. Roseburg of the battery was wounded. During the rest of the day there was only a succession of skirmishes. We remained in this position until the following day.

Now this brings us to the morning of the 20th. Historians tell us that Gen. Rosecrans was overwhelmed and carried from the field in the rout at about 11 a.m. Rosecrans thinking his whole army in retreat would of course hasten to order Granger to fall back by the Rossville and Ringgold road which order he promptly sent and which was promptly disobeyed by Granger. Whitaker and Mitchell were soon in column on their way to Thomas. This was, to my best recollection, about 12 a.m.

The distance from McAlpine Church to the Snodgrass is something like three miles and the column moved with but one short halt. Some of the enemy's cavalry and a battery were seen on our left. The battery opened fire on our column and Granger halted for a few minutes, surveyed them with his field glasses, then ordered the column to advance. My section was detained here probably about twenty minutes by a shell from the enemy's battery on our left which broke the pole to one of my gun carriages. I repaired it by splicing a sapling on to it. This happened a short time before you met us. I remember your saying to me that Hazen had left the position that he held when you left him to go for the ammunition train and as you did not know where he was at the time you would stay with the battery. You remember that Granger reported to Thomas not far from the Snodgrass house and then went into position at the edge of a cornfield. Was there a cornfield in Hazens post at the Kelley farm? Your probably remember that Lieutenant Chestnut was wounded only a short time before the battery got into position, and it seems to me that this happened near the Snodgrass house—a little east of it. I remember that we were agreeably surprised to find that the battery's position was with Hazen's troops.

There were no breastworks of any kind there. The enemy made one assault on Hazen through the cornfield and we harvested the corn with canister. We left this position under the guidance of somebody's chief of artillery to be placed farther to the right, just where we, or at least I, never knew as the officer was wounded or killed before placing us. Allshire asked me if I thought it possible to get the battery on that hill south of the Snodgrass house. I told him I could get my part of it there, and his reply was "Go ahead." I got it there by taking the hill at an angle and the shoulders of my men at the wheels. On the crest, which was sharp, I found a line of infantry lying

What Albert Bierce Saw

Company A, 9th Indiana. These are some of the "band of brothers" with whom Bierce campaigned during the war. His regiment was nicknamed "The Bloody Ninth," an epithet they earned many times over. After the war, Bierce maintained contact with his comrades through their veterans association, although it is not believed he attended any reunions. National Archives and Records Administration.

flat on their stomachs and a desperate conflict going on at its southern base, almost hand to hand. I could have killed an hundred men with one round of canister but some of them would have been wearing the blue. The officer in command of the troops on the hill—a col. whom I did not know—said to me, "This is no place for artillery, you can't do a thing." And he was right. He made no attempt to make room for my guns on the crest said roll down and told Allshire the condition of things and he ordered me to bring my guns down. You may remember that where I came down the battery passed near the Snodgrass house—a little to the east of it—and took a position in open ground after making a half circle to the right. In this place we remained until about dusk when we got the order to retire by the McFarland Gap road.

You're right in your letter to Gracie when you say that the Confederates did not take possession of this hill till after our forces had withdrawn. I believe there were some officers in high command who did not do their whole duty at Chickamauga but Thomas, Granger and Brannon were not in that class surely.

I think that this whole muddle of placing the battery at the Kelley farm comes about by the mistake of Hazen putting the time of his arrival at the Snodgrass house about two hours too late. Our loss was in the three days, two lieut. wounded, two men killed. Our loss of horse compelled us to abandon one caisson, which was destroyed.

Appendix I

I think that Col. Gracie will get little satisfaction from your criticism of his work.

Yes, I have the fifth volume and shall be very glad to get the others; and doubtless you will be glad when your work is finished.

Affectionately,
Albert

March 27, 1911

P.S. On reading this over I found I've made a blunder. When the battery was first moved from Hazens line it was placed farther to the right near the east base of the ridge, and it was from this position that we were moving when I took my guns up the hill.

Appendix II

Major Bierce's Critique of Confederate Strategy

Walter Neale, Bierce's publisher and an early biographer, devoted a chapter to "Bierce the Soldier." While Neale actually tells us precious little about Bierce's wartime career, he does quote what Bierce had to say about Confederate strategy and the relative merits of Lee vs. Grant and Lincoln vs. Jefferson Davis.

Neale, as a chronicler of Ambrose Bierce, has a generally bad reputation for veracity. Whether this is Neale's fault or the product of Bierce's own proclivity to spin tall tales to his publisher is a moot point. Whether the following excerpts from Neale's chapter are actually Bierce's own words or words that Neale put into his mouth is unresolved. Therefore, the comments attributed to Bierce below must be taken with more than a grain of salt.

I believe, however, that these comments recorded by Neale have the tone of Major Bierce expounding to friend and associate Neale after sipping "the poisoned chalice" sufficiently enough to loosen his tongue and pontificate about the Late Unpleasantness. Although there is nothing comparable in his published works to this discussion of grand strategy, the comments are at least consistent with his expressions of opinion found elsewhere. If legitimate, they form an interesting commentary on issues of the war that are still debated by scholars and Civil War enthusiasts to this day. As such these observations may be of more than passing interest to those who continue to wage the war with ink from the confines of their armchair.

"To hear Southerners talk," Bierce would say, "one would suppose that the entire South had been overrun by Federal troops. Such was not the case. But relatively little of the area of the South was ever occupied by Union soldiers until near the conclusion of the war. Old men, boys, negroes, and women were at liberty to supply the armies at the front with all the food and equipment necessary to success. So the Southerners thought at the time the war began, and two years, even three years, later. After the war they thought (or talked) differently. But they had been right at first. They simply failed to make the most of their opportunities.

"Where were the railways laid down that would connect the Southern, Eastern, and Western armies of the Confederacy? Were the Southern military commanders so stupid as to believe that the war would be won for them before railways could be constructed? Did they think they could bring the war to a successful conclusion without the use of natural resources, without taking full advantage of their military opportunities, without availing themselves, to the fullest extent, of their interior lines? What preparation did they make for mining? What plants did they build for the production of munitions and ordnance? What attempt did they make even to conserve and keep in repair their existing railways, manufacturing plants, and other means of supply already developed? There was no shortage of labor. Nor was there a shortage of fighting men, if all capable of bearing arms had been forced into military service; and, as in the case of nearly all wars, more boys grew into manhood during the course of the war than there were soldiers either killed or wounded in battle.

"Did President Davis think, did General Lee believe, that successful warfare in modern times depended only upon the armies in the field?—or that a war waged against the United States could be determined by a single battle, or by a series of battles, or even by the destruction of whole armies, while a single army remained? Apparently so! At any rate, no intelligent effort was made to keep intact and efficient the organized South, which was sufficiently well organized at the time the conflict began to conduct a war of major proportions, and absolutely no effort was made to develop the vast resources of the South that were then lying in waste.

"The logical city for the capital of the Confederacy was Atlanta—not Richmond, but Atlanta, six hundred miles from Washington; Atlanta, in the centre of the South, readily accessible to all parts of the South, and to the sea, to the Gulf, to the Mississippi, and last but not least, accessible to Mexico, with its great natural resources, a neutral country, which could have supplied the South with limitless agricultural and mineral products and with arms and ammunition, without violation of neutrality, and even with men. The battlefield, to be sure, should have continued to be Virginia, and there, and in the fastnesses of the rest of the South, the Southern armies, in defensive warfare, could have held out against the enemy forever.

"The invasion of Maryland and Pennsylvania and the attempt to capture Washington were crucial military blunders. The north was overrun with Southern sympathizers and others who believed that 'the erring sisters' should be permitted to depart in peace. Why alienate this host? Instead, why not continue to thunder out in the North the theory of State Rights, State Sovereignty—in which all the States believed, with the only proviso of the greater number that the Union should not be dissolved. No, the Southern high command should have fought a defensive war, under duress, on Virginian soil, or other Southern soil, from the time of invasion and should have defended that soil by proper use of its great military advantage of interior lines.

"Hindsight? Not at all! But if it were, a great military commander must be possessed of every sort of vision, hindsight as well as foresight. He does not measure up to first-class generalship when he fails to see his opportunities and when he fails to make the most of them.

"Suppose that the head of a great business failed to superintend its every department, or to concentrate his knowledge of the business as a whole upon its weakest points; he would soon fail, and bankruptcy would be his punishment. So with any supreme military command: the commander-in-chief must be the whole works; he must not leave to others the task of supplying the means with which to wage war. He may delegate, as he must, immediate supervision to sub- ordinates, but his must be the genius directing every inferior, weeding out the incompetents, laying down general rules to guide efficient and inefficient alike. His is a pitiful plea in avoidance when he says that he lacks resources and men. It is his business to see to it that both are provided.

"Since the invader should have three soldiers to one of the invaded, and all other resources in proportion, Lee made the cardinal mistake of invading the North when he was the weaker of the contending forces in the military proportion of one to nine. It would be hard to imagine any military or political situation that would have rendered the invasion justifiable. Certainly there was no such political condition at home; nor in Europe, since temporary successes of the invaders would hardly have brought about recognition by Great Britain, or aid from any other part of Europe. The invasion must be counted as an unpardonable blunder on the part of the Confederate high command.

"After all, was not Lee as a soldier a mere opportunist, and did that not account for the invasion of Maryland and Pennsylvania?" asked Bierce. "There was the opportunity, or the possibility, even the probability, of administering a signal though temporary defeat to the Union army; but not its destruction. The threats against Philadelphia and Washington were more fanciful than real; nor would the war have been won if both Philadelphia and Washington had been taken: whole armies—all armies—not a single army, not a few cities, not a capital, must be destroyed in modern warfare before a war can be brought to a successful termination. Hence, the question may well be asked, if Lee were not an opportunist, fighting without grand strategy?—without any general plan, as, for example, a plan by which the war could be extended indefinitely until the enemy should be worn out; not exhausted, but become tired of war?

"The apparent failure of the Confederate high command early to realize the importance of the Western field of war was another cardinal blunder. Always Richmond!—the belief that the fall of Richmond would result in the fall of the Confederacy—as if the capital of a new nation were of great consequence, even in the light of public opinion at home and abroad! With Richmond and not Atlanta as the seat of Government, the capital should have been mobile, even 'in the saddle,' if necessary. There should have been rapid movements of Confederate troops between the East and the West along interior lines, as occasion required, without undue thought of Richmond. Lines of communication were relatively easy to maintain.

"The time came (but should never have come) when the Confederates could not effect a convergence of the Eastern and the Western armies."

"At the time of Lee's orderly retreat from Gettysburg, he was in command of as fine an army as the world had ever known; and it was well-equipped. Even then the South was in a position to wage a successful war; Gettysburg had decided nothing; the morale of the South had not been affected. In fact, the South did not admit defeat in that battle, nor does to this day. The Union army was quite as good as the Confederate, as well equipped, even better equipped; but there was no great numerical disparity between the two, nor any other disparity, the relative positions of invader and invaded being taken into account. The West was in bad shape, to be sure, but in no hopeless condition. The fact that the South held out nearly two years after Gettysburg shows that she was in no desperate plight at the time Lee had successfully withdrawn his army from the North. Grant became the South's principal liability.

"We should remember, too, in attempting to appraise Lee's ability, that he was never pitted in battle against his equal in generalship, much less his superior. In fighting Grant, for example, he was infinitely superior to his enemy in planning and conducting a battle. Lee, the opportunist, could fight his army with rare skill, take advantage of the errors of his inferior opponents among generals, and in the conduct of a battle—or even a campaign—he seldom erred. But at times he did err, grievously, making fundamental mistakes; not mistakes resulting from unlooked-for eventualities such as are common to all campaigns and battles, known as 'the accidents of war'; his most censurable errors were in his deliberated plans.

"In adversely criticising the failure of the Confederate high command to make use of all its resources, we may not say that Grant if in command of all the armies of the South would have provided men, munitions, food, clothing, and all the other necessaries of successful warfare. He was never tested. The North was so organized and her resources so administered that it was unnecessary for Grant to concern himself with anything other than strategy and the fighting of his armies. We may assume, however, that his generalship would have been so comprehensive as to embrace the raising and the equipping of necessary forces, with ample fuel for his great machines.

"Jefferson Davis was the most competent of all Southerners to head the Confederate Government. Forsooth, there was no other man! It is a question if he would not have been a greater commander than Lee in the field. With long and ample military training, with hard and brilliant fighting to his credit, with a wide knowledge of men and their motives, an experienced and a great statesman, the greatest of the secretaries of war that the United States could claim up to the time that he left office, he was incomparably better equipped than any other Southerner to fill the office of President and that of Commander-in-Chief of the Confederate armies and navies. His ability in selecting commanders was so acute as to be weird. If, instead of Lincoln, he had been President of the United States, the probability is that the war would have been brought to an early termination. On the other hand, it might not have been, since it has been pretty thoroughly demonstrated that generalship in the field is but one of the many qualities necessary to successful modern warfare."

"Davis and Lee, then, had to contend with the high hosts of Heaven; with one great genius, Lincoln, and with one great strategist, Grant, both God-made. Neither Davis nor Lee was a genius. Talent they both had; both had minds far better informed in the things that men can learn than had either Lincoln or Grant; technically they were in every respect better equipped; but both lacked the qualities that only the gods possess: knowledge without learning; and in those essentials of successful warfare Lincoln and Grant excelled Davis and Lee.

"Again, let us visualize Lincoln as the President of the Confederacy and Grant as the active commander of the Southern armies: Would the South have *won* the war? Perhaps! It would not have been impossible, nor improbable, particularly as the Fates had given the greater military leaders to the South."

Appendix III

Ambrose Bierce's Journal of the Carolina Campaign

Bierce's notebook, as preserved in the University of Virginia archives, contains a number of entries that clearly do not square with his official military records either as preserved at the University or at the National Archives. For one thing, it records a "Topographic Survey of the Country south of Procter's Creek to East Point and Tiloy Creek, bounded East & West by Macon & Western RR and Chattahoochie River" that begins in Atlanta (or whatever was left of the city after Sherman blew it up) on Peachtree Street. The start date of the survey is not listed, but after the end of the survey there is a notation of "tools issued" that is dated January 28, 1865, which gives us a terminus post quem *of sorts.*

That same notation also mentions a first, second, and third brigade as well as a "pioneer corps," which all indicate that Bierce was attached to one or another of Sherman's divisions, although which division is never mentioned. I interpret this summary as relating to the ensuing Carolina Campaign entries in Bierce's notebook. Hazen, in his postwar memoirs, quotes one of his field orders mentioning the creation of a "pioneer corps" from among his three brigades' "unarmed men and superfluous servants" and "able-bodied negroes" of the region, which is highly suggestive but not conclusive proof.[1]

The hard evidence for Lt. Bierce's participation in Sherman's Carolina Campaign is contained in Bierce's daily log, beginning with a January 30 entry and continuing on up to March 24; the log consists of engineering accomplishments as well as topographic notes and some combat details, which all clearly relate to Sherman's Carolina Campaign. The notebook entries more or less cease until the diary of his journey to Panama, which begins on September 13, 1865 and which is a brief but full report of his vacation from duties as Treasury agent. While his notebook fills a gap in our knowledge of Bierce's activities in the early parts of 1865, the entries raise more questions than they answer.

Appendix III

I present the daily log, hitherto unpublished, in hopes that other researches may further elucidate details contained in it. The entries seem to have been entered on a daily basis and they give some idea of the enormous physical difficulties that Sherman's armies in the Carolina Campaign encountered during their advance. In their own modest way they are also testimony to Bierce's great skill as a combat engineer. In editing Bierce's entries, I have rendered them in journal rather than chart form, judging this to be a more easily readable format. Changes in punctuation and spelling have been kept to a minimum and are included mainly for the sake of clarity. The serious researcher can, of course, always consult the archived originals to view them in context.

1865

JAN. 30TH Distance: 17 Character of roads: good, previously cordoroyed. Wether: Clear. Braoing Incidents: Teames overloaded—Troops closed up. Camp: Pooabodigo Sta.[2]

JAN. 31ST Distance: 0 Character of roads: Camp in old line of works. Weather: (ditto). Incidents: Reconnoitered roads in front. Foarce skirmished at crossing. Camp: (ditto).

FEB. 1ST Distance: 13 Character of roads: Good! Swamp at intervals. Weather: (ditto). Incidents: Impeded by 3rd Divis. 15th ac. Firing in advance 3 P.M. Camp: Strand Hill Ch.

FEB. 2ND Distance: 17 Character of Roads: Frequent swamps and streams. Weather: Rain threatened. Incidents: In advance skirmishes 8 miles with cavalry. Camp: Lopers Crossing.

FEB. 3RD Distance:—Character of Roads: Demonstrated across h.w. of Coosawatchie Weather: Rained Incidents: Forced the passage of Duck Branch Skirmished 6 m. Camp: Lopers Crossing.

FEB. 4TH Distance: 7 ½ Character of Roads: Needing frequent repairs Weather: Cloudy Incidents: Two regiments repairing roads. Camp: Anglesay P.O.

FEB. 5TH Distance: 8 Character of Roads: Tolerable Weather: Warm Incidents: Crossed Saltketcher by difficult bridg Camp: Beaufort Bridg.

Feb. 6th Distance: 8 Character of Roads: Good. Sandy Weather: Rained Incidents: Crossed Little Saltketcher by difficult bridg Camp: Spring Cr.

Feb. 7th Distance: 7 Character of Roads: Soft, Easily cut up Weather: Rained Incidents: Destroyed 1mile of R.R. Camp: Bamburg Sta.

Feb. 8th Distance:—Character of Roads: 2nd Brigade reconnoitered cannons Brg. Weather: Windy Incidents: Exceedingly swampy Enemy strongly posted Camp: Bamburg Sta.

Feb. 9th Distance: 11 Character of Roads: Good Swampy near the river Weather: Cold Incidents: Enemy at river construct Flying Bridg x on . . . Camp: Holmans Bridg.

Feb. 10th Distance: 1 Character of Roads: Road ½ mile water and bridg Weather: Cold! Incidents: Pontoon the Edisto. Cross Willow Branch. Camp: In fields.

Feb. 11th Distance: 16 Character of Roads: Good -3 bad swamps Weather: Clear Incidents: Cross Snake Creek, Camp: Poplar Springs.

Feb. 12th Distance: 8 Character of Roads: Cordoroy about the river. Weather: Mild Incidents: Forced the passage of N. Edisto construct foot bridg Camp: Rad Side.

Feb. 13th Distance: 12 Character of Roads: Orangeburg Road Weather: Very Cold. Incidents: Crossed & marched down Caw-Caw Swamp Camp: Farm House.

Feb. 14th Distance: 16 Character of Roads: very good Weather: Rained. Incidents Crossed Beaver Cr. and Sandy Run Camp: Deserted House.

Feb. 15th Distance: 7 Character of Roads: Causway through overflowed land. Weather: Cloudy Incidents: Crossed Congres Cr. Drove the Enemy from the position. Camp: In Line of Battle (Hoffmans).

Feb. 16th Distance: 8 Character of Roads: Good. Along the Conres oposite the town. Weather: Clear. Incidents: Demonstrated in front of Town & Forced passage of Saluda Br. Camp: Saluda Fork.

Feb. 17th Distance: 3 Character of Roads: Cordoroyed the approaches to the Bridge. Weather: Windy. Incidents: During the night preceeding

Appendix III

crossed Broad River on Pontoons Entered Columbia S.C. City Burned. Camp: Columbia.

FEB. 18TH Distance:—Character of Roads: One Brigade on Provo duty. Weather: Clear Incidents: Destroy six miles of the C & S.CRR. Camp: Columbia.

FEB. 19TH Distance:—Character of Roads: Destroy Municians Weather: (ditto) Incidents: (Destroy) 1 ½ (miles of the C&S. R.R.) Camp: (ditto).

FEB. 20TH Distance: 20 ½ Character of Roads: Sandy Frequent Streams. Weather: (ditto) Incidents: Cordoroy creek bottoms Pines Camp: Mudy Springs.

FEB. 21ST Distance: 21 Character of Roads: Sandy—Quick Sand—W Hilly. Weather: (ditto) Incidents: Cross Rice Creek Dutchmans Cr. Camp: Near Poplar Springs.

FEB. 22ND Distance: 11 Character of Roads: Latter part very Hilly. Weather: Cloudy Incidents: Cross Wateree 17 Pontoons Camp: Singleton Cr.

FEB. 23RD Distance: 11 Character of Roads: Hilly—3 inches soft mud over hard ground. Weather: Rain. Incidents: Cross Beaver Cr. Camp: White Oak Creek. (Marengo Mills).

FEB. 24TH Distance: 19 ½ Character of Roads: A good bottom covered with soft mud. Weather: (ditto) Incidents: Foragers captured Camden. Camp: Pine Tree Creek.

FEB. 25TH Distance: 9 Character of Roads: A good bottom covered with 3 inches of soft mud. Weather: Rained. Incidents: Secure the bridges across Lynches Cr. Camp: Pinetree Church.

FEB. 26TH Distance: 10 Character of Roads: Good. Weather: Clear. Incidents: Creek flooded. Cross two Brigades. Camp: Kellys Bridge.

FEB. 27TH Distance:—Character of Roads: Reconnoitered down the Creek. Weather: Rained. Incidents: Constructed 200 yards of Bridg. Camp: (Kellys Bridge).

FEB. 28TH Distance:—Character of Roads: Mud. Weather: (Rained) Incidents: (Constructed) 362 (yards of bridge). Camp: (Kellys Bridge).

FEB. 29TH Distance:—Weather: (Rained)

FEB. 30TH Distance:—Weather: (Rained) Incidents: Work on bridg. Camp: (Kellys Bridge).

MARCH 1ST Distance:—Character of Roads: Bridge broke down with Dept. Train. Weather: (Rained) Incidents: Attempt crossing of the Creek. Camp: (Kellys Creek).

MARCH 2ND Distance: 9 Character of Roads: Quick sand. Piney. Weather: (Rained) Incidents: March to Black Creek. Camp: Black Creek (Campbells).

MARCH 3RD Distance: 18 ½ Character of Roads: Good—Sandy—Piney. Weather: Cloudy. Incidents: Crossed Black Creek—Cheraw road. Camp: Juniper Creek (Judg Dunken).

MARCH 4TH Distance: 12 Character of Roads: Needing some repairs. Weather: Showers. Incidents: Cross Thompson's Creek. March into Town. Camp: Cheraw.[3]

MARCH 5TH Distance: 5 Character of Roads: Muddy Weather: Clear Incidents: Cross Great Pee Dee River. Camp: Harringtons.

MARCH 6TH Distance: 0 Weather: (Clear) Camp: (Harringtons).

MARCH 7TH Distance: 11 Character of Roads: Sandy Weather: (Clear) Incidents: March at Noon. Camp: Crooked Creek.

MARCH 8TH Distance: 15 Character of Roads: Quick sand in creek bottom. Weather: Rainy. Incidents: Cross RR. Send two regiments forward to build bridg. Camp: Laurel Hill.

MARCH 9TH Distance: 14 Character of Roads: East of Lumber River roads bottomless Weather: (Rainy) Incidents: Cross Lumber River. Camp: Raft Swamp.

MARCH 10TH Distance: 1 Character of Roads: Roads Impassible Weather: (Rainy) Incidents: Make six miles of corduroy. Camp: Bethel Ch.

MARCH 11TH Distance: 19 Character of Roads: Good east of Rock Fish Cr. Sandy. Weather: Clear. Incidents: (Make) Four (miles of corduroy) cross Rock Fish Cr. Camp: Little Rock Fish Cr.

Appendix III

MARCH 12TH Distance: 6 Character of Roads: Good Sandy Weather: (Clear) Incidents: Crossing of Creek difficult. Camp 1 mile from Fayetteville.

MARCH 13TH Distance: 0 Weather: (Clear) Camp: (Fayettteville).

MARCH 14TH Distance: 3 ½ Character of Roads: Require a good deal of work. Weather: Rainy Incidents: Cross the Cape Fear. River Falls 14ft. Camp: Warsaw Road.

MARCH 15TH Distance: 10 Character of Roads: Sandy. Weather: Rain. Incidents: 4 Divis at Maxwells Bridg. Camp: Bethany Ch.

MARCH 16TH Distance: 9 Character of Roads: Very bad require much corduroying. Weather: (Rain) Windy Incidents: Cross South River Camp: Near Wesleys Ch.

MARCH 17TH Distance: 6 Character of Roads: Bad. Weather: Clear. Incidents: Cordoroy 2 ¼ miles. Camp: Roberts x Roads.[4]

MARCH 18TH Distance: 11 Weather: (Clear) Incidents: Cross the Coheras Camp: N. Alec Benton's.

MARCH 19TH Distance: 7 Character of Roads: Very Bad. Weather: (Clear) Incidents: Cross the H.W. of Fulling Cr. Cordoroy 3 miles. Camp: Irving Kings.

MARCH 20TH Distance: 16 Character of Roads: Very difficult. Dark. Weather: Windy Incidents: Marched at 7 a.m. for the relief of Slocum. Camp: N. Bentonville.

MARCH 21ST Distance: 3 Character of Roads: Cut and corduroy a road 1½ mile. Weather: Rainy Incidents: Take a position in line on Left of Right Wing. Camp: (N. Bentonville) S.E.

MARCH 22ND Distance: 9 Character of Roads: Forward as working party. Weather: Clear Rainy. Incidents: Enemy evacuate. Withdraw to Smithfield. Camp: Granthams.

MARCH 23RD Distance: 6 ½ Character of Roads: (Forward as working party) Weather: Windy. Incidents: Cross Falling Cr. Camp: Wm. Halls.

MARCH 24TH Distance: 9½ Character of Roads: Good. Weather: Clear Incidents: Cross Nuse River and take position E. of Goldsboro.

Total Number of Miles Marched. 461½.
" " " Days. 56. Aver. Per day 8¼
" " " Marching days 46 " " " 10.03

No. of Rivers crossed
First class 6. Second class 8. Creeks 36.
Swamps with current 36.

Total am'nt of corduroying 17,417 Yards.
Average per day 311 "
" " Marching day 380 "
Amount of side road cut for troops 223 miles

Total Amt. of bridging 4850 ft.

Notes

Introduction

1. Walter Neale, *Life of Ambrose Bierce* (New York: Walter Neale, 1929), 45, vehemently denied that his friend was bitter, morose, disappointed, sulky, or similar attributes; although he does aver that Bierce had an inferiority complex when confronted by persons with lesser talent but more formal education than he.
2. Carey McWilliams, *Ambrose Bierce a Biography*, second edition (Hamden: Archon Books, 1967—originally published 1929), 61.
3. Napier Wilt, "Ambrose Bierce and the Civil War," *American Literature* 1 (1929): 260–85. While Wilt repeatedly references the "rolls of the regiment" as his chief source, it does not seem he actually consulted the "Record of Events" (regimental diary) of the Ninth. From his brief mention of the records, it seems more likely he looked at Bierce's military service record, now in the National Archives, which included his muster rolls with the Ninth.
4. See for example, Bierce's rebuttal to the criticism of his story "Son of the Gods" as "unrealistic" in "A Rational Anthem," from S. T. Joshi and David E. Schultz, eds., *A Sole Survivor: Bits of Autobiography* (Knoxville: Univ. of Tennessee Press, 1998), 254.
5. Roy Morris, *Ambrose Bierce: Alone in Bad Company* (New York: Crown, 1995); Cathy N. Davidson, *Critical Essays on Ambrose Bierce* (Boston: G. K. Hall and Company, 1982); David M. Owens, *The Devil's Topographer: Ambrose Bierce and the American War Story* (Knoxville: Univ. of Tennessee Press, 2006).

Chapter 1

1. Strictly speaking, the persons who came over on the Mayflower were not Puritans and even the term Pilgrim is something of a misnomer; but generally the Pilgrims and Puritans have been treated as one in the popular imagination. In *Ambrose Bierce: The Devil's Lexicographer* (Norman: Univ. of Oklahoma Press, 1951), Paul Fatout thoroughly researched the Bierce family genealogy in his first chapter (1–27), charting the family history back to their earliest arrival in the 1600s. I see no need to chew the cud twice in this regard. Curiously, Walter Neale, in his Bierce biography, spends more time on his *own* family's genealogy than on Bierce's, just one of the many peculiarities of his book

(Neale, *Life*, 13–22); but what little he records of Bierce's own views on his family background contradict that negative view (33–34). Regarding the bare facts of Bierce's early youth, Fatout (28–35) and others have gleaned what little they could from Bierce's later writings. There is also abundant genealogical data accessible on the Bierce and Sherwood clans, some compiled by descendents: see the Bierce Family Genealogy Forum, http://genforum.genealogy.com/bierce/. Where I mainly differ from his predecessors in this regard is in his interpretation of those fundamental facts and to a certain extent in Bierce's immediate prewar chronology. I do not think we can take the mature Ambrose Bierce's statements about his parents and his unhappy youth at face value, much less inferences derived from his fiction. While such negative statements were perhaps psychologically true for Bierce, they do not constitute objective fact.

2. Joshi and Schultz, *Sole Survivor*, 312; originally appeared in the *San Francisco Wasp*, September 16, 1883.
3. Fatout, *Ambrose Bierce*, 8–9.
4. Lord Byron was a scandalous and immensely popular Romantic poet; Joseph Addison was a famed eighteenth-century English journalist, playwright, and poet. It is a curious choice of a child's name for an ostensibly dour Puritan.
5. Fatout, *Ambrose Bierce*, 8.
6. Bertha Pope, ed., "Introduction," *The Letters of Ambrose Bierce* (San Francisco: The Book Club of California, 1922), vi.
7. Fatout, *Ambrose Bierce*, 13; after Bierce, "The Social Unrest," *Cosmopolitan* XLI, no. 3 (July 1906): 299.
8. Neale, *Life*, 34.
9. Margaret Parker, "My Quest to Find the Birthplace of Ambrose Bierce," *Meigs Historian* (September 2003), accessed via Don Swaim's *The Ambrose Bierce Site* (http://donswaim.com/bierce-parker.html).
10. Ibid. The history of land speculation in America is a long one. Some of the general sources relating to it are: Roy M. Robbins, *Our Landed Heritage: The Public Domain, 1776–1936* (Princeton: Princeton Univ. Press, 1942); Daniel Felk, *The Public Land in Jacksonian Politics* (Madison: Univ. of Wisconsin Press, 1984); James W. Oberly, *Sixty Million Acres: American Veterans and the Public Lands Before the Civil War* (Kent: Kent State Univ. Press, 1990); Daniel M. Friedenberg, *Life, Liberty and the Pursuit of Land: The Plunder of Early America* (New York: Prometheus Books, 1992).
11. Neale, *Life*, 39, 129–30.
12. Albert Bierce to sister Almeda, July 20, 1909 in Fatout, *Ambrose Bierce*, 18.
13. Albert Bierce, in Carey McWilliams, *Ambrose Bierce, a Biography* (1929; reprint, Hamden: Archon, 1967), 23.
14. Fatout, *Ambrose Bierce*, 18; after Bierce, *The Argonaut*, June 8, 1878.
15. Neale, *Life*, 33–34.
16. Reuben Williams, "Forty Years," *The Warsaw Daily Times*, January 1, 1896.
17. "In my green and salad days I was sufficiently zealous for universal and unqualified Freedom to engage in a four years' battle for its promotion," Bierce

once confessed in a candid moment. See Russell Duncan and David Klooster, eds., *Phantoms of a Blood-Stained Period, the Complete Civil War Writings of Ambrose Bierce* (Amherst: University of Massachusetts Press, 2002), 9.
18. Reuben Williams, "A Warsaw Boy in London," *The Northern Indianian,* March 19, 1874.
19. Adolphe DeCastro, *Portrait of Ambrose Bierce* (1929; reprint, New York: Beakman, 1974), 7.
20. Williams, "A Warsaw Boy in London"; Reuben Williams's son, L. H. Williams, later averred that Bierce was accused of theft (see Fatout, *Ambrose Bierce,* 32), but that is not what Reuben wrote.
21. "Grand Lodge of Ohio, Past Grand Masters," accessed online at http://www.freemason.com/past-grand-masters/74-1853-lucius-v-bierce.
22. For an early biography of Lucius Bierce, see Gen. L. V. Bierce, *Historical Reminiscences of Summit County* (Akron: T. & H. G. Canfield, 1854), 3–8. Also see "Grand Lodge of Ohio, Past Grand Masters," accessed online at http://www.freemason.com/past-grand-masters/74-1853-lucius-v-bierce; *The Daily Cleveland Herald,* September 23, 1857; *The Daily Cleveland Herald,* September 13, 1861; his papers are located in the Western Reserve Historical Society Archives (MS 1081).
23. Lucius Verus Bierce, *Travels in the Southland, 1822–23,* ed. George W. Knepper (Columbus: Ohio State Univ. Press, 1966).
24. Daniel B. Hadley, "Reminiscences of John Brown," *McClure's Magazine* 10 (1897): 275–84.
25. *Summit Beacon* (OH), December 7, 1859; Lucius later saw fit to publish the full address in pamphlet form: General L. V. Bierce, "Address Delivered at Akron, Ohio on the evening of the Execution of John Brown, December 2, 1859" (Columbus: Ohio State Journal Steam Press, 1865).
26. DeCastro, *Portrait,* 4.
27. Carey McWilliams, in *Ambrose Bierce,* 25, cited a letter from William E. Guy, who confirmed that Bierce attended the Kentucky Military Institute; James Darwin Stephens, *Reflections: A Portrait—Biography of the Kentucky Military Institute, 1845–1971* (Georgetown: KMI Inc., 1991), 65, likewise affirms that Bierce was an alum, as does the Alumni Association secretary Jim Flora (personal correspondence).
28. For general background on KMI and similar Southern military academies, see Bruce Allardice, "West Points of the Confederacy: Southern Military Schools and the Confederate Army," *Civil War History* 43, no. 4 (December 1997): 310–31; also see KMI alumni website: www.kmialumni.org/kmi-history.
29. See advertisement in *Louisville Daily Journal,* January 4, 1858.
30. Personal correspondence, Liz Haeuptle, Curator of Collections, Elkhart County Historical Museum; list of Bierce papers and artifacts in museum, Item No. 29.
31. Bruce Allardice, "West Points of the Confederacy: Southern Military Schools and the Confederate Army," *Civil War History* 43, no. 4 (December 1997): 310–31.

32. *The Louisville Daily Journal,* June 18, 1860.
33. *The Charleston Courier, Tri-Weekly,* December 1, 1860.
34. Fatout, *Ambrose Bierce,* 29.
35. Stephens, *Reflections,* 301.
36. Neale, *Life,* 35–6, after Captain Chamberlain and others.
37. The 1860 census lists "Marcys" (Marcus) and Laura, as well as Ambrose and Andrew; see Indiana Historical Society, *1860 Census,* Alphabetical Listing by County (Kosciusko), page 5717 (THP 89, Page 354, 321). Courtesy Warsaw Community Public Library.
38. Fatout, *Ambrose Bierce,* 33–34.

Chapter 2

1. The chapter title comes from a letter: "No, my pet scheme for making soldiers of the Major's little rascals is not practicable. The confounded Government is so particular about the moral character of its recruits that I couldn't enlist myself. This is a great disappointment to me. I had quite set my heart on getting Co. A into Cuba, to prove that bad boys make the best soldiers. But I'm assured that it cannot be done." Letter from Ambrose Bierce, Los Gatos, CA, to Harriet Hershberg, Waterman, CA, May 1, 1898, ALS. acc. #5992-j, *Papers of Ambrose Bierce,* Special Collections Dept., Univ. of Virginia Library.
2. Scholars had long thought talk of a secret society, called he Knights of the Golden Circle, to be mostly moonshine, concocted by paranoid Northern Unionists who saw treason everywhere and needed an excuse to justify violating the civil rights of legitimate political opponents. Recently, however, one researcher has taken an in-depth look at this organization, from its filibuster origins to its role in fomenting Secessionism and war. See Daniel C. Keehn, *Knights of the Golden Circle: Secret Empire, Southern Secession, Civil War* (Baton Rouge: LSU Press, 2013). As early as 1850, South Carolina had been actively acquiring heavy ordinance and other munitions in preparation for a violent uprising against Federal authority; see Ashley Halsey, Jr., "South Carolina Began Preparing for War in 1851," *Civil War Times* 1, no. 1 (April 1962): 8–10, 12–13.
3. Reuben Williams, "Memories of War Times" Part 1, *Warsaw Daily Times,* December 27, 1902.
4. Duncan and Klooster, *Phantoms,* 9.
5. *San Francisco Examiner,* May 9, 1897.
6. Or, as the Rebel recruiting song put it, "If you want to smell hell, *jine* the cavalry."
7. Neale, *Life,* 129–30.
8. Catharine Merrill, *The Soldier of Indiana in the War for the Union* (Indianapolis: Merrill & Co., 1864), 26; Ezra J. Warner, *Generals in Blue* (Baton Rouge: LSU Press, 1967), 326.
9. Tim Beckman, "Camp Morton—Civil War Camp and Union Prison, 1861–1865," via *Rootsweb* at Ancestry.com.

10. Cf. "Camp Morton, 1861," Indiana State Archives, http://www.in.gov/icpr/2533.htm.
11. Merrill, *The Soldier of Indiana*, 15–16.
12. Jasper County Library, Robert H. Milroy Collection: access no. RHM_1861–109a, *To Milroy From Bank of Indiana*, May 17, 1861; accession no. RHM_uc1-May23–1861_a, *To Bank of Indiana From 9th Ind Regt*, May 23, 1861.
13. Henry Lovie sketch "Tigers of the Bloody Ninth," (Becker) CW-HL-WV-7/61c, Becker Collection, McMullen Museum, Boston College. Sketch of the Ninth Indiana in action during the skirmish on Gerard Hill; Lovie made notes on the uniform as a guide for the engraver.
14. "The Troops in Grafton," *New York Herald*, June 7, 1861.
15. Besides Bierce's writings and the OR reports, also see: Ruth Woods Dayton, "The Beginning—Philippi, 1861," *West Virginia History* 13, no. 4 (July 1952): 254–66; Ronald S. Coddington, "Captain Hunnum Attends the Philippi Races," *The New York Times*, June 2, 2011; Catherine Merrill, *The Soldier of Indiana*, 30–35.
16. "Battlefields and Ghosts" from Joshi and Schultz, *Sole Survivor*, 4. For Bierce's fictional take on "friendly fire," albeit with fog instead of darkness as the source of confusion, see Bierce, "One Kind of Officer" in Duncan and Klooster, *Phantoms*, 41–50; S. T. Joshi, Lawrence I. Berkove, and David E. Schultz, eds., *The Short Fiction of Ambrose Bierce* II (Knoxville: Univ. of Tennessee Press, 2006): 833–41; first published in the *San Francisco Examiner*, January 1, 1893.
17. Gerald D. Swish, "An Omen at Philippi," *America's Civil War* 24, no. 2 (May 2011): 49.
18. "On a Mountain" from Joshi and Schultz, *Sole Survivor*, 7, published in his *Collected Works*, 1, 1909; it was previously published in a newspaper, but this appearance has not been located so far. See S. T. Joshi and David E. Schultz, eds., *Ambrose Bierce: An Annotated Bibliography of Primary Sources* (Westport: Greenwood Press, 1999), 296 (item E16).
19. *The Daily Cleveland Herald*, Wednesday, June 26, 1861 (issue 151).
20. Joshi and Schultz, *Sole Survivor*, 7.
21. Joshi and Schultz, *Sole Survivor*, 3.
22. "Marching and Skirmishing," *The Daily Cleveland Herald*, July 16, 1861.
23. Merrill, *The Soldier of Indiana*, 49; Joshi and Schultz, *Sole Survivor*, 4; *Indianapolis Journal*, July 27, 1861.
24. Merrill, *The Soldier of Indiana*, 50; *Cleveland Daily Herald*, July 16, 1861.

Chapter 3

1. Dr. George L. Andrews, "Welcome Address," *6th Annual Reunion of the Ninth Indiana Veteran Association* (LaPorte, IN: Ninth Indiana Vet. Vol. Assn., 1889), 5–6.
2. For example, Adolphe DeCastro, *Portrait of Ambrose Bierce* (1929; reprint, New York: Beakman, 1974), 7.

3. NARA, *Bierce, Ambrose Gwinnet, Compiled Military Service File* (NATF 86).
4. Quartermaster Kelly's remarks, *6th Annual Reunion*, 18.
5. Joshi and Schultz, *Sole Survivor*, 7–8.
6. Captain Amasa Johnson, "The First Year of Service," *9th Annual Reunion, Ninth Indiana Veteran Infantry Association* (Chicago: Ninth Indiana Veteran Volunteers, 1892), 37.
7. "Bivouac of the Dead" from Joshi and Schultz, *Sole Survivor*, 2; first published in the *New York American*, November 22, 1903.
8. Joshi and Schultz, *Sole Survivor*, 8.
9. Janet B. Hewett, ed., "Record of Events for Ninth Indiana Infantry," *Supplement to the Official Records of the Union and Confederate Armies, Part II, "Records of Events" Vol. 16, Serial No. 28 (Indiana)*, (Wilmington: Broadfoot Publishing, 1995), 16. (Hereafter cited as OR *Supplement*.)
10. Joshi and Schultz, *Sole Survivor*, 8.
11. OR *Supplement*.
12. Ibid.
13. Joshi and Schultz, *Sole Survivor*, 8.
14. Ibid.
15. Marplot: one who frustrates or ruins a plan or undertaking by meddling.
16. Ibid.; Captain Amasa Johnson, "The First Year of Service," 39.
17. Joshi and Schultz, *Sole Survivor*, 8–9.
18. Ibid., 9.
19. William H. Peck to Orrin Peck, November 10, 1861; Corporal William H. Peck correspondence; excerpt via Nate D. Sanders Auctions website: http://www.icollector.com/Extensive-Collection-of-Letters-by-9th-Indiana-Soldier-KIA_i10535962.
20. Joshi and Schultz, *Sole Survivor*, 6.
21. Ibid., 9.
22. Ibid.
23. Ibid., 5.
24. Ibid., 9.
25. "The Battle of Alleghany Mountain," *Richmond Daily Dispatch*, December 17, 1861.
26. "Battle of Alleghany Summit," *Wheeling Intelligencer*, December 24, 1861.
27. Joshi and Schultz, *Sole Survivor*, 6.
28. Ibid., 10.
29. "The Coup de Grâce" in Duncan and Klooster, *Phantoms*, 136–40; Joshi, Berkove, and Schultz, *Short Fiction* II, 668; first published in the *San Francisco Examiner*, June 30, 1889.
30. Joshi and Schultz, *Sole Survivor*, 10.
31. Ibid., 6.
32. George Anderson, "Welcome Address," *6th Annual Reunion*, 7.
33. Captain Amasa Johnson, "The First Year," 41.
34. *Newark Advocate* (OH), March 14, 1862, issue 33. This works out to something on the order of a twenty percent casualty rate.

35. Carey McWilliams, *Ambrose Bierce*, 243.
36. Joshi and Schultz, *Sole Survivor*, 2–3.

Chapter 4

1. Joshi and Schultz, *Sole Survivor*, 24.
2. See OR *Supplement*, 19.
3. See John Miller McKee, "An Eyewitness," *The Great Panic* (Nashville: Johnson & Whiting, 1862; reprinted, Nashville: Elder/Sherbourne, 1977).
4. For an early account of the occupation on the twenty-fifth by Nelson's division and the raising of William Driver's "Old Glory" over the capitol building, see McKee, *The Great Panic*, 79–80.
5. William Babcock Hazen, *A Narrative of Military Service* (Boston: Ticknor and Son, 1885), 19.
6. "Correspondence of the Louisville Anzeiger," (March 12, 1862), Louisville Anzeiger, March 18, 1862; article republished online and translated from the German original by Joseph R. Reinhart: www.geocities.com/jreinhart_us/kyomar181862?20095. Accessed September 5, 2009.
7. "Defending General Buell" in Duncan and Klooster, *Phantoms*, 111; Joshi and Schultz, *Sole Survivor*, 25, first published in the *San Francisco Examiner*, December, 1898.
8. Thomas B. Van Horne, *History of the Army of the Cumberland* (1875; abridged reprint, New York: K&K, 1995), 78. The abridged reprint is hereafter cited as Van Horne, Army (1995).
9. See Van Horne, *Army*, 71–2; James Lee McDonough, *Shiloh—In Hell Before Night* (Knoxville: Univ. of Tennessee Press, 1977), 32–39; Steven E. Ambrose, *Halleck: Lincoln's Chief of Staff* (Baton Rouge: LSU Press, 1962), 26–27.
10. Hazen, *Narrative*, 21.
11. Joshi and Schultz, *Sole Survivor*, 39.
12. For General Hazen, see John Fitch, *Annals of the Army of the Cumberland* (Philadelphia: J.B. Lippincott & Co., 1864), 219–24; Ezra J. Warner, *Generals in Blue* (Baton Rouge: LSU Press, 1964), 225–26.
13. "Two Military Executions" in Duncan and Klooster, *Phantoms*, 114–18; Joshi, Berkove, and Schultz, *Short Fiction* III, 1012, first published in *Cosmopolitan Magazine*, November 1906.
14. Duncan and Klooster, *Phantoms*, 114.
15. Letter of March 8, 1862, Corporal William H. Peck correspondence, excerpt via Nate D. Sanders Auctions website: http://www.icollector.com/Extensive-Collection-of-Letters-by-9th-Indiana-Soldier-KIA_i10535962.
16. Journal of First Sgt. John Daeuble, Sixth Kentucky Volunteer Infantry Regiment US, translated by Joseph R. Reinhart from original manuscript in The Filson Historical Society, Louisville, Kentucky, 3. Cited hereafter as John Daeuble, *Journal*. Accessed via the 6th Kentucky Volunteer Infantry U.S. website: http://6thkentuckyus.yolasite.com/journal.php.

17. "Presidential War Order 3," March 11, 1862, in Roy P. Basler, ed., *Collected Works of Abraham Lincoln* 5, (New Brunswick: 1953), 155; Wiley Sword, *Shiloh, Bloody April*, (New York: 1974), 21; Van Horne, *Army*, 78; Ambrose, *Halleck*, 29, 33–34, 39–40.
18. McDonough, *Shiloh*, 37–39; Sword, *Shiloh*, 16–17; Ambrose, *Halleck*, 36–37.
19. Joshi and Schultz, *Sole Survivor*, 12. While it is not explicit in Bierce's writings on the subject, his criticisms of Grant's performance at Shiloh seem to be heavily influenced by Buell's detailed analysis of Grant's performance in the battle and of Grant's and Sherman's misrepresentations: see General Don Carlos Buell, "Shiloh Reviewed," *Battles and Leaders of the Civil War* I, eds. Robert U. Johnson and Clarence C. Buel (New York: Century, 1887), 487–536. A manuscript penned by Buell in the Filson Society archives in Louisville may contain the original draft of this essay, although I have not had an opportunity to view the manuscript and study its contents.
20. Buell, "Shiloh Reviewed," 490; McDonough, *Shiloh*, 43–44; Sword, *Shiloh*, 7–11.
21. The analogy is, perhaps, an imperfect one; in any case, I take full blame for the comparison of Grant's amphibious strategy in the Civil War to MacArthur's in World War II. In fact, the "island-hopping strategy," as enshrined in the 1935 revision of *War Plan Orange*, was the Navy's idea, not MacArthur's; see Edward S. Miller, *War Plan Orange: The U.S. Strategy to Defeat Japan, 1897–1945* (Annapolis: Naval Institute Press, 1991). Apparently the Navy never told MacArthur about the changes in Plan Orange when he decided to make a stand at Bataan, thinking the Navy would sail to his rescue. One could similarly argue that the Navy deserves more credit for the successful use of amphibious tactics in the Western Theater during the Civil War than does Grant or the Army, so either way the analogy stands. For a recent survey of riverine amphibious operations in the Western Theater, see Gary D. Joiner, *Mr. Lincoln's Brown Water Navy: The Mississippi Squadron* (Lanham: Rowan & Littlefield, 2007); also see Craig Symonds's recent lecture at the Civil War Institute, Gettysburg College: "1862 Western Theater River Operations," re-broadcast June 23, 2012, on American History TV, CSPANN (http://www.c-span.org/video/?306716-5/1862-western-theater-river-operations).
22. For a recent discussion of the controversy over Buell's advance to Pittsburg Landing, see Donald A. Clark, "Buell's Advance to Pittsburg Landing: A Fresh Look at an Old Controversy," *Tennessee Historical Quarterly* 68, no. 4 (Winter 2009): 355–90.
23. For General William "Bull" Nelson, see: Van Horne, *Army(1995)*, 10-11, 14, 18, 55–6; Warner, *Generals in Blue*, 343–4; Hazen, *Narrative*, 54–60.
24. Van Horne, *Army(1995)*, 84; McDonough, *Shiloh*, 57; Buell, "Shiloh Reviewed," 491.
25. Van Horne, *Army(1995)*, 81–82.
26. D. B. McConnell, *Proceedings of the Ninth Indiana Veteran Volunteers Infantry Association, 16th Annual Reunion* (n.p., Ninth Ind. Assoc., 1902), 25.
27. Hazen, *Narrative*, 24.

Chapter 5

1. Ambrose Bierce, "What I Saw of Shiloh" from Joshi and Schultz, *Sole Survivor*, 10–25, who cite its first publication as the *San Francisco Wasp*, December 23 and 30, 1881; however Mr. S. T. Joshi (personal communication) has since informed me that it was in fact first published in the *London Sketch-Book* 1, no. 4 (April 1874): 1–4; and 1, no. 5 (May 1874): 21–25, a fact only discovered after both the annotated bibliography and collection of Bierce's autobiographical texts had gone to press. The memoir is hereafter cited as "What I Saw." Unless identified otherwise, all following quotes in this chapter are from this memoir.
2. This chapter is largely crafted around Bierce's "What I Saw of Shiloh," supplemented by the OR reports for Nelson's division, Buell's "Shiloh Reviewed," *Battles & Leaders* I, 487–536, and Hazen's *Narrative*, 24–48. A number of general studies of the battle were also referred to in constructing the general battle narrative and context for Bierce's writings about it: James Lee McDonough, *Shiloh—In Hell Before Night* (Knoxville: Univ. of Tennessee Press, 1983); Wiley Sword, *Shiloh, Bloody April* (New York: Morrow, 1974); and Larry Daniel, *Shiloh: The Battle That Changed the Civil War* (New York: S&S, 1998).
3. "Looking for the Elephant" is one of those expressions that was so commonplace in the early nineteenth century as to not need any explanation at the time but that now requires some clarification. It seems to have begun as a kind of running joke in the eighteenth century, when wild-eyed hunters claimed to have seen wooly mammoths or mastodons in the deep woods of the early frontier. There was actually some basis to this: during the early frontier period at Big Bone Lick in Kentucky, salt miners came upon both mastodon and mammoth bones, which came to the attention of naturalist-turned-politician Thomas Jefferson. Even into the 1880s some creative newspaper editors would continue to publish reports of mammoth sightings. Over time, however, the meaning of the phrase evolved, and it came to signify any quixotic quest; settlers going west in the 1830s and 1840s were commonly said to be "looking for the elephant." It could also be a euphemism for one's first sexual encounter. At the beginning of the Civil War, however, it came to mean something akin to a search for adventure, manhood, and more specifically, one's first taste of combat. For this usage of the idiomatic expression during the Civil War, see John Fitch, *Annals of the Army of the Cumberland* (Philadelphia: J. B. Lippincott & Co., 1864), 681–82.
4. Bierce, "What I Saw," 15.
5. Hazen, *Narrative*, 25.
6. Bierce, "What I Saw," 15.
7. General William Nelson, "Report of the 4th Division," *War of the Rebellion, Official Records of the Union and Confederate Armies* 10, Pt. 1: 324 (series hereafter cited as *OR*); Webb Garrison, *Friendly Fire in the Civil War* (Nashville: Rutledge Hill Press, 1999), 61.
8. Nelson, *OR*, 324.

9. Buell, "Shiloh Reviewed," 494, 506.
10. See, for example, Timothy B. Smith, "The Myths of Shiloh," *America's Civil War* 19, no. 5 (May 2006): 34. Of course, one man's "troops massed in compact positions" is another's leaderless mob; not seen, but Smith's book-length study of Shiloh is presumably in the same vein. Although he attests to the demoralization of Grant's troops, Wiley Sword also buys into the "big guns" rationalization; see Sword, *Shiloh*, 360–1. For an opposing view of the "big guns" myth, see Robert Collins Suhr, "Saving the Day at Shiloh," *America's Civil War* 12, no. 6 (January 2000), 34–41. The still-unresolved issues of how many effectives Grant actually had and how much of his "massed artillery" was manned and actually in use at the end of the day on the sixth greatly affect the discussion of whether Grant's army could have survived a second day of battle had Buell not arrived in the nick of time. Certainly morale was at a low point in Grant's army before Ammen's brigade arrived and to assume otherwise is to ignore the overwhelming evidence—evidence that Bierce's narrative corroborates. As for Smith's assertion that Grant's army was not "surprised," see Hazen, *Narrative*, 47–48.
11. "Two Military Executions," Duncan and Klooster, 113–14; Joshi, Berkove, and Schultz, *Short Fiction*, III, 1013.
12. See Van Horne, *Army*, 97–98; Buell, "Shiloh Reviewed," 519, 522–23, 528–29, 532; Bierce, "What I Saw" 15–16. Regarding Bierce's views of Grant at Shiloh, also see Michael W. Schaefer, *Just What War Is* (Knoxville: Univ. of Tennessee Press, 1997), 82–83.
13. Bierce, "What I Saw," 19.
14. See "Coup de Grâce," Duncan and Klooster, 136ff; Joshi, Berkove, and Schultz, *Short Fiction* II, 666ff; Joshi and Schultz, *Sole Survivor*, 296; "The Morality of Suicide" from Joshi and Schultz, *Sole Survivor*, 225; "On the Right to Kill the Sick," *NY Journal* (October 1, 1899), 30.
15. Peter Cozzens, "The Tormenting Flame," *Civil War Times* 35, no. 1 (April 1996): 50.
16. On the need for artillery support, see Buell, "Report," *OR* 10, Pt. 1, 294; Nelson, "Report," *OR* 10, Pt. 1, 324–25.
17. Bierce, "What I Saw," 21.
18. Ambrose Bierce, "Officers Taking Cover in Battle," The *Denver Evening Post*, (reprinted from *New York Journal*), November 12, 1899, 4.
19. Ibid., 21–22.
20. Ibid., 25.
21. Captain D. B. McConnell, "Record of the Regiment," *Proceedings of the Ninth Indiana Veteran Volunteer Infantry Association, 16th Annual Reunion*, 24–25.
22. See Edmund Wilson, *Patriotic Gore* (New York: 1960), 618; Roy Morris Jr., *Alone in Bad Company*, 43–44; for Bierce's account of military executions, see Duncan and Klooster, *Phantoms*, 116.
23. "Two Military Executions" from Duncan and Klooster, *Phantoms*, 113–15; Joshi, Berkove, and Schultz, *Short Fiction* III, 1012–14. Also see Joshi and Schultz, *Sole Survivor*, 14–15, 44ff; Nelson, "Report," *OR* 10, Pt. 1, 324.

24. For examples of Bierce's editorializing on Shiloh see: "The Mocking Bird" in Duncan and Klooster, *Phantoms*, 51; Joshi, Berkove, and Schultz, *Short Fiction* II, 790, first published in the *San Francisco Examiner*, May 31, 1891; "An Affair of Outposts" in Duncan and Klooster, *Phantoms*, 117; Joshi, Berkove, and Schultz, *Short Fiction* III, 914–15; "Death of Buell" from Joshi and Schultz, *Sole Survivor*, 25. Regarding the issue of Grant's army being surprised on April 6, Grant's supporters have always denied it, including more recently Timothy B. Smith. In all fairness, contrary to Bierce's sarcasm, a few of Grant's units did indeed have pickets posted, but they were not posted far out enough to provide advanced warning of attack and those officers who did attempt to warn of an impending assault were ignored by their superiors. The best response to this issue of the "surprise" on April 6 was penned by General Hazen, *Narrative*, 47–48.

Chapter 6

1. From "Affair of Outposts" in Duncan and Klooster, *Phantoms*, 117–26, Joshi, Berkove, and Schultz, *Short Fiction* III, 914, first published in the *San Francisco Examiner*, December 19, 1897.
2. Bierce, "What I Saw," 13.
3. This is not strictly true anymore; since this narrative was first crafted, a new study has come out chronicling both Corinth battles. See Timothy B. Smith, *Corinth 1862: Siege, Battle, Occupation* (Lawrence: Univ. Press of Kansas, 2012).
4. John Daeuble, *Journal*, 8.
5. See Thomas B. Van Horne, *Army* (1995), 101–4; Ambrose, *Halleck*, 41–53; Alfred Roman, The *Military Operations of General Beauregard in the War Between the States* I (New York: Harper & Bros., 1884), 380–95.
6. Duncan and Klooster, *Phantoms*, 117.
7. Morris, *Alone*, 42.
8. *The Chicago Times* was particularly zealous in documenting Governor Yates's extracurricular (and extramarital) activities, chronicling in particular the rise and fall of the relationship between Governor Yates and Mrs. Reynolds in its pages between May 19 and 28, 1862.
9. Duncan and Klooster, *Phantoms*, 117.
10. See *The Chicago Times*, May 19, 1862, p.1, c5; Frank Moore, ed. *The Rebellion Record* 5 (1862), (New York: G. P. Putnam, 1863).
11. Article by "WPL," *The Chicago Times*, May 21, 1862, p. 1, col. 5.
12. For Ambrose Bierce's participation in the Corinth campaign and the Battle of Shiloh and the context behind his postwar writings, see also Christopher Kiernan Coleman, "Ambrose Bierce in Civil War Tennessee: Nashville, Shiloh and the Corinth Campaign," *Tennessee Historical Quarterly* 68, no. 3 (Fall 2009): 250–69. For general background to Buell's advance on Chattanooga and "retreat" to Louisville, see Van Horne, *History of the Army of the Cumberland* I (Cincinnati: Robert Clarke & Co., 1875): 139–75; henceforth cited as Van Horne, *Army* (1875); Henry M. Cist, "The Army of the Cumberland," *Campaigns of the Civil War* VII (New York: Charles Scribner's Sons, 1882), 40–74.

13. Van Horne, *Army* (1995), 116–17.
14. Ambrose Bierce, "Occurrence at Owl Creek Bridge" from Brian M. Thomsen, ed., *Shadows of Blue and Gray, the Civil War Writing of Ambrose Bierce* (New York. Tom Doherty Assoc., 2002): 34–43; Joshi, Berkove, and Schultz, *Short Fiction* II, 725–33; first published in the *San Francisco Examiner*, July 13, 1890.
15. Throughout 1862, Union forces were continually plagued by bridge burnings, not just in Alabama, but elsewhere in the Mid-South. Generally they were ascribed to "Confederate cavalry" as the culprits. This may well have been true in many instances, but often such explanations were a cover to avoid Federal retribution for civilian sabotage. In one case, a young girl of eighteen acted as arsonist; see Sue Berry, Martha Fuqua, and Pam Oglesby, eds., *Homespun Tales* (Franklin: Territorial Press, 1989), 22–23.
16. See John Fitch, "Police Record of Operations of Spies, Smugglers, Traitors, etc. Occurring Within the Lines of the Army of the Cumberland," *Annals of the Army of the Cumberland* (Philadelphia: J. B. Lippincott, 1864), 483–646. The sometimes-harsh counterinsurgency tactics eventually roused the ire even of some Federal officers: see for example, Walter T. Durham, *Rebellion Revisited* (Franklin: Hillsboro Press, 1999), 158–65, 186–91.
17. John Fitch, *Annals*, 589–96.
18. Edmund Wilson, *Patriotic Gore: Studies in the Literature of the American Civil War* (New York: Oxford Univ. Press, 1962), 617–34. Wilson (or rather one of his students) was the first to take note of this coincidence and divines significance in it. More recently, researcher David Owens has substantially expanded on this thesis and while his facts are undoubtedly quite correct, he still does not prove Wilson's thesis; see David N. Owens, "Bierce and Biography: the Location of Owl Creek Bridge," *American Literary Realism* 26, no. 3 (Spring 1994): 82–89. In actual fact there *is* an Owl Creek in northern Alabama as well, but it does not cross what would have been the line of the Memphis and Charleston Railroad in 1862. Whether Bierce was even aware of the creek's existence is unknown. For a list of all bridges along the line of the Memphis and Charleston in 1861, see www.csa-railroads.com. Owens posits the alleged bridge along the connecting north-south route of the Tennessee & Alabama Railway (today part of the CSX RR Birmingham Division), which terminated at Decatur and which did indeed pass by Athens where the Ninth Indiana was posted; see Figs. 2 and 3 (87–88) of Owens.
19. Van Horne, *Army* (1995), 124.
20. Roy Morris Jr., "War Crimes? Colonel Turchin and The Sack of Athens," *Civil War Times Illustrated* 24, no. 10 (February 1986): 26–32; Ezra J. Warner, *Generals in Blue*, (Baton Rouge: LSU Press, 1964), 512–13. A correspondent with the Cincinnati *Gazette* visiting the town shortly after the incident averred that accounts of the "outrages" were "greatly exaggerated." The reporter observed that "some three or four stores were broken into and the most valuable part of the merchandise abstracted"; additionally, articles of value were also taken from some dozen private homes, but that was the extent of the pillaging.

While white residents may have been verbally insulted by the Union troops, none seem to have actually suffered any physical abuse. Ironically, the only alleged sexual abuse that may have occurred was against a slave. See "General Turchin in Alabama," reprinted in the *New York Herald,* August 4, 1862.
21. Van Horne, *Army* (1995), 120.
22. "Story of General Hazen," *The Nashville American,* January 9, 1900. It's likely that he did, knowing what we do about the Bierce's; during the San Francisco Earthquake, his brother Albert heroically remained at his post at the Federal Treasury to protect it from both fire and looters.
23. NARA, Ambrose Bierce Military Records, Field and Staff Muster Roll, Sept./Oct. 1862.
24. Ambrose Bierce, "A Resumed Identity" from Thomsen, *Shadows,* 163–68; Joshi, Berkove, and Schultz, *Short Fiction* III, 1036–43; first published as "The Man" in *Cosmopolitan* (New York), May–September 1908.
25. For a full discussion of the phenomena of "acoustic shadow" in the Civil War, see Charles D. Ross, *Civil War Acoustic Shadows* (Shippensburg: White Mane, 2001).
26. For the Battle of Perryville, see Kenneth W. Noe, *Perryville: This Grand Havoc of Battle* (Lexington: Univ. of Kentucky Press, 2001).
27. Captain D. B. McConnell, address, *6th Annual Reunion of the Ninth Indian Veterans Association* (LaPorte: Ninth In. Vet. Vol. Assn., 1889), 10–11.
28. Joseph P. Fried, "How One Union General Murdered Another," *Civil War Times Illustrated* 1, no. 3 (June 1962): 14–16; Webb Garrison, *Friendly Fire,* 34.
29. Van Horne, *Army* (1995), 158.

Chapter 7

1. Joshi and Schultz, *Sole Survivor,* 33.
2. Van Horne, *Army* (1995), 162–72; Peter Cozzens, *No Better Place to Die* (Urbana: Univ. of Il. Press, 1990), 29–31.
3. OR *Supplement,* 16; "Record of Events," 26.
4. Alcohol was readily available in town, as was the company of women of easy virtue. The latter, in fact, quickly proved a major nuisance for Federal authorities. See Thomas P. Lowry, *The War the Soldiers Wouldn't Tell: Sex in the Civil War* (Mechanicsburg: Stackpole, 1994); Walter Durham, *Nashville the Occupied City* (Nashville: Tennessee Historical Society, 1985); Jeanine Cole, "'Upon the Stage of Disorder': Legalized Prostitution in Memphis and Nashville, 1863–1865," *Tennessee Historical Quarterly* 68, no. 1 (Spring 2009): 40–65.
5. NARA, Field and Staff Muster Roll, Nov./Dec. 1862; Company Muster Roll, Nov./Dec. 1862.
6. Roy Morris, *Alone,* 47–48, citing *The Elkhart Review,* Dec. 1862.
7. *The Elkhart Review,* February 26, 1863.
8. Cozzens, *No Better Place,* 19–20; for Bierce on the harsh punishment often meted out to soldiers, see Joshi and Schultz, *Sole Survivor,* 27–28.

Notes to Pages 99–110

9. Cozzens, *No Better Place*, 46.
10. Joshi and Schultz, *Sole Survivor*, 27; first published in the *San Francisco Examiner*, May 5, 1889.
11. Joshi and Schultz, *Sole Survivor*, 63; first published in the *San Francisco Examiner*, Oct. 29, 1899.
12. For Bierce's invective against "save the dayers" at Stone's River, see Joshi and Schultz, *Sole Survivor*, 26–27; also see Cozzens, *No Better Place*, 151–61.
13. Captain Amasa Johnson, "The Campaigning of the Ninth from the close of the Buell and Bragg Campaigning to the battle of Chickamauga," 6th Annual Reunion Ninth Indiana Veteran Association (LaPorte: In. Ninth Vol. Vet. Assn., 1889), 36.
14. Hazen, *Narrative*, 80.
15. Peter Cozzens, "The Tormenting Flame," *Civil War Times* 35, no. 1 (April 1966): 51.
16. UVA Archives, Military Papers, Sgt. N. V. Brower to Ambrose Bierce, November 1, 1905.
17. For battlefield conditions at Stone's River on the night of December 31, see Cozzens, *No Better Place*, 166–71.
18. Bierce, "A Cold Night," *San Francisco Examiner*, April 22, 1888; bundled with five other short pieces as "Bodies of the Dead" in *Can Such Things Be* (New York: 1893); also Joshi, Berkove, and Schultz, *Short Fiction* II, 579–80; republished separately in Everett F. Bleiler, ed., *A Treasury of Victorian Ghost Stories* (New York: Scribner, 1981).
19. *The Daily Inter-Ocean* (Chicago, IL), August 11, 1893 (issue 140), 3.
20. Cozzens, *No Better Place*, 169.
21. Bierce, "A Resumed Identity" from Thomsen, *Shadows*, 163–8; Joshi, Berkove, and Schultz, *Short Fiction* III, 1036–43.
22. After two world wars and numerous lesser modern conflicts, the clinical literature on amnesia in combat is voluminous; it need not be due to a head wound but can simply be induced by the stress of combat. In Bierce's day the medical profession far less understood this phenomenon. His inclusion of it as a motif in his story probably indicates that Bierce had some personal knowledge of it, either having experienced it himself or aware of it happening to fellow veterans.

Chapter 8

1. The application of the terms "sitzkrieg" and "phony war" to this period is mine alone and borrowed from the history of World War II, but insofar as this period in the Mid-South is concerned I believe the terms entirely appropriate. The secondary literature on this phase of the war in the Western Theater is not abundant as it lacks the drama featured in the periods before and after. In addition to the various accounts in the Ninth's reunion pamphlets and Bierce's own words, I have also relied on Hazen's memoirs here to fill the

Notes to Pages 110–17

gap. Also see Cisco, *The Army of the Cumberland,* 136–58; Van Horne, *History of the Army of the Cumberland* I, 287–301.

2. See, Captain Amasa Johnson, "The Campaign of the Ninth from the close of the Buell and Bragg Campaign to the Battle of Chickamauga," *6th Annual Reunion of the Ninth Indiana Veteran Association,* (LaPorte: Ninth Regt. Ind. Vet. Vol. Assn., 1889), 38.
3. Ambrose Bierce, "A Baffled Ambuscade" from Thomsen, *Shadows*; Joshi, Berkove, and Schultz, *Short Fiction* III, 1009–11; first published in *Cosmopolitan,* November 1906, 37–38.
4. See for example, *OR* 23, Pt. 1, 203ff, 70ff, 197ff.
5. Hazen, *Narrative,* 98.
6. NARA, Company C "Muster Roll, March/April, 1863"; "Detachment Muster-Out Roll, May 20, 1863."
7. Johnson, "The Campaign of the Ninth," 38–39.
8. NARA, "Return, 2nd Bde, 2nd Div, for month of April, 1863" (dated May 1863). For a general sketch of the Army of the Cumberland's Provost Marshal General's Department, see Fitch, *Annals,* 282–83. While Record Group 110 in NARA contains extensive microfilm records of the various Union provost marshals, historians have analyzed very little of it. Also see Daniel Lewis, *Military Discipline during the Civil War* (guide to microfilm collection) (Bethesda, MD: LexisNexis, 2009).
9. Ambrose Bierce, "Crime at Pickett's Mill" from Joshi and Schultz, *Sole Survivor,* 37.
10. Joshi and Schultz, *Sole Survivor,* 27–28.
11. Ibid.
12. Ibid.
13. Ibid., 64.
14. Bierce, "George Thurston" in Duncan and Klooster, *Phantoms,* 162–6; Joshi, Berkove, and Schultz, *Short Fiction* I, 420–23; first published in the *San Francisco Wasp,* Sept. 29, 1883.
15. Earl B. McElfresh, *Maps and Mapmakers of the Civil War* (New York: Abrams, 1999), 196.
16. "Killed at Resaca" in Duncan and Klooster, *Phantoms,* 212; Joshi, Berkove, and Schultz, *Short Fiction* II, 507–12; first published in the *San Francisco Examiner,* June 5, 1887.
17. NARA, Company C "Muster in Roll, May/June, 1863," for Bierce.
18. NARA, "Appears on Returns," stamped with date "May 4, 1895," with the notation "Peck, copyist." "War Topics," *San Francisco Examiner,* May 1, 1898.
19. For detailed plans of these defenses, see Davis, Percy and Kirkley, eds., *The Official Atlas of the Civil War* (1891–95; reprinted New York: Barnes & Noble, 2003), (Cite hereafter as *Official Atlas*); plate 31.5 (102–3); plate 35.3 (111); plate 35.7 (111).
20. Major Julian D. Alford, "Executive Summary," in "The Tullahoma Campaign, the Beginning of the End for the Confederacy" MA Thesis, 2002 USMC

Command and Staff College (not paginated). Primary sources for the campaign are abundant; in-depth historical appreciations are few.
21. In addition to Major Alford's military analysis of the Tullahoma campaign, for other discussions of the Tullahoma Campaign, see: Rosecrans "Report," *OR* XXIII, Pt. 1: 403–9; Lt. Col. Gilbert Kniffen, "Manoeuvring Bragg out of Tennessee," *Battles and Leaders of the Civil War* 3: 635–7; Van Horne, *Army*, 223–9; Bob Redman, "The Tullahoma Campaign, June 23-July 4, 1863," *Army of the Cumberland*, www.aotc.org; and Michael R. Bradley, *Tullahoma; the 1863 Campaign for Control of Middle Tennessee* (Shippensburg: Burd Street Press, 2000).
22. UVA Archives, Military Papers, letter of July 14, 1863, C. E. Hayes to Lt. A. G. Bierce.
23. *Official Atlas*, plates 35.6, 34.4 and 34.5 (108–11).
24. Hazen, *Narrative*, 99.
25. Also referred to as Waldon's Ridge, Waldron's Ridge, and Walton Ridge.
26. Hazen, *Narrative*, 108.

Chapter 9

1. *Chic, Chick, chica, or chisca* are common Native American prefixes found in ethnic and place names throughout the South (Chickasaw, Chickahominy, etc.). The Chickamauga were a warlike faction of the Cherokee during the late eighteenth century. For one etymology, see James Mooney, "Myths of the Cherokee," *Nineteenth Annual Report, Bureau of American Ethnology, 1897–98* Pt. 1 (Washington, DC: 1900), 413. The first postmaster of Chattanooga, who lived with the Cherokees for a time, said it meant "sluggish water," while a former captive of the tribe said it meant "dwelling place of the war chief." Some modern Cherokees say it is not native to their language but a loan word from another Native American tongue. In any case, it does *not* mean "river of death."
2. For a more detailed explanation of the term, see Christopher K. Coleman, "Introduction," *Strange Tales of the Dark and Bloody Ground* (Nashville: Rutledge Hill Press, 1998), 9–12.
3. Joshi and Schultz, *Sole Survivor*, 29; originally published in the *San Francisco Examiner*, April 24, 1898.
4. Ibid., 30.
5. Ibid.
6. Ibid.
7. Though I have not yet seen it, the following provides a different account of these opening engagements: David A. Powell, "A Mad Irregular Battle, From the Crossing of the Tennessee River Through the Second Day August 22–September 19, 1863," *The Chickamauga Campaign* I (El Dorado Hills: Savas Beatie, 2014).
8. Cozzens, *This Terrible Sound*, 105. It is generally believed that Bierce incorporated this incident regarding Mrs. Reed into his short story "Chickamauga" as a motif: see Joshi, Berkove, and Schultz, *Short Fiction* II, 648–53.

9. See *Tenth Annual Reunion, Ninth Indiana Volunteer Veteran Association* (NP: Ninth Ind. Vet. Inf. Assn., 1895), 27–9. The veterans of Companies C and A don't mention any Union cavalry engaged, but both they and the Confederate cavalry veterans they talked with equally regarded it as the opening skirmish of the battle and determined that the Confederate cavalry captain killed was the first casualty of the Battle of Chickamauga. Prior to crossing the river, both Minty's brigade and Wilder's "Lightning Brigade" were part of Hazen's command and cooperated with it; they may well have also done so on September 17 and 18 near Reed's Bridge. The regimental diary is very brief regarding events after crossing the Tennessee, simply saying that after crossing the river they "advanced into Georgia to Lee and Gordon's Mill" and neglecting to mention anything else before the nineteenth. The record for Company C is more detailed but still not very specific: on the eleventh they were at Ringold, the twelfth at Lee and Gordon Mill; on September 15 they marched to Crawfish Springs and were involved in some skirmishes prior to the main battle. See "Record of Events" *Supplement,* Part II, Vol. 16, 22, 36–37.
10. For details of the action, see Hazen, "Report" 164, *OR* 30, Pt. 1: 759–62.
11. Hazen, *OR* 30, Pt. 1: 762.
12. Ibid.
13. Joshi and Schultz, *Sole Survivor,* 30.
14. Ibid.
15. Hazen, *OR* 30, Pt. 1: 762; Joshi and Schultz, *Sole Survivor,* 31.
16. Joshi and Schultz, *Sole Survivor,* 31.
17. Hazen, *OR* 30, Pt. 1: 763
18. Ibid.
19. Ibid.
20. Col. I. C. B. Suman, "Report," *OR* 30, Pt. 1: 769; Capt. D. B. McConnell, "Ninth Indiana at Chickamauga," *Tenth Annual Reunion of the Ninth Indiana Veteran Infantry Association,* (NP: Ninth Ind. Vet. Inf. Assn., 1895), 36–37.
21. Archibald Gracie, *The Truth About Chickamauga,* (NY: Houghton Mifflin, 1911), 172–192; Laurence D. Conley, "The Truth About Chickamauga: A Ninth Indiana Regiment's Perspective" Indiana Magazine of History, 98, No.2, (June, 2002), 113–43; Capt. D. B. McConnell, (comments regarding the controversy over location of placing of Ninth's monument at Chickamauga), Eleventh Annual Re-Union of the Ninth Regiment Indiana Veteran Volunteer Infantry Association, (np: Ninth Regt Vet. Vol. Assn, 1900), 5–9; "Ninth Indiana, Controversy as to location of a Monument at Chickamauga Park Settled," Indiana State Journal (Indianapolis), November 3, 1897. Bierce disagreed with Gracie and a number of his comrades of the Ninth on this, but given the possibility of Bierce's memory of that day also being faulty, the issue remains very much a moot one.
22. Hazen, *OR* 30, Pt. 1: 764.
23. Joshi and Schultz, *Sole Survivor,* 33; originally published in the *San Francisco Examiner,* May 8, 1898.

24. Cozzens, *This Terrible Sound*, 363–65; Cist, *Army*, 222–23; Turchin, *Chicamauga* (Chicago: Fergus Printing Co., 1888), 113–14; more recently Dan Lee, *Thomas J. Wood: A Biography of the Union General in the Civil War*. (Jefferson, N.C., and London: McFarland, 2012) has also made the case for blaming Wood for the debacle.

25. Bierce, "One Kind of Officer" in Duncan and Klooster, *Phantoms*, 41–50; Joshi, Berkove, and Schultz, *Short Fiction* II, 833ff; first published in the *San Francisco Examiner*, January 1, 1893. The fictional artillery officer was punished for his deadly obedience; General Wood was not.

26. Joshi and Schultz, *Sole Survivor*, 33.

27. Charles Dana, *Recollections of the Civil War*, (1898; reprint Lincoln: Univ. of Nebraska Press, 1996), 115.

28. For the political nature of Garfield's field appointment, see Peter Cozzens, *This Terrible Sound, The Battle of Chickamauga* (Urbana and Chicago: Univ. of Illinois Press, 1992).

29. "A Little of Chickamauga" from Joshi and Schultz, *Sole Survivor*, 31.

30. Ibid. Bierce is making a small in joke here. As any Army of the Cumberland veteran would know, Fort Negley was the massive fortress guarding the southern approaches to Nashville atop St. Cloud Hill. It was the largest inland stone fort built during the Civil War, equipped with heavy caliber siege guns and numerous shielded redoubts. It was unique in that it had a 360 degree field of fire—in case the garrison needed to fire on the citizens of Nashville they were supposedly defending.

31. Joshi and Schultz, *Sole Survivor*, 31–32.

32. Ibid., 32.

33. Ibid.

34. Ibid.

35. Peter Cozzens, "The Tormenting Flame," *Civil War Times Illustrated* 35, no. 1 (April 1996): 51.

36. Gordon Berg, "A Tall Tale of Chickamauga," *America's Civil War* 22, no. 5 (November 2009): 36–43.

37. Cozzens, "The Tormenting Flame," 52.

38. Ibid.

39. "The Death of General Grant" from Joshi and Schultz, *Sole Survivor*, 189, originally published in the *San Francisco Wasp*, August 1, 1885.

40. Sam Kessler, *Tenth Annual Reunion, Ninth Indiana Volunteer Veteran Association* (Chicago: Ninth Indiana Assoc., 1895), 27.

41. Sam Watkins, *"Co. Aytch" Maury Grays, First Tennessee Regiment or, A Side Show of the Big Show*, second edition (Chattanooga: Printing Co., 1900), 92.

42. See Bob Redman, "Sheridan's Ride at Chickamauga" (NP, 2003); accessed via Army of the Cumberland website (www.aotc.net).

43. Hazen, *OR* 30, Pt. 1: 765.

44. UVA Archives, Ambrose Bierce, Military Papers: letters from Gracie to Bierce May 26, June 22, August 17, August 30 and Sept. 23, 1911.

45. Ibid.
46. Thomas, *OR* 30, Pt. 1: 252–53. Another version of the incident, based on General Steedman's recollection of the incident, asserts that the man who discovered and guided them to Thomas was a "colonel"—unnamed—on Thomas's staff for the day; see J. T. Woods, *Steedman and his Men at Chickamauga* (Toledo: Blade Printing, 1876), 45–46.

Chapter 10

1. For the general narrative of the siege of Chattanooga and the raising of same, see James Lee McDonough, *Chattanooga, A Death Grip on the Confederacy*, (Knoxville: Univ. of Tennessee Press, 1984), but also Hazen's reports in *OR*. Recently, Frank Varney, *General Grant and the Rewriting of History*, (El Dorado Hills, CA: Savas Beatie, 2013), has argued that Grant and associates have distorted the record regarding Rosecrans's performance at Chattanooga.
2. Peter Cozzens, *This Terrible Sound*, (Urbana & Chicago: Univ. of Illinois Press, 1992), 520; after Capt. B. L. Ridley, "Daring Deeds of Staff & Escort," *Confederate Veteran*, Vol. IV No. 10, 359.
3. Jim Miles, *Paths to Victory* (Nashville: Rutledge Hill Press, 1991), 61.
4. UVA Archives, Ambrose Bierce papers, Military Papers; General Hazen to General Lyne Straching, A.A.G., October 15, 1863.
5. UVA Archives, Ibid., Captain William G. Misagadant to Lt. A. G. Bierce, October 18, 1863.
6. UVA Archives, Ibid., "Map of Brown's Ferry."
7. The Brown's Ferry amphibious night assault is justly famous; the present narrative is based on Hazen's Report, *OR*, Ser. 1, Vol. XXXI, Pt. 1, Report No. 7, 82–85; Major Albert G. Hart, "The Surgeon and Hospital in the Civil War," *Report of the Military Historical Society of Massachusetts* XIII (1902); *Harpers Weekly*, Nov. 28, 1863, 756, 764.
8. Hazen, *Narrative*, 162, 164.
9. For a recent account of the battle see, Dan O'Connell, "Night Fight at Wauhatchie," published in four parts on TOCWOC, May 17, 20, 22, 24, 2012 (http://www.brettschulte.net/CWBlog/2012/05/17/night-fight-at-wauhatchie-part-1/); Also see Cozzens, *Chattanooga*, 91–3 and sources cited in footnote 8, below.
10. Ulysses S. Grant, "Chattanooga" in *Battles and Leaders* III: 690; General Oliver O. Howard, *The Atlantic Monthly* 36, iss. 226, 209. The Rebels denied the whole incident and doubtless the story grew in the telling. For the Southern view of the incident see John K. Stevens, "Of Mules and Men—The Night Fight at Wauhatchie Station," *The South Carolina Historical Magazine*, Vol. 90, No. 4, (Oct. 1989), 282–98.
11. Miles, *Paths*, 96.
12. Ibid.; Glenn Tucker, *The Battles for Chattanooga* (Jamestown: Eastern Acorn Press, 1987), 22. The complete poem can be accessed via the Civil War Poetry website, http://www.civilwarpoetry.org/union/battles/mules.html.

13. Ambrose Bierce, "Jupiter Doke, Brigadier General," *The Collected Writings of Ambrose Bierce* (1946; reprint New York: Replica Books, 1999), 733–43
14. Ibid., 741.
15. "Death of Grant" from Joshi and Schultz, *Sole Survivor*, 188; first published in the *San Francisco Wasp*, August 1, 1885.
16. Joshi and Schultz, *Sole Survivor*, 28.
17. Ibid., 29.
18. Ibid., 28
19. Ibid., 29.
20. McDonough, *Chattanooga*, 56.
21. Charles A. Dana, *Recollections of the Civil War* (1898; reprint Lincoln: Univ. of Nebraska Press, 1996), 151.
22. Joshi and Schultz, *Sole Survivor*, 36.
23. OR 31, Pt. 1, 282.
24. McDonough, *Chattanooga*, 180.
25. Col. Whitaker's Report, *OR* 31, Pt. 1: 288.
26. Hazen, *Narrative*, 178–80; the rest of his chapter on Missionary Ridge consists largely of supporting testimony as to his brigade's priority on attaining the summit and disproving Sheridan's claims. Sheridan, like Grant, excelled at creative fiction, especially when writing action reports; see Report of Maj. Gen. Philip H. Sheridan: Report No. 27, O.R. Ser. I, Vol. XXXI, Pt. 2, 188–93. In his memoirs, Sheridan casts aspersions on the numerous eyewitnesses who corroborate Hazen in his memoirs: P. H. Sheridan, *Personal Memoirs of P. H. Sheridan* I (New York: Charles Webster, 1888): 320–4. He largely responds by reprinting excerpts from his subordinates' official reports. Hazen was not the only one to take exception with Sheridan's creative fiction regarding Missionary Ridge: General Wood also took issue with it; see Mike West, "Hazen faces Controversy at Missionary Ridge," *Murfreesboro Post* (June 17, 2007) accessed at: http://www.murfreesboropost.com/hazen-faces-controversy-at-missionary-ridge-cms-4846. Grant chose to side with Sheridan and give him prime, if not sole, credit for the victory, probably because it better fit with his magnifying Sherman's achievements at Tunnel Hill.

Chapter 11

1. Carey McWilliams, "Ambrose Bierce and his First Love," *The Bookman* (June 1932) 259.
2. OR *Supplement* 16, 23.
3. See McWilliams, "Ambrose Bierce and his First Love," 254–59; McWilliams, *Ambrose Bierce*, 56–57.
4. McWilliams, *Ambrose Bierce*, 36
5. U. S. Census of 1860, Schedule 1, "Free Inhabitants of Wayne Township . . . County of Kosciusko, State of Indiana," 144. (Accessed via *www.Ancestry Institution.com*).

6. Bierce reputedly disliked James Whitcomb Riley and abhorred his nostalgic poetry that praised the virtues of rural life. While the two men were very different in temperament and literary style, they did have one thing in common: love of strong drink. Frank Jerome Riley once told me of the time that he was a boy and "Uncle Jamie," in his cups, kept trying to throw a literary prize (a Pulitzer I think) in the fireplace, much to his nephew's dismay. Bierce criticized Riley's wildly popular poetry on technical grounds; Bierce's own poetry in contrast, while technically correct, never found favor with the public.
7. Oscar Burton Robbins, *History of the Jackson family of Hempstead, Long Island, NY, Ohio and Indiana: descendants of Robert and Agnes Washburn Jackson* (Loveland, CO: Robbins, 1951), 222 (accessed via *www.AncestryInstitution.com*); also see George A. Nye, *Warsaw in the 1860's* (Warsaw, IN: self-published typescript, 1951), 10–16 (p. 9).
8. Joshi and Schultz, *Sole Survivor*, 46.

Chapter 12

1. This chapter on the Atlanta Campaign was abstracted largely from Hazen's report in *OR* 38, Pt. 1, Report No. 61; Hazen's *Narrative*, 244–64; Bierce's writings (see citations below); and Sherman's memoirs—William T. Sherman, *Memoirs of General William T. Sherman by Himself* II (1885; reprinted, Bloomington: Univ. of Indiana Press, 1957). Although long neglected by scholars obsessed with the Eastern Theater, in recent years there have been several excellent narratives published about the complex Atlanta Campaign; however, I consulted none of them for this chapter.
2. Hazen, "Report 61," *OR* 38, Pt. 1: 421–25.
3. Ambrose Bierce, "Killed at Resaca" from Thomsen, *Shadows*, 97–103; Joshi, Berkove, and Schultz, *Short Fiction* II, 507–12; first published in the *San Francisco Examiner*, June 5, 1887.
4. Hazen, *OR* 38, Pt. 1: 422.
5. Reuben Williams, "A Warsaw Boy in London," *The Northern Indianian*, March 19, 1874.
6. "The Crime at Pickett's Mill" from Joshi and Schultz, *Sole Survivor*, 37–44; first published in the *San Francisco Examiner*, May 27, 1888. That it was published on the anniversary of the battle was not a coincidence.
7. Ibid., 44.
8. Ibid., 39.
9. Ibid., 40.
10. On General Patrick Cleburne see: Ezra Warner, *Generals in Grey*, (Baton Rouge: LSU Press, 1959), 53–54; Wiley Sword, "The Other Stonewall," *Civil War Times Illustrated* 36, no. 7 (February 1998): 36–44; Phil Leigh, "The Stonewall of the West," *Disunion* column/blog, *The New York Times*, September 3, 2012.
11. Hazen, *OR*, 423.

12. Ibid.
13. Joshi and Schultz, *Sole Survivor*, 40.
14. Ibid., 43.
15. Hazen, *OR*, 423.
16. For an eyewitness account of the battle by an officer in Knefler's Brigade, see Kenneth W. Noe, "Somebody Blundered," *The Ambrose Bierce Project Journal* 3, no. 1 (Fall 2007). (www.ambrosebierce.org/journal).
17. Hazen, *OR*, 424.
18. Ambrose Bierce to Clara Wright, June 8, 1864, from Joshi and Schultz, *Sole Survivor*, 46.
19. William T. Sherman, *Memoirs*, 59.

Chapter 13

1. McWilliams, "Ambrose Bierce and his First Love," 254.
2. UVA Archives, Military Papers, Eastman to Bierce, letters of June 17 and July 13, 1897.
3. McWilliams, *Ambrose Bierce*, 56.
4. NARA, Ambrose Bierce to AAG and approval, both dated June 29, 1864; reverse of Return.
5. NARA, Muster in Rolls for May/June and July/August, 1864.
6. Ambrose Bierce, "The Other Lodgers" from Thomsen, *Shadows*, 187–89; Joshi, Berkove, and Schultz, *Short Fiction* III, 1026–28; first published in *Cosmopolitan*, August 1907, 445–46.
7. NARA, Ambrose Bierce, Surgeon's Certificate, August 9, 1864.
8. McWilliams, "Ambrose Bierce and his First Love," 256.
9. George Sterling, "Shadow Maker," *American Mercury* (September 1925), 11.
10. McWilliams, "Ambrose Bierce and his First Love," 259.
11. Oscar Burton Robbins, *History of the Jackson family of Hempstead, Long Island, NY, Ohio and Indiana: descendants of Robert and Agnes Washburn Jackson* (Loveland, CO: Robbins, 1951), 222 (accessed via ancestryinstitution.com).
12. Maurice Frink, "Little Recalled of Ambrose Bierce, Author, in Home Town, Elkhart," *The Indianapolis Star*, February 12, 1928.
13. McWilliams, *Ambrose Bierce*, 56.
14. James McPherson, *Battle Cry of Freedom*, (New York: Oxford Univ. Press, 1988), 449; 816–19.

Chapter 14

1. Telegrams both dated July 12, 1864 at 8:45 and 9:30 PM respectively: Clifford Dowdy, ed., *The Wartime Papers of R. E. Lee* (New York: Bramhall House, 1961), 821–22; originally published by Douglas Southall Freeman in *Lee's Dispatches*, numbers 158 and 159; now also accessible online at Washington and Lee

Univ. Lee Family Digital Archives: http://leearchive.wlu.edu/papers/letters/by_recipient_list_23.html
2. Ambrose Bierce, "Four Days in Dixie" from Joshi and Schultz, *Sole Survivor,* 47—54; (first published in the *San Francisco Examiner,* Nov. 4, 1888).
3. Quoted in "Sherman's Campaign," *The New York Times,* Nov. 16, 1864; citing *The Cincinnati Commercial.*
4. Wiley Sword, *Embrace an Angry Wind* (New York: HarperCollins, 1992), 99.
5. "What May Happen Along a Road" from Joshi and Schultz, *Sole Survivor,* 55, first published in *Cosmopolitan Magazine,* December 1906.
6. Ibid.
7. Ibid.
8. Ibid.
9. Ibid.
10. Sword, *Angry Wind,* 152.
11. Joshi and Schultz, *Sole Survivor,* 55.
12. Ibid.
13. Bierce was certainly aware of the Confederate veterans' dispute over Spring Hill and likely the accusations regarding Hood's intoxication as well, but said nothing. Given his own comments regarding generals and their drinking (see Chapter 10), Bierce likely would not have been overly critical of Hood even if he had been in his cups. In any case, Bierce was always far more interested in excoriating Federal officers than Rebel ones. The charge regarding Hood is an old one and over the years historians have tended to pile on more scorn, assuming what their predecessors said to be true. Stanley Horn, familiar with the local lore of Maury County, would not have given the accusations any credence at all had the oral tradition not been so strong among old veterans; Horn, *The Army of Tennessee* (Norman, OK: Univ. of Oklahoma Press, 1952), 392. Wiley Sword asserted far more about Hood in his book on the Autumn Campaign (e.g. *Angry Wind,* 136 and caption to portrait facing 244), but other historians have made similarly negative assertions. More recently, there has been a strong pushback on the part of Hood's defenders: Steve Davis, "John Bell Hood's 'Addictions' in Civil War Literature," *Blue & Gray* magazine, October 1998 (http://counter.johnbellhood.org/davis.htm); and most recently Stephen M. Hood, *John Bell Hood: The Rise, Fall, and Resurrection of a Confederate General* (El Dorado Hills: Savas Beatie, 2013).
14. Joshi and Schultz, *Sole Survivor,* 56.
15. Henry M. Field, *Bright Skies and Dark Shadows* (New York: Scribners, 1890), 219.
16. Joshi and Schultz, *Sole Survivor,* 57.
17. Ibid.
18. Ibid., 57-8.
19. Ibid., 58.
20. Ibid.
21. Ibid., 57–58.
22. Ibid., 58.

Chapter 15

1. Secondary works on the Battle of Nashville and the Autumn Campaign have grown in recent years. Still useful is Stanley F. Horn's *The Decisive Battle of Nashville* (Baton Rouge: LSU Press, 1956); Sword, *Angry Wind*, 272–422; Colonel Henry Stone, "Repelling Hood's Invasion of Tennessee" in *Battles and Leaders* IV: 441–64. There are also, of course, the after-action reports in the *OR*, of most relevance for the present work were the ones relating to IV Corps and Sam Beatty's division, particularly Post's brigade.
2. Ambrose Bierce, "The Major's Tale," 753 in *The Collected Writings of Ambrose Bierce* (1946; reprinted New York: Replica Books, 1999), 752–58; Joshi, Berkove, and Schultz, *Short Fiction* II, 706–12; originally published in the *San Francisco Examiner*, Jan. 5, 1890, as "A Practical Joke: Major Broadwood Recalls the Heroic Past."
3. UVA Archives, Military Papers, General Beatty to A. G. Bierce, Special Order No.119, December 6, 1864.
4. Belmont was the residence of Adelicia Acklen, one of the richest, smartest, and most beautiful women in the South. At the time of the battle she was absent, having gone down to Louisiana, where she persuaded a Union commander to loan her wagons to transport her cotton crop to market and a Confederate commander to provide a cavalry escort for it. Insofar as Adelicia's ability to manipulate the male of the species, the fictitious Scarlett O'Hara was a naïve schoolgirl by comparison.
5. Bierce, "The Major's Tale," 753.
6. Ibid., 754.
7. Ibid.
8. Joshi and Schultz, *Sole Survivor*, 299–300.
9. "On Black Soldiering" Joshi and Schultz, *Sole Survivor*, 63; originally published in the *San Francisco Examiner*, June 5, 1898.
10. "General Debility" from Joshi and Schultz, *Sole Survivor*, 62; originally published in the *San Francisco Wasp*, July 14, 1883.
11. Alexander Whithall, "The Battle of Nashville," Ninth Indiana Veterans Association, *Sixth Annual Reunion*, (1889), 51.
12. Joshi and Schultz, *Sole Survivor*, 62.
13. Ibid.
14. "A Son of the Gods" from Thomsen, *Shadows*, 69–75, Joshi, Berkove, and Schultz, *Short Fiction* II, 599–604; originally published in the *San Francisco Examiner*, July 29, 1888.
15. As with his editors, Major Bierce had a love-hate relationship with critics (perhaps hate-hate relationship might be more apt). In this case the offending reviewer was a scrivener for "Life." See Joshi and Schultz, *Sole Survivor*, 253–54; published in the *San Francisco Examiner*, March 1, 1897. He had earlier taken issue with Hazeltine, the book editor for the *New York Sun*, for similar criticisms of his military stories in *Tales of Soldiers and Civilians*;

see Joshi and Schultz, *Sole Survivor*, 251–53, *San Francisco Examiner*, June 26, 1892. Bierce seems to have taken note more of the negative reviews than the positive ones; for example, J. S. Cowley Brown in the British Weekly *Black and White*, wrote an insightful review of Bierce's military writings, comparing him favorably to Rudyard Kipling: J. S. Cowley, "The American Kipling," *Black and White: a Weekly Illustrated Record and Review*, January 7, 1899.

16. Joshi and Schultz, *Sole Survivor*, 254.
17. S. T. Joshi and David E. Schultz, *The Unabridged Devil's Dictionary*, (Athens GA & London: Univ. of Georgia Press, 2000), 194. First published in book form as *The Cynic's Word Book*, (New York: Doubleday, 1906). Begun in 1881 in the *San Francisco Wasp* and continued "in a desultory way" over the years by Bierce in various periodicals, this has been reissued in various editions ever since and is what he is best know for today. The Joshi and Schultz edition includes quips left out of the first edition and deletes later additions that were Biercean in tone but not attributable to him; this volume should therefore be considered the definitive edition. When we compare this corpus of Bierce's acidic barbs to the humor of the late nineteenth century in general, the conciseness of Bierce's wit as compared with his contemporaries—even compared to Mark Twain—is striking, and we can't help but speculate whether the "one-liner" and modern stand-up humor in general owe a deep debt to Bierce's writings.
18. Joshi and Schultz, *Sole Survivor*, 62.
19. Matthew C. O'Brien, "Ambrose Bierce and the Civil War: 1865," *American Literature*, vol. 48, no 3 (Nov. 1976) 377–81, apparently viewed Bierce's journal in the UVA Archives and tried to explain the mystery of his Carolina service away by theorizing that "somehow it came into the possession of one of his fellow engineers" and was then returned and that Bierce was in Selma Alabama throughout 1865. While I am not a handwriting expert, neither is Mr. O'Brien, and the Carolina Journal, with its numerous misspellings and cramped style, can best be explained by the work of a military engineer, still recovering from a head wound, hastily writing daily entries under combat conditions. The letter to Bierce from Eaton is most certainly a dating error on Eaton's part, for even if Eaton were working as Treasury Agent in January, Bierce was not. Written soon after the beginning of the new year, it is likely Eaton put 1865 instead of 1866 at the heading of his letter out of habit, an error I have done myself on many occasions. Moreover, Bierce was never in Atlanta in 1864, either before or after his sick leave and the survey entry is probably to be dated sometime after his Carolina service and before becoming an aide to Eaton. More importantly, Selma would have been a very insalubrious place for anyone in blue uniform during the winter and early spring of 1865. Wilson's Cavalry did not take the city until April and Forrest's marauders were still roaming the region for several weeks after that. While, as noted above, Bierce's chronology remains unresolved for this period, and it is very doubtful he assumed duties as assistant to Eaton in Selma much before June of 1865.

20. UVA Archives, Military Papers, Gen. Hazen to SPR ADJ Gen. HQ, Atlanta, September 16, 1864.
21. UVA Archives, Military Papers, Notebook, 1865 Jan.-Dec. This and ensuing Bierce quotes in chapter are from this source. It is probable that Carey McWilliams saw this journal among the papers he viewed belonging to Bierce's daughter; if so, it doesn't seem that understood its full import. Although McWilliams nods to the importance of Bierce's war service, he glosses over it in his biography.
22. Hazen, *Narrative*, 340. General Hazen published his order of February 4, 1865, directing his three brigade commanders to organize "pioneer corps" from the free Negro males traveling with the army "for labor on roads." Although carried on the payrolls of the quartermaster, they would not have been considered military personnel. Someone with engineering experience had to direct their activities, but Hazen does not say who; was it Bierce?
23. Bierce Papers, UVA Archives.
24. Hazen, *Narrative*, 339.
25. Hazen, *Narrative*, 340.
26. Hazen, *OR* 47, Pt. 1: 271–76; additional reports, 277–81. All of them are part of "Report No. 21."

Chapter 16

1. Ambrose Bierce, "Way Down in Alabam" from Joshi and Schultz, *Sole Survivor*, 69; the earliest known publication was 1903, but its first appearance in print has not been identified so far; see Joshi and Schultz, *Annotated Bibliography*, 297, item E31. Unless otherwise specified, all the Bierce quotes in this chapter are taken from this same article.
2. See *Order of Exercises at Exhibition; Phillips Academy, Andover Mass. July 26, 1859* (Andover, MA: Warren F. Draper, 1859), where Eaton delivered the "Greek Dissertation," presumably in Greek; Brvt. Major Henry S. Burrage, Comp., *Civil War Record of Brown University*, (Providence: Brown, 1920), 45.
3. *Opelika Union*, June 1, 1865.
4. Joshi and Schultz, *Sole Survivor*, 69.
5. Walter L. Fleming, *Civil War and Reconstruction in Alabama* (New York: Columbia Univ. Press, 1905), 291.
6. Walter L. Fleming, *Civil War and Reconstruction*, 299–301, footnote 785.
7. See for example, Sherburne B. Eaton, *A Discussion of the Constitutionality of the Act of Congress of March 2, 1867, Authorizing the Seizure of Books and Papers for the Alleged Frauds Upon the Revenue* (New York: Press of the Chamber of Commerce, 1874). Eaton penned several similar works of literature, and while not as popular as comrade Bierce's, were undoubtedly more lucrative for his law practice.
8. Joshi and Schultz, *Sole Survivor*, 69.
9. "The South As It Is: A Correspondent's Tour Through Alabama," *The New York Times*, Nov. 2, 1865.

10. See Van Horne, *Army* (1995), 557–60; Jerry Keenan, "Wilson's Selma Raid," *Civil War Times* 1, no. 9 (January 1963), 37–44; also see Brian S. Wills, "The Confederate Sun Sets on Selma: Nathan Bedford Forrest and the Defense of Alabama in 1865," in Kenneth Noe, (Ed.) *The Yellowhammer War* (Tuscaloosa: Univ. of Alabama Press, 2013) 71–89.
11. Joshi and Schultz, *Sole Survivor*, 70.
12. See V. C. Jones, "The Rise and Fall of the Ku Klux Klan," *Civil War Times Illustrated* 2, no.10 (Fall 1964), 12–17.
13. Joshi and Schultz, *Sole Survivor*, 74–76.
14. See Bierce, Notebook, Ambrose Bierce Military Papers, UVA Archives Accession no 5992-a. The Aspinwall Diary is written in the same hand as the previous Carolina journal and also has some original spelling ("holy nude woman," "parot," etc.), and so the same person composed both—presumably Bierce. While I leave it up to those more qualified than I to weigh in on the Aspinwall travelogue's literary merits, we should note that it is the earliest surviving piece of continuous narrative we possess of Bierce's and his short essay is therefore of some interest on that account.

Chapter 17

1. UVA Archives, Military Papers: Telegraph from Nashville to Elkhart, July 31, 1866; letter from Washington, DC to La Porte, IN, dated January 11, 1867; Washington to "Assistant Treasurer" San Francisco, dated April 3, 1867. Adding to the confusion regarding Bierce's final war rank is the notice in *The Evening Star*, Washington, DC, November 12, 1866. It is an official notice from the Adjutant General's Office, War Department, notifying officers who have not yet accepted their commissions that the offer will be voided if they do not contact the War Department by December 1. In the notice, Bierce is listed as "late captain, 9th Indiana volunteers," which, if not a typo, would indicate that he was indeed promoted to captain at some point, although there is no record of it.
2. UVA Archives, Military Papers, Presidential Commission, August 3, 1866; War Department to Bierce notifying him of his majority, October 22, 1866.
3. Neale, *Life*, 87.
4. See Williams, "A Warsaw Boy in London."
5. Duncan and Klooster, *Phantoms*, 344.
6. UVA Archives, Military Papers, Executive Department, Indianapolis, to Ambrose G. Bierce, Jan. 14, 1886.
7. Bierce, "The Moonlit Road," Frank McSherry Jr., Charles G. Waugh and Martin Greenberg, *Dixie Ghosts*, (Nashville: Rutledge Hill Press, 1988), 199–208; Joshi, Berkove, and Schultz, *Short Fiction* III, 1015–22; first published in *Cosmopolitan*, Jan. 1907. Bierce, "A Baby Tramp" from Joshi, Berkove, and Schultz, *Short Fiction* II, 799–803; first published, *The Wave* (San Francisco), August 29, 1891. For the Fortean rain of blood in Bath, Kentucky, cf. Christopher K. Coleman, *Strange Tales of the Dark and Bloody Ground* (Nashville: Rutledge Hill Press, 1998), 109–15.

8. Ambrose Bierce, "The Difficulty of Crossing a Field" from Joshi, Berkove, and Schultz, *Short Fiction* III, 1165–6; first published in the *San Francisco Examiner*, Oct. 14, 1888. While the exact history of this particular Mulhattan tale has yet to be fully unraveled, the following deal with aspects of it and its connection to Bierce's story: Garth Haslam, "The Mystery of David Lang," *Anomalies* (http://anomalyinfo.com); T. Peter Park, "Looking at the Lang and Lerch Legends," *Mythfolk*, October 14, 2006 (http://www.mail-archive.com/mythfolk@yahoogroups.com/msg00764.html); Joe Nickell, *Secrets of the Supernatural* (New York: Prometheus, 1988). Ironically, in 1999, modern composer David Lang composed on opera based on Bierce's "The Difficulty of Crossing a Field."
9. Duncan and Klooster, *Phantoms*, 332–33.
10. Joshi and Schultz, *Sole Survivor*, 66–67.
11. Duncan and Klooster, *Phantoms*, 334–36.
12. UVA Archives, Ambrose Bierce Papers, Bierce to Harriet Hershburgh, June 15, 1898.
13. See for example, Martin Buinicki and David Owens, "De-Anthologizing Ambrose Bierce: A New Look at 'What I Saw of Shiloh,'" *War Literature and Art* 23 (2011); online edition.
14. Neale, *Life*, 73–74.
15. UVA Archives: Military Papers, President, Army War College to Major Ambrose Bierce, September 29, 1908, October 1, 1908, and October 16, 1908.
16. UVA Archives, Military Papers, letter of Alex L. Whitehall to Helen Bierce Cowden, January 9, 1915.

Epilogue

1. By the early part of 1915, there seems to have been a general sense that the Major was dead. See for example, H. M. East, Jr., "Bierce—The Warrior Writer," *Overland Monthly* (June 1915), 507–9.
2. McWilliams, *Ambrose Bierce*, 346.
3. Stanford Univ. Archives, letter of Ambrose Bierce to Charles Dexter Allen, October 25, 1911.
4. Bertha Pope, ed., *Letters of Ambrose Bierce* (San Francisco: The Book Club of California, 1922), 204.
5. Joshi and Schultz, *Sole Survivor*, 296; also in Pope, *Letters* (A. G. to niece Lora, Oct. 1, 1913), 196–97.
6. UVA Archives, letter of Alex L. Whitehall to Helen Bierce Cowden, January 9, 1915.
7. Helen Bierce, "Ambrose Bierce at Home," *The American Mercury* (Dec. 1933), 458.

Appendix 3

1. William Babcock Hazen, *Narrative*, 340.
2. Date, Distance, Character of Roads, Wether [*sic*], Incidents and Camp are the headings at the top of each page and the entries are listed vertically below them in chart form, much as one might do on a modern Excel spreadsheet. I have integrated the headings into each entry here. Bierce has the correct the spelling of weather on the ensuing pages, although not on the first; some of his other orthography is also idiomatic, which I have battled autocorrect to preserve.
3. On a separate page under March 4 is the notation "Route du Marche. 15th A.C. Via Harrington. Quicks Church, Springfield, Sanomburg Gilchrists Bridge."
4. On a separate page is a notation: "17th Bennettville Burns Bridg Stewartville Gallipolis."

Selected Bibliography

A Note about the Sources

In my efforts to faithfully chronicle Ambrose Bierce's war years, I have drawn on a wide variety of sources, some of which have been more fundamental to exploring A. G.'s military career than others. Basic to any modern researcher of Bierce are the reference works of S. T. Joshi and David E. Schultz, particularly their *Annotated Bibliography*, which for the first time straightened out the often-complicated publishing history of Bierce's writings. Many of Bierce's pieces have several variorum editions, and previous researchers, relying only on reprints in one or another of his anthologies, frequently missed deleted passages, as well as the article's original context. One Civil War tale had been overlooked completely because it was bundled in with several non-Civil War pieces in one of his early anthologies. I fully acknowledge the expertise of Messrs. Joshi and Schultz regarding all things Bierce and certainly this work would be far more deficient without the benefit of their groundbreaking research.

While I have chased down a number of the original newspaper and magazine articles by and about Bierce, for citation purposes I have found it more convenient to cite his autobiographical pieces from Joshi and Schultz's collection, *Sole Survivor*. Although I consulted several other collections of Bierce's war-related writings in composing this biography, the 2006 three-volume collection of his short stories, *The Short Fiction of Ambrose Bierce: A Comprehensive Edition*, done by Joshi and Schultz in collaboration with Lawrence Berkove, should now be considered the standard and definitive reference on the corpus of Bierce's creative works. Several libraries, archives, and museums have been most helpful in my quest, but I would be remiss if I did not single out the University of Virginia's Bierce collection, which contains the bulk of papers relating to Bierce's wartime career.

Although posthumous collections of Bierce's works are voluminous, in recent years a few have focused on his Civil War pieces, both fiction and nonfiction: Brian Thomsen's *Shadows of Blue and Gray* and Duncan and Klooster's *Phantoms of a Blood-Stained Period* have proved the most useful collections. Duncan and Klooster subtitled their work "The Complete Civil War Writings of Ambrose Bierce" which is inaccurate; they missed at least one piece and added another not dealing with the Civil War at all. Nonetheless it is a valiant attempt. Those many articles and books that have dealt with Bierce's Civil War work mainly from a literary perspective were largely irrelevant for our present purposes and were therefore not consulted; likewise several biographies, which were either mainly of literary focus or limited to his postwar life, or else added nothing new, were also glossed over and are not listed.

Although for many years historians neglected the war in the west, in recent decades that oversight has been remedied. There are now numerous studies of those battles and campaigns to choose from, and with the Sesquicentennial more are being released every year. With such a plethora of available sources, necessarily I have had to be selective in their use. Fundamental for any serious study of the Civil War or its participants is, of course, *The Official Records of the Union and Confederate Armies* (to give its short title). In reviewing it in one of his columns, Ambrose Bierce referred to it as "the book that is more than a book," and at some 137 volumes (plus multiple parts to each volume), that is something of an understatement. However, in passing, I should point out for those unfamiliar with this resource that many of the action reports contained within that monumental volume are distinguished by their equivocal nature—as Bierce was only too aware of. Less well known, but highly useful to this present study, is Broadfoot Publisher's more recent *Supplement to the Official Records of the Union and Confederate Armies*, a separate multi-volume work based on microfilms of records overlooked by the original compilers of the Official Records. I discovered this quite by accident at the TSLA while looking for something else. Volume Sixteen contains the "Record of Events" of the Ninth Indiana—their regimental war diary.

Although a Luddite by inclination, as time goes by I find the use of the Internet increasingly essential to my research and writing. In my previous work on Lincoln, the online search of the Library of Congress and Basler's Lincoln papers proved invaluable in locating documents hitherto overlooked (and unburned by Robert Lincoln) and that supported the thesis of that book. The Internet is particularly useful for locating and accessing many volumes of quaint and curious lore long out of print. In this present study of Bierce, the Internet Archive, HathiTrust, The Gutenberg Project, the TSLA's own online resources, plus miscellaneous other online archival and research resources were all indispensable in tracking down and accessing rare and otherwise unobtainable primary sources relating to Bierce, the Ninth Indiana, and campaigns in the Western Theater in which they were involved.

There is a myriad of websites relating to Ambrose Bierce and his literary genius, two of which are worthy of particular praise: Don Swaim's *The Ambrose Bierce Site* and The Ambrose Bierce Project's *The ABP Journal*.

Selected Bibliography

While doubtless there are primary and secondary sources relating to Bierce's military career that I have missed or overlooked, I have made as thorough a search as time and resources permitted. Regretfully, I had neither the benefit of an academic sabbatical or an institutional grant to pursue every lead regarding Bierce and his war years. Being paid a year's wages to read, study, and write as fancy dictates would indeed have been "in high cotton" (to use a sanitized version of the Southern expression). Prior to beginning this work in earnest, I did occasionally have a chance to discuss my research in a public forum and sometimes learned from the audience as much as I imparted, as with my lecture before the Tennessee Historical Society about Ambrose Bierce in Tennessee.

This particular work has been a long time coming, not only in regards to actual research and writing, but going back even to boyhood, when, during the centennial of the Civil War, I first experienced Ambrose Bierce's Civil War writings. Back then I did not realize they had a specific context, as doubtless many other modern readers still do not know; hopefully this present tome will rectify that misapprehension. In any case, it only began to slowly dawn on me after I moved from New York to the Mid-South and found I was frequently treading upon the same pathways that Bierce had during the war, that, despite the universality of his works, he was in fact for the most part describing real people, places, and events of the war. In fact, it was only during the later phases of this project, when I was actually writing the manuscript, that I became aware that within a mile or so of where I was writing was also where the Ninth Indiana had pulled escort and guard duty and where one of Bierce's uncanny civilian tales had (perhaps) taken place. Unfortunately, David Lang/Orion Williamson is still missing and whether his bones may someday be found along Cottontown Road or whether Dr. Hern is correct and he resides somewhere in the limbo of the "luminiferous ether" remains a moot point.

Due to a near-fatal car accident, I did not have the opportunity to visit either Warsaw or Elkhart Indiana's libraries and museums in person, which I deeply regret; hopefully in the future I shall be able to remedy that deficiency. In the meantime, I enjoin the interested readers of this book to rectify this deficiency by making the pilgrimage to these estimable Biercean boyhood destinations themselves. From prior forays into Indiana before this present enterprise was begun in earnest, I can personally assure the reader that these regions of the Hoosier state are hardly the "wasteland" Bierce made them out to be. While they perhaps may not be quite the bucolic paradise that fellow Hoosier and sometime Bierce nemesis, James Whitcomb Riley, made them out to be, they were never so dire as The Major later remembered them.

Selected Bibliography

Archival Sources

Elkhart County Historical Museum, Bristol, IN

The Jail Museum (Kosciusko County Historical Society), Warsaw, IN

Library of Congress (LOC)

The Nashville Room, Nashville Public Library

National Archives and Records Administration (NARA)

Robert Milroy Papers, Jasper County Public Library, IN

Stamford Univ. Library, Department of Special Collections, Ambrose Bierce Papers (1872–1913); online calendar

Tennessee State Library and Archives

Univ. of Virginia, Alderman Memorial Library, Papers of Ambrose Bierce, 1842–1914; Military Papers

Newspapers

The Charleston Courier (SC), Tri-Weekly

The Chicago Daily Inter-Ocean

The Daily Cleveland Herald (OH)

The Denver Evening Post

Harpers Weekly

The Louisville Daily Journal

Milwaukee Daily Sentinel

The Nashville Banner

The New York Herald

The New York Times

The New York Tribune

The Northern Indianian (accessed via The Ambrose Bierce site)

Summit Beacon (OH)

The Warsaw Daily Times

The Washington Evening Star

The Washington Times

Significant Online Resources Consulted

The Ambrose Bierce Project

Don Swaim's The Ambrose Bierce Site

Selected Bibliography

Army of the Cumberland website (www.aotc.net)

ICPR (Indiana Commisssion on Public Records), Indiana State Archives Digital Records (http://www.in.gov/icpr/2533.ktm)

The Internet Archives

Jasper County (IN) Archives

Library of Congress, *American Memory* et al.

Project Gutenburg

ProQuest Civil War Era, (Pamphlets of the Civil War, 1861–65)

Rootsweb and AncestryInstitution.com (www.Ancestry.com)

Articles

Allardice, Bruce. "West Points of the Confederacy: Southern Military Schools and the Confederate Army." *Civil War History* 43, no. 4 (December 1997): 310–31.

Berg, Gordon. "Allegorical Trip Through Alabama." *The Washington Times*. Thursday, December 10, 2009.

Berg, Gordon. "Phantoms of a Blood-Stained Period." *Civil War Times* 44, no. 4 (October 2005): 42–48.

Bierce, Helen. "Ambrose Bierce at Home." *American Mercury* 30, (December 1933): 453–58.

Buell, General Don Carlos. "Shiloh Reviewed." *Battles & Leaders* I, 487–536.

Buinicki, Martin and David Owens. "De-Anthologizing Ambrose Bierce: A New Look at 'What I Saw of Shiloh.'" *War, Literature and Art, An International Journal of the Humanities* (online edition) 23 (2011).

Clark, Donald A. "Buell's Advance to Pittsburg Landing: A Fresh Look at an Old Controversy." *Tennessee Historical Quarterly* 68, no. 4 (Winter, 2009): 355–90.

Cole, Jeanine. "'Upon the Stage of Disorder' Legalized Prostitution in Memphis and Nashville, 1863–1865." *Tennessee Historical Quarterly* 68, no. 1 (Spring 2009): 40–65.

Collins, Cary C. "Grey Eagle: Major General Robert Huston Milroy and the Civil War." *Indiana Magazine of History* 90 (March 1994): 48–72.

Conley, Laurence D. "The Truth About Chickamauga: A Ninth Indiana Regiment's Perspective." *Indiana Magazine of History* 98, no. 2 (June 2002): 113–43.

Cozzens, Peter. "The Tormenting Flame." *Civil War Times* 35, no. 1 (April 1996): 45–54.

Daeuble, John. *Journal of 1st Sgt. John Daeuble, 6th Kentucky Volunteer Infantry Regiment U.S.* Translated by Joseph Reinhart. http://6thkentuckyus.yolasite.com/journal.php.

East Jr., H. M. "Bierce—The Warrior Writer." *Overland Monthly* (June 1915): 507–9.

Fried, Joseph P. "How One Union General Murdered Another." *Civil War Times Illustrated* 1, no. 3 (June 1962): 14–16.

Guelzo, Allen. "Bierce's Civil War: One Man's Morbid Vision." *Civil War Times* 44, no. 4 (October 2005): 34–40, 60. (Reprint of *Civil War Times Illustrated* article from 1981.)

Hadley, Daniel B. "Reminiscences of John Brown." *McClure's Magazine* 10: 275–84.

Halsey Jr., Ashley. "South Carolina Began Preparing for War in 1851." *Civil War Times* 1, no. 1 (April 1962): 8–10, 12–13.

Jones, V. C. "The Rise and Fall of the Ku Klux Klan." *Civil War Times Illustrated* 2, no. 10 (February 1964): 12–17.

McKee, John Miller. "An Eyewitness." *The Great Panic* (Nashville: Johnson & Whiting, 1862; reprinted, Nashville: Elder/Sherbourne, 1977).

McWilliams, Carey. "Ambrose Bierce and His First Love." *Bookman* 35 (June 1932): 254–59.

Morris Jr., Roy. "War Crimes? Colonel Turchin and the Sack of Athens." *Civil War Times Illustrated* 24, no. 10 (February 1986): 26–32.

Noe, Kenneth W. "Somebody Blundered—Marcus Woodcock, Ambrose Bierce, and the Crime at Pickett's Mill." *The ABP Journal* 3, no. 1 (Fall 2007).

O'Brien, Matthew C. "Ambrose Bierce and the Civil War: 1865," *American Literature*, 48, no. 3 (Nov. 1976) 377–81

Owens, David M. "Bierce and Biography: The Location of Owl Creek Bridge." *American Literary Realism* 26, no. 3 (Spring 1994): 82–89.

Parker, Margaret. "My Quest to Find the Birthplace of Ambrose Bierce." *Meigs Historian Newsletter* (September 2003). accessed online via *The Ambrose Bierce Site*.

Pittard, Homer. "The Strange Death of Peter Garesche." *Civil War Times Illustrated* 1, no. 6 (October 1962): 23–25.

Redman, Bob. "The Tullahoma Campaign, 23 June-3 July, 1863." www.aotc.net.

Redman, Bob. "Sheridan's Ride at Chickamauga." http://americancivilwar.com,

Shanks, William. "Chattanooga: Our Special Report of the Terrible Conflict." *New York Herald*, September 27, 1863.

Timothy B. Smith. "The Myths of Shiloh." *America's Civil War* 19, no. 5 (May 2006): 30–36, 71.

Sterling, George. "Shadow Maker." *American Mercury* (October 1925).

Suhr, Robert Collins. "Saving the Day at Shiloh." *America's Civil War* 12 No. 6 (January 2000), 34–41.

Swick, Gerald D. "An Omen at Philippi." *America's Civil War* 24, no. 2 (May 2011): 44–51.

Truman, Benjamin C. "The South As It Is: A Correspondent's Tour Through Alabama." *The New York Times*, November 2, 1865.

Williams, Reuben. "Memories of War Times." published serially in *Warsaw Daily Times,* December 27, 1902 onward. Accessed online via *The Ambrose Bierce Site.* (Later reissued in book form.)

Wilt, Napier. "Ambrose Bierce and the Civil War." *American Literature* 1 (1929): 260–85.

Wood, General T. J. "Nashville—The Crowning Victory, Speech of General Wood, delivered . . . February 5, 1868." *Report of the First Meeting of the Society of the Army of the Cumberland.* (Cincinnati: Ohio Valley Press, 1868): 91–97.

Books

Ambrose, Stephen E. *Halleck: Lincoln's Chief of Staff.* Baton Rouge: LSU Press, 1962.

Basler, Roy P., ed. *Collected Works of Abraham Lincoln* 5. New Brunswick: Rutgers, 1953.

Berry, Sue, Martha Fuqua and Pam Oglesby, eds. *Homespun Tales.* Franklin: Territorial Press, 1989.

Bierce, Ambrose (Clifton Fadiman, ed.). *Collected Writings.* 1946; reprinted New York: Replica Books, 1999. (This collection is faulty in many respects and hoary with age, but oft reprinted and widely available and for that reason consulted in the writing of this manuscript. Now, however, see Joshi, Berkove, and Schultz, 2006, for the more authoritative edition of these works.)

Brickham, William Denison. *Rosecrans Campaign with the Fourteenth Army Corps, or the Army of the Cumberland: A Narrative of Personal Observations.* Cincinnati: Moore, Wilstack, Huys & Co., 1863.

Burrage, Major Henry S., comp. *Civil War Record of Brown University.* Providence: Brown, 1920.

Cist, Henry M. "The Army of the Cumberland." *Campaigns of the Civil War* VII. New York: Charles Scribner's Sons, 1882.

Cozzens, Peter. *No Better Place to Die, The Battle of Stones River.* Urbana and Chicago: Univ. of Illinois Press, 1990.

Cozzens, Peter. *This Terrible Sound, The Battle of Chickamauga.* Urbana and Chicago: Univ. of Illinois Press, 1992.

Cox, General Jacob D. "The March to the Sea—Franklin and Nashville." *Campaigns of the Civil War* X. 1882; reprint Edison, NJ: Castle Books, 2002.

Dana, Charles A. *Recollections of the Civil War.* 1898; reprint Lincoln: Univ. of Nebraska Press, 1996.

Davis, George B., Leslie J. Percy, and Joseph W. Kirkley, eds. *Atlas to Accompany the Official Records of the Union and Confederate Armies.* 1891–95; reprint New York: Barnes & Noble, 2003 (under *The Official Atlas of the Civil War*).

DeCastro, Adolphe. *Portrait of Ambrose Bierce.* 1929; reprint New York: Beakman, 1974.

Selected Bibliography

Dowdy, Clifford, ed. *The Wartime Papers of R. E. Lee.* New York: Bramhall House, 1961.

Duncan, Russell and David J. Klooster, eds. *Phantoms of a Blood-Stained Period: The Complete Civil War Writings of Ambrose Bierce.* Amherst: Univ. of Massachusetts Press, 2002.

Durham, Walter T. *Nashville, The Occupied City, 1862–1863.* Nashville: Tennessee Historical Society, 1985.

Durham, Walter T. *Rebellion Revisited.* Franklin: Hillsboro Press, 1999.

Fatout, Paul. *The Devil's Lexicographer.* Norman: Univ. of Oklahoma Press, 1951.

Fitch, John. *Annals of the Army of the Cumberland* (Fifth Edition). Philadelphia: J. B. Lippincott & Co., 1864.

Fleming, Walter L. *Civil War and Reconstruction in Alabama.* New York: Columbia Univ. Press, 1905.

Freeman, Douglas Southall. *Lee's Dispatches: Unpublished Letters of General Robert E. Lee, C.S.A., to Jefferson Davis and the War Department of the Confederate States of America, 1862–1865.* New York and London: G. P. Putnam's Sons, 1915.

Garrison, Webb. *Friendly Fire in the Civil War.* Nashville: Rutledge Hill Press, 1999.

Gracie, Archibald. *The Truth About Chickamauga.* Boston & New York: Houghton Mifflin, 1911.

Hazen, William B. *A Narrative of Military Service.* Boston: Ticknor & Son, 1885.

Horn, Stanley F. *The Army of Tennessee.* Norman: Univ. of OK Press, 1952.

Horn, Stanley F. *The Decisive Battle of Nashville.* Baton Rouge: LSU Press, 1956.

Howett, Janet B., ed. *Supplement to the Official Records of the Union and Confederate Armies, Part II: Records of Events* 16, serial no. 28, Indiana. Wilmington, NC: Broadfoot, 1995. (Cited as OR *Supplement*).

Indiana, Adjutant General's Office. *Report, Adjutant General State of Indiana* 4, 1861–1866. Indianapolis: Samuel M. Dorghen, 1866.

Johnson, Robert Underwood and Clarence Clough Buel, eds. *Battles and Leaders of the Civil War* I-IV. New York: The Century Co., 1887–89. (Also accessed online and in various reprint editions; cited as *Battles and Leaders.*)

Joshi, S. T. and David E. Schultz, eds. *Ambrose Bierce: An Annotated Bibliography of Primary Sources.* Westport, CT: Greenwood Press, 1999.

Joshi, S. T. and David E. Schultz, eds. *A Sole Survivor: Bits of Autobiography.* Knoxville: Univ. of Tennessee Press, 1998.

Joshi, S. T., Lawrence I. Berkove, and David E. Schultz, eds. *The Short Fiction of Ambrose Bierce: A Comprehensive Edition,* 3 vols. (Knoxville: Univ. of Tennessee Press, 2006).

Joshi, S. T. and David E. Schultz. *The Unabridged Devil's Dictionary.* Athens: Univ. of Georgia Press, 2000.

Selected Bibliography

Lowry, Thomas P. *The War the Soldiers Wouldn't Tell: Sex in the Civil War.* Mechanicsburg, PA: Stackpole, 1994.

Mammoy, Major Michael J. *Union Artillery at the Battle of Chickamauga.* MA Thesis for degree in Military History. West Point: US Military Academy, 1990.

McCann, William, ed. *Ambrose Bierce's Civil War.* New York: Regnery, 1956.

McDonough, James Lee. *Chattanooga—Death Grip on the Confederacy.* Knoxville: Univ. of Tennessee Press, 1984.

McDonough, James Lee. *Shiloh—In Hell Before Night.* Knoxville: Univ. of Tennessee Press, 1983.

McPherson, James. *Battle Cry of Freedom, The Civil War Era.* Oxford: Oxford Univ. Press, 1988.

McWilliams, Carey. *Ambrose Bierce: A Biography* (Second Edition). Hamden: Archon, 1967.

Merrill, Catherine. *The Soldier of Indiana in the War for the Union.* Indianapolis: Merrill & Co., 1864.

Miles, Jim. *Paths to Victory.* Nashville: Rutledge Hill Press, 1991.

Moore, Frank, ed. *The Rebellion Record, 1862.* New York: G. P. Putnam, 1863.

Morris Jr., Roy. *Ambrose Bierce, Alone in Bad Company.* New York: Crown, 1995.

Neale, Walter. *Life of Ambrose Bierce.* New York: Walter Neale, 1929.

Noe, Kenneth W. *Perryville: This Grand Havoc of Battle.* Lexington: Univ. of Kentucky Press, 2001.

Noe, Kenneth W. (Ed.) The Yellowhammer War: The Civil War and Reconstruction in Alabama. Tuscaloosa: Univ of Alabama Press, 2013.

Noyales, Jonathan A. *'My Will is Absolute Law:' General Robert H. Milroy and Winchester, Virginia.* A Thesis: Virginia Polytechnic Institute and State Univ., April 2003.

Nye, George A. *Warsaw in the 1860's.* Warsaw: self-published typescript, 1951.

Pope, Bertha C., ed. *The Letters of Ambrose Bierce.* San Francisco: The Book Club of California, 1922.

Report of the Proceedings of the Society of the Army of West Virginia, at its first three meetings . . . Cincinnati: Peter E. Thomas Publishers, 1880.

Reunion of the 9th Indiana Veteran Volunteer Association, Proceedings (title varies). Vols. 6, 9–18. 1889, 1892–1904.

Robbins, Oscar Burton. *History of the Jackson family of Hempstead, Long Island, NY, Ohio and Indiana: descendants of Robert and Agnes Washburn Jackson.* Loveland, CO: Robbins, 1951. Accessed via www.ancestryinstitution.com.

Robertson, William G., Lt. Col. Edward P. Shanahan, et al. *Staff Ride Handbook for the Battle of Chickamauga, 18–20 September 1863.* Fort Leavenworth, KS: Combat Studies Institute, U.S. General Staff College, 1992.

Selected Bibliography

Roman, Alfred. *The Military Operations of General Beauregard in the War Between the States* I. New York: Harper Bros., 1884.

Ross, Charles D. *Civil War Acoustic Shadows.* Shippensburg, PA: White Mane, 2001.

Ruger, Edward. *History of the Army of the Cumberland, Atlas.* Cincinnati: Robert Clarke & Co., 1875.

Schaefer, Michael W. *Just What War Is, The Civil War Writings of DeForest and Bierce.* Knoxville: Univ. of Tennessee Press, 1997.

Sheridan, P. H. *Personal Memoirs of P. H. Sheridan.* New York: Charles Webster, 1888.

Sherman, William T. *The Memoirs of William T. Sherman by Himself.* 1885; reprint Bloomington: Indiana Univ. Press, 1957. (Two volumes in one, but with separate pagination.)

Stephens, James Darwin. *Reflections: A Portrait—Biography of the Kentucky Military Institute, 1845–1971.* Georgetown: KMI Inc., 1991.

Sword, Wiley. *Shiloh, Bloody April.* New York: Morrow, 1974.

Sword, Wiley. *Embrace An Angry Wind, The Confederacy's Last Hurrah: Spring Hill, Franklin, and Nashville.* New York: HarperCollins, 1992.

Thomsen, Brian M., ed. *Shadows of Blue and Gray, The Civil War Writings of Ambrose Bierce.* New York: Tom Doherty Assoc., 2002.

Tucker, Glen. *The Battles for Chattanooga.* Jamestown, VA: Eastern Acorn Press, 1987.

Van Horne, Thomas B. *History of the Army of the Cumberland* I-III. Cincinnati: Robert Clarke & Co., 1875.

Van Horne, Thomas. *History of the Army of the Cumberland.* Abridged reprint, New York: K&K, 1995.

Warner, Ezra J. *Generals in Gray.* Baton Rouge: LSU Press, 1959.

Warner, Ezra J. *Generals in Blue.* Baton Rouge: LSU Press, 1964.

Watkins, Sam. *Co. 'Aytch; Maury Grays, First Tennessee Regiment; or a Side Shoe of the Big Show* (Second Edition). Chattanooga: Times Printing Co., 1900.

Wilson, Edmund. *Patriotic Gore: Studies in the Literature of the American Civil War.* New York: Oxford Univ. Press, 1962.

Index

Federal units were officially known by their numerical designation, although this was often changed during the course of the war. Ohio infantry regiments are designated by the standard abbreviation OVI (Ohio Volunteer Infantry). Confederate units above the regimental level were officially referred to by their commander's surname, so those units are subsumed under the respective officer's name. Union brigades and divisions were informally known by their commander's names too, but with the exception of Hazen's brigade, these are listed here by their numerical designation at the time.

Abbott, Prvt. James (Co. C, 9th Indiana), 42
Adairsville, GA, 168
Aleshire's Battery (U.S.). *See* Eighteenth Ohio Independent Light Artillery Battery
Allatoona (Altoona), GA, 169
Allen, Col. Robert D. D., 19
Ambrose Bierce Project, xv, 3
Ammen's brigade (Army of the Ohio), 63, 75
Anderson, Capt. Andrew, 28
Army of the Cumberland (U.S.), xiii, 7, 9, 93, 95, 102, 109–10, 116–17, 119–20, 122–39, 141–146, 151–152, 154–55, 191, 208
Army of Kentucky (U.S.), 93
Army of the Ohio (U.S.), 51, 57–59, 79, 84–85, 89–90, 92; reconstituted (1864), 191
Army of the Potomac (U.S.), 146, 152
Army of Tennessee (C.S.A.), 89, 109, 127, 174, 195–96, 204–7
Army of the Tennessee (U.S.), 59, 65, 150–52
Aspinwall. *See* Colon, Panama
Athens, AL, 86–88
Atlanta, 165–66, 180–90, 209, 236, 238
Autumn Campaign, xv, 190

Baldwin, MS, 87
Battle of Chancellorsville, 110, 169
Battle of Chickamauga, 7, 104, 122–37, 139, 146; Albert Bierce's account of, 231–34
Battle of Franklin, 196–97
Battle of Mill Springs, 51
Battle of Nashville, 201–5, 208
Battle of Perryville, 90–91, 98
Battle of Philippi, 33–35
Battle of Pickett's Mill, 170–74
Battle of Resaca, 166–69
Battle of Shiloh, 6, 64–77
Battle of Spring Hill, 193–95, 197
Battle of Stones River, 7, 90, 99–106, 99, 109–10
Battle of Wauhatchie Station, 146–48
Beatty, Gen. Samuel, 200, 203, 205, 209
Beaufort, SC, 209
Beauregard, C.S.A. Gen. Pierre Gustave Toutant, 80–81, 83–84, 88
Belmont Mansion (Nashville), 200
Benham, Edwin, 184
Benwood, OH, 33
Berg, Gordon, 131, 136
Bierce, Albert ("Grizzly," "Old Sloots"), 15, 130, 135–36, 184, 219, 228, 231
Bierce, Ambrose, xiii, 1; as Treasury Dept. agency aide, 8; "Almighty God," 1, 3; Atlanta Campaign,

Index

Bierce, Ambrose (*cont.*)
165–75, 177–80; Autumn Campaign, 191–97, 201–8; "Bitter Bierce," 1, 5, 11; ancestry and youth, 11–14; Brown's Landing, 141–46; Carolinas Campaign, 208–10; Chickamauga, 121–37; his first love, 14–15, 177, 182–85; Kentucky Campaign, 89–92; Pickett's Mill, 170–74; printer's devil, 16; promoted to sergeant, 40; promoted to sergeant major, 89; promoted to 2nd lieutenant 97; first lieutenant, 112–13; as Provost Marshal, 113–15; Resaca, 166–68; Shiloh, 63–77; spymaster, 116–17; Stones River, 98–106; topographical engineer, 115–16; Tullahoma Campaign, 117–18; campaign in western Virginia, 32–49; wounded, 178–82
Bierce, Andrew, 184
Bierce, Helen, 180, 229, 231
Bierce, Laura Sherwood, 11–12
Bierce, Lucius Varus, 13, 16–19, 21, 26
Bierce, Marcus Aurelius, 5, 12–14, 16
Blake, Capt., 28
"Bloody Ninth." *See* 9th Indiana Volunteer Infantry
Boothroyd, Corp. Dyson (Co. A, 9th Indiana), 37
Bowling Green, KY, 89–90
Braden, Lt., 102
Bragg, C.S.A. Gen. Braxton, 88–92, 95–96, 99, 101, 106, 109, 117, 119, 122, 127, 130, 139–40, 150, 158, 165
Brannon, U.S. Gen. John M., 126, 136
Bratton, C.S.A. Gen. John, 147
Breckenridge, C.S.A. Gen. John C., 96
Brower, Sgt. (9th Indiana), 102
Brown, John, 18–19
Brown's Landing (Brown's Ferry), 141, 151, 152; amphibious assault on, 142–46
Buckner, C.S.A. Gen. Simon Bolivar, 127
Buell, U.S. Gen. Don Carlos, 51–53, 56, 59–60, 69, 79, 82–85, 87, 92, 95–96

Buffalo Mountain (Top of the Alleghenies), 44. *See also* Camp Baldwin
Burnside, U.S. Gen. Ambrose, 98, 150
Buzzard Roost, GA, 105

Cameron, Capt., 28
Camp Baldwin (Buffalo Mountain), WV, 45–46
Camp Bartow, WV, 41, 45
Camp Colfax, IN, 40
Camp Jackson, TN, 52–53, 55–56
Camp Morton, IN, 30–32
Camp Turner, 88
Camp Wildcat, KY, 91
Camp Wyckliffe (Wickliffe), KY, 52
Carrick's Ford (Corrick's Ford), WV, 39
Charge of the Mule Brigade. *See* Battle of Wauhatchie Station
Charleston, SC, 110
Chase, Capt. (9th Indiana), 28
Chattanooga, TN, 181, 190, 228; 1862 advance on, 84–87, 89; 1863 advance on, 117–20; Brown's Landing assault, 141–46; Grant promoted because of, 165; Missionary Ridge assault, 151–58; siege of, 139–41
Chattanooga and East Tennessee Railroad, 166
Cheatham's Corps (Army of Tennessee), 192
Cheatham, C.S.A. Gen. Benjamin F., 193
Cheat Mountain, WV, 41, 43–44
Chestnut, Lt. (18th Ohio Volunteer Artillery), 232
Chickamauga: battlefield, 228; etymology, 121–22. *See also* Battle of Chickamauga
Chonwel, Prvt. Michael O., 24th OVI, 55–56
Cincinnati, OH, 90
Cleburne, C.S.A. Gen. Patrick, 152, 154, 170–71, 192–93
Cobb, Lt. (2nd Bde., 3rd Div., IV Corps), 134, 189
Cockerill's Battery. *See* First Ohio Volunteer Artillery, Battery F
Crossville, GA, 168

Index

Collis's Zouaves (114th Pennsylvania Volunteer Infantry), 113
Colon, Panama, 117
Columbia, TN, 191, 192
Coosa River, AL, 189–90
Corinth, MS, 57–59, 79–82, 84, 228
Cozzins, Peter, 131
Croft, U.S. Col., 53
Cushing's Battery, 123

Dallas, GA, 169
Dalton, GA, 166
Dana, Charles, 128, 133–34, 154
Danville, KY, 91–92
Davidson, Cathy N., 3
Davis, U.S. Gen. Jefferson, 92
Davis, Jefferson, 165, 187–88, 221, 236, 239
Davis's Ford (Duck River), 192
Delphi, IN, 28
Dennison, Gov. William (OH), 32
Department of the Cumberland, 51–52; reconstituted, 92, 95
Department of Missouri, 51–52
Department of the Ohio, 52
Drake's Creek (TN), 89
Duck River, TN, 59–60, 63, 109, 118–19
Dumont, Col. Ebenezer, 34
Dunn, Capt. (9th Indiana), 28
Dunham, Sgt. (9th Indiana), 35–36
Dunning, Sgt., 111

Eastman, Capt. John (93rd OVI), 179
East Point, GA, 209
Eaton, Capt. Sherburne Blake (124th OVI, Special Treasury Agent), 8, 211, 212–13, 216
Eighteenth Ohio Independent Light Artillery Battery (Aleshire's), 130, 135–36, 228
Eleventh Corps, 146, 169
Elkhart, IN, 20, 23, 27–28, 159, 184–85
Elkwater Camp, 41

Fatout, Paul, 5, 11
Fetterman, WV, 48–49
Fifth Kentucky Volunteer Infantry, 171, 178

Fifth U.S. Light Artillery, Battery H (Terrell's Battery), 74
First Brigade, Third Division, Fourth Corps (Gibson's), 173–74
First Division, Fourth Corps, Army of the Cumberland, 141
First Indiana Regiment (Mexican War), 28
First OVI, 171
First Ohio Volunteer Light Artillery, Battery B (Standart's), 123
First Ohio Volunteer Light Artillery, Battery F (Cockerill's), 123, 125
First Virginia Volunteer Infantry (U.S.), 33
Fitch, John, 85, 139
Florence, AL, 191
Forrest, C.S.A. Gen. Nathan Bedford, 87, 139, 192, 214
Fort Wayne, IN, 28
Fortress Rosecrans, TN, 107
Forts Donelson and Henry, TN, 53
Forty-First OVI, 52, 171
Fourth Corps, Army of the Cumberland, 141, 173, 191–92, 202, 205, 209
Fourth Division, Army of the Ohio, 58, 63, 69, 90
Fourth Division, Army of the Tennessee (U.S.), 210
Fourth Kentucky Volunteer Infantry, 75
Fourth U.S. Artillery, Battery G (Howe's), 42
Fourth U.S. Artillery, Battery H/M (Mendenhall's Battery), 72, 74
Fourth U.S. Artillery, Battery M (Russell's), 123
Fourth U.S. Artillery, Battery H (Cushing's), 123
Foy, Col. James C, 23rd Kentucky (U.S.), 154–55
Franklin, TN, 88, 195–96. *See also* Battle of Franklin

Gallatin, TN, 89, 222
Garfield, Gen. James A. (President), 128, 220

291

Index

Garesche, U.S. Col. Julius, 100, 103
Garnett, C.S.A. Gen. Robert S., 38
Gatewood, Jeff, (C.S.A., guerilla), 190
Gault Hotel (Louisville), 92
Geary's Division, Army of the Potomac. *See* 2nd Division, XII Corps
Gettysburg, 117
Gibson, U.S. Col. William H., 173–74
Gibson's Brigade. *See* First Brigade, 3rd Division, IV Corps
Gillespie's Land Surveying, 20–21
Girard Hill. *See* Laurel Hill(s)
Girard, William T (9th Indiana), 36
Grafton, WV, 33, 41, 49
Glasgow, KY, 92
Goldsboro, NC, 210
Gracie, Col. Archibald, 134–35, 233–34
Granger, U.S. Gen. Gordon, 129–31, 135–36, 152, 231–33
Grant, U.S. Gen. Ulysses S., 51–53, 56–58, 60, 66, 79–83, 98, 109–10, 122, 143, 147, 149–52, 156, 188, 205, 208, 221, 238–39; promoted to General of the Armies, 165; use of alcohol, 153–54
The "Grey Eagle." *See* Milroy, Col. Robert H.
Guy Gap, TN, 109, 117

Halleck, U.S. Gen. Henry W., 51, 56–58, 79, 82, 84, 92, 110, 118, 122, 146, 188
Hanger, C.S.A. Pvt. James, 33–34
Hannum, Capt. J. C. (9th Indiana), 28
Hardee, C.S.A. Gen. William J., 109, 188
Hardee's Infantry Tactics, 31, 112
Harpeth River (Harper's), TN, 195
Hazen, U.S. Gen. William Babcock, 7, 21, 53–54, 57, 60–61, 65, 89, 92, 100–101, 105, 118–20, 123–26, 129, 131, 134–35, 137, 140–41, 151–52, 156–57, 212, 219, 222; Atlanta Campaign, 165–75; Pickett's Mill, 170ff; Sherman's March to Sea, 208–9; Carolina Campaign, 209ff; transferred to the Army of Tennessee, 187

Hazen Monument, 105, 228
Hazen's Brigade (Post's Brigade): as Nineteenth Brigade, Fourth Division, Army of the Ohio, 52–53; at Shiloh, 63–77; advance on Corinth, 79–81; Kentucky Campaign, 90–92; as Second Brigade, Second Division, Left Wing, Army of the Cumberland, at Stone's River, 99–102, 106; as Second Brigade, Second Division, Twenty-First Corps, Tullahoma Campaign, 117ff; advance on Chattanooga, 119–20; Battle of Chickamauga, 122–30; as Second Brigade, Third Division, Fourth Corps, siege of Chattanooga and assault on Brown's Landing, 141ff; Missionary Ridge, 150–57; Atlanta Campaign, 165ff; Battle of Resaca, 166–69; Pickett's Mill, 170–74; ceases to be Hazen's command, 187; as Post's Brigade, Second Brigade, Third Division, IV Corps, Autumn Campaign, 187, 192, 194, 200, 203–4
Hearst, William Randolph, 224
Helmenstein, C.S.A. Capt., 132
The Hermitage, 56
Hermitage Hotel (Nashville), 228
Hood, C.S.A. Gen. John Bell, 8, 187–89, 190–95, 200–201, 203–4, 207
Hood, Stephen, xv, 8
Hooker, U.S. Gen. Joseph, 146–47, 150–52, 155, 166
Hoover Gap, TN, 109, 117
Howard, Oliver O. (Oh-Oh! Howard, U.S.), 95, 169–72, 174, 191, 214, 221
Huntsville, AL, 207
Huttonsville, WV, 41
Howe's Battery. *See* 4th U.S. Artillery, Battery G

Indianapolis, IN, 28–30, 39, 159

Jackson, C.S.A. Gen. Thomas J. ("Stonewall") 169–70
Jenkins, C.S.A. Gen. Micah, 147
Jerrold, Douglas, 13
Johnson, U.S. Capt. Amasa (9th Indiana), 100

Index

Johnson, Andrew, 182
Johnson, U.S. Capt. G. M. I., 131, 136
Johnston, C.S.A. Gen. Joseph P. ("Uncle Joe"), 65, 166, 168, 170, 173–75, 187
Jupiter Doke (character), 148–50

Kelley, U.S. Col. Benjamin, 33–34, 36
Kelley Farm (Chickamauga), 135, 232–33
Kennesaw Mountain, 175, 178, 180
Kentucky Military Institute, 5–6, 19–23
Kessler, Sam (9th Indiana), 132
Kingston, GA, 168
Kipling, Rudyard, 224
Knefler, U.S. Col. Frederick, 173–74
Knoxville, TN, 150
Kosciusko County, IN, 23, 26
Kosciusko Guards (Co. E, 12th Indiana), 26

La Fayette and Rossville Road, 123
La Porte, IN, 28, 39
Laurel Hill(s), 35, 36, 38
Lawrence Mansion (Nashville), 200
Lebanon Pike (Davidson County, TN), 56
Lee, C.S.A. Gen. Robert E., 187, 236–39
Liberty Gap, TN, 109–17
Lincoln, Abraham, 23, 25–26, 82, 92, 99, 109–10, 120, 188, 208, 239
Logansport, IN, 28, 103
Longstreet, C.S.A. Gen. Peter, 127–29, 139, 146–47, 150
"Looking for the elephant" (colloquialism), 2, 5, 40, 64
Louisville, KY, 89–90, 92, 188
Little Harpeth River (Little Harper's Creek), 88
Lookout Mountain (Chattanooga), 146–48, 150

Macon and Western Railroad, GA, 209
Madden, Capt. (9th Indiana), 46–47
Manchester, TN, 118–19
Mann, Capt. Theodore (9th Indiana), 11, 27
Mansker's Creek, TN, 89–90

Maxwell's Bridge (Carolina Campaign), 210
McClellan, U.S. Gen. George B., 38–39
McCook, U.S. Gen. Robert L., 86
McConnell, Capt. D. B. (9th Indiana), 74–75
McConnell, U.S. Col. Henry K., 189
McCulloch, U.S. Sec. of Treasury Hugh, 213
McDonald's Station, GA, 165
McFarland Gap Road (Chickamauga), 233
McLaw, C.S.A. Gen. Lafayette, 147
McNamara House (Chickamauga), 123
McWilliams, Cary, 1, 7, 159, 161, 183
Meade, U.S. Gen. George Gordon, 168
Memphis and Charleston Railroad, 84–86
Mencken, H. L., 2
Mendenhall's Battery. *See* 4th U.S. Artillery, Battery H/M
Michigan City, IN, 28
Miller, Jacob (9th Indiana), 103
Milroy, U.S. Col. Robert H., 28, 31–32, 37, 39, 41–43, 45–47
Minty, Gen. Robert H., 119, 122–23
Missionary Ridge (Mission Ridge), Chattanooga, 121, 150–58
Mitchellville, TN, 96
Moccasin Bend, Tennessee River, 141
Montgomery Hill, (Battle of Nashville), 203
Moody, Capt. Gideon (9th Indiana), 28, 43–49
Moore, C.S.A. Lt. Col. John C., 71
Morgan, C.S.A. Col. John Hunt, 87
Morris, Roy, 3
Morris, U.S. Gen. Thomas, 33, 38
Morton, Gov. Oliver P., 27, 32, 82, 159
Murfreesboro Pike (Nashville), 96, 99
Murfreesboro, TN, 88–89, 96, 99, 106–7, 109, 110–11, 115. *See also* Battle of Stones River.

Nashville, TN, 41–52, 54, 89, 96, 180–81, 188; siege of, 199–200. *See also* Battle of Nashville
Nashville and Chattanooga Railway, 100, 109

293

Index

Neale, Walter, 14–15, 27–28, 184, 220, 225, 235
Negley, U.S. Gen. James S., 129, 134
Nelson, Gen. William ("Bull"), 58–60, 61, 63, 69, 72, 75, 89, 92–93
New Orleans, 217, 228
Nineteenth Brigade. See Hazen's brigade
Nineteenth Illinois Volunteer Infantry, 87
Nineteenth OVI, 75
Ninety-Third OVI, 171, 178–79
Ninth Indiana Regiment of Foot Volunteers (Ninety Day). See 9th Indiana Volunteer Infantry
Ninth Indiana Volunteer Infantry (Volunteer Veteran Infantry), xiii; as ninety day regiment, 28, 30–32; Battle of Belington, 36–38; Three Year Regiment: mustered in, 40; western Virginia Campaign, 48; Cheat Mountain, 41; action at Camp Bartow, 41–43; assault on Camp Baldwin, 45–47; transferred to Army of the Ohio, 51; assigned to Nineteenth Brigade, 51ff; Battle of Shiloh, 63–77; advance on Corinth, 79–81; Kentucky Campaign, 90–92; Battle of Stone's River, 99–102, 106; Tullahoma Campaign, 117ff; capture of Chattanooga, 119–20; Battle of Chickamauga, 122–30; capture of Brown's Landing, 141; transferred to Third Brigade, First Division, Fourth Corps, 140–41; regiment re-enlists as veterans, 159, 162
Northern Indianan (newspaper), 15–16, 26
Nuse River, NC, 210

One Twenty-Fourth OVI, 171
Opalika, AL, 212
Opdycke, U.S. Gen. Emerson, 195–96
Orchard Knob, TN, 150–56
Overton Knob (Battle of Nashville), 203
Owens, David, 3
Owl Creek Bridge, 13, 75

Palmer, U.S. Gen. John, 99, 101
Peach Tree Street (Atlanta), 209
Peck, Prvt. William H. (9th Indiana), 44
Perryville, KY. See Battle of Perryville
Philippi, WV, 33, 41. See also Battle of Philippi
Pilot Knob (Sumner County, TN), 89
Pioneer Corps (Carolina Campaign), 209ff
Pittman's Ferry (London, KY), 91
Pittsburg Landing, 58, 63–65, 68–69, 79–80, 228
Poe, Edgar Allen, 224
Poe Tavern, 119
Polk, C.S.A. Gen. Leonidas, 109, 127
Pope, Alexander, 224
Pope, U.S. Gen. John, 79, 83, 87
Porter, U.S. Gen. Horace, 148
Porterfield, C.S.A. Col. George, 33
Post, Gen. Philip Sidney, 189, 192, 202–4, 209
Post's Brigade. See Second Brigade, Third Division, Fourth Corps
Proctor's Creek, GA, 209
Provisional Army of Tennessee (C.S.A.), 52
Pulaski, TN, 191

Readyville, TN, 110–12, 114, 117
Reed House (Chickamauga), 131–32
Reed's Bridge, 122–23
Rensselaer, IN, 28
Resaca, GA. See Battle of Resaca
Reynolds, Arabella (Belle), 83
Reynolds, U.S. Gen. Joseph J., 41, 43, 45–47, 124
Reynolds Station, TN, 88
Richmond, VA, 98, 236, 238
Riley, James Whitcomb, 160
Risley, Capt. (9th Indiana), 112–13
Rocky Face Ridge, GA, 106
Rosecrans, U.S. Gen. William S. ("Old Rosey"), 92–93, 95–100, 102, 106, 109–10, 116–18, 141, 143, 220; Battle of Chickamauga, 122, 127–29, 134, 139, 174
Rossville, GA, 126

294

Index

Russell's Battery. *See* 4th U.S. Artillery, Battery M
Rutherford County, TN, 89

Salomon, E. S., 223
San Antonio, TX, 228
Savannah, TN, 58–60, 63, 68
Schofield, U.S. Gen. John, 191–95, 197, 199
Second Division (Wood's), Twenty-First Corps, Army of the Cumberland, 140
Second Division (Geary's), Twelfth Corps, Army of the Potomac, 146
Second Virginia Infantry Regiment (U.S.), 45, 46
Segur, Capt. (9th Indiana), 28
Seidel, U.S. Maj. Charles, 111
Selma, AL, 212–14
Seventh Indiana Volunteer Infantry, 33
Seventy-First OVI, 189
Shelbyville, TN, 109, 117–18
Sheridan, U.S. Gen. Philip, 134, 152, 154, 157
Sherman, U.S. Gen. William T., 52, 95, 150–52, 154, 165; Atlanta Campaign, 166, 169–71, 175, 180, 187–91, 208
Sixteenth Corps (U.S.), 212
Sixth Kentucky Volunteer Infantry (U.S.), 52, 71, 80, 157, 171
Sixth OVI, 171
Slocum, U.S. Gen. Henry W., 210
Smith, C.S.A. Gen. Kirby, 89–90
Smith, U.S. Gen. William F. ("Baldy"), 141
Snodgrass Hill (Chickamauga), 129–30, 135–36, 139, 232–33
South Bend, IN, 28
Smith, Sgt. (9th Indiana), 42
Standart's Battery. *See* First Ohio Lt. Arty, Battery B
Stanley, U.S. Gen. David S., 191, 200
Stanton, William, U.S. Sec. of War, 92, 110, 118, 120, 122, 146, 169, 188
St. Cloud Hotel (Nashville), 52, 57
Steedman, U.S. Gen. James B., 130
Suman, Capt. (9th Indiana), 60, 126, 209

Sumner County, TN, 89
"Swamp Angels" (9th Indiana), 37
Sword, Wiley, 191

Tennessee River, 122, 141, 207
Tenth Indiana Volunteer Infantry, 75
Terrell's Battery. *See* 5th U.S. Artillery, Battery H
"Third Division," Army of the Tennessee, 210
Third Division, Fourth Corps, Army of the Cumberlands, 200, 204–5, 207
Third Ohio Volunteer Cavalry, 111
Thirty-Third Indiana Volunteer Infantry, 184
Thirty-Third OVI, 42
Thomas, U.S. Gen. George "Pap," 51, 106, 116, 123–24, 126, 128–31, 134, 135–37 139, 152, 171, 191, 197, 199, 200–202, 205, 232–33
Tombigbee River, 216
Travels in the Southland, 17
Tullahoma, TN, 109; Tullahoma Campaign, 117ff
Tunnel Hill (Chattanooga), 151–52, 154
Turchin, U.S. Col. John Basil, 87, 141, 143, 145
Twelfth Corps (U.S.), 146
Twelfth Indiana Volunteer Infantry, 26
Twelfth OVI, 44
Twenty-Fifth OVI, 43
Twenty-First Corps (U.S.), 140
Twenty-Fourth OVI, 55
Twenty-Third Corps (U.S.), 166, 191
Twenty-Third Kentucky, 154–55, 171

Valparaiso, IN, 28
Vicksburg, MS, 110, 117–18

Wagner, U.S. Gen. George D., 193, 195–96
Walden Ridge, 119, 140, 146
Wallace, U.S. Gen. Lew, 53, 68
Ward, U.S. Adjutant C. J., 22
Warsaw, IN, 16, 160, 184
Watkins, C.S.A. Prvt. Sam, 132
Waynesboro, TN, 60
Webster, WV, 41

295

Western Theater, 6
Wheeler, Gen. Joseph ("Fightin' Joe"), 170
Whitaker, U.S. Gen. Walter, 231–32
Whitaker, U.S. Maj., 157
Whitehall, Capt. Alexander (9th Indiana), 226, 229
Wilder, U.S. Col. John T., 119
Williams, Reuben, 16, 23, 26; Col., Indiana Volunteers, 169
Wilson, Edmund, 76
Wilson, U.S. Gen. James, 150, 192–93, 202, 214

Wilt, Napier, 1
Winchester, TN, 86
Wood, U.S. Gen. Thomas J., 127, 152, 169–71, 173–74, 195, 200, 202, 209
Woodbury, TN, 110–11
Woodward, Capt. (9th Indiana), 28
Wright, Benjamin, 160
Wright, Clarissa (Clara), 160–62, 182
Wright, Fatima (Bernice), 7, 15–27, 159–62, 182, 184
Wright, Oliver (9th Indiana), 160–61

Yates, Gov. Richard (IL), 82–83, 149